M000277950

WHAT'S KILLING AMERICA

WHAT'S KILLING AMERICA

INSIDE THE RADICAL LEFT'S TRAGIC DESTRUCTION OF OUR CITIES

JASON RANTZ

NASHVILLE • NEW YORK

Cover design by Studio Gearbox

Center Street
Hachette Book Group
1290 Avenue of the Americas, New York, NY 10104
centerstreet.com
twitter.com/centerstreet

First edition: September 2023

Center Street is a division of Hachette Book Group, Inc. The Center Street name and logo are trademarks of Hachette Book Group, Inc.

Library of Congress Control Number: 2023942541

ISBNs: 9781546006145 (hardcover), 9781546006169 (ebook)

Printed in the United States of America

LSC-C

Printing 1, 2023

DEDICATED TO MY FAMILY,
LISTENERS,
READERS,
VIEWERS,
AND ALL WHO PUT UP WITH ME.

CONTENTS

OPENING ARGUMENT

AMERICA ON LIFE SUPPORT

IF YOU LIVE IN A BIG CITY, does your neighborhood look and feel the same way it did when you first moved in? Has it stayed clean in recent years, or is it defiled by trash, graffiti, used needles, and human waste? Do you feel safe letting your kids ride their bikes alone? Have you had to explain to them what that homeless man is smoking on the sidewalk?

Or did you move to a suburb, hoping to escape the crime, homelessness, and despair of big city life only to find these problems followed you to your new home? Have more homeless addicts popped up? Have your taxes soared? Is your kid's school pushing values in conflict with your own? For millions of Americans, and perhaps yourself, the answer to these questions is a resounding yes. In many cities and towns, the Radical Left has taken control of the Democrat Party and transformed the places you live and love into unmitigated failures by ramming through disastrous virtue-signaling, woke policies.

But some of you answered no. Sure, there are problems popping up around your community, but they seem manageable. After all, there's no perfect community. You're confident that your neighborhood could never devolve into chaos. Well, I hate to burst your bubble. Crime, drug addiction, homelessness, left-wing school indoctrination, so-called "inclusive" housing policies, and outrageous taxes don't stay within big city limits forever. They don't even stay in liberal cities. It's not Las Vegas. What happens in Los Angeles, Chicago, Portland, New York, Seattle, San Francisco, and other cities run by the Radical Left doesn't stay there. The effects of ideologically-driven left-wing policies always spread. Activists pushing policy changes in Democrat strongholds inspire like-minded ideologues in other cities to step up and organize for change. It's why they see more policy victories than we expect.

Activists on the Radical Left are more organized than those on the Right. They're more organized than those of you who don't have a firm ideological position. You vote for who you think best serves your community and believe no one party can completely define your interests and views. You like some ideas on the Left, others on the Right, and you vote with your gut, not with a political identity you casually identity with. How in the world do you find like-minded people to join you in a political fight to retake your communities? And even if you could find them, would you have the time to do what's necessary to make meaningful change?

The Radical Left has a set of ideologically motivated, professional activists who show up to meetings in the middle of the day when you're at work, on a Tuesday evening when you're preparing dinner for your family, or when you're picking up your son or daughter from soccer practice. They endlessly scroll social media, looking for protests to attend or new causes to embrace. They share information with a community they've curated to help promote their activism, while you're online paying bills, finding family recipes on a budget, or looking for a movie to watch with the kids.

It's hard for you to organize because you have jobs and lives, families and responsibilities. Who wants to spend a Thursday evening at a city council meeting, when you could be at home spending quality time with your spouse and kids or grandkids, going to a concert, relaxing in front of a movie, or reading a book? Believe me, I get it. But when you choose not to engage more in the community, you've unintentionally ceded power to the Radical Left. They know you don't show up to meetings or town halls, so they fill the empty seats with the purpose of convincing lawmakers to take their positions and transform our cities.

Sure, in Democrat-run cities it's much easier for the Radical Left to convince lawmakers to take their side. They share a general political view and see the world through the same social justice lens. But why should we make it so easy for them? Why not put up a little resistance and inspire those who are not politically motivated, who see what's going on and are displeased, so that we can win small victories before, ultimately, winning the war for the future of our country? Why not connect the dots for those who don't understand or even see what's going on, so that we can explain away most of what's destroying our neighborhoods by directly tying it to a radical policy that won't ever produce the results we deserve?

I have two primary motivations for writing this book. I hope you'll view them as important, as I do.

First, there are millions of Americans who have no idea how bad our largest, Democrat-run cities have deteriorated. That may be hard to believe, but think about your neighbors or coworkers. Do they admit that the homeless crisis in your area is as bad as it is? Perhaps they think the complaints are hyperbole, and that it's only really a problem in certain neighborhoods they don't visit anyway. They don't seem to realize how quickly homelessness spreads. Are your childless friends aware of what's happening in our schools? They think it won't ever affect them, but those woke kids become the next generation of lawyers, doctors, CEOs, and politicians. Do we want their worldview to be defined by the Radical Left?

In my hometown of Seattle, I've spoken to people who think my reports about the very city they live in are fake, manipulated, or exaggerated. I've infiltrated Antifa marches to witness the vandalism, arson, and chaos. I've been followed home by Black Lives Matter radicals who tried to intimidate me into silence. I've hiked deep into unsanitary homeless encampments, stepping over needles and human waste to talk with men and women about what's keeping them on the streets. I've reviewed hundreds of secretly recorded videos and audio of Radical Left educators trying to indoctrinate your kids. I've covered more stories than I can count about my deteriorating city as part of my Seattle-based talk radio show. Yet, some claim I'm making all these problems up. Even after playing video of my experiences on Fox News, I'm told the problems don't really exist. It's pretty surreal.

Too many live in a bubble where they're not exposed to reality; others live in an echo chamber where they refuse to acknowledge the politicians and policies they support are destroying their communities. And if they watch CNN or MSNBC or get their news from left-wing Twitter, they are rarely exposed to the crises overtaking American cities. They don't know that Los Angeles gave up its streets to homeless encampments that spread medieval diseases or that Seattle radicals passed criminal justice "reforms" at the state level that allow criminals to speed away from the scene of a crime without any fear the police will follow. Few know of the reforms to single-family housing zones that threaten the American dream of homeownership in Minneapolis or that the way you cook or drive is now dictated in New York and Denver. And the truth is, though you are concerned with the news you see and are rather engaged, you might not even know the extent of the crises destroying our cities. This book will highlight those stories.

Second, for those of you who share my concerns about the state of our cities, it's important to understand *why* the Radical Left believes what they do, *how* their policies are failing, and *what* alternatives exist to combat and counter their agenda. You'll never be able to convince a radical that they're wrong or dangerous because they're blinded by their own ideology. They are unmovable and, frankly, not worth our time. You want to win over the moderate Democrats, the independents, the unmotivated Republicans, or the I-Don't-Know-What-the-Heck-I-Am family member, neighbor, friend, and coworker (the one who won't report you to Human Resources for talking politics, at least). The best way to convince people something isn't working is to specifically explain why and how. The only way to inspire people to push for positive change is to argue from a place of facts with examples of failures and reasons why a different approach will work.

In the following chapters, I will dive deep into some of the country's largest American cities, take a few detours to some midsize and small ones, and focus on states where extremist policies are wreaking havoc. My focus is almost exclusively framed around Democrat policies from the Radical Left because they're the ones who run most major cities. It's not meant to suggest there are no problems in Republican-led cities. There most certainly are. And I'm not critical of all Democrats who are, on average, well-intentioned, kind, generous, and thoughtful—we just may have an honest difference of opinion. Instead, my focus is on a subset of powerful radicals who, right now, have the most power in major population centers. I believe they're wielding their power and control recklessly.

Each chapter is organized by a big picture topic, such as homelessness, illegal immigration, crime, or education. Some examples about Radical Left policies gone awry will be explored in great detail. Other times, I'll give you everything you actually need to know in order to see how the problems spiraled out of control. I'll focus on policies that don't work, while striving to highlight policies that do. I hope you'll learn as much about a city you don't live in as the one that you do live in.

I cover these topics, for the most part, through a political lens.

That's not to say every issue is political. I don't see policing, school curriculum, or housing policy as inherently political. Likewise, most Americans don't consider any overt political objective when supporting a policy, initiative, or strategy—regardless of one's political background. Democrats and Republicans alike just want what's best for their family and community. But the Radical Left crafts and passes their policies through a political lens, and the only way to properly understand them is by analyzing them in the way they're advanced. Plus, I do hope that more people are inspired to vote for the better candidates as a result of what you learn in this book.

To be clear and upfront: I have biases. *We all do*. There is no such thing as a purely objective journalist, talk show host, or television talking head. (I hold all of those titles.) The best of us try to report or analyze stories in good faith and without bias, but we screw up. Me? I don't pretend that I don't have a view. I very clearly do. My analysis, informed by 41 years of experiences living in big cities, surrounded almost entirely by people who don't think the way I do, is why you hear me on the radio, read me on popular websites, and watch me on television. I think there's value to my perspectives and observations, but I don't always expect you to agree with me. In fact, I hope you take advantage of the many endnotes included in this book to learn more about stories I cover and the source material that led to my observations and conclusions. It's okay to disagree with me. So, if you're so inclined, review the sources and form your own viewpoints to help shape your communities.

And a personal note: In addition to being intelligent, witty, attractive, and humble, I do have a tendency to get snarky or sarcastic. In other words, I can be a smart ass. You will experience that personality from time to time in the forthcoming chapters. But ultimately, I hope you'll appreciate the presentation that's meant to inform, shock, anger, *and* inspire you into bringing back sanity and reason to your community and, ultimately, the country.

If we don't pay more attention to what's going on in our most liberal cities, the policies will continue to spread. We've been complacent for far too long, assuming that the craziest elements of the Radical Left would stay confined to both coasts and that their ideas wouldn't sweep the country like a woke plague. It's time to take a closer look at what's going on in our country.

These policies are what's killing America.

PART I

THE RISE IN CRIME

PROGRESSIVES DISMANTLE THE CRIMINAL JUSTICE SYSTEM

CHAPTER 1

SEATTLE GETS AUTONOMOUS

Infiltrating Antifa

On January 24, 2021, I found myself in the middle of an Antifa mob, marching through an unfamiliar neighborhood with no police in sight, when I heard my name whispered by one of the many unfriendly, unidentifiable faces dressed in black-bloc, a style of dress that covers any personal features. The group I had infiltrated found out I was among them, they were looking for me, and they wanted to hurt me.

I won't lie: I was absolutely terrified.

About an hour earlier, roughly 200 Antifa radicals made the drive from in and around Seattle, where I live, to Tacoma, a mid-size city about 40 minutes south. They staged near a parking lot downtown, ready for "direct action" against police after a recent incident of what they pretended was police brutality.

At the same intersection the night before, a large crowd gathered to watch and cheer drivers doing donuts and burnouts. When an officer arrived in his patrol vehicle, the crowd swarmed around the car, banging on its doors and windows, rocking it back and forth, threating the officer, and throwing at the vehicle what the officer believed to be a Molotov cocktail. He tried to back out, but the crowd would not let him leave. They were laughing and cheering. To them, this was a game. To the officer, with nearly 30 years on the job, this was a threat. Fearing for his safety, he accelerated out of the mob. Elation from intimidating the officer turned to horror as they saw the cruiser roll over a member of the crowd.[1]

The crowd posed a clear threat to the officer, which is why the local prosecutor cleared him of all wrongdoing. But nearly a year after the death of George Floyd while in police custody in Minneapolis, Minnesota, the Radical Left and their allies in the media were on the lookout for any use of force they could turn into a national outrage. CNN falsely claimed the officer drove "through the crowd," rather than out of the crowd.[2] ABC News was most dramatic, characterizing the officer as "plowing through the crowd."[3] Some local media was as explosive; the *Tacoma News Tribune* characterized a video of the incident as "a Tacoma Police patrol car running into and through a group of pedestrians."[4]

The media coverage and out-of-context videos shared on social media prompted the anti-police Antifa gathering that I was covering for my radio show in Seattle. By then, I had been all over Fox News, and my local brand had turned me into the leading conservative voice in the region. While I do love to brag about my success, I only say this to point out that I was easily recognizable. To my advantage, however, people still wore masks thanks to COVID-19 and dressing in black-bloc requires you to cover your entire face and body, making it easy for me to hide. While I always thought I looked like a narc while undercover in the field, I always fit in.

When a colleague and I arrived at the rally, there wasn't much going on. The crowd loitered as if waiting for someone to take charge. But before I knew it, the crowd took over the intersection, placing large trash bins and construction signs around them to warn cars that they will not be able to pass. Though Democrats claim Antifa doesn't exist, some in the crowd waived flags that read "anti-fascist," while others literally chanted "Antifa." Soon, the crowd lit a large fire from debris they found at a nearby construction project and from trash bins. After some short speeches extolling the virtues of abolishing police, the crowd started to march.

Local reporters stayed near the fire to file their reports. Few dared to walk with the crowd, either out of justifiable fear for their safety or a disinterest in exposing Antifa's destruction. Me? I felt a need to be in the crowd to document their anarchy, since few others would. I perfected the art of recording video on my cell phone without being noticed. (It took months of practice in the field to attain this important skill.) When Antifa members see you filming, they will confront you, threaten you, and usually try to destroy your phone or camera if you don't show them that you deleted the footage. It happened to one independent journalist who tried to cover the mob but made the mistake of bringing attention to himself.

As the crowd snaked through the streets of Tacoma, individuals tagged businesses with graffiti reading "ACAB" (an acronym for "all cops are bastards") and smashed windows of a bail bond agency, South Sound 911 offices, and the county courthouse, along with the vehicles in its parking lot. They were armed with various tools and weapons, including a pipe and crowbar. They stopped at the Pierce County Sheriff's Department Corrections Bureau to attempt to tear down protective fencing while shouting demands that prisoners be released. While passing homes, the mob shined flashlights on residents who were looking out of their windows to see what was going on. They yelled to the residents, "Out of your homes, and into the streets!" No one, as far as I could tell, joined the marauders. But I did witness a woman tell her friend, "I'm not going to jail for this," before leaving. These were presumably well-intentioned women wanting to be a part of what they thought was a legitimate social justice movement, only to realize what the media didn't tell them: It was an Antifa-led mob hell-bent on destruction and chaos.

The agitators at the front of the march seemed to have a plan in place, but I was out of sorts. I had no idea where we were headed. The march took us to a neighborhood I had never visited, and I didn't know where I was. But after about 30 minutes of marching, I assumed we were heading back to where we came from. That assumption was a huge mistake. I posted a photo too soon, not realizing the march wasn't over.

When out in the field, I strategically post photos or videos on my Twitter account. I sometimes take photos from afar to indicate I'm farther away than I really am. Other times, I post far later than when I captured the video to throw people off. I do this for safety, especially when I'm with a colleague or friend. Antifa and their enablers who do not attend marches or riots monitor social media and communicate with members on the ground, either directly or via hashtags. If you post from or near the crowd, and you're deemed an enemy of the movement, Antifa Twitter users post your name, face, and most recent location.

Oftentimes, these Twitter scouts pretend to be independent journalists; sometimes they're mainstreamed by outlets like the Associated Press or PBS. One such pretend journalist is Portland-based Griffin Malone, who outed me to the Antifa mob. He tweeted my photo and noted, "Jason Rantz is also in Tacoma tonight recording crowds."[5] To those of us who closely cover Antifa, we know this tactic is meant to put people like me in harm's way and intimidate me into not covering their riots. Of course, Malone denied any nefarious intent, since he didn't directly tell people to harm me. But Antifa saw his tweet.

Moments later, I heard someone in the march whisper my name. He knew I was among the group, and soon others started to wonder out loud if I was there. My colleague and I exchanged glances before she asked if we should leave. I didn't think it was wise at the time: We were in the middle of an empty neighborhood, with no cops in sight. We were going to awkwardly leave the *moment* the group started to look for me? I felt like it would have outed us, so I decided to stay, continue to walk with my head down and my cell phone in my pocket so as not to arouse suspicions, as my colleague watched my back.

Suddenly, the march stopped for no apparent reason. We were standing in the middle of a residential neighborhood and no one was moving, everyone casually loitering. Paranoid, I felt like they had stopped to search the group for me. As every second ticked away, my colleague and I exchanged nervous glances. I had never felt more tense or vulnerable than I did in that moment. A loud noise startled me. It was a pair of Antifa members kicking over two trash bins. Then, as abruptly as we stopped, we marched again. They weren't looking for me. It turns out the leaders of the group were as lost as I was.

We were headed back to the county courthouse they previously vandalized. This time, however, the local police had finally arrived, a sign that the fun was over. An Antifa member pulled out an American flag and set it on fire, letting it burn in the middle of the street, while his buddies yelled invective at cops. They were, for the most part, silent and at a distance, ready to act if they needed to, but willing to wait it out.

In the end, the group dispersed, having caused significant damage by vandalizing buildings and setting fires. That was their only goal—to roam the streets and exert dominance. They knew they'd be allowed to get away with a lot, so that's what they did.

Marches that turned into riots went on for months after the death of Floyd. Antifa and other agitators owned the Pacific Northwest and were able to get away with virtually anything. Police were not allowed to engage until after damage was done, local politicians said virtually nothing to discourage the so-called "direct action," and many media outlets either ignored or downplayed the violence and threats. None of this would have been possible had it not been for the way the Radical Left treated an autonomous zone in Seattle, one that would capture the attention of the nation.

"All Cops Are Bastards"

When Radical Left lawmakers showed up outside the East Precinct police station in Seattle's Capitol Hill neighborhood on June 6, 2020, they hoped to earn political currency for being part of the Black Lives Matter movement. Though the death of George Floyd had zero bearing on anything related to policing in Seattle, progressives in the Emerald City are always looking to be a part of a larger movement. This was their opportunity.

For days, local activists entered the fray with marches, rallies, and riots. While they started out peaceful, there was a growing number of the Radical Left, like Antifa and their enablers, that took to the streets to antagonize cops into using force so that they could have an actual reason to protest Seattle police. They were looking to create problems to exploit.

But Seattle police were trained. The 1999 Seattle World Trade Organization (WTO) protests provided a wake-up call for the need to be prepared for mass movements. And the previous year's May Day riots, where anarchists sought to destroy parts of the city, left the department ready for large crowd management. Little did they know what would come.

"In response to protests, the Seattle Fire Department is advising all downtown area business owners to immediately secure all open areas like outdoor seating areas, garages, dumpsters, and recycling bins as much as possible and to remove all combustibles that cannot be secured," the Seattle Fire Department tweeted on May 30.[6] We all knew what was coming and the activists-turned-domestic-terrorists did not disappoint.

The chaos started in downtown Seattle. While legitimate and peaceful protesters chanted "Black Lives Matter," a contingent of hooligans lobbed glass bottles at police as they vandalized downtown businesses.[7] By the next day, activists ratcheted up their behavior to see how much they could get away with. It turns out, the answer was almost anything.

Downtown storefronts were destroyed, and businesses were looted. Police faced a cacophony of insults and an onslaught of rocks, bottles, and other items used as weapons. Then-mayor Jenny Durkan announced a 5 p.m. curfew for May 30 and May 31. Residents were told to stay at home, but those who hoped to loot for racial justice did not listen. They didn't have to. They knew the police would not be able to enforce the curfew, and after weeks of COVID-19 restrictions, the crowd was ready to explode.

While chanting "No Justice! No Peace!" dozens of rioters destroyed police cars, some yelling "Set it on fire!" while tagging the car with "ACAB." Tyre Wayne Means Jr., a felon from Georgia living in Washington State at the time, was captured on film lighting a paper towel on fire and placing it in the backseat of an empty police cruiser. Nearby, other rioters used lighter fluid and other accelerants to keep the fires burning. Why would they bring lighter fluid to what was billed as a peaceful protest?

At one point, a rioter pulled out an AR-15 from the burning patrol vehicle and began firing at it.[8] Within moments, a highly trained security guard working on a detail for a local news reporter swooped in, handgun out, and snatched the AR-15 from the man. He felt the public was in danger, so he intervened and called 911. It was all caught on video. It was the second rifle the security detail had confiscated from radicals in the crowd.[9]

Members of the National Guard were activated, though not yet deployed. Police were still trying to handle the situation, with fears that any further show of force could agitate the rioters who had taken the downtown shopping core. Fires engulfed cars and trash cans, but it wasn't safe for firefighters to enter the riot, so they let them burn.

It had quickly become clear that the crowd that started the day peacefully marching had been replaced in the evening by Antifa radicals and anarchists who would take advantage of the chaos for personal benefit. They used Molotov cocktails[10] and threw frozen water bottles at police,[11] indicating that this wasn't some protest that got so emotional that it turned violent; it was planned. They attacked media covering the unfolding story on the ground. Some tried to block photojournalists from filming as masked criminals stole clothing from the Urban Outfitters, Old Navy, and Nordstrom department stores.[12]

As the riot unfolded, Seattle's Socialist council member Kshama Sawant sent out a tweet to justify the violence, doing nothing to stop Antifa terrorists (members of her base) from destroying the city. Instead, she turned to a tweet version of her stump speech, blaming the "political establishment" for letting down the "working people."

"The outrage on Seattle's streets today represents the deep community anger about police violence on top of profound & longstanding suffering because the political establishment has failed to meet basic needs of working people before & during this crisis," she regurgitated from previous speeches.[13]

By the next morning, downtown looked like a war zone. Broken glass, buildings tagged with messages like "Kill cops," and the burning embers from torched cars and trash bins. As I walked around downtown, I couldn't believe what it had become. But it wasn't over. That afternoon, another rally formed and the mayor again promised to enforce the curfew, but as the day turned to early evening, that hadn't yet happened. This time, the police strategy was to allow the group of roughly 1,000 to wander the streets and tire themselves out. It was mostly successful. At 10:27 p.m., well after the 5 p.m. curfew, police finally started to break up the demonstration. The crowd reacted by throwing debris at officers, but it ended shortly after that.[14]

If the city had a unified set of competent leaders, perhaps the destruction of downtown Seattle would have been the worst of it. There was little reason for locals to turn to destruction after Floyd, with a police department that was about to see a federal consent decree lifted thanks to years of successful reform. But Radical Left council members wanted the violence to continue. They didn't seem to mind what happened downtown. And rather than condemn the rioting and looting, they condemned the police.

"The very thing that everybody was protesting, excessive police force, was met by a militarized response," council member Teresa Mosqueda claimed during a June 1, 2020, committee hearing, angry that cops helped quell the riot.[15] "Colleagues, I hope we're all saying we understand why that destruction happened and we understand why people are upset," Mosqueda continued, justifying the lawlessness.

"We have had hundreds, if not thousands of accounts from ordinary people, community members, of unacceptable conduct from the Seattle Police Department," council member Sawant claimed.[16] "It is tragically ironic that we live in a society where a protest against police brutality and violence was met with police brutality and violence."

These comments were at best unhelpful, at worst incendiary. They were implying they were okay with what happened downtown, telegraphing future support for even more riots. But it was comments from Socialist city council member Tammy Morales that were most outrageous. She was openly condoning the violence.

"But what I don't want to hear is for our constituents to be told to be civil, not to be reactionary, to be told looting doesn't solve anything," Morales said before gaslighting the public.[17] "It does make me wonder and ask the question why looting bothers people so much more than knowing that across the country, black men and women are dying every day, and far too often, at the hands of those who are sworn to protect and serve."

The Radical Left listened to Morales and again turned violent the following evening, with agitators throwing rocks and lit fireworks at cops. Antifa brought umbrellas both to shield their criminal comrades and to use as weapons against the police. In return, police used tear gas and flash bangs to disperse the unruly crowd;[18] it was ineffective. The crowd was hell-bent on taking the East Precinct.

Situated in the heart of Capitol Hill, across the street from popular Cal Anderson Park, the police station had always seemed out of place. This particular neighborhood is home to the city's most Radical Left activists, many of whom see cops as the enemy. But the area is also plagued by crime, with nearby rowdy nightlife often in need of police intervention. Nevertheless, activists didn't want the police department there, and they were using the Floyd-inspired activism to push it out.

Iconic and dramatic images were captured as a vastly outnumbered police force formed a human barrier between thousands of protesters and the police precinct. If the mob reached the precinct building, it would have either been destroyed or occupied. Police relied on tear gas and flash bangs as the crowd became increasingly violent. Despite that violence, some local media portrayed the events as mostly peaceful, while lawmakers continued their unrelenting criticism of the police.

"I've never in 25 years of participating in protests experienced such an indiscriminate use of tear gas and pepper spray and flash bombs against people who are not doing anything wrong, with so little effort to de-escalate, negotiate with protesters, utilize peacekeepers…and focus your efforts on people doing wrong," council member Lisa Herbold complained to Police Chief Carmen Best at a council meeting, believing that cops should actually negotiate with violent rioters she portrayed as peaceful protesters.[19]

Police found themselves in a difficult position. It's undoubtedly true that "peaceful protestors" were caught up in the tear gas. But that's because they were standing next to agitators trying to physically harm police. Some protestors legitimately didn't see what was happening; others very clearly did, before pretending that any police response to rocks being launched at their heads was an overreaction. And some local media was either too apprehensive to report the truth, fearful of getting on the wrong side of a movement, or unwilling to be honest because they sided with the protesters.

The mayor had been meeting with local organizers, asking them to help calm the tense standoffs between the crowds and police. But there really weren't any official organizers, per se. There were activists who generally helped amplify calls to meet up to protest, but there was no one person or group calling the shots, and every activist group out there had a different set of demands.

One local leader, failed mayoral candidate Nikkita Oliver, demanded the mayor defund police, redistribute the funds to the black community, and release any rioters who had been arrested. Oliver is a reactionary who did not have the city's best interest at heart; a true ideologue from the Radical Left, she was a partisan warrior who would have seen the city burn to the ground if it meant defunding the police. Rashyla Levitt and David Lewis, two community activists identified by the city and media as representatives of the community, also participated in the meetings, seemed level-headed, and became de facto Durkan allies. But there was a problem: No one really knew who the hell Levitt or Lewis were.[20]

Over several nights, Seattle witnessed the same script unfold: Peaceful rally-goers were replaced by dangerous radicals who always taunted cops and sometimes used violence. By the weekend, all hell broke loose. It became a defining moment for the Radical Left.

On the morning of June 6, the city got a better understanding of the movement's strength. First, thousands of left-wing healthcare workers marched to City Hall, some donning scrubs or white lab jackets, in defiance of the very claim that these gatherings would spread COVID-19. But they said it was worth the risk because racism is a public health emergency, as if a bumper sticker talking point justified their COVID-19 hypocrisy. They said their profession was part of the problem, with speakers citing medical experiments conducted on black patients and how the industry has failed black Americans.[21] Then the crowd grew as they marched to the East Precinct. It was no longer a healthcare workers' march.

Agitators arrived looking for a fight and launching heavy glass candles at police, while trying to break the barricade surrounding the precinct. The Seattle Police Department (SPD) reported several officers were injured due to "improvised explosives,"[22] with two sent to the emergency room with wounds.[23] From the crowd, multiple people were trying to blind cops by pointing lasers at their eyes.[24] Police again responded with flash bangs and pepper spray.[25] Council member Mosqueda condemned the police on Twitter, saying there was "no need to use these dangerous tactics" because she received "multiple reports that it was absolutely peaceful."[26] It was not "absolutely peaceful."

As the situation grew more tense, with demonstrators refusing to disperse, local lawmakers decided it was time for them to step in, not to help mediate or calm things, but instead to agitate from the crowd. They were *joining* the protests.

A who's who of Radical Left lawmakers arrived. Council members Mosqueda, Herbold, Dan Strauss, and Andrew Lewis, along with King County council member Girmay Zahilay, state senator Joe Nguyen (D-White Center), and state representative Nicole Macri (D-Seattle) arrived. They took selfies celebrating their participation in the protest, live-tweeted the events, and even livestreamed on Facebook.

Strauss claimed that police were using "weapons of war" in a stilted performance on Facebook Live.[27] Police, of course, were not using weapons of war. County council member Zahilay livestreamed as he joined the crowd in chanting, "Take off your riot gear, I don't see no riot here," and demanding to defund the police.[28] He then panned the camera to police officers, saying, "We need to demilitarize. We need to de-escalate."[29] Senator Nguyen taunted cops via tweet, photographing them holding shields used to protect themselves from the rocks and glass candles his constituents were launching at them, and writing, "Protestors are peaceful but this doesn't look like peace."[30]

Mosqueda offered live commentary and interviews from the

protest via Facebook Live. At one point, a man on a bullhorn behind the council member taunted police as she interviewed an activist from the crowd. She was visibly distracted by the man as he threatened to murder cops.[31]

"SPD, I need you to do me a favor. Take your guns, put them onto your chins, and pull the trigger," the man shouted. "I need you to kill yourselves. That's your only redemption. Go ahead, save us the trouble of tearing you apart, and f—king kill yourselves. Did I stutter? I said k-k-k-kill yourselves."

Mosqueda turned to him but didn't say anything. The man continued: "F—king kill yourselves. It's the only chance you have left to do something good for the world and that's remove yourself from it."

Mosqueda was finally moved to comment. But she actually defended the threats, saying, "The anger that you hear is justified."

Moments later, Mosqueda interviewed Zahilay. While he claimed that "I've seen nothing but peaceful people out here," the protester shouted, "You have declared war on the American people. We do not forgive; we do not forget. Expect us."

Media outlets characterized the protest as peaceful, and local lawmakers placed themselves firmly in the middle of the fight between demonstrators and police. They made it clear who they stood with. And what did the mob want? The East Precinct. Days later, with the help of the council, that's exactly what they got.

The Free Nation of CHAZ

The next day, the city came under seemingly insurmountable pressure. They were put on the defense, with media outlets amplifying the claims that Seattle police instigated the violence the night before, despite video evidence proving otherwise.[32] Seattle police chief Carmen Best called those claims "simply not true."[33] But the media was not interested in the truth. Under the mayor's direction, the department removed the barrier around the East Precinct, a capitulation they hoped would placate the mob. But can you ever satisfy a group of ideologues who would turn to violence in order to see a department fully defunded and abolished?

The East Precinct's windows were boarded up in anticipation of more items being hurled their way. A fence was erected around the building to help keep protesters from breaching. The fire department put fire retardants around the building should Molotov cocktails or other incendiary devices be used.[34] And the police abandoned the building on the 11th day of demonstrations, taking with them important files and equipment from inside. Chief Best did not support the move.[35] But in the end, Mayor Durkan made the call, ignoring her police chief to mollify the Radical Left. In a private video to her officers that was leaked, Best slammed that decision.

"You should know, leaving the precinct was not my decision. You fought for days to protect it. I asked you to stand on that line, day in and day out, to be pelted with projectiles, to be screamed at, threatened, and in some cases hurt. Then to have a change of course nearly two weeks in? It seems like an insult to you and our community. Ultimately, the city had other plans for the building and relented to severe public pressure," Best explained.[36]

It actually could have been worse. Durkan contemplated handing over the building to Black Lives Matter Seattle-King County.[37] Her office insisted it was only a fleeting thought, though the process to start the transfer had been explored.

When the precinct was abandoned on June 8, the foundation for an autonomous zone was set. Demonstrators began erecting their own barriers on the streets around the East Precinct. Armed Antifa in body gear showed up as rumors swirled that mythical white supremacists were planning to cause trouble.[38]

"We are seeing quite a few bulletproof vests out here," said local independent activist-journalist Omari Salisbury on his stream that night.[39] "A lot of protesters out here before not armed, who are now armed. It's a different situation."

And the mob grew more agitated when they saw the press. Though they were getting almost entirely one-sided, positive coverage, a small group of local television reporters told both sides, including reports about the violence. Among them was my friend Brandi Kruse, at the time a reporter with Q13 FOX TV. She was the type of journalist unafraid to go into the crowd, rather than report from blocks away for safety like most of Seattle media. On this particular night, she wasn't particularly close to the nightly demonstrations because she was set to do a live hit from the field and didn't want to be interrupted by an increasingly aggressive crowd. She ended up getting surrounded and assaulted; she posted the raw video to her Twitter feed.

"Our crew was targeted, stalked, harassed, and assaulted," Kruse explained.[40] "The level of vitriol from one member of the mob, who claimed she was a 'social worker,' was like nothing I've ever experienced. When elected leaders lump this type of behavior into what they're calling 'peaceful,' not only is it a lie, but it's deeply offensive to those who have been subjected to it. I hope this video is spread widely. Seattle needs to do better."

With no more resistance, the movement gained unstoppable momentum. The American Civil Liberties Union (ACLU), a once nonpartisan group focused on preserving rights that turned into an arm of the Radical Left, filed a lawsuit against Mayor Durkan and Chief Best for unleashing "unnecessary violence" on peaceful protestors.[41] Council member Sawant hosted a rally to discuss next steps with activists, while organizer Oliver rallied the crowd to demand reparations.[42] The Seattle Department of Transportation (SDOT) provided maid service for the area, cleaning up debris and emptying trash more frequently.[43] Things were looking promising for the Radical Left.

On the evening of June 9, Seattle became what resembled a music festival—one designed for left-wing, young, mostly white activists looking to help define both a movement and their privileged lives. Sawant led a crowd of over one thousand to occupy

City Hall, where she used her key to unlock the doors, in violation of Council and state COVID-19 protocols.[44] Two smaller groups of protesters marched around the neighborhood, taking different routes. By 11 p.m., organizers set up a large projector at an intersection near the East Precinct to watch *13th*, an Ava DuVernay–directed propaganda documentary about racism in the criminal justice system.[45]

Then, protesters set up tents. Others brought tarps and blankets. A memorial to George Floyd occupied one piece of a nearby block. Another area was designated for street art. A station was set up for free snacks, and another for medical services. Police were nowhere to be seen, and the city left Cal Anderson Park's lights on so organizers could stay through the night.[46] So that's exactly what they did. The activists were setting up a camp, and they started to call it the Capitol Hill Autonomous Zone, or CHAZ.

Mainstreaming an Insurrection

CHAZ was born out of a violent insurrection to overtake a police precinct. And yet many in the media were covering the six city blocks taken over by radicals as a beautiful expression of anti-racism and social justice. Politicians celebrated it.

Activists constructed borders made of eco-blocks, fences, trash containers, cones, sandwich boards, and everything else left by police, the city, and nearby businesses. (Borders are not appropriate for the United States, but in the free nation of CHAZ, they were necessary to stem the flow of outsiders coming in.) One of the makeshift borders said, "Capitol Hill Autonomous Zone" and "You are now leaving the US." The SPD sign at the precinct was vandalized, with the word "police" replaced by "people," so it read the Seattle People Department. Graffiti went up declaring it a "cop free zone." Flyers advertised free snacks for protesters and their demand to defund police, while others surmised, "The cops will always be racist because capitalism requires inequality."

During the day, CHAZ mostly resembled a block party or Christiania, the peace and love commune in Copenhagen, Denmark. The snack station became the "No Cop Co-op," with free sodas, chips, and fruit donated by visitors—along with anti-police vitriol. The Conversation Cafe, a collection of secondhand couches arranged as if they were in a coffee shop or library, allowed folks to discuss their activism and joblessness. (It was mostly used by stoners getting high.)

At Cal Anderson Park, community gardens were planted, with one exclusive to black and indigenous gardeners. One section of the park was labeled "Black Out: an all black healing space" meant for, as the name suggests, black folks to "heal" from institutional racism and whatever else they pretended they were suffering from. Self-righteous white "allies" literally guarded the space, allowing entry only "if you experienced oppression because you are black."[47] Meditation sessions were held nearby.

Documentaries were screened on the giant projector, and a stage was erected for daily speeches.[48] A giant "Black Lives Matter" mural was painted on CHAZ's thoroughfare, which gave the media a beautiful image to distract from the vulgar "F—k the police" and "All Cops Are Bastards" graffiti everywhere.

"This is the most beautiful thing. It's so hopeful. I've been to a lot of festivals around the world, and what I see is just something very similar," artist Adam One told CNN.[49] "Love and giving and self-organized policing and just a lot of good vibes, rainbows."

But President Donald Trump didn't feel the good vibes and declared via Twitter that "Domestic Terrorists have taken over Seattle, run by Radical Left Democrats, of course. LAW & ORDER!" At a press event, Trump argued that Seattle "would be so easy to solve," declaring "you can't let that happen...you have to dominate the streets."[50]

Mayor Durkan, humiliated from her poor handling of the rallies and riots, responded on Twitter: "Make us all safe. Go back to your bunker."[51] Governor Jay Inslee also reacted on Twitter, saying, "A man who is totally incapable of governing should stay out of

Washington State's business."[52] It was an ironic message because when a reporter asked Inslee about CHAZ radicals commandeering a neighborhood, he said, "That's news to me," suggesting no credible source was making that claim.[53] The state's largest city ceded six blocks to armed radicals, a story that was trending for a full 24 hours locally and nationally, and the governor wasn't aware?

Media outlets, eager to contradict Trump and support activists and Democrat lawmakers, published press releases masquerading as serious journalism, loaded with half-truths and spin. The *New York Times*, in a dubiously titled puff piece entitled "Free Food, Free Speech and Free of Police" (there were no free speech rights at CHAZ), reporter Mike Baker contrasted Trump's tweet by highlighting the poetry readings and children making chalk drawings on the street.[54] CNN's Dan Simon seemed impressed, marveling at the "remarkable...infrastructure of the whole thing."[55] He bragged, "It really has the feel of a street festival."[56] Kelly Weill, a reporter with the *Daily Beast*, celebrated the zone for helping generate business for restaurants in and near CHAZ that had been shuttered due to COVID-19.[57] Not that I ever trusted these outlets to accurately portray what was happening, but I legitimately couldn't believe how dishonest and selective the coverage was.

CNN's Chris Cuomo downplayed Trump's "tone-deaf" concern over CHAZ, inviting Durkan on to his show to defend the insurrection.[58] She called it a "block party atmosphere, it's not an armed takeover." Cuomo mildly pushed back, saying partygoers don't take over police departments, and he wondered if the city had the ability to take the area back. But Durkan deflected.

"During this time, a number one priority every American city has is to protect the First Amendment right. Our country was born out of protest. The right to gather, the right to protest, the right to challenge government when it's wrong is our most fundamental constitutional right. It's a reason it's the First Amendment. And as a mayor of this city, I will do everything to protect that right and balance the public safety," she said.

When asked how long CHAZ would be in place, she uttered words that would come to define her political career: "We could have a summer of love."

A Deadly "Summer of Love"

The "summer of love" quickly turned violent. And thanks to untrained "security," the situation grew unnecessarily tense.

The Puget Sound John Brown Gun Club, an Antifa-aligned group of militant cosplayers, provided some of the CHAZ security. They describe themselves as "an anti-fascist, anti-racist, pro-worker community defense organization" committed to "active resistance," which is what they provided on-site.[59] Armed guards were posted at border entrances[60] where I saw them sometimes ask to see ID or question visitors about why they were entering the autonomous zone.

"We're just making sure that there's no violence or, you know, anything against people of color. That's why we're here," a volunteer guard told CNN.[61]

They weren't alone. Local rapper and former pimp[62] Raz Simone also took up security duty, arming anyone who said they were over age 18 with automatic rifles, if they promised to defend CHAZ.[63] Without training, but with plenty of the "toxic masculinity" the Left constantly complains about, it didn't take a soothsayer to know what was coming.

During the day, random fights broke out in the crowd. Sometimes, it was over politics. Other times, it was due to intoxication. And we weren't allowed to film the violence when it broke out, an effort by CHAZ "security" to keep all coverage positive. This assault on a free press didn't make the *New York Times* coverage. When Townhall.com reporter Julio Rosas and I attempted to film skirmishes, organizers repeatedly bumped into us so that we would drop our phones, which were recording the action, and stand in front of us so we wouldn't get clear shots.[64] When I was spotted in the crowd, activists would post photos of me on Twitter, warning people that I was around.[65] The intent was to put a target on my back. It was simply not safe, with a COVID-19 mask and hat the only thing providing me some cover.

At night, when most reporters were tucked away safely in their hotel beds, CHAZ grew increasingly chaotic. Fights were common, gang members and drug dealers were everywhere, and crime was rampant. Businesses within the CHAZ borders were frequently vandalized. When I was out in the field after dark, I could feel the tension. The mood had shifted considerably, and many of the people who showed up—who weren't living in the tents in the park—looked up to no good and wholly disconnected from the movement. These were outsiders taking advantage of a lawless zone in the middle of Seattle.

Car Tender was an auto-garage business that, at the time, was within the CHAZ zone. Early one morning during the occupation, the owners received an alarm notification of a break-in. They called 911 while driving down to the store to protect their business. When they arrived, they say they found a suspect, later identified as Richard Hanks, setting one of the desks on fire, using a cassette tape and what appeared to be liquid hand sanitizer. The owner and his son stopped Hanks and held him as they waited for cops to arrive. But the cops were never going to arrive.[66]

The city forbade police from entering CHAZ unless there was a mass casualty event or under very specific circumstances in which protesters allowed them to enter. Despite calling over a dozen times, the Car Tender business owners were left to their own devices. While the police didn't show up, a mob of about 100 to 200 CHAZ activists did. Some were armed when they demanded Hanks be turned over to them.

"They were shouting at us from outside the gate of my dad's shop, saying that they were going to kill us and to let him go and, you know, obscenities," Mason McDermott, son to the owner, told me on my Seattle talk show.[67] "Basically, they said, 'let him go or we're gonna kill you guys. You need to let him go.' And we were just holding him so the police could get there, you know, so this guy could be accountable for trying to burn our family business to the ground and stealing."

To appease the mob, Hanks was released to their custody. It didn't go so well for him. A police report says Hanks was searched and "forcibly detained" before someone in the crowd "assaulted the suspect, repeatedly punching him in the face."[68] When a brawl broke out, Hanks escaped, but was arrested during a suspected car burglary in nearby White Center later that day.

Disturbed by reports of lawlessness, Iconic Global, a security firm based in Auburn, Washington, volunteered it's time to help protect Car Tender. They also provided my security when I was reporting live from CHAZ for *Tucker Carlson Tonight* on Fox News. When Iconic Global security was patrolling the area outside the auto shop, they say they made a startling discovery. They say they found an AK-47, with five fully loaded magazines, a Glock magazine, fireworks, and "explosive hardware," hidden in nearby bushes. They turned the weapons over to the SPD.[69]

The thuggish behavior by the Radical Left was common, and CHAZ started to be seen for what it was. That might explain the sudden name change. Around June 13, the occupiers started calling the area the Capitol Hill Occupied (or Organized) Protest, or CHOP. Some said it was a necessary change to better characterize what they were doing, which was occupying a space for protest. They started replacing signage to reflect the new name.[70] While some activists fought (literally and figuratively) over the name change, CHOP stuck, but the dangers only got worse.

Isaiah Willoughby confessed to dousing a pile of debris in gasoline and igniting it outside of the East Precinct, scorching the exterior of the building. Fortunately, nearby protesters put out the fire.[71] Robert James was taken into custody for allegedly attempting to sexually assault a deaf woman after luring her into his tent at CHOP. A nearby protester heard the alleged crime-in-progress and intervened.[72]

Yet the city still seemed disinterested in clearing the area. In fact, the Durkan administration made it clear that activists were welcome to stay. On June 16, the city provided concrete barriers around CHOP, providing extra security so cars could drive through.[73] In return, CHOP organizers allowed the city to reopen portions of the streets to people who live and work within the area. In a blog post, Durkan's office said they were "committed to maintaining space for community to come together, protest and exercise their first amendment rights."[74]

The agreement was short lived. Hours later, CHOP activists blocked the newly reopened areas by strategically positioning vehicles to obstruct incoming and outgoing traffic.[75] The lack of a clear organizational structure and the city's inconsistent approach to dealing with various organizers made it difficult for the activists to reach a unified decision on how to compromise with the city, if at all. However, the activists did agree to the city's offer to provide portable toilets.

The situation appeared to be evolving CHOP into a permanent fixture, with the city unwilling to clear the area and the activists unwilling to leave. However, the situation changed dramatically when black teens were shot to death.

These Black Lives Didn't Matter in CHOP

In the early hours of June 20, around 2:30 a.m., 19-year-old Horace Lorenzo Anderson visited CHOP and bumped into 18-year-old Marcel Long, with whom he had a bad relationship. A verbal altercation ensued between the two, but ended in gunfire.

According to police reports, video footage captured Long drawing a handgun and shooting Anderson multiple times as he was walking away from the altercation. CHOP medics decided to call 911. But when police arrived to secure the scene for city medical personnel, they were immediately met with resistance from a large group of CHOP activists, as captured on police body cameras.[76]

Anderson was eventually transported to the nearby hospital by activists, but was pronounced dead.

Council member Sawant, who helped establish CHOP, wanted to avoid any culpability for the shooting. Sawant used Anderson's death as an opportunity to blame the "right wing." In a statement, she baselessly claimed that "there are indications that this may have been a right-wing attack."[77] There was never any evidence to support her claim. It was clear from the outset that Anderson's death was the result of a fight. Nevertheless, Sawant persisted in her efforts to deflect blame.

"If this killing turns out to be a right-wing attack, President Trump bears direct responsibility, since he has fomented reactionary hatred specifically against the peaceful Capitol Hill occupation, and even threatened to intervene with federal troops. Also responsible are the conservative and corporate media outlets, both locally and nationally, which have themselves whipped up right-wing hate by completely misrepresenting the nature of the peaceful protest occupation, and who are continuing to do so even now, claiming that this shooting proves the CHOP is descending into chaos. Seattle's establishment mayor Jenny Durkan and Police Chief Carmen Best also share responsibility for having portrayed our protest movement as violent," she wrote.[78]

Sawant's statement was a transparent attempt to manipulate the narrative in real time. After she released her false information, CHOP activists released a statement confirming the more accurate details of the altercation that led to the shooting.[79] The following day, *another* black teenager was shot. This time, a 17-year-old was struck by a bullet to the arm.[80] But Durkan's office did not immediately move to clear CHOP, instead continuing negotiations with the Radical Left. Durkan proposed to allocate $20 million from the current SPD budget and vowed to not hire any officers in 2021. She also asked the police department to prepare "models" for what it would mean to reduce policing by up to 50 percent, if the budget was gutted.[81] These efforts failed to sway the Radical Left, who remained steadfast supporters of CHOP.

"Let it be clear, we will not be bought off. We will not attend meetings where the goal is to buy us off, we are here to dismantle systemic racism," said Naudia Miller of Black Collective Voices, one of the many groups behind CHOP.[82] "Until these demands are met we will continue to organize and strategize the people."

Black Collective Voices circulated a list of 30 demands of the city. Most of their demands were unrealistic and disconnected from reality. Claiming police are "beyond reform," they demanded abolition. Until then, the police were to be disarmed. They also demanded an end to the school-to-prison pipeline, though it's unclear how a city can end a poorly formed metaphor. They demanded a "retrial of all People in [sic] Color currently serving a prison sentence for violent crime" and that felons currently serving time receive full voting rights. But they *also* demanded we abolish prisons. They asked for rent control, the "de-gentrification" of Seattle, and that "hospitals and care facilities of Seattle employ black doctors and nurses specifically to help care for black patients."[83] These were the demands of unserious people. And yet the city tried to reason with them, while local media took them seriously.

Following the fatal shootings, there was a palpable change in the atmosphere, as if Radical Left activists had a sense that CHOP was coming to an end. The numbers started to dwindle, and the movement did not have the same energy as before Anderson was murdered. Many of the people who remained in the zone were homeless drug addicts. That's when Durkan decided to act, telling the remaining activists and homeless that "It's time for people to go home. It is time for us to restore Cal Anderson and Capitol Hill so it can be a vibrant part of the community."[84]

Durkan waited until the murder of a black teen before acting because she didn't have the political courage to intervene sooner. Hoping to earn some points with an activist crowd that was unhappy with her leadership, Durkan used Trump's tweet to gaslight the country into thinking CHOP was just a festival. And too many in local media uncritically covered the movement they appeared to want to succeed.

The End of CHOP

While Durkan ordered CHOP to be cleared and promised the police would return to the East Precinct, days went by without any meaningful action. On June 26, the SDOT was finally sent in to remove the barricades. The city had also agreed to reoccupy the East Precinct with police officers by the end of the day.

SDOT encountered resistance from aggressive CHOP residents and holdouts, forcing the city staff to retreat.[85] Durkan's plan to retake the East Precinct was then called off.[86] A friend and colleague reported live from the scene. He witnessed fights break out, a man brandishing a rifle and a hammer, and individuals who threatened anyone who tried to document the events on camera.[87]

Due to the postponed sweep, CHOP was attracting more sinister elements. At the time, I warned that the longer this continues, the chances of further violence and fatalities would increase. Sadly, my predictions came true.

On June 29, another shooting occurred in CHOP and it was believed to be carried out by untrained Antifa security personnel. Two young, black teenagers were tragically impacted by the violence; 16-year-old Antonio Mays Jr. lost his life, and an unidentified 14-year-old boy was seriously injured. The teens were reportedly in a white Jeep Cherokee that drove through Cal Anderson Park before crashing into a barrier. The police investigation was hindered because witnesses tampered with evidence. It seemed likely that Antifa security and others cosplayers fired at the teens, believing they might have been the white supremacists they deluded themselves into thinking were on the way.[88] The movement proclaiming that Black Lives Matter was responsible for taking and hurting multiple black lives.

After this preventable tragedy, Durkan finally swept CHOP. On July 1, the autonomous zone came to an end with a long overdue executive order declaring an unlawful assembly. City staff were not greeted as liberators. The police operation to sweep CHOP began around 5 a.m., with 44 individuals arrested throughout the day because they were unwilling to leave. One of the arrestees possessed a large metal pipe and kitchen knife, according to police.[89] During the clean-up, some armed activists were reported to be driving cars without license plates around the area in an attempt to intimidate the police and city workers.[90] Other activists chanted slogans like "No cops, no Nazis, no racists, no KKK USA" at the officers.[91]

My three and a half weeks at CHOP seemed unreal. I was there almost daily, and I remember struggling to truly grasp the reality of what was happening in my city and the lack of critical coverage by uncurious media. Durkan's leadership was embarrassing. She surrounded herself with an equally inept staff, making her unable to navigate this crisis. The escalation of CHOP ultimately led to the end of her unimpressive political career, as she announced she would not run for re-election.

As CHOP unfolded, I covered the day-to-day action on Fox News (sometimes from a distance due to threats of violence). But most other national outlets lost interest after the first weekend, especially after the violence made their previous coverage look foolish and pedestrian. Local media failed to adequately cover incidents in which reporters were attacked. It failed to provide objective coverage of what was happening at CHOP. Instead, their reporting morphed into advocacy.

Though the autonomous zone was done, the movement continued. For weeks, Antifa and Black Lives Matter radicals marched nightly. In late July, over 4,000 radicals and their enablers took to the streets of Capitol Hill, walking from the site of a future youth detention facility to the East Precinct. Antifa, dressed in black to conceal their identities, were everywhere. They burned down two construction trailers at the detention center construction site.[92] I watched as the structures burned. Then, I witnessed them gut a Starbucks, setting a small fire inside. That café was attached to an apartment complex, but luckily, there was no major damage.[93] Once the mob reached the East Precinct, someone hurled an explosive at the building, cratering through the building's exterior. After declaring a riot, the police responded with blast balls and pepper spray. With the explosion of flash bangs behind me, I ran with the crowd for cover. I remember thinking how could the crowd be okay with the violence many in the their group were responsible for? Inexplicably, they thought the cops were in the wrong.

Activists claimed cops indiscriminately attacked protesters, portraying this as another peaceful protest. The *Seattle Times* called it a demonstration, downplaying the violence, at first attributing it to the police. They only characterized the actions of Antifa and other agitators as "scattered vandalism and fires." In fact, they seemed to justify the violence, writing, "While most protesters have been peaceful, some see fires, graffiti and broken windows as forms of resistance to an oppressive regime."[94] It was a shameful failure of journalism. By not offering sufficient coverage so that the public knew what was really going on, the violence only escalated, including to the point where they tried to burn cops alive.

On the evening of August 24, a group of Antifa members and other agitators again surrounded the East Precinct. They used quick-dry cement to seal shut an entrance/exit to the building and destroyed the electronic key card pad with the clear intention of locking police inside. At the same time, 20-year-old Desmond David-Pitts set fire to the exterior of the building. A source told me that officers trapped inside kicked the door open to escape the building.[95] David-Pitts was later sentenced to just 20 months in prison for conspiracy to commit arson.[96]

Later that evening, the Seattle Police Officers Guild (SPOG) offices were attacked with Molotov cocktails. Fortunately, the police union offices were empty at the time. Surveillance footage that I exclusively obtained showed two suspects in all black hurling the explosive devices at the stairway entrance before fleeing. A fire raged for two minutes before officers arrived and extinguished the flames.

"What's shown in the SPOG videos are two criminal actors determined to kill police officers by using Molotov cocktails to destroy private property that could possibly have people inside working. These people have no fear. They do not adhere to law and order. They could care less about the human beings that could possibly be hurt or killed by their criminal, domestic terrorism actions," Officer Mike Solan, union president, told me.[97]

A month later, black-bloc Antifa and other agitators descended on the East Precinct again, and this time with weapons. During the unrest, as police officers on bicycles retreated, 19-year-old Jacob Greenberg ran up behind Officer Jose Jimenez and violently struck him on the head with a baseball bat.[98] The officer was wearing a helmet at the time, but had he not been, prosecutors say it would have been a fatal blow. Months after the attack, Jimenez still suffered from brain fog and sensitivity to bright lights.[99]

Greenberg, who is the stepson of former Democrat state lawmaker Laura Ruderman, was there to hurt cops. Prosecutors claim that he and his accomplice, Danielle McMillan, planned a well-orchestrated attack against police, devoting time during the fall to "plotting various assaults and fire bombings on police officers." The charging documents state that their discussion showed "a high degree of sophistication and planning for their attacks, identifying targets (Seattle Police Officer's Guild, East Precinct), itemizing the needs for set numbers of Molotov cocktails, calculating expected loss for failed bombs, and where to obtain supplies."[100] In texts exchanged between the two after the attack, McMillan told Greenburg, "Very proud of you." Greenberg responded: "Appreciate it. I'm proud too, hehe. Wish he didn't have a helmet on, lol."[101]

As a result of the attack, Greenberg was sentenced to five years in prison for first-degree attempted arson, second-degree assault with a deadly weapon, and second-degree reckless burning. McMillan earned 60 days in jail and 12 months of community custody for first-degree reckless burning as part of a plea deal.[102]

These were not isolated events. They were a frequent occurrence, and yet city council members stayed silent, the mayor was conspicuously absent, and the media only presented transactional stories limited to basic details without further examination or analysis. They never mentioned Antifa, and they never blamed the Radical Left.

Living in Seattle became a source of fear and anxiety at the time. There was a surge in crimes like murders, thefts, and assaults, on top of dealing with Antifa terrorists who were targeting law enforcement and political opponents. Despite this reality, nationally, Democrats like Representative Jerry Nadler (D-NY) denied Antifa even existed, claiming it was a "myth that's being spread only in Washington, DC."[103] Does he have any respect for the public? His statements exemplify the gaslighting employed by Democrats to advance their extremist political agenda, in this case tied to Black Lives Matter.

How did city and national leaders allow this to happen in a major American city? How was other Antifa violence allowed in Portland, Oregon; Los Angeles; Minneapolis; and New York City? Democrats cast no judgments, and many in the media withheld the truth. The Radical Left viewed this as advancing a political agenda that would benefit them, so they turned a blind eye or justified what was happening. It became a strategy for the Radical Left: Ignore the damage being done in service to an ideological cause. And it wasn't just Antifa damage that they ignored.

CHAPTER 2

THE WAR ON THE WAR ON DRUGS

So, You Found Some Meth in Your Jeans . . . Who Hasn't?

When Shannon Blake was arrested in Spokane, Washington, in 2016, after police executed a search warrant to uncover a stolen vehicle, little did she know she would dramatically change the course of Washington State drug laws. It certainly wasn't her intent. She just wanted out of a drug charge.

At the time of her arrest, Blake was wearing used jeans that she said were a gift from her friend. While Shannon was searched at the county jail, police found a small bag of methamphetamine in the coin pocket. It earned her a charge of unlawful possession of a controlled substance.

But at a bench trial, where a judge determines the outcome of a case in lieu of a jury, Blake claimed the drugs did not belong to her and that she was surprised the drugs were there.[104] After all, who among us hasn't reached into a pair of jeans we're wearing to find a bag of meth that doesn't belong to us?

Blake and her boyfriend testified that she was not a drug user, but the court did not find the testimony credible. It found she had a chemical dependency. She was sentenced to three days in jail, with credit for three days she already served, so she was freed. But she was hit with 12 months of community custody for treatment.

Blake appealed with a simple argument: Requiring a defendant to prove "unwitting possession" violates due process. But the Court of Appeals disagreed, finding simple possession of a drug is a strict liability crime. That means, regardless of your intent, possession is the crime.

This low-level drug charge reached the left-wing Washington State Supreme Court. They took this case, *State v. Blake*, as an opportunity to upend decades-old drug policy.[105] The Court found that unknowing possession of drugs is not a crime.

"The question before us today is whether unintentional, unknowing possession of a controlled substance is the sort of innocent, passive nonconduct that falls beyond the State's police power to criminalize. Because unknowing possession is just as innocent and passive as staying out late with a juvenile or remaining in a city without registering, we hold that this felony drug possession statute is just as unconstitutional," the Court concluded.

As a result of the ruling, the state's felony possession law was moot. It required a legislative fix; otherwise, drugs would be fully legalized. That was likely the Court's intent. More troubling, the Court's ruling was retroactive, meaning drug users sentenced for simple possession could have their sentence reduced or their conviction vacated. Progressives have long argued that the so-called War on Drugs does not work. They believe we should offer drug treatment to addicts instead of "criminalizing addiction." It's a position that many people likely support, including conservatives. If someone is truly an addict, we have a moral responsibility to at least try to help. But what started as a promise to treat addiction led to legalization, where Democrat policies allow open drug use free from stigma and prosecution. Washington State voters legalized marijuana in 2012, so Democrats thought why not treat that drug nearly the same as methamphetamine, heroin, cocaine, and fentanyl?

After the *Blake* decision, Washington state's Democrat-controlled legislature changed the law to make drug possession crimes misdemeanors, but only after the drug user is offered diversion programs twice.[106] If caught with personal possession amounts a third time, the addict can be arrested and prosecuted. But the legislature did not create a mechanism to track police encounters. Consequently, police weren't making arrests because there was no official record of an addict having previous contact with police. It should come as no shock that when you effectively legalize drugs and stop enforcing the law, drug crimes and fatal overdoses soar. One need only look at Seattle and King County as proof.

King County prosecutor Dan Satterberg first took office in 2007 as a moderate Republican. At the time, being a Republican was not the kind of scarlet letter in Seattle it is today. But in 2018, facing a progressive challenger, Satterberg changed parties so he would not be seen by voters as supportive of then-president Donald Trump, who was loathed across the city and county.[107]

Satterberg might as well have been a Democrat from the start. He advocated to abolish the death penalty. He argued that immigration laws were actually counterproductive to public safety.[108] And he supported increasing the age to 21 to legally purchase semi-automatic weapons (which the Radical Left mostly describes as "scary looking guns"). But it was his dramatic positions on drug laws that helped set the stage for the county's drug crisis.

In 2018, Satterberg announced he would not charge for personal possession of any controlled substances, be it meth, heroin, cocaine, or fentanyl. For him, the decision was personal.[109] When his sister Shelley was 14 years old, she ran away from home, upset that her parents wouldn't let her attend a concert. She didn't return for two months. She turned to hard drugs to cope with the trauma of a gang rape she says she suffered while living on the streets.

When she finally returned home, Satterberg saw what worked to address her addiction. It was treatment. Though she was never arrested, that experience ultimately informed his approach as a prosecutor when dealing with addicts.

"It gave me some insight about what works better than jail," Satterberg told the *New York Times* in a 2019 puff piece.[110] "What Shelley needed was not a jail cell and not a judge wagging a finger at her, but she needed some support."

One can understand how this could change his view. But it ultimately blinded him to the reality of his position as prosecutor. Just because treatment worked for his sister, who did not deal with the criminal justice system as he implied to the *New York Times*, doesn't mean it's sound policy when managing a prosecutor's office for a large county. Not every addict has a close family capable of interceding.

When word got out that Satterberg wasn't prosecuting most drug crimes, addicts and their dealers adapted, making policing nearly impossible. Drugs flooded the county. The homeless turned to petty crime to fuel their habit, breaking into cars, homes, and businesses, stealing whatever they could to sell, using profits to buy their drug of choice.

Sections of downtown Seattle turned into homeless bazaars.[111] You could buy jeans and shirts on street corners in downtown Seattle. I saw the stolen clothing still had tags on them from a nearby Target when I investigated a site for a story I was working on. You could purchase or trade for hats, gloves, scarves, and luggage. In need of laundry detergent or toilet paper? You could buy those too. And of course, booze was plentiful, including different whiskies like Maker's Mark 46 Bourbon. High West Whiskey went for "around $20," according to the homeless proprietor. That's quite a steal (literally), since a bottle normally goes for $70.

Open-air drug markets popped up downtown where residents and tourists were greeted by addicts resembling zombies. Their eyes were glossy and empty. Their bodies were hunched over, slowly swaying back and forth like a broken-down swing set you'd never let your kids close to, before inevitably collapsing on a sidewalk, park bench, alleyway, or storefront. Others huddled together smoking fentanyl on a small piece of tin foil in front of struggling businesses. They did not hide their drug use because they knew it came with no consequences.

Because drug users avoided charges, the only way to slow the growing crisis was to arrest the dealers. Though drug dealing was common, it was no longer easy to make arrests.

First, drug dealers knew that if they carried personal possession amounts, they wouldn't get arrested. Police said that known and suspected drug dealers were simply carrying less product and restocking for sale more frequently; or they distributed the products among nearby associates who all carried a little, but collectively, were able to sell copious amounts.

Second, police could no longer leverage addicts to turn on their dealers. Cops could either catch addicts using or establish probable cause to search their property and find an illicit substance. The addict was then given two choices: Go to jail or give up information on the dealer. The prospect of coming off a high while in a jail cell is as terrifying as an actual jail sentence for most addicts. The headache, sweating, shaking, and nausea would be torturous. It would be just enough to convince the addict to give up information on who and where the drugs were being sold and stored. But addicts know how to survive until their next hit. They knew the cops wouldn't arrest them, so they had no incentive to cooperate.

Even before the *Blake* decision, drug use was mostly tolerated in Seattle. When Seattle City Attorney Pete Holmes took office in 2010, he immediately announced he would not prosecute marijuana charges. He was both a supporter of marijuana legalization and an active pot user. In fact, he was caught bringing two, two-gram bags of OG's Pearl weed to his "drug-free workplace" in the city attorney's office, a purchase he made the first day the drug became legal at retail stores in 2014. "When I brought the unopened marijuana to city offices—trying to keep up with a busy schedule—I nonetheless violated the city's rules," Holmes admitted in a press release. "I apologize to my employees, all city employees, and to the public."[112]

The drug crisis quickly spiraled out of control with fatal overdoses reaching historic highs. It was relatively flat in the years preceding Satterberg's drug decriminalization move, though slowly trending upward. But from 2018 through 2022, the numbers soared.[113] The year Satterberg announced his new drug policy, there were 393 fatal overdoses, with methamphetamine and heroin the drugs of choice. By 2022, fatal overdoses more than doubled, reaching an astonishing 877, with 385 from fentanyl and 365 from methamphetamine. There were so many fatal drug overdoses to begin 2023, the Seattle-King County Public Health Director Dr. Faisal Khan made a startling revelation during a county presentation. "The Medical Examiner's Office is now struggling with the issue of storing bodies because the fentanyl-related death toll continues to climb. Obviously, they have finite space in the coolers they use and that space is now being exceeded on a regular basis," he warned.[114]

Though the drug crisis had worsened in Seattle and King County, Democrats in the state legislature hoped to bring Satterberg's policy statewide. With the *Blake* decision, the Radical Left seized on that opportunity. But why move forward with a policy that was verifiably unsuccessful?

The Radical Left believes that the criminal justice system is oppressive, and that it intentionally and systemically targets black people. After the death of George Floyd in Minneapolis, which sparked nationwide racial justice rallies and riots, politicians and activists took a social justice posture. Everything was viewed through a racial lens, and issues that were already steeped in claims of institutionalized racism only saw those claims intensify.

In September 2018, the city of Seattle moved to vacate misdemeanor, nonviolent convictions for marijuana offenses between 1996 and 2010. Then-city attorney Holmes argued the move was meant "to right the injustices of a drug war that has primarily targeted people of color." It is a claim that's made without any further comment or context; it's presented as fact.[115] But is it? The Seattle Municipal Court judges said that 46 percent of the marijuana prosecutions between 1996 and 2010 were against black defendants. But the judges also wrote that, "The Court makes no finding that these numbers are 100 percent accurate, or that individual defendants were specifically impacted because of their race."[116] Yet Holmes called this "one small step to right the injustices of a drug war that has primarily targeted people of color." (He fails to mention, of course, that the drug war he loathes also saved scores of black lives from fatal overdoses.)

Like so many arguments pursued by the Radical Left, you're asked to assume or infer intent just by looking at raw data, sans context. If the black community is "disproportionately" impacted by a law, it must mean the law is racist, they argue. Disproportionality arguments, however, are as lazy as they are misleading. Raw data, absent context, doesn't make an argument. For example, if there's more crime in low-income communities, and those communities have a large black population, it makes sense that there will be more interactions between black residents and cops. Was the Seattle Police Department purposefully ignoring white drug dealers so they could hunt for black people selling heroin or marijuana? Of course not. But it's much easier for the Radical Left to invent a specific problem, and then play white savior. When it comes to black communities, Democrats love playing the literal White Knight coming to the rescue to fight racism (and earn their votes in future elections, of course). It is, however, quite ironic that the drug overdose fatalities disproportionately impact the black community in King County. So perhaps their drug policy is racist?

Oregon Suffers a Bad Trip

Voters in the Beaver State legalized drugs before it earned progressive street cred. It's been an utter disaster by any reasonable measure. But the Radical Left won't admit failure.

Measure 110, the Drug Decriminalization and Addiction Treatment Initiative, made Oregon the first state in the nation to decriminalize all drugs. It reclassified hard drugs such as heroin, fentanyl, cocaine, and methamphetamine from a Class A misdemeanor to a Class E violation. Caught with personal possession amounts? Addicts get hit with either a $100 fine or they can agree to a voluntary health assessment for drug treatment. Beyond the reclassification, it also would allocate marijuana sales tax to fund addiction treatment because the goal, advocates claimed, was to fund addiction services.

The vote to decriminalize was characterized as both historic and groundbreaking, with support from a collection of local and national organizations including the Oregon chapter of the American College of Physicians, NAACP Portland, American Civil Liberties Union, and Human Rights Watch. Even left-wing musician John Legend endorsed the measure, though the only time he's in Oregon is for a rare tour stop. The reason for the national attention was that Oregon was seen as a test market for the movement. It's why the New York-based Drug Policy Alliance wrote and funded the measure, pouring $4 million into the campaign. Its executive director Kassandra Frederique called the plan a "huge sledgehammer to the cornerstone of the war on drugs."[117]

As was the strategy in Washington State, advocates argued against criminalizing addiction. Mona Knudson, executive director of nonprofit Bridges to Change, argued we must "begin to shift the way we think about addiction" and "stop being naive that we can think that we can continue to incarcerate ourselves out of this issue."[118]

For Andy Seaman, an addiction specialist and assistant professor of medicine at Oregon Health and Sciences University, this was an opportunity to finally offer appropriate treatment and stop leaning into a carceral system. He claimed that "by incarcerating them [addicts], we take away the very things that allows their recovery."[119]

For local activists who knew the homeless fueled the addiction crisis, they tugged on the heartstrings of Oregon's loyally progressive population. Decriminalizing hard drugs actually *saved* lives, they argued. They're not even truly addicts; they're just taking methamphetamines as a tool of survival. "Some people use methamphetamines to stay up at night because it's not safe," explained Laura Carlson, program supervisor at Club Hope, a recovery center in Portland.[120] "If you're out on the street, it's not safe to go to sleep at night. People die. People get killed. People get assaulted."

And former addicts-turned-advocates, like Janie Gullickson, sung Measure 110's praises. If she had access to the services promised under the measure, her life would be different. Indeed, she told local media that she didn't even know how to get access to treatment when she was struggling to survive the disease of addiction. Vote for Measure 110, and addicts will at long last have a shot, rather than a jail cell that continues the cycle of addiction.[121]

Voters believed Measure 110's proponents. Buoyed by especially strong support in Multnomah County, home to Portland, the measure passed with over 58 percent of the vote and went into effect in February 2021. It didn't take long to fail.

The civil infractions were meant to convince addicts to seek treatment rather than be hit with a $100 fine. Each ticket included the hotline to call to start your health assessment. But by October 2021, the hotline only received an average of two calls per week with only seven defendants using it to get out of paying the fine.[122] A year later, fewer than 200 people had called. Of the 3,169 drug users receiving tickets, most didn't appear in court nor did they pay the $100 fine.[123] It turns out addicts think the $100 is better spent on the drugs flooding Oregon communities. Who knew?

Measure 110 failed to leverage infractions to get addicts into treatment, and as in Seattle, it also coincided with more fatal drug overdoses and crime. In 2021, the Mental Health and Addiction Certification Board of Oregon (MHACBO) released an all-you-can-eat buffet of data pointing to a surge in drug use. At over 9 percent, Oregon ranked number one in most adult and teen drug use, well above the 6.64 percent national average. Just within the last year of the study, 21.17 percent of the population tried a hard drug, while 27.82 percent of the population smoked marijuana. And despite Measure 110 offering addiction services, Oregon was the lowest state with the percentage of addicts needing but not receiving substance abuse treatment.[124] In 2010–2011, the Oregon legislature ranked the state as having the 10th most residents with substance abuse disorder. The rank was fourth by 2016–2017.[125] In 2021, the MHACBO said the state had the second highest.

The Oregon Health Authority painted an even direr picture. Fatal overdoses surged 76 percent from 2011 to 2021, with fentanyl driving the numbers. Just between 2020 and 2021, fentanyl-related fatal overdoses rose 83 percent.[126] Fatal opioid overdoses nearly doubled from 2020 to 2021, growing from 472 to 745, respectively. Preliminary data from the first quarter of 2022 showed Oregon on the path to meeting or exceeding 2021's record numbers.[127] As is the case in Washington State, Oregon's drug addicts are disproportionately black.

To addiction experts, this data is not surprising. Keith Humphreys, professor and director of the Stanford Network on Addiction Policy, testified in front of a Senate committee overseeing Measure 110's implementation. Unsurprisingly, overly permissive drug policies fail to provide an addict an incentive to seek treatment. Yes, addiction is a health issue, but unlike chronic pain, he argues, drugs provide the addict euphoria and end withdrawal symptoms. Treatment for chronic pain provides relief, just as a drug provides pleasure to an addict.[128]

"This matters because Oregon has removed all legal pressure to stop drug use and seek treatment," said Humphreys, who served in the White House Office of National Drug Control Policy under Presidents George W. Bush and Barack Obama. "Because many addicted individuals are not working or in touch with family, those pressures to stop using drugs and alcohol are also often absent in their lives. Because the West Coast has an individualistic culture with significant tolerance for substance use, social pressures to seek treatment are often minimal as well. So, on the one hand, we have highly rewarding drugs which are widely available, and on the other hand little or no pressure to stop using them. Under these conditions, we should expect to see exactly what Oregon is experiencing—extensive drug use, extensive addiction, and not much treatment seeking."[129]

Walk around downtown Portland on any given afternoon or evening, and you'll see the human toll of Measure 110 and years of a laisse-faire approach to the crisis. My last weekend trip to Portland was heartbreaking. Homelessness extended far outside of the downtown core, with tents, trash, human waste, and used needles found in formerly picturesque suburban neighborhoods. Residents find strategically placed used needle containers around their homes, but are obviously ignored. The broken-down RVs that line city streets are hotbeds of drug activity, often used as drug dens where homeless addicts purchase what may lead to their final high, the inevitable fatal overdose, if they don't seek help.

It's gotten so bad that some homeowners and renters have given up. One resident told a local station that, "We're done with Portland." She's moving out of state, sick and tired of the homeless addicts making her feel unsafe in her own neighborhood. "Our number one reason is because of the homeless. We're sick of it," she explained.[130] "We've had many camps moved out of here, and as soon as they clear them out, they move right back in."

With addicts come crimes to help them pay for their next fix. Burglaries, car thefts, and larceny are through the roof in Portland. In 2021, the Portland Police Bureau received over 5,000 reports of property crime but, due to staffing shortages within the department, they only made 36 arrests.[131] The Radical Left will have you believe this *isn't* tied to the drug crisis.

Let Them ~~Eat Cake~~ Shoot Up!

The Radical Left failed to push addicts into treatment; instead, they enabled them under a "harm reduction" model. This approach aims to reduce the health consequences of drug use, be they physical or mental. For example, sharing needles spreads diseases, so public health officials and nonprofit groups hand out clean needles. This helps prevent the spread of HIV or other blood-borne diseases. Instead of allowing someone to shoot up heroin or smoke fentanyl alone, they're offered a "safe consumption site" to use in front of a medical professional. This allows a nurse to intervene during an overdose.

But as more progressive-minded politicians and activists gained control over local programs, the envelope was pushed. At first, the idea of a heroin injection site was, frankly, insane. The idea that government agencies and nonprofits would set up space for addicts to comfortably shoot up seems almost like a parody. All that these sites are missing is a soothing soundtrack of waterfalls and chirping birds, mood lighting, and a shoulder massage while they inject themselves with a poison that is ruining their lives. Yet after the model was adopted in Vancouver, British Columbia, left-wing American politicians quickly jumped on the bandwagon, rushing to see which city could establish the nation's first heroin den.

Philadelphia hoped to open the country's first site in 2018, a year after more than 1,200 people died from opioid overdoses.[132] These sites were originally called Comprehensive User Engagement Sites, but the name never stuck because what the hell does that even mean? Democrat mayor Jim Kenney characterized the plan as a "bold action to help save lives."[133] At the time, the city was the number-one metro for heroin use.[134] But finding a location would be tricky. Who wants to live near a heroin injection site? Perhaps it's why advocates nationwide quickly changed the name to variations of "safe consumption sites." The name is dubious, of course. It's never "safe" to shoot up. But by framing the move as a way to save lives, they hoped it would sound more appealing to residents suspicious of bringing such a site to their neighborhood.

A small team of researchers led by University of Pennsylvania's Injury Science Center epidemiologist Douglas Wiebe used mathematical modeling to determine the best location.[135] They looked at narcotic arrests and fatal and nonfatal overdose reports for the answer. But they also mapped public transit locations within neighborhoods because addicts, usually homeless, would need relatively easy access to the sites. In the end, they went with the obvious location: Kensington.

Local leaders pegged the low-income, dangerous neighborhood, known to locals as Kenzo, as the ideal spot for such a site because it had been ravaged by drug use. It's so bad, it earned the dubious honor of being featured in a Mexican government anti-drug ad campaign meant to scare youth away from drug use.[136]

The truth is there is no ideal site, at least not by reasonable standards set by the people who live nearby. Just visit Vancouver, British Columbia's first heroin injection site to learn what these facilities do to neighborhoods. In 2017, I visited the location.[137] It was terrifying, depressing, and an experience I won't ever forget.

A stone's throw from Vancouver's Chinatown neighborhood, the city blocks leading to Insite Supervised Injection Site provides all a heroin addict would need to stay perpetually high. Unsurprisingly, I watched a drug deal a few yards away from the location, which offered an addict a quick spot to shoot up indoors, supervised by a nurse. Homeless, some looking lifeless, were sprawled around the sidewalks. Litter was everywhere. Businesses were dead or dying. I stopped by a coffee shop, but it was empty. I remember thinking, there's no way customers feel comfortable enough to stay here long. It's hard to enjoy a cup of coffee as addicts walk by.

How could anyone want this in their neighborhood? Who could feel comfortable opening a business or living nearby? It took one visit to know I would never want to live anywhere near a heroin injection site.

Shockingly, a delegation of leaders from Philadelphia had different thoughts. The group visited Vancouver in November 2017, and they were impressed. Though he had "operational" concerns about the site, Mayor Kenney concluded, "overdose prevention sites actually do save lives."[138] At the time, few people outside of public health understood the concept of harm reduction. When you're promised a heroin injection site will save a life, the assumption is that the addict gets treatment, not that taxpayer dollars will help subsidize a deadly disease. It was that societal ignorance that helped liberal voters in Philadelphia warm up to the idea. Soon, city leaders declared they'd move forward with their plans. San Francisco and Seattle joined in. They were each determined to move forward, hoping it would inspire other like-minded cities to do the same.

"There is strength in numbers," San Francisco mayor London Breed said at a press conference. "And we are talking to other cities who want to consider this as an option. I mean, here in other cities like New York and Seattle, we are trying to address the crisis."

After months of promotion, as heroin injection sites started to seem as if they could become a reality, Department of Justice officials finally stepped in. US Deputy Attorney General Rod Rosenstein explained there's no legal basis allowing for illicit substance abuse just because it's done in front of a medical professional.[139] "Just because someone tells you in San Francisco that San Francisco is not going to prosecute you for doing something, that does not make it legal. It remains illegal under federal law," Rosenstein argued to NPR. "If anybody thinks this is a good idea, there's a way to accomplish that: try to persuade the US Congress to legalize it."

City officials did not heed the warning. Newly elected

progressive district attorney Larry Krasner, propelled into office with the backing of billionaire left-wing disruptor George Soros, vowed his office would not prosecute anyone involved with the heroin injection sites. He endorsed the approach to tackling the drug overdose epidemic, claiming the locations would "keep them [the addict] alive long enough" to eventually seek treatment.[140]

It's obviously true that heroin injection sites are *safer* than shooting up alone. That's because you have a healthcare provider who can quickly administer naloxone, a drug treatment that can help stop a fatal overdose before medics can tend to the addict. There's nothing wrong with naloxone, of course, but treatment needs to be in the conversation. And unless you have heroin injection sites all around town and open around the clock, an addict will return to shooting up wherever they are at the time they're looking for their next hit. There are also scant studies to suggest addicts, when given a safe space to shoot up, will seek and stay in treatment. What we do know is that when you legalize drugs—be it via heroin injection sites or a promise not to prosecute personal possession—drugs flood your streets.

The New York City Department of Health took harm reduction messaging to the extreme with a series of subway posters meant to empower addicts. "Don't be ashamed you are using, be empowered that you are using safely," one poster read. Another explores the benefits of testing your drugs before smoking them.[141] "Fentanyl test strips can save your life," the poster announces, instructing addicts to test their drugs and consume in groups, one at a time, to help intervene in case of a drug overdose.[142] Warning people not to use drugs can also save lives, but is apparently too stigmatizing to message to the addict community.

To question harm reduction is sacrilege in liberal cities; if you offer even the slightest criticism, the Radical Left labels you a monster who wants to see addicts die. It's why progressive activists and politicians respond, perched upon the highest of high horses, by claiming *they* just want to save lives while you want to stigmatize addicts. The National Harm Reduction Coalition claims "stigma creates the social conditions that make people who use drugs believe they are not deserving of being treated with dignity and respect, perpetuating feelings of fear and isolation."[143] You are, advocates insist, to cast no judgment on an addict because it gets in the way of treatment by making the addict feel "unwelcome or judged by program staff that offers services." We're supposed to believe it's not the consequence-free drug use and open embrace of addiction that's stopping them from treatment. It's the stigma.

This contrived argument is meant to shut down the opposition. Progressive activists pursuing harm reduction strategies rely on little opposition. They use arguments guilting the public into submission, insisting progressive neighbors that they should consider their privilege and embrace discomfort to help those in need. The guilt works in cities with the most left-wing voters, all eager to be in the vanguard of a revolution in tackling societal ills. This tactic allows Radical Left public health officials and politicians to keep veering policy farther to the left.

Hypodermic Needles, "Booty Bumping Kits," and Crack Pipes—Oh My!

Even before providers more formally identified their programs as part of a harm reduction strategy, Democrat-run cities and counties across the country allowed addicts to trade in used needles for clean ones. But the programs that promised to keep dirty needles off the streets quickly turned into nonreciprocal transactions. Addicts stopped returning their needles, dangerously discarding them wherever they wanted. Rather than demand accountability from the user, requiring them to return their used needles, program managers argued it was more important to give them clean supplies to enable their addiction than to keep the public safe from improperly discarded needles. Some providers were so eager to hand out needles that they would even give them to kids.

Using the COVID-19 pandemic as justification, Seattle and King County Public Health expanded its needle distribution program to include mobile deliveries of needles and medications such as naloxone. Public health officials said COVID made in-person exchanges dangerous, as if catching COVID was more dangerous than shooting up heroin. "When COVID-19 hit our community, we transitioned to a model that minimizes the time someone needs to be out in public—reducing their risk as well as staff risk of exposure to COVID-19," a Public Health spokesperson told me.[144]

Public Health effectively established an Uber for illicit drug supplies; call a number and have paraphernalia delivered directly to you. Between January and March 2021, via its mobile efforts and office locations, the department handed out 137,910 needles. Helping bolster its efforts was a move to proactively deliver to locations where the homeless were living, giving needles out to all who asked, including children.

South King County city leaders sounded the alarms after learning that the South County Outreach Referral and Exchange (incredibly titled SCORE), one of the county-run programs, was secretly delivering drug supplies to local addicts. Local mayors condemned the program, explaining they were never told about the mobile needle exchanges. Increasingly, they heard complaints from residents who found used needles around parks, sidewalks, and parking lots.

Federal Way had been known for being family-friendly, but over the years, thanks to far-left policies, it witnessed rising crime and drug use. In early 2021, neighborhood activists were unhappy with what their tight-knit community was becoming. A group of residents did their own sleuthing, tracking the SCORE drop offs and making a startling discovery.

"It was a boy, he went up to the van, got his needles, and then he walked off to the side of the parking lot and then he proceeded to shoot up," a resident told a local talk station. "I think if people actually watched something like that in progress, they would think twice about whether this program is actually helping or aiding people in supporting their addiction. And it's really sad."[145]

It seems outlandish—a lie made up by a well-intentioned activist who wished needles wouldn't be distributed in her neighborhood. But it was true. A spokesperson from Public Health acknowledged that they won't turn anyone away, confirming that "SCORE does not check IDs for syringe supplies nor for other life-saving medications including naloxone." The spokesperson told me that the department "[does] not have a policy that states age requirements for exchange so I can't say that there hasn't been, or will not be a situation where a minor exchanges syringes." If it's not handing needles directly to kids, it's kids finding needles themselves.

Four-year-old Hayes and his parents were enjoying a day at Plaza De Vera Cruz Park in Santa Barbara, California. But then he was pricked by a used hypodermic needle, drawing blood.[146] According to the family's lawyer, Hayes was subjected to intensive drug therapy to ensure he hadn't contracted diseases and underwent frequent tests for HIV/AIDS. His doctors said they wouldn't know if he would suffer any significant health issues for at least a year.[147] Think of the terror this kid and his parents felt every time they went for a blood test that, whether you're four or 40, you never get used to, wondering if, after this blood draw, you'll be hit with devastating and life-changing news.

A Cup of Coffee, a Blueberry Muffin, and a Used Needle

Coffee behemoth Starbucks came under fire in 2018 after two black men were arrested at a Philadelphia café. One of the men went to use the bathroom without first making a purchase and refused to leave when asked, prompting a call to the police. The two were arrested, and it was caught on cell phone video. Media outlets and left-wing talking heads pretended this was a common occurrence; they were making the "white supremacy culture" argument before it became the insufferable go-to claim in 2020 after the death of

George Floyd. Under pressure, Starbucks announced an open-bathroom policy. Starbucks bathrooms were now for the community. Addicts quickly took up residency.

Thanks to the permissive bathroom policies, homeless addicts were commandeering single-stall toilets to shoot up. The *New York Post* called Starbucks in New York City a "haven for junkies," reporting one NoHo location was so unsafe that customers were scared away.[148] In Seattle, there was a rash of incidents where baristas were getting poked while cleaning out the bathrooms after a homeless addict would camp out.

Baristas complained that addicts would dispose of needles either in the trash or in the tampon dispenser nearly every day. At least three employees at a single location told a local television news station that they were pricked with the needles and offered hospital, pharmacy, and insurance receipts as proof they were placed on anti-viral medications to proactively protect them from HIV and hepatitis. Baristas begged management to install sharps containers for the safe disposal of needles.[149]

Carlos Nieto was 21 when he said he was poked by a used needle as he was loading trash bags into the bin behind his Starbucks location. He was fitting in all the trash when he felt a prick on his left index finger. After inspecting the bag, he realized what had happened. He told a local alternative weekly that his manager suggested he go to the emergency room, but it was late and he was tired from a long night of making increasingly convoluted coffee orders for a steady flow of customers. Three days later, he finally visited the doctor only to be told he should have listened to the manager. The medication they could have put him on is only truly effective within 72 hours of exposure to HIV. He nearly broke down. He spent the next month getting frequent blood tests.[150] "I was on the verge of tears outside the Bartell Drugs on Capitol Hill [a Seattle neighborhood]. And I was like, 'What if I have HIV? Starbucks might have just ruined my life,'" he explained.

When you give needles to addicts, they don't take the

responsibility to dispose of them seriously. Who knew homeless addicts would be so irresponsible? Okay, well, everyone. But as scores of needles littered the streets of Seattle, public health officials and advocates decided to *expand* their offerings. Taxpayers split the bill for something called booty bumping kits.

I thought I'd seen it all, but then I was tipped off that the Downtown Emergency Service Center (DESC), which operates a low-barrier shelter, was passing out heroin pipes and so-called "booty bumping" kits to homeless addicts. The DESC posted flyers at one of their shelters promoting the kits. What's worse, DESC staff encouraged addicts to use the tool. As you might have guessed, the DESC serves the homeless through a harm reduction strategy.[151]

Booty bumping allows an addict to inject drugs rectally, usually meth or cocaine mixed with water, through a needleless syringe. The rectum is especially efficient at absorption, which delivers a more intense and longer-lasting high. The flier pitched booty bumping as a "good choice if your veins are hard to hit." And how's this for a bonus mentioned on the flier: It "doesn't leave tracks."[152]

"We try to reduce the stigma around substance use to encourage clients to share openly and honestly about their experiences and needs. We speak to clients frankly and directly about the risks and dangers of substance use and the options available to them about changing their use," DESC Executive Director Daniel Malone told me. "We have substance use disorder counselor and opioid treatment nurse positions at the shelter who provide motivational interviewing and individual and group counseling."[153]

If you're able to get the image of someone using a booty bumping kit out of your head, imagine what it was like for me to explain to millions of people on *Tucker Carlson Tonight* about this inventive way to get high. You should have seen the emails and tweets in response.

Public health officials in Boston, Massachusetts, went from handing out clean needles to distributing literal crack pipes and cookers, a spoon-shaped device used to mix and heat drugs. The program is also paid for with state tax dollars. "Every step that we take has to also be about immediately saving lives," Democrat mayor Michelle Wu claimed.[154] "We have seen a big drop and data proven success with the parts of this program, the goals of this program, which are to ensure there is a stop to communicable diseases that are preventable."

While these addicts aren't spreading HIV or hepatitis with a clean needle or crack pipe, they're also succumbing to their addiction. Democrat-run public health agencies are exacerbating the problem by enabling addicts to fall deeper into the grips of fentanyl, methamphetamine, cocaine, and heroin. The crisis has deteriorated to the point where public health agencies, like the Washington State Department of Health, actually encouraged all citizens to carry naloxone on them should they encounter someone experiencing an overdose. Advocates see this as helping when it truly exemplifies the problem. Some went from harm reduction as one of the strategies to being the *only* strategy.

Gift Cards for Meth Addicts

Contingency Management is an approach that at least partially pursues drug cessation for meth addicts, albeit in unorthodox ways. The program generally works like this: Meth addicts enroll in a 12- to 24-week program where they earn small-value gift cards for abstaining from drugs. The longer they abstain, the more money they earn. If they slip up, they end up reverting back to a lower amount in gift card value. In other words, addicts are being bribed to stay off meth. To qualify, they must agree to regularly meet with clinicians or health officials during the program.

The strategy caught the attention of the Seattle City Council after public health officials in California announced a program.[155] Meth addiction cannot be treated with medications, and it's a leading cause of fatal overdoses in the city (especially among the homeless), second to fentanyl. Seattle council members Andrew Lewis and Lisa Herbold asked for an audit to see if the program could work in the city. Of course, the audit's researchers said it could; left-wing city leaders always try to out-progressive each other and they love new, shiny, left-wing programs to endorse and implement.

Released in October 2022, the report concluded that Contingency Management has "strong research evidence" that it works to combat meth addiction. That's not entirely true. Indeed, the very audit provides data that conflicts with its rosy conclusion. The audit detailed studies showing the approach can be effective for some in the short-term, but not in the long-term, and less so for those who are extreme addicts.

"[O]ne of the studies indicated that Contingency Management was less effective for participants who reported a longer history of methamphetamine use (e.g., seven years of lifetime methamphetamine use versus four years of use), and another study indicated that Contingency Management was also less effective for participants who reported higher methamphetamine use at baseline," the audit noted.[156]

Talk about burying the lede. In other words, the very cohort of homeless people this program would be designed to help would benefit the least. As worrisome, the audit notes "a gap in the research evidence regarding Contingency Management and long-term abstinence from methamphetamine use."

"Some current research on long-term abstinence suggests that reductions in methamphetamine use are not sustained after six months post-treatment," the audit continued.

Nevertheless, the audit endorsed Contingency Management, albeit with a social justice twist. The research, the audit noted, suggests white addicts benefit the most. Consequently, the audit said it's important to address racial disparities. To be successful, the program must also be designed to escape the confines of a clinical setting. That is, it must be adopted in homeless encampments.

We Don't Have a Drug Problem. We Have a Drug *Policy* Problem.

In an editorial for the *Philadelphia Inquirer*, Mayor Kenney and District Attorney Krasner criticized the war on drugs of the 1980s, arguing "we failed many people during the crack epidemic by treating it solely as a law enforcement problem rather than a health problem."[157] Unfortunately, their approach—shared by the Radical Left nationwide—wholly dismisses the criminal justice element to fighting the crisis. It's why they've failed so spectacularly. Cities must approach the drug epidemic as a public health emergency *and* a criminal justice problem.

When you create a society that accepts drug use, you get more of it. The reason why so many addicts smoke fentanyl on Seattle buses, shoot up on sidewalks in Kenzo, or pass out in a drugged-up stupor at a Manhattan Starbucks is because we allow it. It wasn't always like this, was it? Addiction has always been here, and there have certainly been some parts of town known for substance abuse, but this crisis is no longer contained to a small section of a neighborhood in our cities. And it's not staying within the confines of big liberal cities because addiction spreads like cancer, thanks to the drugs that flood our streets. When someone knows there is no legal consequence to personal possession or use, they may partake—particularly our youth. Unfortunately, it takes one pill that a teen believes to be OxyContin, but is actually oxycodone laced with fentanyl, to take a life or trigger an addiction.

When you allow open-air drug use, drug dealers take notice. So, too, do the Mexican drug cartels responsible for the bulk of drugs sold in the United States. While fentanyl is manufactured via Chinese-sourced ingredients, illicit substances still come through the southern border with the Sinaloa Cartel and the Jalisco New Generation Cartel responsible for the bulk of products.[158] When the Biden administration spent the first two years of its presidency pretending the border wasn't open, it allowed cartels to smuggle billions of dollars' worth of products into the United States. In concert with local street gangs, cartel drugs flooded the Democrat-run cities known for consequence-free drug use. Then, the drugs quickly spread into the suburbs. And while drug cartels will always exploit an insecure southern border, the sheer number of products flowing into the country is terrifyingly high. But who can blame them for taking advantage of policies from the Radical Left? They may be evil and murderous, but they follow the news closely enough to know what they can get away with. It's a lucrative business model for them.

The Radical Left created a recipe for disaster that is overtaking cities, and the only way to undo the damage is to reject their policies in their entirety. Since left-wing politicians and public health officials have been in charge, the crisis has worsened. It's time for them to be sidelined. In reality, it's not a drug crisis we're dealing with; it's a Radical Left drug *policy* crisis.

It's important to reject the notion that stigma prevents an addict from seeking treatment. It's the ever-flowing drugs and *lack* of a criminal justice response that's keeping them hooked. Drug addiction is worthy of stigma. It's a disease that will ultimately claim the life of an addict, and the only way to stop most people from that inevitable death is to make it crystal clear that their behaviors are unacceptable. Scared to hurt an addict's feelings? Well, I'd rather stigmatize addicts, if it means they won't die from their addiction. If you talk to recovering addicts, many of them explain that they appreciated those who offered some tough love.

We must embrace law enforcement's role in tackling drug addiction. Decriminalizing drugs makes it more difficult for officers to bust drug dealers who have adopted the new rules, while taking advantage of police departments left depleted by the Black Lives Matter movement. As problematic, jail time (or even the threat of confinement) can be why an addict finally gets help. While recognizing it's not the only option, it must be *an* option. It may be just enough to convince would-be addicts not to use in the first place, a reminder that their relationships, job, and life will be ruined if they go down this path. Is it worth risking the job as an accountant, construction worker, or promising high school athlete for a quick high that could lead to an arrest? Moreover, policing can tackle the culture of open-air drug use. When you have officers breaking up druggies hunched over, passing crack pipes or tin foil to one another as they search for the high, it sends an important message, not just to the addicts that the city won't make their addiction easy, but to the residents that they can have their neighborhood back.

It's equally important to invest in addiction treatment facilities, not spaces to shoot up or gift card bribes. Do you know what's missing in the push to open heroin injection sites or convince someone to give up meth for a $20 Visa gift card that they'll sell for more drugs? Addiction treatment facilities. Instead of a heroin den, we must open facilities designed to detox addicts and get them in the right headspace for long-term, effective treatment. Some form of Contingency Management can be a part of the process once an addict goes through detox, assuming the city uses private dollars, rather than public funds, to help entice recovering addicts to remain sober.

Democrat embrace of a harm reduction strategy is getting in the way of progress; they've mostly given up on treatment and, instead, have endorsed enabling. Heroin injection sites are already established across the country, defying the law. Many are operating in secret, staffed by activist volunteers. Drug tools are being handed out, including crack pipes courtesy of the Biden administration. And Contingency Management programs may be underway in a city near you.

But you don't have to accept this; addicts don't have to die at the altar of a Radical Left approach adopted merely to show how "evolved" Democrats are on public health. There are better ways, some of which are pretty simple to adopt. It's just returning to what has worked in the past. But since that includes policing, the Radical Left is standing in the way.

CHAPTER 3

DECRIMINALIZING CRIME

Do You Feel Lucky, Punk? Actually, Yes. Yes, I Do.

"This s—t looking real good. Now we got a new DA in LA...so they're going to drop a gang of, um, like my gun enhancement, my gang enhancement," Luis Angel Hernandez boasted from a Los Angeles jail in an audio recording obtained by *Tucker Carlson Originals.*[159] "...That's the n—a right there, bro. He's making historic changes for all of us, fool. I'm just grateful, fool. Like, I got good news off that s—t."

Hernandez pleaded guilty to the murder of a marijuana delivery worker in 2018. He was initially facing life without the possibility of parole because he is the exact kind of monster society wants locked away. Yet, he did have a reason to celebrate. An ally was just elected to an important post.

George Gascon was elected Los Angeles County district attorney (DA) in 2020, after turning San Francisco into a criminal wasteland while serving in the same role. Dubbed the "godfather of progressive prosecutors" for his far-left views, Gascon earned the attention of George Soros, Netflix CEO Reed Hastings, and Hastings's philanthropist wife Patty Quillin, who happily poured millions into his campaign to unseat incumbent Jackie Lacey. She warned that a Gascon win would welcome an era of lawlessness.[160] It turns out she undersold Gascon's impact on Los Angeles and the surrounding cities.

The Cuban-born former cop saw his significant victory as a mandate to reimagine the criminal justice system. And Gascon quickly got to work, meeting with Black Lives Matter activists before his own prosecutors.[161] It was a harbinger of changes to come and a clear message about the views with which he was aligned.

Just one day after his swearing in ceremony, the DA released dozens of sweeping new directives aimed at reforming his office. He said the intent was to undo systemic and institutionalized racism that disproportionately impacted racial minorities and help create a justice system that believes in second chances. In reality, however, Gascon believes in endless chances. On his inauguration day, Gascon vowed to "usher in a new era of criminal justice, and transform the largest criminal justice jurisdiction in America."

His new policies did away with sentence enhancements, a tool prosecutors can use to add longer criminal penalties to those responsible for especially egregious or dangerous crimes. His prosecutors were not allowed to try juveniles as adults, no matter the circumstances of the crime. The death penalty was officially taken off the table. Cash bail? Not anymore. And no matter their commitment to a case or passion for keeping a dangerous criminal in jail, prosecutors were barred from attending parole hearings, leaving victims and their families alone to plead their case in front of an intimidating parole board. The DA's office was no longer serving the public. Instead, they were serving the criminals.

While Gascon's prosecutors protested and victims' advocacy groups panicked, felons like Hernandez rejoiced, promising to "get that n—a's name [tattooed] on my face."[162] He and other law breakers had reason to celebrate as Gascon and a new generation of Radical Left lawmakers and public officials were siding with them over their victims.

Criminals Are Victims Too, You Know?

The Radical Left exploited the death of George Floyd to pursue reforms that fundamentally changed the criminal justice system. They were not content with only defunding and dismantling police departments nationwide. They sought to do the same to the very institutions that punish criminals.

The policies adopted by Gascon were popping up nationwide. It wasn't just about cash bail and sentence enhancements. Left-wing DAs and prosecutors were pushing suspects and prolific criminals into diversion programs where they avoided jail time and, in some cases, never even saw a judge. They effectively decriminalized property crimes, refused to charge dangerous juveniles as adults, and even retroactively altered prison sentences.

When you combine these reforms with police defunding, you get skyrocketing crime. The Edwin Meese III Center for Judicial and Legal Studies at the Heritage Foundation released a study that found that Democrat mayors ran 27 of the 30 American cities with the highest murder rates. Of the 27 cities, 14 had "rogue prosecutors" that embraced far-left social justice reforms.[163] The basis for these reforms? A belief that the criminal justice system is inherently racist. Consequently, there's a fundamental belief that criminals are victims.

If a young black man robs a convenience store in Atlanta, Georgia, it simply shows that a racist society failed him. If a Latino from Austin, Texas, gets a harsh sentence for a drive-by shooting, it's only due to a racist judge and jury. Little attention is given to their victims. Democrats said they wanted to address the root causes of why the thief targeted a convenience store or drove the vehicle involved in a shooting. How virtuous!

While there's value in addressing the root causes of crime, doing so after serious crimes are committed is a little too late. We can address root causes of crime while simultaneously punishing criminals. And when the Radical Left nearly always blames "white supremacy culture" as the underlying reason for what led to the crime (poverty, over-policing, COVID-19, etc.), it's nothing more than a lazy political statement that doesn't address anything at all. But to the Radical Left, the criminals were abandoned and victimized by systems and institutions, especially when they come from a marginalized community.

While defending his controversial directives early in his term, Gascon routinely painted criminals as disadvantaged, arguing they struggle to find housing and work as a consequence of entering the criminal justice system. In Gascon's world, criminal behavior doesn't appear to be voluntary; they're compulsory acts thanks to white supremacy culture. The DA claimed that being "tough on crime" has led to an over-incarceration problem, one, he argues, that disproportionately impacts black Americans. He discusses criminals as if they did not commit a crime worthy of societal ire to begin with.

Soros-backed Philadelphia DA Larry Krasner holds similar views on the criminal justice system. Writing in the *Philadelphia Tribune*, he claimed there was an active and "conscious" strategy to target black and Latino suspects while giving a pass to the white ones.

"Racist prosecutors who are deliberately harsh and unequal in their handling of Black and brown defendants and poor people in general play a part [in infecting prosecution]. And our comparative and systemic leniency toward crimes primarily committed by white, affluent people—insider trading, financial and tax fraud, pollution—is quite different than our traditional prosecutors' harsh approach to prosecuting a single mom's unsupported check or a homeless person's theft of food," he wrote in the *Philadelphia Tribune*.[164]

Krasner's column doesn't reference any serious crimes committed by "Black and brown defendants." Instead, he focused on a trope of the single mom or homeless person who steals loaves of bread just to survive. He seems utterly uninterested in the gang violence, rapes, and assaults that commonly occur in Philadelphia because it's harder to argue to keep those suspects out of jail.

Likewise, Chicago's top prosecutor Kim Foxx pushes the line that the racist criminal justice system is punishing innocent people based on their skin color. She points her finger at the police. "When 86 percent of the people in our jails are Black and Brown, and 90 percent of the victims of homicide also are Black and Brown, the distrust of law enforcement in these communities is unsurprising," Foxx wrote in the *Chicago Sun-Times*.[165]

She does not explain whether or not 86 percent of jailed black and Latino criminals are responsible for the 90 percent of black and Latino victims. We're supposed to pretend that black-on-black or Latino-on-Latino homicides are seemingly nonexistent, even though gang violence in Chicago is a leading cause of homicides. A black or Latino criminal serving time is, Foxx implies, as much a victim as a black or Latino Chicagoan mowed down on a street corner.

There's an implication that blacks and Latinos are punished for crimes, while whites are not. It's not a particularly convincing argument. Most reasonable people would argue that if white suspects are getting away with crime because of some kind of systemic bias, we should ramp up efforts to arrest, charge, and imprison them. But if we did that, it would mean we'd have to keep black and Latino criminals in jail. Radical Left DAs don't want that. Putting "marginalized" community members in jail, when a racist society already stacks the odds against them, makes it harder for them down the road.

Ironically, when a racial minority is the victim of an egregious crime, the criminal *still* gets the support from Radical Left DAs. Nothing says "black lives matter" quite like siding with the black criminal over the black victim. How's that for equity? Too many criminals are treated as victims, while too many victims are discarded. Had it not been for media and public outrage, one bodega worker might still be on Rikers Island. It remains the most disturbing case that a Radical Left DA intentionally mishandled.

Jose Alba, a 61-year-old hardworking immigrant, was manning the counter at a Manhattan bodega in July 2021 when Austin Simon, a 34-year-old troublemaker, and his girlfriend stopped by. Simon's girlfriend tried to buy snacks for her child using an EBT card (an electronic version of food stamps), but it was denied. Police said a "verbal dispute" ensued as a result. Court documents reveal she yelled at Alba that she was going to tell her boyfriend, and that he was going to "f—k you up!" That appeared to be the plan. Simon confronted Alba behind the counter.[166]

Simon was seen on surveillance camera pushing Alba, and then grabbing him by the collar. Alba told him he "didn't want a problem," but Simon did not care or relent. Feeling threatened, the bodega worker reached for a knife that was stored out of sight and stabbed Simon five times. Simon's girlfriend retaliated by stabbing Alba in the arm, police said. Simon died at the hospital.

The footage was crystal clear: Alba was the victim and was clearly defending himself against a much stronger and taller Simon. And though Alba didn't know this at the time, it was especially prescient to sense danger, because Simon was out on parole for assaulting a police officer. Yet Manhattan DA Alvin Bragg sided with the criminal, charging Alba with second-degree murder. The girlfriend escaped all charges.

Though Bragg rarely demanded high bail (it's racist, after all), his office demanded that a judge impose $500,000 to secure Alba's spot at Rikers Island. A judge agreed to half the amount, which Alba could not afford, landing him in the notorious jail.

The public was outraged by the bodega worker's treatment, shouting their protestations over the charges on social media and on local media. New York City mayor Eric Adams made an appearance at the bodega to show his support for Alba.[167] Michael

Discioarro, the former assistant district attorney of New York City, told NewsNation that this was a case of "textbook self-defense," calling the decision to charge Alba "really shocking."[168]

The pressure was too much for Bragg to withstand. His office dropped the case against Alba, though it should never have been leveled in the first place. But when you view criminals as victims, even while they're quite literally victimizing an innocent bodega worker, you get decisions like this one.

An especially egregious example of the Radical Left's light-on-crime approach was a bill introduced by Washington State representatives Tarra Simmons (D-Bremerton), a former inmate turned lawmaker, and David Hackney (D-Tukwila).

House Bill 1692 lessened criminal penalties for drive-by shootings, an idea that Simmons and Hackney perplexingly claimed promotes "racial equity in the criminal legal system." It would have banned the use of a drive-by shooting as the basis for elevating a first-degree murder charge to aggravated first-degree murder, which carries a harsher sentence. The bill would have even been retroactive, lowering punishments for those who were already serving time for committing a drive-by shooting. Their basic argument was that too many black people commit drive-by shootings, and it was leading to disproportionate prison sentences.

I'm proud to say that my segment on *Tucker Carlson Tonight* on Fox News delivered so much attention to the issue, local media was forced to cover the bill, generating community anger.[169] In the end, Democrats were forced to abandon the bill, though it could be resurrected in future legislative sessions, if voters aren't alert.

Art Therapy for Armed Assaults

Radical Left DAs and prosecutors embrace restorative justice (a fancy way of saying "diversion programs") as a way for criminals to avoid jail time and stay out of the system, especially when they're dealing with youth. They argue, as Gascon did when he took office, that incarceration leads to "foreclosed job [and] housing opportunities, exacerbated recidivism, crime [and] homelessness, [and] create[s] more victims."[170] Instead, these programs aim to address the root causes of the criminal behavior while making the victim of the crime whole again. The particulars of these programs can vary, but they are community-based, usually run by a nonprofit in partnership with the courts and/or prosecutor's office, and aim to rehabilitate offenders so that they get back on the right path. Some of the programs involve intense therapy or hours-long sessions to discuss their actions. Others involve art therapy, as if finger painting means the teen is too busy to pull a trigger.[171]

On paper, these programs at least sound promising: You help reform the criminal, provide intensive wraparound services or support, and guide them to being productive, self-sufficient members of society, keeping them out of trouble in the future. But prosecutors and judges are referring truly dangerous suspects to these programs. Many times, the programs are run by abolitionist groups that care more about keeping kids out of jail because they loathe the system rather than care about the life of the child. And it's a big reason why they often fail to reform.

There is little appetite for throwing teens in jail for every offense. A 16-year-old kid caught stealing White Claws and Snickers from a 7-Eleven or Wawa doesn't deserve a jail cell; the right restorative justice program can help that kid. They can and should be saved. It is a moral responsibility, particularly when these kids come from broken or unloving homes, which is often the case. But Radical Left DAs and prosecutors treat most juvenile crimes the same, regardless of the level of severity.

A 15-year-old named Kristopher Baca mowed down a mother and her eight-month-old son while taking a stroll in their Venice, California, neighborhood in August 2021. The video surveillance is truly disturbing. Baca sped down the wrong way on a narrow backstreet before veering into the mother, Rachel, and her boy Charlie, who was in a stroller. Both went careening off the hood and windshield of the car. Baca continued to drive away but was stopped by a good Samaritan who drove his truck into the teen's car to stop him. Miraculously, Rachel and Charlie survived with minor physical injuries, but with lasting emotional trauma for the mother.[172]

"I thought those were the last moments of our lives; we were dead," Rachel wrote in a victim's impact statement to the court. "That feeling, along with the memory of a car accelerating directly into us, will haunt me forever." She left Los Angeles, unwilling to stay in such a dangerous city.

Baca committed his crime at a time progressive reforms were keeping dangerous juveniles out of jail. Thanks to Gascon, rather than jail time, the teen was sentenced to just five to seven months in a "juvenile probation camp" for rehabilitation. Gascon's office justified the punishment because, "Fortunately, the baby was uninjured, and the mother received a laceration to her elbow."

"In this case, this teen will be held accountable for his actions and receive the needed services to foster positive development to keep him from committing future offenses," read a statement provided to Fox News.

This result is, of course, outrageous. Mowing down a mom pushing a stroller is not merely violent. When it's done by a 15-year-old, it's a harbinger of even more serious crimes. That teen could have benefited from services to foster positive development in juvenile detention until he is 18 years old. Instead, progressive politicians embrace a general "No Youth Incarceration" posture.

Baca would have been better off serving time in juvenile detention, not only because it could have helped set him straight, but it would have literally saved his life. He was released from scofflaw summer camp after just a few months. About a year and a half later, he was found shot to death after reportedly getting into an argument.[173] Rachel responded to the news by saying, "The universe delivered the justice we weren't given in court, but a much harsher punishment than he'd have been dealt in a court of law.

I think I feel shorted by the system because they didn't hold him accountable and sad, not for him, but for his mom a little, because if George Gascon actually did his job, this kid would still be alive in jail."

Juveniles are increasingly allowed to get away with violent crimes with no meaningful consequences. And they know it. Logic suggests teen criminals will continue to escalate their bad behaviors when they know there's little to no consequences. Unfortunately, the Radical Left only intervenes after an avoidable tragedy.

In Federal Way, Washington, Radical Left prosecutors did not request to review a decision for electronic home monitoring and adult supervision for two teenagers accused in a vicious strong-arm robbery. Montrell D. Hatfield, 16, and Marshon Jones, 15, were charged after allegedly robbing a pawn shop, pistol whipping customers, and firing a gun to threaten staff. After their arrest, Judge Averil Rothrock ordered the teens to wear ankle monitors while the case unfolded. It kept them out of juvenile detention, even though that's where they clearly belonged.[174] Most anyone could see this kind of violent act, which was caught on surveillance video, as warranting detention. But to the Radical Left, an ideological aversion to teen incarceration outweighs the risk to the public. This decision, unsurprisingly, turned out to be a deadly mistake.

Police say the teens cut off their ankle monitors and fled their home confinement. In the process, they allegedly robbed a pot shop in nearby Tacoma, where they were accused of shooting a 29-year-old employee to death.[175] Both teens were eventually caught and charged in nearby Pierce County, which is considerably tougher on crime. This time, they weren't offered a free pass and were tried as adults. They pleaded not guilty.[176]

During a press conference arguing the "three strikes" policy is dated and should be abandoned for diversion programs, Chicago police superintendent David Brown revealed the department had recently arrested an 11-year-old accused in a carjacking. It wasn't the kid's first run-in with police, leading Brown to say the allegation "shocks the conscience."[177] When you give a pass to criminals, does it really shock the conscience that they get younger and younger? It would shock the system if there *wasn't* more crime because of Radical Left policies.

In New Orleans, the progressive mayor Latoya Cantrell shocked the conscience by supporting a 14-year-old who committed five armed carjackings a year earlier, traumatizing helpless women in the process.[178] The mayor showed up to sentencing to console the carjacker's family, disrespecting the victims in the process. When one victim read her impact statement to the court, Cantrell walked out. "The mayor sitting on his side, consoling his family. It kind of makes you think like who's side is the city on? Are they on your side? Do they care about victims?" the carjacked woman asked.[179] After the mayoral appearance, Chief Juvenile Court Judge Ranord Darensburg sentenced the teen to just three years of probation.

Cantrell's callous decision to support the carjacker ignited a firestorm of local media coverage where carjacking victims spoke out as feeling offended and disgusted. But Cantrell showed her support because the boy was previously enrolled in the mayor's diversion program, Pathways, a 15-week program designed to keep 14- to 17-year-olds out of the criminal justice system. It worked in keeping the boy out of jail, though only thanks to a permissive judge.

Cantrell has a history of supporting the wrong teens. At 18 years old, Tyrese Harris was arrested in early February 2022 for a violent carjacking at a local Costco. As he drove off, he dragged the victim about 50 feet through the parking lot, leaving her with a fractured skull. After his arrest, police discovered that he may have been connected to a separate attempted armed carjacking. He also admitted to murdering a 12-year-old boy a month earlier, shooting him in the head. At the time of the arrest, Harris was out on a $12,500 bond in connection with an armed robbery the year before.[180]

Cantrell disclosed that she "personally worked with the family here to try to steer this individual into a different pathway." Only after several crimes did Cantrell acknowledge that "now it's time for the other elements within our criminal justice system to do their part to ensure that our people can live freely in the City of New Orleans and not have to fear for their lives."[181] But imagine if she showed the same passion for punishing clearly dangerous teens instead of pretending that she can save them?

The Radical Left argues juveniles are too young to understand the consequences of their actions; that they're brains aren't fully developed. They don't hold that view when it comes to 13-year-olds who seek surgical intervention to better align with a gender identity. But when that same 13-year-old assaults an elderly man to steal his wallet, the kid just didn't know better. This belief has led to disturbing legal shifts as part of the reform movement.

The Washington State Supreme Court found in 2018 that it was unconstitutional to sentence a 16- or 17-year-old to life in prison without parole.[182] The decision was borne out of a case involving 16-year-old Brian Bassett, who killed his parents and young brother in 1995. He was sentenced to three consecutive life sentences, with the judge in the case calling him a "walking advertisement" for the death penalty. But the state's Supreme Court views this as cruel punishment because of his age, which is outlawed by Washington's constitution. Their ruling granted the chance to resentence all youth serving life in prison without parole.[183]

The argument heavily relied on studies that "hold that age may well mitigate a defendant's culpability, even if the defendant is slightly older than 18." The justices argued that juveniles have a "lack of maturity and an underdeveloped sense of responsibility" in addition to being "more vulnerable or susceptible to negative influences and outside pressures." In other words, they believe a 16-year-old might not truly understand murder, assault, rape, or robbery is wrong.

Some Radical Left lawmakers codified this belief into law by taking discretion away from reasonable prosecutors and judges.

Oregon Democrats pushed through Senate Bill 1008, which gives youth offenders a "Second Look" where a judge can place the offender into a community supervision program halfway through the sentence, if rehabilitation occurred. It also ended life without parole for offenders 17 and under, even if they committed a mass murder hours before their 18th birthday. The Radical Left believes that one day is all that separates naivety and wisdom about a mass shooting. Luckily, Stoneman Douglas shooter Nikolas Cruz was tried in Florida instead of Oregon.

It is reasonable to consider age at sentencing. But Democrats consider age before *charging*, pushing more juveniles than is wise into ineffective programs that keep dangerous kids on the streets. It's not even just juveniles that get diversion programs in lieu of jail.

While one can at least understand the reasons behind teen rehabilitation, including when the suspect is violent because no one *wants* to give up on such a young life, it's harder to justify giving passes to most adults with criminal histories. Teens can, perhaps, be saved. It's less likely when they're older.

Anthony M. Kennedy of Cleveland, Ohio, was popped in 2019 after police said he strangled his then-girlfriend in a shocking domestic violence incident. With both hands around her neck, he strangled her so hard that she couldn't even yell for help. He then "put his forearm against her throat and began using his body weight to strangle her again," according to the arrest warrant. He was charged with domestic violence and unlawful restraint, but both crimes are misdemeanors in Ohio.[184]

After pleading guilty to a reduced criminal mischief charge, Kennedy received a suspended jail sentence and a one-way ticket to a diversion program for domestic abusers called the Domestic Intervention, Education, and Training program. The program is characterized as a "psychosocial education program" to avoid incarceration, but it's basically a glorified seminar on how to be a better partner. (Its acronym is DIET. Does anyone think the program takes its responsibilities seriously?) For 16 weeks, domestic abusers attend one weekly two-hour session where they're taught the virtues of "non-violence, non-threatening behavior, respect, support and trust, accountability and honesty, sexual respect, partnership and negotiation, and fairness."[185]

"Issues discussed include successful implementation of safety plans and what constitutes a healthy relationship. Incentives such as note pads or coffee mugs are given to encourage participation," the program's website says. The coffee mugs didn't help Kennedy understand what constitutes a healthy relationship.

Two years after the program in 2022, Kennedy was accused of murdering his live-in girlfriend. With a bullet wound to the head, her body was found inside of a tote bag, packed in a giant construction bag, and buried under concrete that was still wet when police discovered it.[186] Domestic abuse victims' advocates—along with any reasonable person—will tell you strangling a girlfriend is a red flag for seriously violent tendencies that warrants more than a few sessions about healthy relationships.

An End to Sentence Enhancements

Radical Left DAs and prosecutors hope to end sentence enhancements that add years to a criminal's jail time. Their Radical Left lawmaker allies try to codify that policy into law. Together, DAs and lawmakers do everything they can to keep incarceration as low as possible. These policies treat all criminals as equally deserving of leniency, and it's precisely why the Radical Left is so dangerous.

Los Angeles county DA Gascon ended sentence enhancements on the first day in office, calling them "unjust and unnecessary." Arguing they're a primary driver of mass incarceration, he claimed that sentence enhancements "have never been shown to enhance safety, but excessive sentences have been shown to exacerbate recidivism thus creating more victims of crime." And, of course, he says enhancements disproportionately impacted "communities of color."[187] In other words, sentence enhancements are racist.

None of his positions are objectively true; it is Radical Left analysis presented as fact. It's quite simple to explain how sentence enhancements lead to safer communities: The longer dangerous gang members stay in jail, for instance, the longer we are free from their criminal acts. While Gascon and others pretend everyone is redeemable, reality tells us otherwise. It's why we don't release serial killers. We know that they will harm again, and the longer they serve, the safer we are.

Gascon relies on the lazy disproportionality argument. He argues that gang enhancements have "led to shocking racial disparities" because 92 percent of the state's 11,000 inmates who fall into that category (as of 2021) identify as black or Latino.[188] Like-minded San Francisco DA Chesa Boudin, who took the job one year after Gascon left, pursued the same policy, calling gang enhancements "infused with racism." He even argued that punishing gang members who happen to be black or Latino will create unnecessary tensions between those communities, as if black and Latino people support the gang activities killing their families and friends, while destroying their neighborhoods.[189]

But it makes sense that those hit with gang enhancements are disproportionately black and Latino because those racial groups disproportionately represent gang membership in California. CalGang is a California database that some law enforcement agencies use to track criminal investigations. Of the 34,163 identified gang members in its 2021 database, 22,905 were Hispanic and 7,383 were black.[190] One study published in *Youth and Society* reported the majority of California youth gang members were from an ethnic minority group, with Latino representing nearly 43 percent of gang membership.[191]

Who Carries Cash Anymore, Anyway?

The move to end cash bail is not new, but it gained momentum during the criminal justice reform movement of 2020. Cities and states rushed to ban cash bail in most circumstances, arguing through a racial and social justice lens, consistently relying on a baseless claim that our jails are full of low-level criminals accused of things like stealing a loaf of bread to feed their starving families or smoking a joint. The Radical Left argues that the system "criminalizes poverty" because people who have money or connections can pay to be released from jail, while low-income suspects cannot. They say it leads to over-incarceration, particularly for racial minorities.

Progressive Congresswoman Pramila Jayapal (D-Seattle) said she was "deeply troubled by the fact that we continue to jail people for low-level offenses, things like sleeping under the highway or driving without a license, simply because they can't make bail."[192] We don't, in fact, do that often, certainly not in the district she represents. But it paints a narrative that's easy to defend, even if it's not based in reality.

"People should not lose their jobs or their homes because they're incarcerated while they await a fair trial. Families should not have to choose between putting bail for a loved one, or putting food on the table, or paying rent," she argued in 2018 at a House committee hearing.

Reps. Carolyn Moloney (D-NY), Alexandria Ocasio-Cortez (D-NY), and Jamie Raskin (D-MD) used the cash-bail argument to try to close Rikers Island in 2021. "High bail amounts lead to a two-tiered system of justice, with those who can afford bail being able to escape the inhumane conditions at pretrial detention facilities, such as Rikers Island, while those who cannot afford bail are forced to remain," they wrote in a letter to New York DAs.[193] There are even some, like Senator Kirsten Gillibrand (D-NY), Congressman Tim Ryan (D-OH), and Vice President Kamala Harris, who said they want to get rid of cash bail *entirely*.[194]

There's a politically self-serving argument made by cash-bail opponents, who claim that requiring bail for criminals actually leads to more crime. The left-wing Center for American Progress

(CAP) argues, "Studies show that pretrial detention can actually increase a person's likelihood of rearrest upon release, perpetuating an endless cycle of arrest and incarceration."[195] Perhaps—and go with me here—*criminals* are more likely to commit future crimes even after they're caught, regardless of the bail, because they're *criminals*.

New York Democrat lawmakers prohibited the use of cash bail in most misdemeanor and nonviolent (and some violent) felony charges. Are the beneficiaries of the new cashless bail, presumed by Democrats to be victims of a racist system, better off? CAP says detention can increase rearrests. Surely, keeping people entirely out of jail must lead to a safer New York as a result, right? Not so much.

In Buffalo, New York, Keaira Bennefield was allegedly killed by a man released from jail just 24 hours earlier. Police say Adam Bennefield, her ex-husband, crashed into her car and shot her to death with a shotgun. At the time of her murder, her six-month-old son was in the backseat. One day earlier, the ex was released from jail without bail despite a misdemeanor charge of third-degree assault, fourth-degree criminal mischief, second-degree menacing, and second-degree unlawful imprisonment.[196]

Frank Abrokwa was arrested and released twice in the Bronx within about 24 hours thanks to the bail reform law. He was first arrested on charges of harassment, forcible touching, menacing, and disorderly conduct after allegedly smearing feces on an innocent woman's face.[197] "S—t happens. Haha," Abrokwa said, according to the criminal complaint. "This is a sh—ty situation. Haha."

The next day, Abrokwa earned his second arrest on charges of menacing as a hate crime and harassment after police say he spat on and made anti-Jewish taunts against a victim, telling him, "Come here you f—king Jew" and "I am going to kill you," according to the complaint. He was released without bail. Another "L" for CAP.

The second crimes allegedly committed by those suspects—and

scores more—were preventable. Had they been in jail, presumably unable to pay bail, these specific crimes would not have occurred. Yet, Radical Left backers of the bail reform movement claim there's no evidence to tie this policy (or similar reforms) to the rise in crime. It's either purely coincidental or, some ludicrously claimed, tied to the COVID-19 pandemic.

Philadelphia DA Krasner pushed to end cash bail much earlier than it was mandated by law in New York. When he was first elected in 2018, he called the system "imprisonment for poverty" and instructed his prosecutors not to seek cash bail for nonviolent defendants.[198] But since the decision, homicides skyrocketed, with 2021 setting a record high of 562 victims (a 78 percent increase since 2017, the year before the reform).[199] The city also experienced year-over-year increases in theft (including retail, auto, and personal theft) and robberies involving a gun.[200] When you go easy on nonviolent offenders, there's no guarantee they stay nonviolent.

And in Cooke County, Illinois, the county chief justice Timothy Evans pushed through bail reforms in 2017 to reduce incarceration rates in Chicago. It may have accomplished a reduction in incarceration, but the city has seen an explosion of violent and nonviolent crime to the point where even then-mayor Lori Lightfoot asked for a change. The data showed the county's approach was failing to keep the community safe.

Cook County sheriff Tom Dart oversees the largest pretrial electronic monitoring system in the country. In late September 2021, over 3,500 suspects charged with crimes were wearing ankle bracelets as part of the county's effort to keep people out of jail. It represented roughly 30 percent more electronic home monitoring than the previous year and a half.[201] Alarmingly, between 75 percent and 80 percent of those on electronic monitoring were facing violent crime charges, including 90 charged with murder.[202]

Chicago Police Department data showed they arrested 133 people for a violent crime that year while they were released on electronic home monitoring. Lightfoot requested an immediate moratorium on electronic monitoring for suspects charged with "murder, attempted murder, aggravated gun possession, felons in possession, sex crimes, illegal gun possession, vehicular carjacking, kidnapping or attempted kidnapping, or other crimes of violence."[203] But Justice Evans downplayed the stats, arguing in a press release that, at less than 5 percent according to one study, only a "small minority" of suspects on electronic monitoring were rearrested. In other words, he was unmoved by the victims from those 133 violent crimes and, instead, chose to side with releasing dangerous suspects.[204] But the 5 percent of cases leading to another offense were, again, avoidable. And their victims won't get the second chance given to the criminal.

A seven-year-old girl named Jasyln Adams was murdered in Chicago's West Side in April 2021. She was riding with her father, idling at a McDonald's drive-thru, when Cook County prosecutors say a silver Audi pulled up behind them. Two men in hoodies jumped out and fired at least 28 shots at the pair. The men had some kind of beef with the father. One of the guns used to take the girl's life, while seriously injuring the father, was an AK-47 with a banana clip.[205]

One of the suspects arrested and charged in the shooting was 21-year-old Demond Goudy. Within two and a half years of the alleged murder, Goudy was accused of robbery, possession of a gun with a defaced serial number, aggravated unlawful use of a weapon, manufacturing/delivery of cocaine, and possession of a controlled substance. He was ordered by a judge in the robbery case to be placed on electronic home monitoring while awaiting his trial.[206] He was even an enrollee in READI Chicago, a restorative justice program aimed at "addressing trauma and increasing opportunity among men most likely to experience gun violence."[207]

Perhaps Justice Evans would like to ignore the 5 percent because it makes his position more palatable. But the criminal justice system is supposed to serve those in society who need protection, not favor bad guys with weapons who prey on the most vulnerable. Bail is set as a means to ensure that suspects return for future court hearings, but it also protects the community from the harm they pose and ensures justice is served for the victims.

Moreover, bail agents connect suspects with family members, who often put up their homes or cars as collateral. This incentivizes the suspect to take the process seriously. After all, unless he or she is truly evil, few want to risk their mother's home or car by not showing up to court hearings and skipping town. It also creates a more supportive circle around the suspect to help make sure they stay on the right path.

There's value to the bail system, but the nation's most Radical Left DAs and prosecutors—in partnership with lawmakers—are fundamentally reshaping our criminal justice system in ways that cannot be quickly undone. You would hope that judges would help mitigate some of these efforts by using the law to stymie the light-on-crime approach that endangers us all. But, often, judges are part of the problem.

Judges Who Aren't Very Judgmental

When John Hickey went on his daily walk one Saturday afternoon with his companion Alice, he didn't know it was for the last time. "She's all I had," Hickey mustered through tears.

Alice was Hickey's 14-year-old Jack Russell terrier, who had been by his side for over a decade. But over that decade, Pioneer Square, the neighborhood where Hickey lived, started to deteriorate. Hickey knew the neighborhood wasn't as safe as it once was, but he never thought he'd be a victim. No one ever thinks that.

While he was walking past City Hall Park, which the city allowed to become a large, dangerous, and unregulated homeless encampment during the COVID-19 pandemic, Hickey was approached by Courtney Jamar Williams. Police said the 29-year-old homeless man tried to steal Hickey's jacket. Hickey pulled out his pepper spray, aimed it at Williams, and fired away. It worked. Williams fled, and Hickey went on his way, the always-cheerful Alice in tow, as oblivious as Hickey as to what would happen next.[208]

"I heard pounding of feet and I turned around and he was running full speed at us and I didn't have time to really do anything. I had her on the leash and he came running toward her, knocked me down and he kicked her so hard that she went up in the air and started hemorrhaging," Hickey recounted.[209]

When Alice hit the ground, Hickey knew she wasn't going to make it. He took her in his arms and said he would likely never forget the look she gave him. "She thought everybody liked her and she was just proud of that. And the most horrible thing, when she died she gave me a look... just was like she was confused that anyone would do something like that to her," Hickey whimpered.

"She would cuddle up and wrap her arms around my neck. She's all I had. And I'm not complaining... that was all I had. I mean, she was all I needed," Hickey said of his dear companion Alice.

After covering the local courts for years, I developed a prescient ability to determine the outcome of first-appearance hearings. If I recognized the judge's name, the court would go easy on the suspect. It's the bad judges that I remember and, unfortunately, I recognized the judge assigned to the case.

At his first appearance, before charges were officially filed, the King County Prosecuting Attorney's Office told Judge Marcus Naylor that Williams was a danger to the community, revealing that police indicated, according to the charging documents, they had multiple run-ins with him recently. They said he's exhibited "aggressive, assaultive behavior." Asking to find probable cause for animal cruelty, the prosecutor requested Williams be held on $25,000 bail. It was $25,000 too much for Judge Naylor, who released Williams on his own personal recognizance. Knowing that he is homeless and aggressive, Judge Naylor still believed Williams was responsible enough to stay out of trouble and attend future court hearings. Unsurprisingly, the prosecutor's office said Williams did not show up for a future hearing.

In cities and counties run by the Radical Left, judges consistently go easy on suspects who pose clear and obvious dangers.

They oftentimes go unnoticed. Who can name *any* judge outside of those assigned to cases that get national attention? Yet, these men and women in robes play a key role in the deterioration of American cities. While the media tend to focus on prosecutors and DAs, Radical Left judges get away with unthinkable decisions that are often in line with far-left views on the criminal justice system. They also think cash bail is oppressive.

Alvin Charles, a homeless man, was charged in late 2022 with murder after prosecutors say he stabbed a stranger to death on a southbound L train to Brooklyn, New York, after a dispute. The victim, a father of three, suffered stab wounds to his head, neck, and torso. The alleged murder did not have to happen; Charles should have been in jail.[210]

In 2021, Charles was charged with attempted murder, an upgrade from the initial assault, attempted assault, menacing, and criminal possession of a weapon charges. Prosecutors say Charles stabbed a teacher in the stomach and arm as he was taking an A train home from school. It was a gruesome attack, but the victim survived.

Charles got lucky when his case drew Judge Jessica Earle-Gargan. Prosecutors argued for $50,000 bail. Charles was an obvious risk. But the judge, a Democrat, saw it differently. She freed him on supervised release. The victim's father didn't seem shocked to learn Charles was charged with murder the following year. "We sought justice for a long time," the victim's father told the *New York Post*.[211] "They brought him in and let him out. This is the liberal bulls—t that goes on."

Crime Crisis? What Crime Crisis?

When Manhattan DA Bragg took office, he promised significant reforms in how his office would treat criminals, actually vowing to undercharge and under-incarcerate. This isn't merely an analysis of what his policies led to; this is explicitly what he promised.

In his first memo to staff, Bragg ordered his DAs to "not seek a carceral sentence" for a number of offenses, including certain robberies, assaults, and even gun possession. Additionally, they were instructed to downgrade many felony charges to misdemeanors, including for drug dealing and armed robberies, and never seek sentences over twenty years unless there were "exceptional circumstances" that warrant harsher penalties.[212]

Career criminal William Rolon benefited from Bragg's new policies. Armed with a knife, he robbed a Duane Reade drugstore of about $2,000 worth of products, such as cold medicine. While brandishing a knife, he told an employee, "F—k you, I'm taking everything." That same day, he was accused of returning to the store to steal even more.

In line with Bragg's directives, instead of facing charges for a serious felony for the armed robbery, Rolon was only hit with low-level misdemeanors, including second-degree menacing and petit larceny, as if all he stole was a candy bar.[213] During arraignment, Manhattan Criminal Court Judge Jay Weiner told Rolon that he was "lucky" because this was "a case that two weeks ago would have been charged as a robbery." He specifically cited the "newly elected district attorney" for being charged with a misdemeanor instead of robbery, a charge he should have earned.[214] "I don't know if anyone would ever feel lucky standing in front of me in a courtroom, but you might reasonably feel lucky today," the judge told him. The *New York Post* reported that at the time of his arrest, Rolon was wanted in Brooklyn after he failed to appear in court on felony assault with a weapon charge. In that original case, he was released to community supervision without bail.

The leaked memo ignited a firestorm of community criticism. The pushback was so significant that after initially defending the memo, Bragg revised some policies, including a promise to prosecute armed robberies. But that was just to quiet the critics. His office mostly stuck to the original directives.

By November 2022, Bragg's office downgraded an astonishing

52 percent of felony cases to misdemeanor charges. To put this into context: Between 2013 and 2020, that number never exceeded 40 percent. Prosecutors downgrade charges for a number of legitimate reasons, including a lack of evidence to warrant felony charges or, depending on the case, an agreement that a felony charge for a first-time, nonviolent offender seems too harsh. But to downgrade over half of the cases shows intent. As telling, Bragg's office only asked for bail 49 percent of the time.[215]

It's not shocking that the city was rife with serious concerns, thanks to Bragg's permissive policies. New York City experienced a rash of subway crimes, in particular, largely due to the reform push. But we weren't supposed to notice a connection. In fact, we weren't even supposed to admit there was a problem.

New York City mayor Eric Adams, a former cop, was elected on the heels of voter disapproval with the escalating crime crisis gripping the city. He promised to bring a much-needed law enforcement perspective to an office that, under the former mayor Bill de Blasio, seemed to loathe cops and the rule of law. But Adams' tenure was shaky from the start. On the topic of law and order, he initially fell far short of expectations.

"New Yorkers are safe on the subway system," the mayor said in January 2022.[216] "I think it's about 1.7 percent of the crimes in New York City that occur on the subway system. Think about that for a moment. What we must do is remove the perception of fear."

By the end of October 2022, subway-related crime was up over 40 percent, driven in large part by larceny, robbery, and assault. And it saw a shockingly high 23 murders since the defund and reform movement took shape in 2020.[217] That's a 25-year high, exceeding the 2018 and 2019 homicides combined. Yet, to Adams and other Democrats, the crime crisis was merely about the *perception* of crime.

"We have an average of less than six crimes a day on a subway system with 3.5 million riders," Adams explained at the time.[218] "But if you write your story based on a narrative, then you're going to look at the worst of those six crimes and put it on the front pages of your paper every day."

Similarly, New York governor Kathy Hochul downplayed the crisis. Her re-election was unusually close because her conservative opponent, Republican congressman Lee Zeldin, made crime his central campaign theme. Hochul claimed he was "hyperventilating" about crime, hoping to "scare people" into voting for him.

"And New Yorkers are onto it. All the legitimate media organizations have called him out for what he is doing. Fear-mongering. And that's not just here in New York. That's been the Republican playbook all across this country," Hochul told a reporter.[219] "All you need to know is that Democratic states are safer than Republican states. Check out the facts."

Through intentional sleight of hand, Hochul and other Democrats changed the debate from the safety of Democrat-controlled *cities* to Republican-controlled *states*. California governor Gavin Newsom, a Democrat, argued the country had a "red state murder problem."[220] Soros-funded Philadelphia DA Larry Krasner, in office as his city hit historic homicides, claimed the actual violent crime is happening in "MAGA states."[221]

"Republicans lie!" Krasner said about Republican criticism of Democrat policies on crime. "I mean, let's just get down to it. Republicans lie. That is what they do."

The Radical Left began to argue a point no one was making. But it was a manipulative argument that Democrats thought they could win. And left-wing media did their best to amplify their claims.

Yahoo! News parroted the talking point to bolster Democrat chances ahead of the 2022 midterm elections. Senior editor Ben Adler cited a study from the left-wing think-tank Third Way that claims despite "the right-wing obsession over homicides in Democratic cities: Murder rates are far higher in Trump-voting red states than Biden-voting blue states." It looked at data from 2020. Of the ten states with the highest murder rates, eight voted for Trump.[222]

The argument is disingenuous, of course. The most murderous state from the study is Missouri, a Trump-loving red state. But its murder rate is driven by Democrat-run St. Louis and Kansas City. In 2019, St. Louis was the deadliest city in the country and, according to progressive website ProPublica, 2020 would have been its deadliest on record, but the city is "classifying more than three dozen killings as what are termed justifiable homicides, sometimes in apparent violation of FBI guidelines for reporting crimes." Also on the list are Louisiana and Tennessee. Likewise, Democrat-run New Orleans, Baton Rouge, Memphis, and Chattanooga ran up the numbers for their respective states.[223]

The conservative Manhattan Institute did what Third Way chose not to. It looked at the data behind the Republican claim that Democrat-run cities are rife with crime. Researchers found that, "The homicide rate in the blue cities was 15.8 per 100,000, compared to 9.4 per 100,000 in the red cities and 10.9 per 100,000 in the two cities with Independent mayors." Moreover, they found, "Counties with a higher share of GOP voters not only have lower homicide rates but also a lower growth in homicide rates between 2019 and 2020."[224]

No one argued that crime didn't or doesn't happen in red America, be it states, counties, cities, or towns. But the very crime argument hinges on a simple fact: Many of the crimes the country experienced can be directly tied to specific policies, reforms, and initiatives from the Radical Left. That makes them almost entirely avoidable crimes.

Though for some Democrats married to their ideology, no matter the data you provide, they will never budge from their belief that their reforms are working. And if you're New Orleans mayor LaToya Cantrell, you simply reject reality.

By September 2022, New Orleans earned the title of US murder capital. By then, the city experienced 52 homicides per 100,000 residents, far higher than St. Louis (45 per 100,000), Chicago (18 per 100,000), and New York (3.5 per 100,000). It didn't help that the police department had under 1,000 officers in a city that, just a few years earlier, had over 1,300.[225] It was no coincidence the city was making steady progress at the time, hitting a historic low number of homicides in 2019, until Radical Left reforms were adopted and police fled the department.[226] But Mayor Cantrell rejected these new stats and new reality, making the case at a press conference that the homicides weren't happening. Her answer was as meandering as it was, frankly, deranged.[227]

"I don't embrace that at all," she told local media. "I don't embrace it because, one, that is...the data even used for that is more of a governmental term for that. It's not based on what is actually happening on the ground, in our community, and even as you look at comparisons to other cities throughout this country."

She then complained about media coverage for unfairly comparing New Orleans to cities like Chicago because they had more murders over Memorial Day weekend 2022. Chicago had nine homicides, only two more than New Orleans.[228] And 2022 started off worse than anyone imagined. In just the first 10 days of the year, the city averaged over one murder a day. But Cantrell doesn't "embrace" those numbers, so I guess no one was dying.

Meanwhile, left-wing media outlets like CNN took the same approach. Before his humiliating termination, CNN's Brian Stelter called Fox News coverage of the crime crisis an "imagined drama."[229] His sycophantic colleague, media analyst Oliver Darcy, called the coverage "distorted."[230] They said this even as the national murder rate surged 30 percent between 2019 and 2020,[231] which came after steady and significant declines since the early 1990s.[232]

In fact, 12 large American cities set record-high homicide rates, and all of them were run by Democrats. Philadelphia experienced 561 homicides in 2021, the city's highest number ever recorded.[233] Rochester, New York, broke its 30-year-old homicide record with a rate higher than New York City at 38.4 homicides per 100,000 people.[234] Fueled by gang and drug violence, Portland, Oregon, exceeded its previous record 66 homicides in 1987 with 90 in 2021 (and 101 in 2022).[235] Rounding up the list are Toledo, Ohio; Columbus, Ohio; Baton Rouge, Louisiana; Austin, Texas; Louisville, Kentucky; St. Paul, Minnesota; Tucson, Arizona; and Albuquerque, New Mexico.

When You Tell Shoplifters They Can Shoplift, They, Well, Shoplift

California voters passed Proposition 47 in 2014, which reclassified certain theft offenses from felonies to misdemeanors. If the amount stolen was worth under $950, the crime would qualify as a misdemeanor charge, if you could even find a left-wing prosecutor who would agree to charges in the first place. Too often, they favor restorative justice programs, or they just drop charges altogether under the auspices of spending their time on more serious cases. Even before the 2020–2022 crime crisis sparked by criminal justice reforms, researchers with the Public Policy Institute of California tied Proposition 47 to an increase in some property crimes, such as a 9 percent uptick in larcenies.[236] Once the other reforms went into effect, theft exploded.

Scores of videos were posted to social media showing common criminals and opportunists raiding retail stores, bringing in trash bags, and emptying shelves of basic goods that could be easily resold on the streets, including toothpaste, toilet paper, and laundry detergent. Drugstores like CVS and Walgreens said that theft in their San Francisco shops outpaced theft in their other locations nationwide.[237] Several Target stores in the city changed closing times from 10 p.m. to 6 p.m., with a spokesperson citing "a significant and alarming rise in theft and security incidents at our San Francisco stores, similar to reports from other retailers in the area."[238] A Whole Foods in the Mid-Market neighborhood abruptly closed in April 2023. Management cited high crime, but the fatal fentanyl and meth overdose in one of the store's bathrooms probably made their decision a no-brainer.[239] Just a few weeks later, Nordstrom announced it was closing two stores, including its 35-year-old flagship store. Like Uniqlo, Gap, H&M, and Saks Off 5th, Nordstrom joined the more than two dozen retailers unable to handle the city's crime wave and related homelessness crisis.[240] A spokesperson for the Westfield mall, where the Nordstrom was located, didn't hold back, blaming city leaders for "unsafe conditions" and a "lack of enforcement against rampant criminal activity."[241] Criminals will take advantage of whatever you'll let them get away with.

Portland's crime crisis ran small and large businesses out of town. Some of the closures were due to violent crime. Coava Coffee, an independent coffee shop, called it quits thanks to customers and staff saying the violence in the neighborhood has been "very traumatizing."[242] But many are the victims of death by a thousand robberies. Citing 19 robberies in just a year, losing $56,000 dollars in merchandise, the owner of Consign Couture in Portland's Washington Square mall opted against renewing her lease, unable to absorb the costs associated with the necessary security she'd need to stay afloat.[243] A much larger retailer, REI, announced in early 2023 that it wasn't going to renew its lease in Portland's Pearl neighborhood. A statement to employees criticized the deteriorating neighborhood for the decision.

"The safety of our employees, members and customers is always our number one priority," REI said.[244] "In recent years, Portland has been dealing with increased crime in our neighborhood and beyond. Last year, REI Portland had its highest number of break-ins and thefts in two decades, despite actions to provide extra security."

My exclusive story about John Ray Lomack, a homeless prolific offender, went viral in Seattle after he was caught stealing a 70-inch, widescreen LG television in January 2022.[245] He's seen on surveillance footage casing a Target in downtown Seattle, a location plagued by petty theft; shelves often bare thanks to shoplifting, with security warned to keep interactions with thieves to a bare minimum. Lomack approached a set of TVs, reached into his pocket, and surreptitiously pulled out a tool to cut the plastic straps tying the televisions together. He then loaded the television on a nearby shopping cart.

Security was waiting for him at the store's exit, but he didn't care. This is Seattle, after all. He continued for the exit without attempting to pay, pushing security officers aside to escape with his loot. He was seen dragging the television down the sidewalk when security flagged a nearby police officer who made contact with Lomack and, after what police called a brief struggle, was arrested and booked. This was not his first run-in with the store. In fact, he was given a notice of tresspass from the store weeks earlier. According to court documents, he had cost the store over $6,000 in stolen items at the time.

Citing "warrant activity" from 32 previous cases, a King County prosecutor asked for $5,000 bail. Lomack had at least 18 felonies and misdemeanors to his name, including second-degree burglary, second-degree possession of stolen property, and fourth-degree assault. Soft-on-crime Judge Kuljinder Dhillon didn't seem to care, releasing him on his own personal recognizance. It turns out, Lomack was an enrollee of the county's Equity Just Care program, which offers transitional housing to those in need, while providing them services to address their problems. They didn't serve him well.

Thanks to the Radical Left leadership of Manhattan DA Bragg and soft-on-crime Democrat lawmakers, empowered criminals knew they'd likely get away with theft, so that's exactly what they did. At a news conference in October 2022, NYPD Chief Michael Lipetri confirmed that shoplifting hit historic highs, with complaints up by nearly 18,000 that year. Drugstore chains like Rite Aid and CVS were closing locations over retail theft and threatening to shut more, if the crisis worsened.

Wilfredo Ocasio is a serial shoplifter who, between August and

December 2022, the *New York Post* reported was busted 33 times for petit larceny.[246] In November, he was arrested for his alleged involvement in 23 separate thefts from two Manhattan Duane Reade stores. But none of the individual charges qualify for bail under state reforms. On a local television station, NYPD Commissioner Keechant Sewell complained that officers are "arresting the same people over and over again."

"Judges need to have the ability to determine if someone is a public safety threat to the community and to determine if a person who is a recidivist can be given bail," she pleaded.[247]

Eventually, after yet another arrest and increased media scrutiny, Bragg's office charged Ocasio with third-degree grand larceny. But it shouldn't have to get to that point before action. Too often, however, it takes a massive media and public response to get Radical Left leadership to act. For some, they won't wait for lawmakers and prosecutors to get their act together.

Gaslighting on Crime

Buckhead houses roughly 20 percent of Georgia's Atlanta population. It's a wealthy, beautiful neighborhood with Georgians who, like so many suburbanites in large Democrat-run cities, thought they would be immune to the Radical Left insanity in the city's core. But residents quickly found out that wasn't the case. As crime rates soared in Atlanta, the people who moved away from the crime crisis found it happening in their own backyard.

In December 2021 at an AMC Phipps Plaza showing of *Spider-man: No Way Home*, a dispute over reserved seating turned into a shooting.[248] Earlier that day nearby, there was another shooting, with a victim suffering multiple wounds. Nearly one year to the day earlier, a stray bullet shot from the parking lot of Phipps Plaza hit a nearby Lexus driven by a family going to the mall for Christmas shopping. A seven-year-old girl was killed. One morning in June 2021, police say, Gaelen Newsom fired shots at three random joggers before crashing his car into a fourth victim, who was seriously injured. After a series of violent crimes at Lennox Square mall, including a brutal beating and armed robbery of an elderly woman[249] and an Apple store security guard getting shot by two 15-year-olds, shoppers stopped visiting.[250] And some of the mostly peaceful riots from the Black Lives Matter movement led to looting in Buckhead.

Buckhead residents were fed up. Sick of handing over tax dollars from the city's wealthiest neighborhood into a government that didn't care enough to protect them, neighborhood activists moved to secede with the formation of the Buckhead City Commission. Led by Bill White, who said his neighborhood had become a "war zone," the group raised millions in funding to explore how they could become a separate city where their tax dollars would be spent more effectively on public safety.[251]

Rather than address their legitimate concerns, then-mayor Keisha Lance Bottoms criticized White as being politically motivated. Mayor Bottoms was largely to blame for pushing police out of the Atlanta Police Department, which helped lead to a rise in crime, so it made sense for her to react defensively. She was trying to help write her political legacy in a city she nearly destroyed. "It's no secret that I was very vocal on how I felt about Donald Trump, and I don't think it's a coincidence that the man who is leading this movement is new to Atlanta and was a very big Trump supporter," Bottoms said at a media roundtable at City Hall.[252] "I think the two are very much related."

She did not mention that White held fundraisers for Barack Obama and Hillary Clinton, since it would hurt her MAGA extremist characterization. But with the help of the media, Bottoms was able to define the secession campaign as racist. When CNN[253] and the *Atlanta Journal Constitution*[254] covered the story, they were quick to remind you that the neighborhood is mostly full of wealthy white residents, as if being wealthy or white is the only reason one might not want to be shot, stabbed, robbed, or assaulted.

Still, White and his group persisted, and it led to positive changes, even if they weren't able to secede. The movement garnered enough attention to force city officials to pursue meaningful strategies to tackle Buckhead crime. At an October 2022 town hall, police said violent and property crimes were down 11 percent in Buckhead. Residents are not yet content, since coming down from such a surge is still not enough to make you feel safe. There was still crime and rampant drug dealing, but these residents became activated, organizing for a common good, and started to see some results.

Activists organized in San Francisco too. Not to secede, but to sever ties with DA Chesa Boudin. Even the reliably partisan progressives of San Francisco thought Boudin's reforms had strayed too far to the left, putting everyday residents at risk.

Boudin spent his tenure trying to out-progressive his predecessor Gascon. He pushed more cases to diversion programs, rather than trials, helping lead to a surge in homicides, thefts, and assaults. But there was one high-profile case that caused enough outrage to inspire a group of activists to recall the radical DA.

Prolific criminal Troy McAlister was driving a stolen car on New Year's Eve 2020, when he hit and killed two pedestrians, 27-year-old Hanako Abe and 60-year-old Elizabeth Platt. McAlister had been navigating the criminal justice system since 1995, when he was just 19 years old. By 2019, when Boudin was elected, McAlister had been awaiting trial for robbing a store with a toy gun. This newest case made him eligible for a three-strikes charge, but Boudin wasn't interested. He pleaded the charges down to second-degree felony robbery, and McAlister was released at sentencing for time already served. Within months of release, McAlister had been arrested five times by San Francisco police for driving stolen cars and burglary. Boudin's office refused to file charges in every arrest.[255]

Don du Bain was a prosecutor under Boudin, but left the office over concerns with the reforms. He would eventually join the recall effort. "As a result of that—of striking all those other charges and prior convictions—he put Troy McAlister back on the street with no treatment, no counseling, nothing, just back on the street in a position where he was able to kill those two women," du Bain told a local television station.[256] "I don't see what's reformist about simply releasing a defendant back on the street without any conditions other than he's placed on parole."

The recall was a massive success, despite efforts by Boudin and some media outlets to pretend the campaign was a right-wing effort. When you win with 55 percent of the vote in a city that has, perhaps, fifty-five and one-half Republican voters, it seems silly to entertain that talking point. But it was indicative of the strategy Democrats employed as cities were being devastated by left-wing reforms.

Whether it was New York and Seattle or Philadelphia and San Francisco, the Radical Left first told us that there wasn't a crime surge. Then, eventually, we were told it's part of a nationwide trend, as if they played no role in starting it. They told us it was actually a red-state problem, while reminding us that, actually, crime had been much worse in the 80s, so why are we complaining?

To be fair to the Radical Left, their laws and policies weren't solely to blame for the rise in crime. You can't blame their reforms without looking at what they did to our police departments. By enacting criminal justice reforms, while dismantling police departments, Democrats effectively created a culture of lawlessness that helped nearly destroy large American cities.

CHAPTER 4

THE LIE THAT ENDED MODERN POLICING

Momentum That Couldn't Be Stopped

George Floyd was killed by Minneapolis officer Derek Chauvin on May 25, 2022. It sparked a national movement by the Radical Left, which effectively ended modern-day policing, leading to historic crime in Democrat-run cities. But the movement was based on a lie about the police that initially convinced millions of otherwise well-meaning Americans into seeing law enforcement as an enemy.

Floyd was arrested for suspicion of using a counterfeit $20 bill. After he resisted, police took him to the ground and handcuffed him. To help keep him subdued, Chauvin placed his knee on Floyd's neck, holding it there for over nine minutes. Despite protests that he couldn't breathe, and screams from a growing crowd to get off of him, Chauvin did not relent. Floyd's last words, "I can't breathe" led to a movement that perpetuated a myth that what happened to Floyd happens to black Americans every day and that this was one of many instances of abject police brutality, only it was caught on video for the world to see.

Reasonable people could understand why Floyd's death inspired many Americans to protest. Few viewed the video through a political lens. But the movement became about more than what happened to Floyd. The Radical Left saw an opening to exploit Floyd's death and enact anti-police reforms it had been working on for decades. While some of their plans had already been instituted across the country, this was a once-in-a-generation moment that could lead to insurmountable momentum. It did just that. Any time an officer used force on a black suspect, regardless of the circumstances, it became a rallying cry for the Black Lives Matter (BLM) movement.

Police were portrayed as white supremacists, wandering the streets of American cities looking for black people to harass, assault, or murder. The Radical Left all regaled of stories about police shootings and the killing of unarmed black men purely because of their skin color. There was no nuance or context necessary: All cops are bastards. And too many well-intentioned Americans fell for it. At times, it felt like it became a mass psychosis event falling along party lines, when it shouldn't have been viewed as political issue at all. Policing, after all, isn't political.

Of course, there was no data to back up the exaggerated claims. In the five years prior to Floyd's death, 2015–2019, there were 113 police shootings of unarmed black suspects, according to the *Washington Post* police shootings tracker. But being unarmed doesn't mean a suspect isn't a threat and that police weren't justified in any use of force.

Police in Blytheville, Arkansas, shot and killed 35-year-old Marzues Scott on April 7, 2019. He was unarmed at the time.[257] To the Radical Left, this is enough to persecute and prosecute the officer involved. There's no more to the story. But the context matters. Surveillance footage showed Scott walking into a Dodge's convenience store and eatery, and then viciously beating an employee, inflicting brutal head injuries and dental damage. The attack was unprovoked. Police say Scott never spoke during the attack.

After the beating, he walked to the nearby hotel where he was staying. When an officer arrived at the scene, he attacked her. The incident was captured on the officer's body camera. "You just assaulted somebody at Dodge Store. Go to my car. Go to my car. Don't get near me," she warned him. "Go to my car now. Go to my car. I need some back up. Go to the car."

He was silent and stared her down. Then, suddenly, the much larger Scott approached the officer, who yelled, "Get back, don't come near me. Get back." He did not comply, punching her twice in the face. She responded by firing two shots at him, as she fell to the ground. In horror, she yelled into her radio, "Shots fired!" Scott later died at the hospital. This incident was deemed justifiable use of force, and the officer faced no discipline.

Simply labeling Scott an unarmed black man shot and killed by police does not tell the whole story. But it's not supposed to. The Radical Left use these tragedies as props to forward a political agenda. Without context, these stories tell an alarming fiction, one that the Radical Left wanted to be told. Yet, the Scott shooting was one of many "police killings" that inspired millions of compassionate Americans into believing smears against the police. They were convinced of a reality that didn't exist.

Scores of activists, organized by various BLM and like-minded groups nationwide, marched on the streets to demand police reforms. What happened to Floyd must never happen again. *Now* is the time for change; *now* is the time to focus on the importance of black lives, as if black lives didn't matter before Floyd's death. And if you dare question the reforms, you were called a white supremacist, a term that now included all who expressed any resistance to the BLM cause. There was no reform too extreme, with mainstream media outlets from CNN and MSNBC to CBS and NBC, embracing or endorsing most every demand of BLM radicals.

Of course, these activists did not merely march, they rioted too. The radical elements of the movement torched cars, burned buildings, looted retail stores, and attacked and murdered police and political adversaries. With the help of so-called anti-fascists (or Antifa), loosely organized groups of dangerous domestic terrorists, the movement used violence to push through legislation and impose policies.

At first, we weren't supposed to notice as some media outlets focused almost exclusively on the non-violent marches. You could excuse that to a point; media members saw a national movement that many in their audience agreed with and they wanted to take part. But soon, some outlets appeared to intentionally downplay violence. MSNBC host and *Today Show* co-anchor Craig Melvin tweeted a statement explaining how the network would frame its coverage of the mass looting, arson, and violence: "While the situation on the ground in Minneapolis is fluid, and there has been violence, it is most accurate at this time to describe what is happening there as 'protests,' not riots."[258] In other words, riots were no longer riots. It became another word redefined by the Radical Left like "woman" and "equity."

Three days after Floyd's death, Minneapolis Third Precinct police building was burned down, as thousands of protestors and rioters cheered it on. As flames burst out of buildings behind him, MSNBC host Ali Velshi described the riot as "mostly a protest" before trying to justify the chaos around him.[259]

"I want to be clear on how I characterize this. This is mostly a protest. It is not, generally speaking, unruly, but fires have been started and this crowd is relishing that," Velshi explained. "There is a deep sense of grievance and complaint here, and that is the thing. That when you discount people who are doing things to public property that they shouldn't be doing, it does have to be understood that this city has got, for the last several years, an issue with police, and it's got a real sense of the deep sense of grievance of inequality."

Joy Reid, MSNBC's most conspiratorial host, claimed the violence wasn't being perpetuated by BLM supporters, but by right-wing plants.[260] "Let me repeat this for those inventing the idea of

'Black Lives Matter riots.' BLM doesn't 'riot.' They march against police violence. And note that those caught setting fires, assaulting and shooting people are consistently to the RIGHT, not the left," she falsely claimed about riots that I covered in Seattle.

If they weren't pretending the riots were a right-wing fantasy, some media members were justifying them. Though the mostly white Antifa groups have little legitimate interest in the lives of black Americans, they used the BLM movement to push forward a Radical Left agenda to abolish police and prisons, and ultimately, our representative democracy. And they had supporters at CNN. Former CNN anchor Don Lemon pretended that because Antifa stands for antifascist, the group should be applauded for their agenda.[261]

"Listen, no organization is perfect. There was some violence. No one condones violence," he claimed while condoning violence. "But there were different reasons for Antifa and for these neo-Nazis to be there. One, racists, fascists; the other group, fighting racist fascists. There is a distinction there."

His then-colleague Chris Cuomo tweeted a meme comparing Antifa to American soldiers storming the beaches of Normandy.[262] But Cuomo never left the comforts of his home or office studio, and his colleagues on the ground ignored the domestic terrorists in black-bloc clothing. He didn't know Antifa the way I did, as I infiltrated their pre-riot marches, dressed incognito, taking photos and videos, while writing down as many notes as I could.

The violence was justified or ignored because it benefited the Radical Left, who happily forwarded the policy agenda of BLM. It did not matter that the mobs chanted "ACAB" (which stood for "all cops are bastards"), or that they actively wished harm upon cops (some actually committing assaults against them). That the movement claimed police departments were institutions of white supremacy that hadn't been reformed since police were tasked with tracking down escaped slaves didn't cause many Democrats to bat an eye.

The movement would help the Radical Left realize a political agenda. Some politicians helped the movement because they long agreed with the underlying principles of police reform. Others helped because they were terrified of standing in the way of what would likely be a voting bloc that would retaliate in the next election cycle. The motives for why politicians supported the violent mob doesn't matter in the end. What matters is the impact these policies and postures had on policing. It made us all less safe.

The Rush to Defund the Defenders

Calls to defund the police quickly turned from a rallying cry to legislative action, funneling tax dollars to the nebulously defined "black community." But the intent wasn't merely to fund programs and services to help struggling black residents; it was to punish police departments for their imagined racist sins.

Less than a month after Floyd's death, the Los Angeles City Council voted 11 to 3 to defund the Los Angeles Police Department by $150 million. Normally, massive budget cuts take time and include thoughtful deliberation. But the council, cheered on by then-mayor Eric Garcetti, rushed the process to placate Radical Left protestors and rioters who were demanding immediate action. One Los Angelino who attended a virtual council meeting threatened, "we won't get out of the streets until you cut it down by billions."[263]

The funds were reprioritized toward superserving the black community with programs that included universal basic income, homelessness services, and anti-gang initiatives. It was the council's form of reparations because the city wanted to apologize for the way they claimed to have mistreated black residents.[264]

Seattle and Portland city leaders took similar approaches in defunding the police. After relentless riots, physical attacks against police, and deadly autonomous zones, activists were successful in rallying city councils and mayors to their side.

Promising to defund the Seattle Police Department by 50

percent, the city's far-left city council got to work on cuts, led by Socialist city councilwoman Kshama Sawant and a council full of cop-loathing, Radical Left lawmakers. They removed parking enforcement and 911 call center operations from police control, and forwarded plans for a civilian response team of social workers to tackle some 911 calls. They argued armed officers made crisis calls more dangerous, pretending cops would quickly pull the trigger when egged on by someone having a mental health breakdown.

Though they fell far short of their 50 percent pledge, the Council and then-mayor Jenny Durkan cut 18 percent, with a pledge to continue cuts during the next budget cycle. They also managed to push out the city's first (and one of the nation's only) black female police chiefs, Carmen Best, who was targeted, along with her staff, with salary cuts and layoffs.[265] Equity, am I right?

Portland's Radical Left sustained months-long violence to persuade city leaders to cut and ultimately abolish the police. Led primarily by Antifa terrorists, scores of mostly white, privileged 20-somethings destroyed businesses, attempted to burn down the city's federal courthouse, and threatened anyone who got in their way for over 150 nights.

Portland's Democrat mayor Ted Wheeler, who also serves as police commissioner under the city structure, gave in to the demands of the activists and far-left city commissioners, vowing a $12 million police bureau budget cut. This included defunding the gun violence reduction team, which foreshadowed an inevitable crisis that hit the very community the city vowed to help, along with removing school resource officers (SROs) from Portland public schools.[266]

"My privilege as a white man, my privilege as the mayor and the leader of the institutions of power in this community, I believe shielded me from time to time from the many difficult and uncomfortable truths about our history and about our society," Wheeler announced at the time, setting himself up as a white savior.

New York City officials cut an astronomical $1 billion dollars from the New York Police Department budget after thousands of protesters and rioters demanded change. Some occupied City Hall, creating makeshift encampments and vandalizing government buildings with vulgar, anti-police messaging. Others looted high-end shops for weeks between May and June 2020, shoving expensive clothing and jewelry into trash bags, not even bothering to hide their faces. It turns out they didn't have to.

Most of the arrests during the worst of the looting in the Bronx were dismissed by DA Darcel Clark, with others pleading down to lesser charges, like trespassing, which don't result in jail time. According to NBC News, there were 90 felony and misdemeanor arrests on the evening of June 1 into early the next morning. Of those, 28 were outright dismissals and 14 were adjourned contemplating dismissal (which allows a record to be erased, if one doesn't get arrested within the next six months). The others were mostly combinations of taking plea deals or receiving conditional discharge.[267]

In Manhattan, the worst of the looting took place in the upscale Soho neighborhood, ending with 485 arrests. Then-DA Cyrus Vance Jr. dropped 222 of the cases, with at least 73 pleading down to lesser charges that didn't carry jail time. In a memo obtained by NBC News, Vance told his prosecutors, "For many of these commercial burglaries, you will be asked to reduce the initial felony charge to a misdemeanor and to dispose of the case . . . with an eye toward rehabilitation."[268]

Despite the violence and rioting, then-mayor Bill de Blasio gave BLM a pass, ordering the anti-police rallies exempt from the ban on mass gatherings. "This is a historic moment of change" de Blasio said on CNN.[269] The message was clear: You will get away with looting and rioting because Democrats believe in the cause. The real enemy was the police.

Once lauded as the best and most dedicated force in the world after the September 11, 2001, terrorist attacks, the men and women in blue were vilified as racist thugs mowing down black

New Yorkers. And somehow, at a time when crime was on the rise, the mayor and city council deemed it appropriate to stop the hiring of an additional 1,160 new officers. The city took responsibilities away from police to monitor the homeless and keep schools safe.[270]

The national trend was consistent. Riots broke out, protesters made demands, Democrat leaders gave in. The movement's end goal lost any real connection to the circumstances surrounding Floyd's death. Police funding had little to do with what happened in Minneapolis. And where the funds they cut went would not have prevented Floyd's death. Helping to propel the movement was Democrats' unhinged ire toward President Donald Trump and any supportive Republican. The Right, generally speaking, support police and adopt a tough-on-crime approach. That they were deemed white supremacists made it more obvious to haphazardly cut funds and funnel the money toward the perceived victims of bigotry.

But such monumental change had dire consequences. Little thought was put into the effects of defunding. Lawmakers could just have easily vowed more funding for programs without cutting police budgets, but that's not what the movement demanded. Predictably, cities experienced a mass exodus of police officers, and crime rates soared.

Where Have All the Cops Gone?

The Minneapolis Police Department was reduced to just a third of what it was before Floyd was killed,[271] with two hundred leaving the force within a year of the defund movement.[272] Only dozens applied to replace them in 2022.

Steve Dykstra was one of the officers who quit. He told CBS News that he became a cop to serve his community, but it became obvious he could not do that anymore. Everything changed on May 25, 2020, when he and his fellow officers were pelted with both insults and rocks as they watched their city burn, not allowed to do much to quell the unrest. He held out as long as he could, but knew it wasn't sustainable. It's a dangerous job made worse by a community that did little to support him. He said he quit "out of principle" and moved to a small town in Iowa where he was able to do his job, while feeling supported.

"All of a sudden it was, 'The Minneapolis Police Department is rotten to the root. Everybody with that uniform is a killer and a racist,'" Dykstra explained.

The defund police movement pushed cops out. Some were cut intentionally, but most who decided to quit abandoned the Democrat-run cities for friendlier locations. Some got out of the profession altogether. They were villainized for taking on a job to serve their communities. Each day they put on their uniforms, they put a target on their backs. They run toward danger, while the rest of us run away, but now, the very people who called the police for help are telling them to stay away, pretending the officer is a bigger threat than the gang member or common criminal in their neighborhood.

When Austin, Texas, leaders defunded their police department by $150 million, roughly a third of its budget, it meant the city lost three incoming cadet classes, it cut the funding for 150 officers,[273] and it disbanded a number of specialty units, including the ones responsible for investigating domestic violence and driving while intoxicated.[274] The police chief said they were losing 15 to 20 officers a month. By August 2021, the department was taking an average of nine minutes to respond to priority zero 911 calls (emergencies requiring immediate police response due to an imminent threat) and 20 to 30 minutes, on average, overall. It became so dire that the department asked residents not to call 911 unless it was absolutely necessary. Unsurprisingly, with officers unable to proactively police—a key component of keeping any city safe—Austin set a homicide record in 2020.

Good luck finding a city that didn't pay a price for defunding its police department. Los Angeles County saw homicides jump nearly 94 percent[275] from 2019 to 2021 after 631 officers quit or retired during fiscal year 2020–2021.[276] NYPD officers walked away in droves during the defund push: 465 officers quit in 2020, and 888 quit in 2021.[277]

While the exodus made Democrat-led cities less safe, it pleased the BLM and Antifa activists who hoped to fully dismantle police departments. A chorus of online, left-wing trolls cheered on departments struggling to maintain staff, arguing that despite the clear uptick in crime, we're better off without police. There were, of course, politicians who also didn't seem to mind the staffing crises, seeing it as an opportunity to forward more defunding efforts than they were previously able to accomplish. One of the more contumelious examples of defund activism occurred in Seattle.

Let's Fire the White Cops!

When the Seattle City Council defunded the SPD, council members proposed cutting the salaries of Police Chief Best and her command staff, while eliminating as many as 100 officers through layoffs and attrition. The invidious proposal, championed by Councilwoman Lisa Herbold, was nothing short of racist.

Herbold positioned herself as a wise, edgy, and progressive leader on the council. A grandmother with a nose ring, Herbold rose to office after serving on the staff of longtime activist and progressive city council member Nick Licata, who taught her to legislate through a social justice lens. When the BLM movement came to power, Herbold was eager to serve as a White Knight who could help activists navigate through the wonky legislative maze to ensure policies are implemented.

To get to a 50 percent cut, Herbold knew there needed to be layoffs; roughly 80 percent of SPD's budget was earmarked for personnel. She ran into a problem, not because she didn't want to fire cops, but because Chief Best warned that city policy mandates the newest hires be the first to be separated. The SPD had worked for years to recruit a more diverse police force, and its newest hires represented racial minorities. Herbold couldn't be seen as firing black or Latino officers, even though they were routinely targeted with derisive, hateful rhetoric from BLM activists as "sell outs." So, she floated an idea: Fire the white officers.

"I want to state very clearly that the chief is empowered, under the Public Safety Civil Service Commission rule 15, to implement layoffs in a way that is called *out of order*," Herbold said at a committee hearing.[278] "This means she does not have to fire the newest officers hired first. She can request the Public Safety Civil Service Commission executive director for permission to lay off out of order, when doing so is in the interest of efficient operations of his or her department."

Herbold's position wasn't merely bigoted. It was also obtuse. The most veteran officers, who are white, are responsible for the most efficient policing in the department because they know the institution and policies and have the community relationships that new officers don't have because of their lack of experience. How would race-based layoffs serve the interests of efficient operations of the SPD, exactly? Perhaps "efficient" should be added to the list of words redefined by the Radical Left.

While the plan was eventually abandoned because it's obviously illegal, the cuts that were passed led to a historic number of officers leaving the department. Between 2020 and 2023, over 500 officers left the SPD, leaving it with the lowest deployable staff since the 1980s. I spoke to a number of officers who said they would never police or even step foot in Seattle again. And officer exit interviews did not hide why they left in such dramatic numbers.[279]

"This agenda sacrifices the health and well-being of the officers and ultimately will destroy the fabric of this once fine city," one sergeant wrote upon separation, saying he would "never" return to work for the SPD again.

A 31-year veteran of the force wrote that one reason he was

leaving was, "The total lack of respect and support from the city council and the mayor." A detective of over 20 years said he was leaving, arguing the "disdain for police from the community is astonishing."

As officers left, there were too few cops to intervene in crimes. The department stopped investigating adult sexual assault cases and routinely pushed non-patrol officers to respond to 911 calls due to a lack of staff. In some precincts, it took officers over 11 minutes to respond to the highest priority calls.[280] That's not an ideal stat when Seattle saw homicides hit a 26-year high in 2020, before exceeding that number in 2022.[281] Though Democrats defunded the police because "black lives matter," 49 percent of the homicide victims in 2020 were black. This doesn't sound like a successful movement.

The Most Predictable Results

Perhaps the least surprising result of the defund movement came out of Portland. Thanks to the defund effort, the city lost a specialized unit meant to tackle gun violence. The Gun Violence Reduction Team (GVRT) was formed in 2019 to replace the Gang Enforcement Team, which was disbanded for having too many contacts with black Portlanders. The GVRT suffered from the same criticism, which anti-police Portland Commissioner Jo Ann Hardesty relentlessly targeted for dissolution. With BLM support, she was finally able to sway Mayor Wheeler to kill the program.[282] Surely, you know what happened next: Gun violence was not reduced.

In the six months after gutting the GVRT, there were 657 reported shootings compared to 413 for all of 2019. The following years saw shootings skyrocket, with 1,315 in 2021 and 1,306 in 2022.[283] When shootings go up, usually homicides follow, and 2020 saw the city's most homicides in 26 years with 55,[284] followed by an all-time high of 90 homicides in 2021.[285] Well, it *was* an all-time high until 2022, when the city hit 101 homicides.[286]

Who could have seen this coming? Literally anyone with two functioning brain cells. Yet, city after city witnessed the same general experiences. Under Democrat mayor Muriel Bowser, Washington, DC, defunded police, followed immediately by homicides hitting a 16-year high in 2020,[287] surpassing that by November 2021.[288] San Francisco cut police funding as, according to the *San Francisco Chronicle*, "a gesture of reparations for decades of city policymaking that have created or exacerbated deep inequities for San Francisco's African American residents." What followed? A 20 percent increase in homicides in 2019, and a 17 percent increase in 2021 compared to 2020.[289] Burglaries saw a sharp increase, up 47 percent in 2020 when compared to the three years prior.

Even the small, Democrat-run city of Burlington, Vermont, felt the impacts of the defund movement with homicides in 2022 they hadn't seen in decades. The number itself, at five, is low; if Chicago saw five homicides in a morning commute, they'd consider it a success. But it's the highest number of homicides the Vermont city had seen in at least 63 years. And it coincided with a decision to gut the police department from 105 officers to 74 through attrition. Just like in big Democrat-run cities, the small city of Burlington ran cops out of the department, with low morale from the sudden decision to treat them like the enemy. By December 2022, the department only had 62 officers.[290]

When police funds were diverted, there were some worthy program beneficiaries. But from city to city, they were so quick to placate Radical Left demands, there was no thought on how cities would address the cuts to basic police services. That problem was made worse by the mass exodus of police officers. In Los Angeles, for example, thanks to the cuts, the LAPD announced a plan to stop responding to traffic collisions, while severely gutting the robberies and homicide divisions (despite robberies and homicides skyrocketing).[291] They simply did not think this through. And yet, it didn't stop them from the next phase of their plan.

Banning and Restricting Nonlethal Tools

A chorus of local and national Democrat lawmakers declared *now* is the time to "reimagine policing," as if they were all reading from the same script. While not all were on board—Representative Rashida Tlaib (D-MI) said we should have "no more policing" at all because it is "inherently and intentionally racist"[292]—many of the plans that were promoted were similar. They weren't just asking for reforms. The Radical Left was looking to fundamentally change how policing in America works. Most without any law enforcement experience beyond watching *Chicago PD* or *Hawaii Five-O*, lawmakers pushed sweeping changes that stopped allowing cops to be cops. They started with tactics or tools they thought they could directly tie to either Floyd's death or the rallies and riots it inspired.

Though they can be lifesaving tools, chokeholds and/or vascular neck restraints (VNRs) have been banned by well over half the nation's large police departments. The two types of restraint are markedly different.[293] Unlike chokeholds, VNRs apply pressure to blood vessels in the neck, rendering the suspect unconscious, but do not impact breathing. Traditional chokeholds, which do impact breathing, are not used often by police, since they're usually trained in VNR.

Though neither chokeholds nor VNRs were used in the Floyd incident, they were treated as dangerous tactics. Police in New York, Los Angeles, Chicago, Seattle, Austin, Honolulu, Hawaii, and scores more were either banned by department diktat or law from using the tactic to gain control over a dangerous and aggressive suspect. Ironically, it was a nonlethal tool taken away from officers at a time when Democrats claimed police are too quick to use force. Research by Wake Forest University School of Medicine showed the VNR to be "one of the least injurious tools that police have." It's also effective, with a 92.6 percent success rate in subduing a combative suspect, meaning officers are less likely to use a baton or firearm.[294]

It did not matter that VNRs, in particular, are exceptionally safe when used by a trained officer. It was *something* to show city leaders, who were listening to the increasingly unhinged demands of an activist class pushing to abolish police. But the ban on nonlethal tools did not stop with chokeholds and VNRs.

Cops were forced into difficult positions, particularly in cities like Portland, Seattle, and Minneapolis, where nightly direct actions were becoming more and more violent. Antifa and other radicals, many but not all local, repeatedly tried to burn down the Mark O. Hatfield US Courthouse in Portland during the 100+ consecutive nights of riots. Similarly, Seattle mobs tried to burn down a police precinct at the center of the Capitol Hill Autonomous Zone. And, of course, Minneapolis was the sight of frequent and violent riots and looting that had an entire city on edge. How were police supposed to respond when the very riots they're managing were borne out of claims of police abuse? They couldn't very well intervene, batons swinging, without fear of instigating more violence, especially when media outlets were looking for images of *any* use of force, even justified, to egg on the movement. Instead, police leaned on the nonlethal means of riot control: tear gas. But soon, that came under fire too.

Seattle City Council members, eager to align themselves with the cause, banned tear gas and other crowd control tools, claiming they were being used to harm innocent protesters and deprive them of their First Amendment rights.[295] The Washington State legislature then went one step further, severely restricting its use statewide. Under state law, only mayors, county executives, or the governor can give the okay to fire tear gas into a riot.[296] Think about that in terms of real-world consequences: A riot is breaking out, and rather than immediately deploying tear gas to save lives and prevent property destruction, the commander on the ground connects with the chief of police, who then makes a call to the highest ranking elected political leader for an ultimate decision. Law enforcement action should be free from political influence, but Washington State made them intertwined.

In fact, Washington Democrats were so quick to remove weapons from police, they initially passed legislation that directly led to the death of a Seattle K9 officer named Jedi. HB 1054 banned police from using large-caliber firearms and ammunition, a response to SPD's use of crowd dispersal weapons. But Democrat lawmakers seldom understand the weapons they want to ban. They assumed large-caliber weapons are all exceptionally deadly because of their size. But what they ended up banning were nonlethal weapons like beanbags or 40 mm sponge-tipped rounds because of the caliber size. Either would have come in handy, and been used, during a standoff with a homeless man terrorizing a neighborhood with a machete.

Police were called by a homeowner in south Seattle reporting a man, armed with a machete, tried to break into his home. When police arrived on scene, they spotted the suspect with the machete and a second knife, wearing nothing but a bath towel, and running around the neighborhood.[297] The suspect is seen on body camera footage briefly running toward a sergeant on the scene while raising the machete. As the officer yells, "Sarge, he's got a f—ing machete," the suspect flees and ignores demands to stop. The suspect was getting closer to oncoming traffic, posing a clear threat. Officers could have used nonlethal munitions to stop the man, as one officer explained to me, but they were prohibited. Due to the nature of the threat, officers unleashed Jedi to subdue the man before he reached any civilians. The suspect hacked at Jedi multiple times, before attacking Jedi's handler. A second officer ended the melee by shooting and killing the man. Jedi died not long after.

"I say this with 100 percent certainty, having years of experience in patrol and SWAT and having worked beside K-9 more times than I can count. Had responding officers had 40 mm launchers to deploy on that suspect, Jedi would almost certainly be alive today.

The suspect might also be alive today, receiving treatment," an officer told me on the condition of anonymity.[298]

Representative Roger Goodman (D-Kirkland) admitted they had erred in their bill, telling a local radio station that "Nobody caught it, nobody pointed it out." Democrats amended the legislation during the next session.

In California, woke Democrat leaders advanced a bill to ban K9 units because dogs are apparently racist. Assembly Bill (AB) 742, introduced by Democrat Assemblymen Corey Jackson and Ash Kalra, banned the use of police dogs for arrests, apprehensions, and crowd control. Jackson claimed using K9s is a "deeply racialized traumatic and harmful practice."

"The use of police canines has been a mainstay in this country's dehumanizing, cruel, and violent abuse of Black Americans and people of color for centuries," AB 742 contends.[299] "First used by slave catchers, police canines are a violent carry-over from America's dark past. In recent decades, they have been used in brutal attempts to quell the Civil Rights Movement, the LA Race Riots, and in response to Black Lives Matter protests."

In the context of AB 742, lawmakers want to end a nonlethal tool that can help keep human officers safe. For example, if a suspect is in a tight spot that could put a cop at risk of death or injury, a K9 may be deployed. Or, as was the case in Seattle, a K9 unit is used to help subdue an armed suspect. These dogs sometimes give their lives so that a human can survive. ACAB apparently extends to dogs, too.

All White Cops (and Some Black Cops) Are Racist

In 2020, America saw a nationwide sprint toward implicit bias (or anti-bias) training, which often relies on the presumption that one is racist to begin with. It's not a new concept, and police departments engaged in this prior to Floyd, but his death gave the training momentum. Democrat lawmakers pretended all cops suffer from unconscious bias where, even though they may not know it, they hold ill will toward blacks and Latinos. If you push back, it only confirms your racism.

New Jersey Democrat governor Phil Murphy signed a law mandating implicit bias training for law enforcement in the aftermath of Floyd.[300] In Michigan, the entire basis for the successful (and bipartisan) push to mandate implicit bias training was that white officers take an antagonistic view toward people who don't look like them.

"If we can change what goes through an officer's mind when they encounter one of our community members who doesn't look like them, we can change the outcome," Senator Stephanie Chang (D-Detroit) said, implying that all interactions between white officers and black civilians is somehow problematic.[301]

The City of Seattle, through its Race and Social Justice Initiative (RSJI), mandates city staff, including police, to undergo anti-racism training. The training itself is, however, deeply racist.

One three-hour session was held in September 2021 for employees "who identify as people of color" and was titled "Internalized Racial Inferiority." The event training page said attendees would explore "the process which American conditioning, socialization and history leads People of Color to internalize racialized beliefs, ideas and behaviors about themselves, undergirding the power of White Supremacy."[302]

The goal of the course, according to internal documents I obtained, was to learn ways for blacks and Latinos to free *themselves* of white supremacy influence. The training explained how "whiteness" interfered with racial minorities, explaining that all white people are responsible for white supremacy and that they should abandon "guaranteed physical safety" to be "accomplices" in creating a society where they can "eliminate racism and create racial equity, justice and liberation."

Black cops told me they were outraged by the training, since it told them they suffer from internal racial inferiority and that they likely engage in "self-defeating behaviors," which include assimilating into white culture and engaging in colorism, defined as the discrimination against people with darker skin than theirs.

How exactly does this training lead to safer policing? It doesn't. The training isn't meant to change policing, but to indoctrinate followers into far-left views on race whereby officers choose not to enforce the law against black or Latino residents. That point was made in a NYPD study.

NYPD officers underwent implicit bias training in 2018 and agreed to allow Albany, New York-based John F. Finn Institute for Public Safety to research its impact. Researchers looked at the so-called ethnic disparities among criminal suspects arrested and found no meaningful change after the training. While officers became more aware of the concept of implicit bias, which you'd expect after this kind of training, the group's director Robert Worden said the training did not alter "officers' enforcement behaviors."[303]

We should not understate these findings: Even after the implicit bias training, NYPD officers still stopped, frisked, and/or arrested nearly the same number of black and Latino residents suspected of crimes. But was the intent to alter "officers' enforcement behavior" purely on the race of the suspect? Meaning, was implicit bias training meant to get officers to *not* arrest a suspect they legitimately thought committed a crime because that person is black? While activists may find the data troubling, First Deputy Commissioner Benjamin B. Tucker did not, noting to NPR that the training "was designed just to have them do some self-reflection and just to understand that any biases that they may have may creep into their job."[304] Perhaps the results show that officers already have the requisite skills to understand any potential biases, and the interactions didn't change because there wasn't a problem to begin with.

A Culture of Lawlessness

Democrats sought to cut down on as many interactions between police and the public as possible. They believe any police interaction, particularly with black people, is dangerous. It suggests they understand very little that goes into police training, yet their anti-police bias led to truly disastrous policies that emboldened criminals and created a culture of lawlessness.

A slew of cities moved to prevent officers from making low-level traffic stops. The Philadelphia City Council passed the Achieving Driving Equality Law under the guise that cops purposefully target black drivers.[305] Officers could no longer pull over drivers of unregistered vehicles (up to 60 days) or those with a missing taillight. A similar policy is in effect in Los Angeles, Seattle, and Lansing, Michigan.

The *New York Times* hoped to amplify the concerns over these stops, which often serve as a legal pretext to search for guns or drugs. In an October 2021 feature story, the paper warned that supposedly innocent drivers were losing their lives during routine traffic stops. "Officers, trained to presume danger, have reacted with outsize aggression. For hundreds of unarmed drivers, the consequences have been fatal," they write.[306]

The story's framing implied that these were not justified homicides. But even some of the article's examples show the officers met aggression with aggression. For example, the authors highlight the case of Marvin Urbina of Bakersfield, California. The *New York Times* says he "wrestled with inflated airbags after a pursuit ended in a crash." The reporters note he wasn't armed, but he was still shot to death by police. That's the only context offered in the piece, and it's disingenuous at best.

Urbina was reportedly driving erratically on Interstate 5 highway at high speeds in the emergency lane, weaving in and out of traffic. When California Highway Patrol tried to pull Urbina over, he ignored commands and sped away, taking them on a high-speed pursuit. Soon after, he lost control of the vehicle and rolled over. He was apparently fine, and officers shouted at him to get out of the car. Initially, he wouldn't comply, but after several minutes he agreed. But upon exiting the vehicle and approaching the cops, he reached into his waistband, prompting an officer to shoot and kill Urbina. Upon a search, officers found a fixed-blade knife in the front passenger seat.[307] Here's a great way to avoid getting shot by cops, a lesson learned when I first started covering police in my early 20s: Don't reach into your waistband for a weapon when police are asking you to comply with their demands.

Post-Floyd, there was suddenly a concerted effort to excuse risky and illegal behavior of suspects, and then blame police officers for reacting the way they're supposed to, as if the cops are to blame for chasing a driver who was speeding to begin with.

Though officers are trained to deal with fleeing suspects, Democrats began pretending otherwise, to further stymie legitimate police work. Washington State Democrats used their legislative supermajority to full effect, impetuously passing a suite of reckless reforms like a ban on vehicular pursuits in almost all cases.

Some cities offered restrictions, but with caveats. The Cincinnati, Ohio, police department restricted pursuits to violent felony suspects because of the risk chases pose to the public.[308] Chicago police could not pursue for theft or traffic charges (other than driving drunk or high), but can chase if they determine, per the Chicago PD handbook, "The necessity to immediately apprehend the fleeing suspect outweighs the level of inherent danger created by a motor vehicle pursuit."[309]

But in Washington State, individual departments were not allowed to implement policies that are best for their communities. Under the law, vehicular pursuits could only be undertaken if there's reasonable suspicion of the driver being drunk or high or there's probable cause to establish a violent crime occurred or sex offense *and* (1) the pursuit is necessary to identify or apprehend the suspect; (2) there's greater risk to the public if you don't pursue; *and* (3) the officer has permission to pursue from a supervising officer. Probable cause is a much higher bar than reasonable suspicion, almost requiring an officer to literally witness the violent felony.

Under that new law, not only did violent offenders have an easy time fleeing a crime scene, nonviolent criminals had carte blanche to quickly commit crimes without fear of pursuit. Washington State saw an astronomical rise in car and catalytic converter theft, smash and grabs, and pot shop robberies. Criminals knew if they could commit a crime before cops arrive, so long as they get in a vehicle (usually stolen), they would be allowed to drive off. They wouldn't even have to speed. Under the law, police were restricted from pursuits, so the criminal could drive away at a leisurely pace.

Between January and November 2022, the Puget Sound Auto Theft Task Force reported a total of 41,330 cars stolen statewide.[310] And despite the crisis, the Washington State Patrol announced in late December 2022 that it was leaving the task force because of the rise of other road-related violent crimes, such as road rage shootings and DUIs.[311] Meanwhile, catalytic converter theft in 2022 rose 10,000 percent from where it was in 2019.[312] These jobs can be done in under 60 seconds, making it very easy to escape before cops are even called.

But most troubling—and dangerous—was the precipitous rise in smash-and-grab robberies, targeting pot shops and drugstores. Armed thieves would quickly ransack pot shops, steal product and cash, and then quickly drive off in a stolen car. In just the first month of 2022, there were over 30 reported robberies.[313] Concurrently, the region saw a rise in ATM theft at retail shops where criminals would drive a car or other vehicles into a storefront, quickly attach a cable or rope to an ATM machine, drive it out of the store, load it into their vehicle, and drive off.

The absurdity of the anti-pursuit law was epitomized by an alleged hostage taker who called 911 to report officers violating the vehicular pursuit ban. Isaac Sissel is a homeless man who was living out of his car when police say they got reports he was holding a girlfriend and her cat hostage. Police believed he was armed. When they located Sissel and the victim, police say he fled, and they pursued. Sissel then called 911 to report the chase.[314]

"SPD is illegally chasing me over I don't know what," Sissel says on the 911 call I obtained.

"Sir, are you able to pull over and talk to officers?" an operator replied.

"No. It is an illegal pursuit and my license is suspended, and this is an illegal pursuit.... They're not supposed to be able to pursue," Sissel says.

The situation reached parody levels when a draft policy memo was leaked to me in October 2022 instructing officers to allow DUI suspects to flee, even if they're in stolen cars. If a drunk or high motorist refuses to comply or is passed out in a running vehicle with a needle still in his arm, officers must leave the scene. Though it was just a draft, multiple officers told me that they were told to follow the policy. After my report, the SPD rescinded the policy.[315] And in the 2022–2023 legislative session, Democrats made small changes to the vehicular pursuit bill, allowing for chases against suspects of violent crimes where reasonable suspicion exists. But Democrats refused to address the more prominent concern with the bill, allowing nonviolent offenders to continue to steal cars and engage in smash and grabs.

The city of Atlanta, Georgia, adopted the same harsh policy as Washington State, with predictable outcomes, though it had an interesting distinction: It was implemented before Floyd, and rescinded after his death. The "no chase" policy was quite direct; cops could not chase any suspect for any reason. Atlanta Police Chief Erika Shields cited in a memo, in part, the safety risks of chases, though acknowledged that "this decision may drive crime up."[316] She was rather prescient.

Less than a year later, amid rising crime and under a new

chief, the policy was altered to allow for chases under limited circumstances. Police could pursue when an officer has "direct knowledge" that the suspect has committed or attempted to commit a violent crime like murder, carjacking, kidnapping, or armed robbery, and gets express permission by a supervising officer.[317]

It wasn't just vehicular pursuits that got the BLM reform treatment. In Chicago, then-mayor Lori Lightfoot severely restricted foot chases. The policy was the result of irrational criticism of cops shooting and killing 13-year-old Adam Toledo.

In late March 2021, two officers responded to reports of gunfire in Chicago's West Side. When they arrived on scene, they saw two people in the alley and began to chase them in separate directions. After a short foot chase, Toledo dropped a handgun and raised his hands to surrender, but Officer Eric Stillman fired, thinking the teen was raising his hand to shoot. It was a split-second decision that, in the end, was a mistake, one that you could only tell by freeze framing the body cam footage and reviewing in retrospect. Though the officer attempted life-saving measures, Toledo died at the scene.[318]

The shooting, while tragic, was unintentional and predicated on the actions of the victim. Even Cook County DA Kim Foxx, no friend to police, said Stillman acted within reason, arguing he only shot one time and that he "reacted to the perceived threat presented by Adam Toledo who he believed at the time was turning toward him to shoot him." No charges were filed against the officer.[319]

There was a similar incident two days after the Toledo shooting involving 22-year-old Anthony Alvarez near the Portage Park neighborhood. Police tried to stop him for driving with a suspended license, which stemmed from an incident the night before. But when officers turned on their lights, Alvarez fled on foot. During the chase, Alvarez pulled a loaded 9 mm handgun and Officer Evan Solano thought he was the target. He shot Alvarez shortly after, prompting Alvarez to ask, "Why are you shooting me?" The officer replied, "You had a gun!"[320] Alvarez later died.

Foxx cleared Solano in the shooting, but also criticized the police. The message wasn't that you shouldn't run from cops or illegally possess a weapon. The message was that cops shouldn't chase criminal suspects. She said that "while the evidence is insufficient to support criminal charges, it is important to highlight that the officers themselves created the conditions which the use of deadly force became necessary."

As was a theme post-Floyd, Foxx engaged in a breathtaking display of gaslighting. The officers did not create the conditions for deadly force; Toledo and Alvarez, who chose to be armed and flee, put the officers in a position where deadly force was necessary. If someone pulls a weapon on an officer, their default position should be an assumption that they will be shot and killed in response. If they're lucky, there will simply be an arrest. But the expectation should be that the officer will protect themselves, their partners, and anyone in the neighborhood. Yet post-Floyd, cops were presumed to be in the wrong.

Those shootings led to more protests and rallies, which ultimately led to even more capitulation to the Radical Left. Thousands took to the streets, claiming to be fed up with police violence and demanding the department be defunded (if only they were this passionate after the 99.99 percent of violence perpetrated by civilians, perhaps 2021 wouldn't have been Chicago's deadliest year in a quarter century).[321] Toledo was portrayed as wholly innocent, as if he did not flee or have a gun.

"I'm just in shock at how many of us made mistakes and we're still here," one protester told the *New York Times*.[322] "He did all the right things. He put his hands up, and he still got shot."

After nearly a year of demonizing, citizens lost their ability to understand the positions police were in. Asked to make split-second decisions when their lives are on the line, officers are often put in impossible positions, especially when a suspect is a child. But in the year since Floyd's death, the new consensus among the Radical

Left community is that a cop should either be willing to face death without using force or simply allow a criminal to go free.

Over a year later, Mayor Lightfoot announced a new foot pursuit policy[323] aimed at preventing future cases like Toledo and Alvarez. Officers were instructed that they could only pursue when "they have reasonable articulable suspicion or probable cause" that the suspect they're chasing "has committed, is committing, or is about to commit" a felony, Class A misdemeanor, or dangerous traffic offense. During the pursuit, the policy mandates an officer to re-evaluate whether or not the pursuit is necessary, as if an officer doesn't have enough to worry about while in the middle of chasing down a dangerous suspect.

Thanks to the constantly shifting policies and legislation around policing, the profession became even more dangerous. Not only were Democrat lawmakers emboldening criminals with new protections, shielding them from law enforcement, but officers were stuck second-guessing every action to ensure that they don't become the next target of a Democrat lawmaker or the Radical Left mob. It became a deadly and untenable combination.

The War on Cops

When Officer Ella French joined the Chicago PD, she "wanted to do good for the world," her brother said.[324] But her life was tragically cut short at just 29 years old, a victim of a city where lawlessness was accepted.

French and her partner Carlos Yanez were shot during a traffic stop on the South Side of Chicago in August 2021. The officers pulled over two brothers, convicted felons Eric and Emonte Morgan, for having expired license plates. Prosecutors say French asked Eric, who was driving, to turn over his keys and get out of the car. He complied, along with Emonte and a third female passenger. But that's where the cooperation ended.

Emonte refused to put down a drink and cell phone that he was holding at the time, "physically jerking his arms away from the officers," according[325] to Assistant State's Attorney James Murphy. Eric then fled on foot and was chased by one officer at the scene. Emonte stayed behind and struggled with Yanez before pulling a semi-automatic handgun from his waistband and firing multiple shots at Yanez and French. Yanez was lucky to be alive, after being struck in the eye, cheek, brain, and back.[326] French died at the scene.

The department was reeling. Not only had they lost one of their own, but officers had come under fire, literally and figuratively, for the last year thanks to the Radical Left. They were smeared by BLM radicals and politicians jockeying for their political support, while soft-on-crime policies led to a surge in gun violence they were forced to navigate. Chicago police superintendent David Brown noted at the time that 2020 and 2021 were record-setting years for officers being shot or shot at, with 80 cases of police being targeted in 2020 and 76 cases in 2021. Compare that to an annual average of 20 between 2014 and 2019.[327] As they were dodging bullets in protection of the city, they faced endless smears from the BLM movement.

"They feel alone. They feel unsupported. They feel like no one appreciates the work they do. They're human, so they have a lot of expressions of discouragement, and I would just ask the people of Chicago to support their police officers with kind words of support," Superintendent Brown said at a press conference.[328]

Officers pointed fingers at Mayor Lightfoot who spent the previous year supporting BLM extremism. At the height of the movement, she begged her fellow progressive mayors to "seize this moment and move forward aggressively and not be timid."[329] Publicly, she said she wouldn't go so far as to defund the police, but *Forbes* reported the mayor "quietly cut" 400 police officers' positions in 2020.[330]

When the mayor visited Yanez in the hospital, she received

the welcome you'd expect of a politician who only supports cops when it might earn her political points. Officers at the hospital collectively turned their backs when she walked in; others walked away from her when she tried to speak to them. The father of the wounded officer, himself a veteran cop, laid into her, blaming her for what had happened to his son.[331]

In city after Democrat-run city, cops were under unfair and aggressive scrutiny, with lawmakers either piling on or ignoring the constant smears.

During the Portland riots, Antifa radicals were getting a pass for their violence. They were attacking cops, destroying storefronts, and terrorizing neighborhoods, but under Democrat Multnomah County DA Mike Schmidt, they escaped prosecution because he agreed with the cause.[332]

"As prosecutors, we acknowledge the depth of emotion that motivates these demonstrations and support those who are civically engaged through peaceful protesting," Schmidt said in a statement. "We will undermine public safety, not promote it, if we do not take action to bring about immediate change."

Portland officers in the Rapid Response Team (RRT) were disgusted to find out that one of their own was indicted for alleged unlawful force on a rioter. The 50 or so members of the RRT were volunteers with specialized training, tasked during the BLM riots to help with crowd control, maintain the peace, and help protect innocent civilians.

During one of the many nights of "direct action" by Antifa and other scofflaws, Officer Corey Budworth was attempting an arrest when alleged rioters interfered.[333] The night was chaotic, with fires set, buildings vandalized, and officers taking rocks, chunks of concrete, glass, and professional grade fireworks.[334] The Portland Police Association said Budworth pushed the interfering rioter, Erin Wenzel, down with his baton. When the officer thought Wenzel was ready to "re-engage," he again used his baton to push her down, accidentally striking her in the head.

Wenzel's advocates presented her as an innocent protester seeking racial justice. But Budworth's attorney pointed out she was wearing a helmet, dressed in a black hoodie, a black shirt, black jeans, black gloves, a black backpack, and had on a gas mask and respirator.[335] In other words, she appeared to be in black-bloc, the uniform of Antifa radicals. On June 16, 2021, after the charges were announced, which Schmidt defended as "rooted in fairness and equity,"[336] the entire RRT quit en masse.

Cop hating became a sport in the aftermath of Floyd. Activists fell over themselves trying to one-up each other with disgusting rhetoric. But one email I obtained from a Seattle city employee might earn the designation of most self-righteously unhinged.

Daniel Holmberg is a senior management systems analyst with the Seattle Department of Finance and Administrative Services (FAS). As a city staffer, he volunteered to join the department's Change Team, a group organized to help the department reach its equity and anti-racist goals. In that capacity, Holmberg wrote an all-staff email that viciously characterized Seattle cops as white supremacists.[337]

"When the arbiters of justice serve the false gods of white supremacy, they are not worthy of the power they wield," Holmberg wrote. "If police protection and restraint extend only to white people, they are no longer guardians; they are mercenaries and zealots, paid in the wages of white privilege, inflicting their wicked commandments upon us."

The email sent cops into a rage; this was a colleague at a city department responsible for the upkeep of its fleet. Beyond that, officers knew if they wrote an email even a fraction as vicious about their colleagues, they'd be investigated for ethical breaches. I had no less than two dozen cops forward me this email to expose. Rather than apologize for the vitriol, an FAS spokesperson defended it.

"If we have learned anything from the past year—when COVID-19 disproportionately ravaged communities of color and the murder of George Floyd, Breonna Taylor, Ahmaud Arbery, and so many others laid bare how entrenched systemic racism is in our country—it is that we cannot afford to stay comfortable," Melissa Mixon told me.[338] "Staying comfortable is costing lives, specifically Black lives, and we stand behind our Change Team for keeping us accountable and challenging all of us to learn, to re-examine, to grow and, above all, to act in this urgent work."

They weren't re-examining, growing, or even acting. They were insulting, and doing it in a way in which they hoped to earn some kind of plaudits for bravely speaking truth to power. But it was just some angry white guy hoping to make his first black friend, thinking that attacking cops was the way to do it.

Cops for Me, None for Thee

Crime was rising, and Democrat cities were not protected. Police departments were depleted, and the remaining cops were hamstrung by Radical Left policies. But as the residents were increasingly targeted by emboldened criminals, the very Radical Left politicians who inspired the culture of lawlessness were themselves getting special protection, many times at taxpayer expense.

Baltimore, Maryland, mayor Brandon Scott was an ardent supporter of the defund movement and BLM, making excuses for the nationwide violence endemic to the movement. After all, he argued, "People are only going to ask politely for so long, right?"[339] Like other Democrat-run cities, Baltimore City Council cut the police budget by $22 million, despite homicides in 2019 hitting a 25-year high of 348.[340] At the time, Scott was the city council president. He celebrated the cuts, but said it was "just a first step . . . to reduce our dependence on policing." But Scott did not reduce his own dependency on policing. As Scott pushed to defund, he was benefiting from a personal police security detail costing the taxpayers nearly $2 million.[341]

While San Francisco mayor London Breed reinvested[342] $120 million of the San Francisco Police budget into the black community, she too benefited from pricey and private police protection. Between 2015 and 2020, taxpayers split the bill for $12.4 million in protection.[343] Seattle's Jenny Durkan and New York's Bill de Blasio also benefited from police protection during their mayorships, despite defunding the police.

It's not that mayors aren't deserving of police protection. Their jobs obviously pose inherent risks to their personal safety, and no public official should be left to their own devices when facing very real and serious threats. It's that they deprived from the community the very thing they wouldn't give up themselves—police protection.

There were other Democrats who not only pushed to defund the police while benefiting from personal protection, they also bragged about it. Squad member and race baiter, Representative Cori Bush (D-St. Louis) is an outspoken critic of police. She views them as racist murderers that cannot be reformed from within.

"We're going to defund the police and refund our social services. Don't like this idea? Well, we don't like dead Black & Brown bodies & broken families at the hands of those sworn to protect us. The police have failed at fixing themselves—so we're going to do it," she tweeted.[344]

Bush didn't benefit from police protection; she loathes cops too much to be around. Instead, she spent hundreds of thousands of campaign dollars on private security to protect her from the crime surge she helped create when she defunded the police. This is her privilege. She even found a husband out of it, marrying one of her security guards. And while she allegedly paid her new husband $60,000 for security services, he didn't hold a St. Louis private security license.[345]

"I'm going to make sure I have security because I know I have had attempts on my life and I have too much work to do, there are too many people that need help right now for me to allow that," she told CBS News.[346] "If I end up spending $200,000, if I spend $10 more dollars on it—you know what, I get to be here to do the work. So, suck it up. And defunding the police has to happen. We need to defund the police and put that money into social safety nets because we're trying to save lives."

Her constituents in St. Louis needed the same level of protection. The city had the highest homicide rate of any other American city, at 87 per 100,000 people, hitting a 50-year high in 2020.[347]

Similarly, Representative Jamaal Bowman (D-NY) maligned cops, saying the "cruel and inhumane" criminal justice system is incapable of reform. He demanded we "Defund the police, and defund the system that's terrorizing our communities."[348] And yet when he felt terrorized after the January 6, 2021, riot at the US Capitol, having "received threats," he asked for and received a police detail outside his Yonkers home.[349]

Talk to any cop in Seattle and you'll likely hear complaints over council member Kshama Sawant's conduct. A vile, angry politician, Sawant has made a national name for herself for embracing and forwarding a socialist agenda. When it came to policing, she'd been responsible for some of the most outrageous rhetoric leveled against cops. During the BLM riots, Sawant forwarded a baseless conspiracy theory that officers were told to "orchestrate violence" against activists in the crowd.[350]

"They seem to be coming prepared with instructions to orchestrate violence, including repeated practices and patterns of repression and violence, with officers wearing riot gear and carrying tear gas spray canisters," Sawant claimed of cops breaking up downtown riots.

Though she apparently believes cops attack their political adversaries, Sawant took a risk to personal safety to ask for special treatment when she needed their help tracking down a phantom poop thrower. On at least six occasions, Sawant's residence was targeted by a man hurling bags of what she claimed was human feces. (I never found out how she knew it was human feces, a failure that haunts me to this day.) Not only did she demand that the police department she defunded offer special resources to investigate—including a forensics investigation of the poop—but she also wanted personal police protection outside her home in the evenings.[351] She received neither in this case because the department didn't have officers to spare.

Refunding the Defunding

The defund movement was an abject failure. Democrat cities that cut funding saw increases in crime, and no amount of spin or deflection changed the reality of life in these cities. Mothers and children were being mowed down, subway riders were being sexually assaulted, businesses were being ransacked. These cities did not have enough officers to keep people safe. Then, mid-2021 and into early 2022, there was a change of a heart, along with midterm election polls indicating Democrats were appropriately taking the heat for the rise in crime.

Chicago mayor Lightfoot recognized the police defunding stunt was a mistake. By the end of 2021, she pleaded with the federal government for law enforcement assistance, despite rejecting help offered previously by President Donald Trump.

"Together the city of Chicago and the state of Illinois have 25,000 police officers, sheriffs, and guardsmen available to quell any violence, they can do it very quickly, very easily, if allowed to do their jobs," Trump said at a news conference amid August 2020 looting.[352] "Again, if allowed to do their jobs. Our police, our law enforcement is incredible, but they have to be allowed to do their jobs."

This wasn't the first offer of assistance from Trump. But given Lightfoot's previous posture, he likely didn't expect her to say yes. In rejecting his offer, Lightfoot suggested Trump back "commonsense gun safety reforms" that had nothing to do with the predicament in which Chicago found itself.

But she knew the reality. Lightfoot, in 2021, said it was "no question" that Chicago PD would see a budget bump.[353] Her comments came after the high-profile snub by police turning their backs on the mayor when she visited a hospital caring for an officer wounded on the job.

In December 2021, San Francisco mayor Breed was suddenly sick and tired of the crime, declaring that "It's time that the reign of criminals who are destroying our city—it is time for it to come to an end."[354] With homicides and larcenies surging, and a police department experiencing an unprecedented 45 percent increase in retirements and 18 percent in resignations,[355] Breed called out "all the bulls—t that has destroyed our city." She was, of course, a big part of the bulls—t.

The trend continued, with a tsunami of refunds hitting Democrat-led city police departments nationwide. New York City returned $200 million to the budget, plus $166 million for overtime during budget "reallocation." The city of Baltimore proposed a $27 million increase, Portland started with a $5.2 million refund[356] with the promise of more to come, and the Los Angeles Police Department saw an $87 million boost.[357] Austin increased the police department's budget by 47.8 percent to $442 million, the highest it had ever been, funding two new recruit cadet classes.[358]

Some of the reversals came from Democrat lawmakers seeing the error of their ways. But ultimately, the walk-backs can be directly attributable to a public that declared enough was enough. Seattle voted in a mayoral candidate, Bruce Harrell, a Republican City Attorney in Ann Davison, and moderate council candidate Democrat Sara Nelson, after they campaigned on a platform of supporting police and tackling crime. Portland's aggressively anti-cop commissioner Jo Ann Hardesty was booted from office in the November 2022 elections. Lightfoot didn't even survive her 2023 primary.

Voters in Minneapolis spoke the loudest, sending the most meaningful message that the Radical Left push to defund should be banished into the history bin of bad ideas.

Voters were given the opportunity to defund the police department and go in a completely different direction. While Democrat lawmakers had previously called the shots during the BLM movement, passing policies and budgets without even asking if the public agreed, a measure was put in front of voters to reimagine policing. If passed, the Minneapolis Police Department would be dismantled and replaced with the Department of Public Safety, which promised a "public-health oriented" approach to crime. There was no guarantee that police officers would even exist in this new department, as it would remove a city charter requirement to hire a minimum number of officers. Social workers would respond to 911 calls.

Proponents and left-wing media outlets friendly to the cause downplayed the tectonic shifts that would result if this measure were to pass. CNN dismissed it as a "boring" technical shift in organizational management.[359]

The vote left some of us anxious, which I admitted at the time on an episode of *The Faulkner Focus* on Fox News. If voters approved dismantling the police department in the city that birthed the movement as we knew it, it's hard to see how that momentum could be stalled before the same idea infected Los Angeles, Seattle, Austin, and New York.

To my relief, the voters soundly rejected the measure 56 percent to 44 percent. It was followed by the mayor championing a budget that returned much of what was cut in 2021.[360] Left-wing media seemed shocked at this outcome. Had they sent reporters to actually talk to residents who loathed the Radical Left's takeover of policing, it wouldn't have been all that shocking.

Dejected supporters on the council didn't hide their disappointment, with outgoing council member Lisa Bender complaining of the "heartbreaking political message that nothing has changed in Minneapolis since the murder of George Floyd."[361] Except a lot did change after Floyd. Police departments were defunded and "reimagined," and light-on-crime policies catapulted Minneapolis and other Democrat-run cities into the history books for the rise in crime. But the *movement*, as we once knew it, was finally over.

There is, however, an unfortunate reality. Much of the damage cannot be easily or quickly repaired, no matter how much funding is put back into the budgets. A culture of lawlessness doesn't reverse itself overnight. It can take decades to fix. Even after budgets were increased and commitments were made to support departments, crime didn't suddenly decrease, especially since Radical Left policies were still in place.

And not every American was ready to ditch the extreme, anti-police politics. Former teacher and defund activist Brandon Johnson humiliated Lightfoot to win the February 2023 Chicago mayor's race. Buoyed by teacher union support, Chicagoans elected someone further to the left of Lightfoot. Weeks later, hundreds of youth went on a violent "teen takeover" downtown. It's unclear why the teens engaged in their rioting, which included arson, vandalism, and shots fired. But Johnson warned the public not to "demonize" the hooligans, claiming they've been "starved of opportunities in their own communities."[362] He wouldn't even flatly condemn looting.[363]

But there have been some bright spots. After pumping $2.4 million into Portland's deadliest street, there was a notable decrease in drug crimes and prostitution.[364] After placing more officers in Seattle's downtown core, blocks previously riddled with open-air drug trafficking and frequent shootings saw a positive change. After significantly ratcheting up police presence in the subway system in November 2022, New York City saw five consecutive weeks of reduced crime, a modest but important improvement.[365] It turns out criminals are less likely to break the law when they know police are around. Who knew?

CHAPTER 5

THAT SANCTUARY LIFE

"There's Blood Everywhere"

Brenda and Terry Aultman purchased their dream home in Daytona Beach, Florida, in late 2021. The property, not far from the beach, brought them tremendous joy as they often walked the shoreline each day.[366] According to a neighbor, the couple was living their best lives together. But just six months after moving in, they were victims of a brutal double murder.

"We found two people...possibly dead. There's blood everywhere," a man told a 911 operator. How did he know they were dead and not just seriously wounded?

"I mean they are not moving. I don't really want to get too close to the situation," the man replied. "It's a man and a female. Neither one of them are moving. There's a puddle of blood."

On March 7, 2022, the Aultmans were enjoying an evening at the Bike Week event near their home. Judging by a Facebook post showing Brenda sitting on her husband Terry's lap, the couple was having a blast.[367] The post declared, "Music is wonderful at Main Street. It's the best!!" However, their joyful evening took a tragic turn on the bike ride home, when they were randomly attacked by a man who stabbed them repeatedly, slitting both their throats, before dragging their lifeless, blood-soaked bodies from the sidewalk to a nearby grassy area.

Daytona Beach Police Department Chief Jakari Young described the murders as "probably one of the most vicious and gruesome incidents that I've witnessed in my 20 years" in law enforcement. Police were vexed by what happened. They first believed it was a hit-and-run, but the discovery of the stab wounds led them to realize the true nature of the deaths. The police initially thought it was a failed robbery, until they discovered the couple's valuables were left untouched. But with no known witnesses to the crime, police could not establish a motive.[368]

"We can't make heads or tails of it at this time," Chief Young said.

Detectives reviewed surveillance footage from a nearby neighbor and identified a suspect[369] based on a credit card purchase he made for a meal while in the area.[370] They named the suspect as 32-year-old Jean Macean of Orlando. After his arrest, police say he confessed to the murders, and he now faces the death penalty.

This murder of Brenda and Terry Aultman was a cruel and senseless act. Tragically, random acts of violence can occur. But this was completely preventable.

Macean is an illegal immigrant. According to Florida governor Ron DeSantis's office, Macean was in this country under the Temporary Protected Status designation for Haiti, a policy reversal under Democrat rule, which allows foreign-born individuals to stay in the United States if they're not able to return home due to unsafe or untenable circumstances back home. Without this policy, Macean would not have been in this country and would not have allegedly murdered an innocent couple.

Enabled by the Radical Left, President Joe Biden treated immigration laws like an obstacle to the political agenda of expanding their voter base. During the previous administration, Democrats saw an opportunity to permanently secure their support among Latino voters. They perceived former president Donald Trump as having vilified all Mexicans as drug dealers and rapists, all while trying to build a border wall. This presented the Democrats with a chance to demonstrate their stark differences with the former president and, ultimately, earn the loyalty of Latino voters. This approach wasn't novel, but it gained momentum and led to highly problematic and dangerous policies.

We Welcome You with Open Arms (until You Come)

During the Trump presidency, you couldn't swing a dead cat without hitting a Democrat proudly declaring their city, county, or state as a sanctuary for illegal immigrants, a safe haven for immigrants seeking a better life—an escape from poverty or conflict in their home countries. Some jurisdictions established laws or policies for the first time during the Trump administration, while others strengthened pre-existing ones. But they virtually all had the same effect: An influx of illegal immigrants took these sanctuaries up on their offers for shelter and freedom, putting a strain on local resources. Accepting so many unvetted illegal immigrants led to an increase in preventable crime and negatively impacted the quality of life for residents.

The City of Denver codified its sanctuary status on August 28, 2018, after community activists demanded protections against Trump's immigration policies. The Public Safety Enforcement Priorities Act prevented city employees from sharing information about a resident's immigration status, prohibited the sharing of information for the purposes of immigration matters, and forbade law enforcement to detain an illegal immigrant for the sole purposes of turning them over to federal immigration officials.

"Last year we watched as our new president called us rapists, drug dealers, and criminals. Our children cried in fear as our new president threatened to separate their families and build a wall of deportation," Councilman Paul López, one of the sponsors of the bill, explained while holding back tears in a nearly 15-minute self-aggrandizing speech ahead of the bill's passage.[371]

Lopez and the others extolled what they treated as the most historic civil rights bill in the city's history. It was a nauseatingly rehearsed performance of left-wing theatrics, filled with calculated pauses that feigned thoughtfulness. It was nothing more than performative politics.

"Look, there's never anything false about hope, right? Our movement needs these allies. We need allies to stand in this gap, and we usually refer to civil rights and human rights as something in history books. But it's not in history books. Ladies and gentlemen, it is today, in these chambers, in this city, at this moment that we were born to be here for. And we all have this responsibility to stand up to injustice, and if we all stand together... we cannot be moved."

Denver's welcoming attitude toward illegal immigrants ended with the Trump presidency. While proudly proclaiming to be a sanctuary for immigrants while Trump was in office, the mood changed with Biden's porous southern border. The city saw a dramatic increase in illegal immigrants in December 2022, and local leaders were unprepared.

A steady stream of illegal immigrants was bused to Denver, and the city coped. But then came a much larger group of Venezuelans between the ages of 20 and 40. City leaders didn't know who sent the group, but they were forced to scramble to provide emergency shelter. Despite initial statements from the Democrat mayor Michael Hancock that their number-one priority was the "health and safety of all our residents, including those who are migrants,"[372] their priorities quickly changed.

Less than a month after the surprise visit of Venezuelans, Democrat governor Jared Polis announced he was shipping the migrants elsewhere. In partnership with the city of Denver, Polis's office arranged for "culturally competent navigators" (whatever that is) to help ship the migrants "in the most humane possible way" to their final destination. Polis promised this would be done "in coordination with the receiving community."[373]

Polis strained to portray his plan as compassionate, but his actions were almost identical to those coming from Texas governor Greg Abbott and Florida governor Ron DeSantis, both Republican. Still, Polis got a pass from left-wing national media. Instead, Republican governors earned national headlines rebuking their so-called callous and uncompassionate stunts using vulnerable migrants as political pawns. Unwilling to continue to shoulder the burden of the costs and crimes associated with illegal border crossings, they bused and flew migrants to Democrat-run sanctuary cities, just like Polis. New York mayor Eric Adams called this "unfair."[374]

What's unfair for local governments is to bear the burden of an open border and lax immigration policy. It is supposed to be the responsibility of the federal government. But is it unfair for local governments to take on the obligation, when they touted their sanctuaries as beacons for immigrants? What was the point of designating itself a sanctuary city, county, or state, if they were unwilling to help bear the burden of migrants illegally crossing the border? The Radical Left didn't think through their plans because their sanctuary declarations were acts of virtue signaling. Their real plan was to burden Republican-led border states, while Democrats earned future voters in areas they haven't yet been able to win. Their strategy came back to haunt them, and their residents paid a price.

Mayor Adams spent the tail end of 2022 complaining about the influx of migrants straining the city's resources. At one point in August, the city's shelters housed 4,900 migrants seeking asylum.[375] At first, Adams turned the busloads of migrants shipped to his city into a publicity campaign to celebrate the city's compassion, personally greeting them and offering food. When the cameras were not recording, Adams' office volunteers were "screaming at the refugees to smile at the mayor," according to Ariadna Phillips, the founder of South Bronx Mutual Aid.[376]

New York became a sanctuary city well before Trump was in office. The proclamation was passed in 1989 under then-mayor Ed Koch. Under Mayor Bill de Blasio, the city went even further with a bill that limited most cooperation with federal officials by "end[ing] cooperation with federal 'detainer requests' for all residents, except those who have been convicted of violent or serious felonies."[377] Some migrants were receiving hotel rooms and free food. Others were housed in complexes with big screen televisions, Xbox consoles, and cushy sofas.[378] Immigrants would see this as more of an incentive to make the dangerous journey into the United States. And that's exactly what they did. The surge continued, as the Biden administration did next to nothing to stem the tide of migrants.

Don't Ask, Don't Tell

Radical Left lawmakers did little to encourage sound border policy or discourage illegal immigration. De Blasio was one of many Democrats pretending federal officials were rounding up migrants at random, demanding to see papers, and then deporting anyone who could not prove citizenship. The truth was that Immigration and Customs Enforcement (ICE) used detainer requests to ask local law enforcement to hold an illegal immigrant who had already been arrested on criminal charges, giving time for ICE to take them into custody. In those cases, ICE believed there was probable cause that the migrants were deportable. But illegal immigrants were often released without notice to ICE, thanks to Radical Left policies. While rejecting most attempts to deport, De Blasio spent the Trump era decrying the president as a bigot and New York as a panacea for immigrants searching for a home, celebrating the Biden administration ending a Trump-era policy to limit grant dollars to sanctuary cities. To the former mayor, any attempt to enforce immigration law was xenophobic.

"New York City is proud to be a welcoming and inclusive city for immigrants," de Blasio said in a statement at the time.[379] "We are thrilled by the news that the Department of Justice has recognized that anti-immigrant policies do not make our communities safer. Donald Trump's vindictive attempt to withhold grants from cities that stand up for our immigrant neighbors was inhumane and unacceptable, which is why we joined localities across the country to challenge these policies in court."

De Blasio's 2014 sanctuary law said it would support detainers only when the subject is accused of "violent or serious felonies." But there's a huge and very obvious problem with that small exception. Just look at the case of Reeaz Khan, a Guyanese national living in this country illegally. ICE lodged a detainer for Khan in 2019 after he was arrested on assault and weapons charges, which are serious misdemeanors, but not "violent or serious felonies." Local law enforcement ignored an ICE detainer and let Khan go free. Months later, he was arrested and charged for sexually assaulting and murdering a 92-year-old woman in Queens.[380] Maria Fuertes was left outside in 32-degree weather, half naked, while she suffered not just a rape, but a broken spine and rib fractures. She died at the hospital.

Unfortunately, these scenarios are too common. Radical Left sanctuary policies do not differentiate between immigrants whose only crime is being here illegally and immigrants who are actively breaking our laws and making our communities less safe.

Washington declared itself a sanctuary state in 2019 with the dubiously titled Keep Washington Working Act. While Democrats presented this bill as a way to save migrant farmers in Eastern Washington, it was a direct rebuke to the Trump administration's threat to deport criminal illegal immigrants. The bill, in part, bars jails from fulfilling ICE detainers without a warrant signed by a judge and prevents Washington officials from notifying ICE or the

Customs and Border Patrol when an illegal immigrant is released from jail. This was never about keeping Washington State working; it was about keeping illegals from deportation, offering them more protections than legal Washingtonians.

Francisco Carranza-Ramirez set his sights on a Seattle-area mother, approaching her for small talk as she was with her toddler at a park. Days later, the homeless man showed up at her apartment, forcibly entered, and raped her. The victim, wheelchair-bound due to a partial disability, was a vulnerable target. After she convinced Carranza-Ramirez to let her use the bathroom, the victim secretly called police on a cell phone that she then tucked into her wheelchair. The operator heard the rape continue. When cops arrived, they found Carranza-Ramirez sexually assaulting the victim.[381]

It took almost nine months for the case to conclude. Carranza-Ramirez was sentenced to 12 months in jail after entering an Alford plea, where a defendant maintains innocence while acknowledging that a jury would find a guilty verdict. But he was released the same day for time served by King County Judge Nicole Gaines Phelps. While prosecutors asked that Carranza-Ramirez be placed on community supervision, the defense attorney argued to the judge that he be allowed to return to Mexico. It turned out, the rapist was living in this country illegally.

"This is just a very interesting circumstance because the defendant himself is asking to leave the country. So, to the extent that he is making a request of the court to return to Mexico, that is the only reason why the court is even thinking of the issue of that, depending on his citizenship, which I'm not asking about because I'm legally prohibited from doing so," the judge said at a June hearing.[382]

In the end, the judge allowed Carranza-Ramirez to self-deport, ordering him to leave for Mexico within three days. The sanctuary law prohibited the court from informing ICE about the judgment, meaning they weren't able to ensure that he left the country or formally begin deportation plans. Had ICE been involved, the next tragedy would have been prevented.

Two days after his release from jail, Carranza-Ramirez returned to the victim's home. She called 911, but he fled before they could get there. The next day, as she was out with her kid, Carranza-Ramirez assaulted her. He pushed the victim from her wheelchair, before starting to strangle her. Luckily, witnesses intervened, but he was again able to flee.[383] Only after the assault did he flee to Mexico.[384]

"I thought he was going to kill me," the victim told a local television station.[385] "The way he had my throat, I couldn't breathe. I couldn't talk."

That wasn't even the most egregious case. The murder of 16-year-old Juan Carlos Con Guzman was as tragic as it was preventable. Prosecutors say Rudy Garcia-Hernandez and Carlos Iraheta-Vega were gang members from Federal Way, Washington, with Iraheta-Vega in this country illegally from El Salvador. They lured the teen victim through SnapChat to meet and settle an argument. But prosecutors say they "beat the victim with a baseball bat and mercilessly chopped his neck repeatedly with a machete."

This tragedy exemplifies the dangers of ignoring immigration laws and ICE detainers. Iraheta-Vega had been previously arrested in King County with an ICE detainer placed on him. But King County officials were forced to ignore it, allowing him to go free. Had Iraheta-Vega been turned over to ICE, this terrible crime would have been prevented.[386]

Radical Left lawmakers do not apologize to the victims of their families for these crimes. They usually ignore them, singularly focused on contrived stories of single moms who escaped their home countries who are just trying to make it in Washington State as a way to emotionally manipulate us into accepting their policies. We're often told these immigrants clean our hotel rooms, bus our tables, and pick our vegetables, and we should be grateful they're here. They do all those things, but some also murder our neighbors, stab our friends, and rape our family members. Those are the very illegal immigrants that ICE seeks to deport, not the single mom cleaning the mansion of a Limousine Liberal living in Beverly Hills.

At the time of the sanctuary state debate in Washington, Gael Tarleton was a Democrat state representative from Seattle. A stalwart supporter of the sanctuary law, Tarleton wouldn't abandon her position even after a series of crimes by illegal immigrants rocked the region. In June 2019, just after the Carranza-Ramirez case, I asked her on my radio show if an illegal immigrant should be deported after committing a felony or misdemeanor. After nearly 15 seconds of awkward silence, she said, "Jason...I don't know."[387]

I remember being stunned by that answer. This doesn't seem controversial. If you commit a serious felony, if you show a disinterest in following the laws of a country you're illegally crashing, it should be a no-brainer that you be deported.

Oregon Democrats engaged in the same quizzical behavior, though they passed a sanctuary law in 1987. That law prohibits state and local law enforcement from arresting people whose only crime is being in this country illegally. But, in practice, Oregon agencies went much further, refusing to share any citizenship status with federal authorities.[388] To Oregon Democrats, all illegal immigrants are members of marginalized communities; thus they're equally deserving of special treatment.

Martin Gallo-Gallardo, a Mexican citizen living illegally in Gresham, a suburb of Portland, was subject to an ICE detainer in March 2018 after he was arrested on accusations of assaulting his wife. But the Multnomah County jail ignored the detainer, and Gallo-Gallardo was released after posting bail. The charges against him were dropped after his partner and daughter refused to cooperate with the investigation. By November, Gallo-Gallardo was back in jail for fatally stabbing his partner 27 times. Police found her body left in a ditch. After pleading guilty, he was sentenced to life in prison, but is eligible for parole in 25 years.[389]

Why was Gallo-Gallardo worth protecting from ICE? Had Oregon officials been permitted to cooperate with ICE, a woman wouldn't have been brutally murdered and a child would still have a mother. Yet the Radical Left refuses to see the difference between a rapist and a hard-working farmer if both are in this country illegally.

Rather than address their sanctuary problems, Oregon Democrats doubled down on their support of illegal immigrants. In 2021, on a party-line vote, Democrats passed the Sanctuary Promise Act, which not only made it illegal for any public official to work with immigration enforcement but also created a private cause of action allowing them to be personally sued for their actions. The law was strengthened after concern that some officials could still cooperate with immigration enforcement under limited circumstances. In 2017, for example, Multnomah County deputies were investigated for tipping off ICE agents to the locations of three illegal immigrants up for deportation. One of them was Julio Montejo-Mex, a 21-year-old who had been charged with assault, strangulation, and kidnapping.[390]

"To me, it's really frightening to see this kind of situation," Kayse Jama with Unite Oregon told a local television station.[391] "It seems like you have vigilante, rogue officers who are taking the law into their own hands."

Imagine how radical one must be to get upset that a domestic abuser might be deported.

Yes, Illegal Immigrants Break the Law

Democrats most loyal to the cause insist illegal immigrants rarely commit crimes. They argue Americans are the real dangers, as if rushing to denigrate their fellow citizens will earn them some extra points among the Radical Left base. But how do they know? Do these claims stand up to scrutiny?

Researchers at the University of Wisconsin at Madison made

a bold claim in 2020: "Relative to undocumented immigrants, US-born citizens are over 2 times more likely to be arrested for violent crimes, 2.5 times more likely to be arrested for drug crimes, and over 4 times more likely to be arrested for property crimes."[392] They're not alone in their findings, with broad agreements from Libertarian think tank Cato Institute[393] and University of California at San Diego scholar Christian Gunadi.[394] The claims are both bold and precise. But to get to their results, the studies acknowledge they are not relying on hard data. Rather, they're *estimating* illegal immigrants who are incarcerated or even the total number of illegal immigrants.

Each paper may utilize competent methods to review the available data. But as confident as they are, it's notable that local and statewide agencies in the areas with high concentrations of illegal immigrants do not inquire about nor attempt to determine a suspect's immigration status. When an illegal immigrant is charged with a misdemeanor (or pleads down to one) in a sanctuary city or county, and avoids jail time through a diversion program, citizenship status isn't documented. Los Angeles County DA George Gascon went so far as to issue a directive to his prosecutors to avoid pursuing cases that could lead to deportation.

"All charging determinations shall be undertaken with the goal of avoiding or mitigating the adverse immigration consequences of a decision when known, possible or permitting" the policy orders.[395] "Under these circumstances and when, consistent with public safety alternatives to filing charges exist, those alternatives shall be pursued."

This policy both discriminates against native-born suspects and downplays crimes committed by illegal immigrants, substantially perverting the stats that Democrats use to dismiss crime concerns. If crimes are purposefully going unpunished as a means to hide citizenship status, how can we rely on data that purports to tell us their rate of crime? Moreover, what about the crimes we know are occurring but aren't getting disrupted?

San Antonio and Houston, Texas, saw nearly unprecedented surges in crime. With 161 homicides in 2021, San Antonio residents likely thought hitting a 28-year high would be the worst of it.[396] But in 2022, that number hit 231, leaving the city with a higher homicide rate than Mexico City.[397]Meanwhile, Houston rang in the new year in 2022 with a 53 percent year-over-year increase in homicides.[398] Despite offering more resources to its police, homicides continued to climb.[399] This crime corresponded with President Biden's open border and lax immigration enforcement.

Texas shares over 1,200 miles of border with Mexico and has become a destination for immigrants from all corners of the world. But among those seeking a more prosperous life via a shortcut across the border, there are elements of the Mexican cartels who smuggle deadly drugs and exploit vulnerable migrants. These are crimes that we know occur, but with a lack of resources and a porous border, it's hard to catch and prosecute them all. These crimes aren't counted in the studies used by the Radical Left to downplay border issues.

Juan Gerardo Treviño-Chavez, also known as "Huevo," is the leader of Cartel Del Noreste, a reckless and violent drug gang based in Mexico. He was indicted in San Antonio on scores of charges, including possession of a machine gun in furtherance of drug trafficking and unlawful distribution of controlled substances.[400] How many crimes did he commit that weren't counted?

Human smugglers steal cars in San Antonio, as part of a car theft ring operated by cartels, to illegally transport migrants to and from the city.[401] Cartel members and associates use social media to convince American youth to steal the cars for them.[402] The stolen cars are often recovered with the backseats ripped out in order to fit more migrants, but the drivers get away. Again, this isn't counted in the data.

Meanwhile, cartel enforcers and drug distributors enter the United States through the Rio Grande Valley, driving up Highway 59, and infiltrating the Houston area.[403] They're responsible for much of the illegal drug trade that is difficult to track. From November 1, 2020, through December 31, 2020, ICE agents were able to nab nine illegal immigrants who re-entered the United States after deportation, most of them gang members with criminal histories in this country.[404] One Houston ICE campaign in 2018 snatched up 26 illegal immigrants with previous criminal histories, including rape, child sexual exploitation, and robbery.[405] The crimes they committed prior to ICE enforcement are not counted in the data.

In May 2022, a segment on *Tucker Carlson Tonight* highlighted a correlation between a rise in Houston homicides and President Biden's porous border. Tucker showed terrifying video evidence of drug cartel wars spilling into Houston, showing a suspect with an automatic weapon shooting at police officers who were serving a warrant. CATO Institute director of economic and social policy studies Alex Nowrasteh, who takes a very lax approach to border security, wasn't impressed by Tucker's argument.

Nowrasteh wrote a blog post in May 2022 claiming that illegal immigration is not a factor in the increase of homicides in Houston.[406] He cited data showing illegal immigrants have been arrested for homicides, but at nowhere near the same rate as American citizens. But doesn't that make Tucker's point that the crimes are happening and they're the result of an open-border policy, making them preventable?

The studies comparing crimes by illegal immigrants to American-born suspects miss the crucial point. It is not argued that illegal immigrants commit *more* crimes than American citizens. It makes sense that illegal immigrants would commit fewer crimes, so they don't risk deportation. They're eager to be in this country to escape difficult circumstances in their home countries. Why risk it? But the fact that they commit *any* crimes, including violent ones, means we have one more case of homicide, rape, assault, robbery, or carjacking than if we had an immigration policy that excluded criminal illegal immigrants. These are crimes that could be prevented.

Mexican-Manufactured Drugs Are Flooding Our Cities

The country's drug epidemic (65 percent of which is connected to synthetic opioids[407]) is a direct result of an open border allowing billions of dollars of product to be smuggled into the country. What was once a concern over marijuana, cocaine, and heroin has morphed into a much bigger concern with the synthetic opioid fentanyl. Addressing the issue of open borders would reduce the number of unnecessary fatal drug overdoses, which reached 108,000 in 2021 alone.[408] But in 2022, the United States hit a staggering record high 110,236 fatal overdoses.[409]

Using ingredients primarily from China, Mexican drug cartels produce the fentanyl that is destroying American families and cities. They are taking advantage of the Radical Left's permissive views on drug use. Fentanyl made its way into the United States around 2014, marking a notable acceleration around 2017, until it hit a full-blown surge in 2019. Fentanyl powder is often mailed from China (and some from India) to Mexico, where it's cut, diluted, and often laced into counterfeit prescription pills. The Sinaloa and New Generation Jalisco (Cártel de Jalisco Nueva Generación or CJNG) cartels are responsible for the majority of drugs smuggled into our country.[410]

Cost is a major driver of the fentanyl market growing precipitously since 2014, while the heroin market has been shrinking. A kilogram of fentanyl can cost around $200 to produce, whereas that same amount of heroin can cost upward of $6,000.[411] The pill's small size makes it easy to smuggle large quantities across the border, either via car through ports of entry or through unguarded land in Texas, Arizona, and California. Border seizures saw significant successes, with US Customs and Border Protection (CBP) confiscating 5,091 pounds of fentanyl in the first nine months of fiscal year 2022.[412] Yet, much more than that is making its way over the border freely, with only 11 percent of fentanyl captured by CBP.[413]

The fentanyl crisis has taken its toll on the American people, killing more Americans than suicide, car accidents, and gun violence. In fact, it's the leading cause of death for 18- to 49-year-olds. But the Radical Left tells Americans that there's no connection between the open border and rise in fentanyl use. Congresswoman Pramila Jayapal (D-Seattle), for example, tweeted that, "Over 90 percent of fentanyl is brought into the country by US citizens. The fentanyl crisis has nothing to do with immigrants. Don't let anyone convince you otherwise."[414] Though she doesn't cite her source, it's obviously misleading since smugglers who illegally cross the border without getting caught aren't counted in her data. But she makes no mention of the Americans she cites as working with Mexican drug cartels or taking advantage of lax border policies. You're supposed to be moved to allow any immigrant to walk into this country illegally because most of them don't carry fentanyl.

The Radical Left is disinterested in tackling border security because it would stop future supporters from coming into this country. No matter the consequences of their sanctuary policies, any American showing even a hint of anxiety about the border crisis gets you labeled an inhumane xenophobe. It's a Radical Left strategy meant to silence opposition.

When President Trump announced ICE mobilization to capture and deport criminal illegal immigrants in the summer of 2019, Democrats responded with self-righteous condemnation portraying themselves as champions of justice. Washington, DC, mayor Muriel Bowser called the move "cruel and antithetical to our American values."[415] (Years later she would decry immigrants bused to her city, demanding federal assistance.) Unlike policies inviting illegal immigration, Trump's move to enforce the law was "politically driven," according to Seattle mayor Jenny Durkan.[416] Chicago mayor Lori Lightfoot told Trump to "back off!" because she would be fighting on behalf of illegal immigrants with her "Chicago values."[417]

Los Angeles mayor Eric Garcetti said, "The families you

threaten are not 'illegal'—they're our mothers and fathers, friends and neighbors, colleagues and confidants. They're us."[418] Well, no, they're not us. They're not even Garcetti, who held an elected office that illegal immigrants may never hold due to their citizenship status.

The Radical Left even objected to raids targeting immigrants *who already went through the system* and ignored orders to self-deport by a judge.[419] Many Democrats don't merely support open borders; they think if an individual is able to make it here illegally, they should be able to stay consequence-free. But that only encourages the cycle of illegal immigration to continue. Thanks to Democrat efforts to offer tips to illegal immigrants to circumvent ICE, Trump's raids were mostly a failure, netting only 35 at the time.[420]

It wasn't just Democrat lawmakers helping illegal immigrants stay in the country. Left-wing media outlets consistently offered campaigns to defend and deflect.

As fentanyl use exploded, National Public Radio (NPR) chided the "misleading and false claims" connecting fentanyl use to illegal immigration. Reporter Joel Rose aimed to set the record straight with an interview with 20-year CBP veteran Victor Manjarrez, the director for the Center for Law and Human Behavior at the University of Texas at El Paso. He noted that the "the chaos and clutter that occurs at a port of entry" makes it easier for smugglers to bring in fentanyl across the border. Though he conceded that it also comes by foot across the border, "brought in by cartels who are using migrants as a distraction." But Rose declared, "Most of the fentanyl entering the country is not smuggled in by migrants," not based on data, merely the observations of one hand-picked expert.[421] Left-wing NPR adopts a Democrat posture to obfuscate concerns over the streams of unvetted migrants crossing into the country illegally, acting like a publicist for the Democrat position.

Rose may very well be right, though the confidence in which these claims are made is confounding. We know drugs are smuggled across the Rio Grande River, with the Rio Grande Valley operating as the most used marijuana corridor in the country in 2014.[422] It's much easier to transport fentanyl pills than weed. We also know about sophisticated tunnel operations connecting cartels in Mexico to safe houses in California. In March 2022, U.S. officials uncovered a tunnel the length of six football fields, with electricity, a ventilation system, and a running rail line connecting Tijuana to a warehouse near San Diego, California.[423] Whether it's drugs across the Rio Grande River or via tunnels, how much is getting through that we're not aware of, only to then be told our concerns over an open border and illegal immigration are misplaced? The Radical Left will have you believe none of the hundreds of thousands of known "got aways" in 2021 and 2022 were carrying fentanyl.

If the majority of drugs aren't being smuggled by illegal immigrants across the border, so what? If any comes across an open border, wouldn't it be smart policy to stop it? Think about the lives it would save. Democrats often argued that their gun policies, no matter how unconstitutional, are worth it, if they can take just one gun off the street or save just one life. But when it comes to drugs flowing across the border because of illegal immigrants, killing thousands of Americans a month, that approach is no longer valid.

Media outlets also go out of the way to ignore stories showing illegal immigration reaching untenable milestones. In late October 2021, as a migrant caravan of thousands was heading toward our southern border, mainstream news outlets and left-wing cable all but ignored it, particularly the morning shows that are designed to bring viewers up to speed on the biggest stories in the preceding 24 hours.[424]

Why Do Democrats Support Illegal Immigrants?

Democrats never miss an opportunity to demand that we "fix our broken immigration system," while doing nothing meaningful to close the border or cut down on the red tape making it difficult to come here legally. The problem is that the Radical Left within the party refuses to offer necessary border security commitments, including building a wall, investing in technology to track migrants, and fully staffing and funding ICE. They want blanket amnesty, which Republicans will not stomach, at least not without assurances that our border will be fully secure.

The Radical Left's embrace of illegal immigrants is, in part, about playing savior to marginalized communities. They speak of racial, gender, religious, and ethnic minorities as vulnerable souls that will languish and extinguish without the steady hand of a Democrat lawmaker who can make everything better. Many of these Democrats are white, and they love adopting the role of White Savior. The immigrants are seeking a better life and, despite the protestations from the Left about America's culture of white supremacy, even Democrats know immigrants are better off here than in Mexico, Honduras, Venezuela, or El Salvador.

Democrats also benefit from the cheap labor provided by these migrants. They claim Americans won't take certain jobs, such as picking lettuce, bussing tables, or cleaning hotel rooms. Democrats who adopt that belief must be content with the exploitation of these workers, who are paid very little for their hard work. The reason that American workers refuse to take these jobs is because the availability of immigrant workers who will work for little drives down wages. That's not my take, but is that of left-wing *New York Times* columnist Paul Krugman who wrote, "immigration reduces the wages of domestic workers who compete with immigrants."[425] It's basic supply and demand. The high number of low-skilled workers willing to take on manual jobs due to their desperation to make a life in the United States leads to them accepting lower wages. It's blatant exploitation of the vulnerable, which Democrats overlook. If the number of these workers weren't so large, the market would naturally drive up the wages to a level that would attract American workers.

So why give up on American workers while allowing for fatal

drug overdoses and crime, particularly among border states, to soar? It's about power.

It's not possible to get an accurate number of illegal immigrants in the United States. While it's been generally believed to hover around 12 million, researchers seem unwilling to update their numbers as scores continue to cross our border. Yale University is an exception; three researchers estimated it at roughly 22 million.[426] Under President Biden, that number obviously went up. CBP agents contacted an unprecedented number of immigrants illegally crossing the border in 2021 (over 1.72 million) and in 2022 (over 2.76 million),[427] with over 600,000 known "got-aways" (the term for immigrants that officials saw cross the border but could not contact) for fiscal year 2022.[428]

These are millions of likely Democrat voters, which is why the Radical Left aims to grant them citizenship and the right to vote. The New York City Council passed legislation to allow noncitizens to vote in local elections in December 2021, though it was struck down by the state supreme court the following year.[429] In San Francisco, noncitizens and illegal immigrants were granted the right to vote in school board elections if they have a child in a public school. Four years later in 2022, a judge declared the law in violation of the state constitution, though elections had already occurred under the change.[430]

The Radical Left doesn't want us to notice their plan, calling it out as a white supremacist talking point akin to the "Great Replacement" theory (a conspiracy that immigrants are purposefully let into the country to take power away from whites). But the Radical Left who offers this rebuke always labels their political opponents as white supremacists. It's a shameless way to silence the other side. Illegal immigrants aren't meant to replace white people, they are meant to replace Republican voters.

Adding millions of votes will help grow or maintain Democrat control. And it's not like party members haven't touted this as their goal. After all, the Democrat party platform declares it's "long past time to provide a roadmap to citizenship for the millions of undocumented workers, caregivers, students, and children who are an essential part of our economy and of the fabric of our nation."[431] Would granting illegal immigrants citizenship not come with voting rights?

Meanwhile, the Biden administration handed out a nearly $171.7 million taxpayer-funded government contract to Vera Institute of Justice, a far-left nonprofit based out of New York, to help unaccompanied minors avoid deportation with subsidized legal assistance.[432] Locally, Democrat-run cities offer the same services. The City of Seattle offers taxpayer-funded legal assistance to avoid deportation, even if you're accused of a serious crime.[433] The Los Angeles City Council funded a pilot program offering free legal representation to immigrants who face deportation.[434] Some even go as far as to help illegal immigrants stay off the radar of the federal government. In Minneapolis, the city was set to unveil municipal identification cards in 2018 but halted the program over concerns it could help the federal government identify immigrants for deportation.[435] Will illegal immigrants eventually reward Democrats with a vote? The Radical Left hopes the answer is yes.

Democrat lawmakers and their media toadies often discuss the "shifting demographics" of the country and how it favors them. To a cheering crowd, perennial election loser Stacey Abrams declared the "blue wave" that will push Democrats into power is "made up of those who've been told that they are not worthy of being here. It is comprised of those who are documented and undocumented."[436] In an editorial literally titled "We Can Replace Them," left-wing *New York Times* columnist Michelle Goldberg bragged about the coalition of "African-American and other minority voters" who backed Abrams to replace white conservative voters. "The potential is there; Georgia is less than 53 percent non-Hispanic white. 'Georgia is a blue state if everybody votes,' DuBose Porter, chairman of the Democratic Party of Georgia, told me," Goldberg wrote.[437]

Senator Dick Durbin (D-IL) didn't hide the strategy either.

Speaking on the Senate floor, he declared, "The demographics of America are not on the side of the Republican Party." He was speaking mostly about Latinos. "The new voters in this country are moving away from them, away from Donald Trump, away from their party creed that they preach," he said.[438] "Instead, they are moving to be independents or even vote on the other side. To argue and fight against that, the Republicans in legislative settings are reducing and restricting the opportunity to vote."

But Republicans were restricting the opportunity to *illegally* vote, while Democrats are hoping to expand the voting base to those in this country illegally. If that isn't the intent, why do Democrats embrace an open border while simultaneously pushing for a path to citizenship no matter how long someone's been here? Rather than even attempt to answer that question, the Radical Left smears the Right.

While conservative critics are not wrong about the Radical Left's intent, we might just be wrong about the end result. In recent years, ethnic minorities, Latinos in particular, have been abandoning the Democrat party after it shifted so far to the Left, particularly when it comes to breaking up the nuclear family and deriding religion. Still, it seems Democrats hope the shifts are only temporary and not large enough to stop their plans to maintain or reach electoral dominance. And if some cities suffer from violence and drug overdoses in the process, so be it.

PART II

HOW THE PROGRESSIVE LIFESTYLE IS DESTROYING OUR CITIES

THEIR RULES, OUR DEMISE

CHAPTER 6

HOUSING FIRST, RESULTS . . . NEVER

An Unmitigated Disaster

Roughly 70,000 homeless people roam Los Angeles County looking for a clean and safe place to sleep and, increasingly, to get high. In Los Angeles alone, there are nearly 42,000 homeless. Many live with mental health issues that have only deteriorated from the lack of treatment. They find alleyways, sidewalks, parks, and any open spaces to set up camp as they struggle to survive. Their encampments and tents are filthy, surrounded by human waste, refuse, drug paraphernalia, and weapons to keep them safe at night. They are deeply vulnerable when on the streets; these are human beings suffering, many feeling hopeless and alone. But Democrat lawmakers thought they had a plan.

Proposition HHH ("Housing and Hope to End Homelessness") was a $1.2 billion bond, funded through a modest property tax in 2016, to build affordable housing for the chronically homeless. It was the brainchild of the Los Angeles City Council's Homelessness and Poverty Committee, and Marqueece Harris-Dawson and José

Huizar, who were concerned about the growing homelessness crisis. At the time, there were roughly 28,000 homeless in the city.[439]

Though HHH wouldn't solve homelessness, it would create a serious dent in the problem, building 10,000 permanent supportive housing units over the course of a decade. The campaign's message was direct, arguing the problem is urgent and HHH would provide "immediate solutions to keep people off the street, reduce the number of encampments, and protect vulnerable women and children."[440]

Lawmakers, local media, and even some celebrities backed HHH. Then-mayor Eric Garcetti touted HHH as a way to "confront a humanitarian crisis."[441] The *Los Angeles Times* provided a full board press of editorials, urging Los Angelinos to pass the proposition, calling it "critical" to invest in permanent supportive housing because "years of studies by academics and service providers" show it works to get the homeless off the streets.[442] Even *The Good Place* star Kristen Bell endorsed HHH as "a really good version of the help that we need. It's worth it." She called the $1.2 billion investment "a small concession to fix a gigantic problem that we all care about."[443]

In the end, the voters listened. It wasn't even close, with 76 percent of the vote favoring HHH. After the victory, council member Huizar, whose district includes Skid Row, promised quick action. "Within the next three to six months, with all the work we've done, we will see an improvement," he said.[444] "And in two years . . . we'll see a significant reduction in people living in the streets."

To call HHH an unmitigated failure would be both an understatement and too kind. There was no improvement; the homelessness crisis got worse. And about six years after HHH was passed, there are barely any housing units to show for it. What was built was extraordinarily expensive.

By early 2022, only 1,142 units opened, with one project costing $837,000 per housing unit. Most of the permanent supportive housing units are either studios or one-bedrooms, yet 14 percent of the units cost over $700,000 to build.[445] In a scathing February 2022 audit, city Controller Ron Galperin ripped the "sluggish" pace of development and increased costs of units. He called the total number of completed units "wholly inadequate in the context of the ongoing homelessness emergency."[446] The excessive costs were not completely the fault of HHH developers, with the COVID-19 pandemic driving up the costs of goods and the supply chain disruption that plagued 2020 and 2021. But projects have been so delayed and slow to complete, it drove up the costs more than they would have been without COVID-19.

While housing was built at a snail's pace, homelessness surged. Disgusting tent encampments popped up in virtually every neighborhood. They were violent and home to drug use and dealing. Homeless deaths spiked in 2020, up 56 percent year over year, and it wasn't from COVID-19, but instead from drug overdoses.[447] Homeless addiction rates were skyrocketing, with the *Los Angeles Times* finding roughly 46 percent had substance use disorders and 51 percent had mental illnesses.[448] Take a stroll around any neighborhood in Los Angeles, and you'll realize these numbers severely understate the problem.

The Affordable Housing Myth

The University of California at Los Angeles conducted a study across 15 states, interviewing over 65,000 homeless adults over the age of 25. Their findings match what most people can see when observing a homeless encampment. Over 50 percent suffer from a combination of a physical health condition, a mental health issue, and a substance-abuse condition. Let that percentage sink in.[449] You think a house will fix their issues?

Let's quickly dispel the oft-cited claim that homelessness is caused by a lack of affordable housing. You wouldn't know that based on the prevailing talking point that we just need more affordable housing to end homelessness. That position is driven by Radical Left lawmakers and activists who believe housing is a human right.

Garcetti believes "housing has gone from being an aspiration to a right in this country," stressing that "we have to address the general crisis of affordability, or else more people will become homeless."[450] Likewise, then-mayor Jenny Durkan of Seattle decried a "lack of affordable housing" for fueling the city's escalating homelessness crisis.[451] And as if following the same script, Austin, Texas, mayor Steve Adler endlessly pitched affordable housing, saying the city can "end" homelessness by 2025.[452]

It's certainly true that it's nearly impossible for the homeless to afford a home without assistance. But housing costs didn't cause the crisis. The homeless weren't born without a home; something changed their life circumstances to make them homeless. Whether or not you believe housing is a right has no bearing on the crisis. Homelessness is driven, in large part, by drug addiction and mental illness (oftentimes afflicting the homeless concurrently). Unless those underlying issues are addressed, the homeless won't be able to navigate self-sufficient lives in which they keep a steady job and pay rent.

San Francisco's homeless people are plagued by drug addiction, with 52 percent acknowledging they suffer from drug or alcohol abuse.[453] Portland (35 percent),[454] Denver (35 percent),[455] Austin (33 percent),[456] and Los Angeles (24 percent)[457] fare slightly better, though none of the data, compiled by a one-night count of the homeless, are likely accurate. They undoubtedly all undercount the extent of addiction, given the high rate of fatal and nonfatal overdoses these cities and counties are experiencing and the limitations of how the count is conducted.

King County, Washington, had over 40,000 homeless in 2022,[458] driven by the Seattle homeless population, a number that has consistently grown since the 10-year plan to end homelessness was announced in 2005. Needless to say, that plan was a failure. But Democrats claim the crisis was worsened by Amazon headquarters employing thousands of high-paid engineers who have occupied the available homes and apartments, driving up the rents. And over the years, their talking points didn't change.

Then-council member Mike O'Brien claimed in 2017 his district had "thousands of homeless people that actually are working and just can't afford housing."[459] Socialist city councilwoman Kshama Sawant argued in 2019, "The only realistic solution to homelessness is to make housing available and affordable."[460] Democrat council member Dan Strauss explained in 2022 that housing helps the "majority of people who are experiencing homelessness."[461] Democrat Governor Jay Inslee proclaimed in 2023, "Until we fix our housing crisis, thousands of people will remain homeless."[462] None of these claims are accurate.

When O'Brien made his comment, only 7.5 percent of the homeless reported working full-time.[463] This makes sense given how difficult it is to find work when homeless. Sawant, Strauss, and Inslee, likewise, downplay the number of homeless people struggling with crippling addiction and deteriorating mental illness. The data has been fairly consistent, even using the inadequate point-in-time count, which cities use to quantify homelessness for the US Department of Housing and Urban Development (HUD).

In 2020, the latest data available for Seattle, only 5 percent of the homeless cited eviction as the main reason for their homelessness.[464] And due to COVID-19 changes, evictions were banned from 2020 to 2022, making that number nonexistent for the Washington-based homeless who were living in a home at the time. In contrast, the leading causes were lost job (16 percent), alcohol or drug use (11 percent), and mental health issues (8 percent). All of these numbers are undoubtedly low, especially since 44 percent say they actively suffer from drug or alcohol abuse, with 64 percent citing that as the reason they can't get a job. Of the 16 percent who cite job loss or the 5 percent citing eviction as the initial reason for their homelessness, how many couldn't keep a job or pay rent *because* of the addiction or untreated mental health issues? The data is also self-reported, making it less reliable. Some addicts live in denial, while others are so high, they won't be able to properly answer questions. And try getting coherent answers out of mentally ill homeless. You won't get very far.

The truth came out in a Seattle lawsuit against opioid manufacturers in 2017 for their alleged role in causing the addiction crisis. The city blamed the bulk of the homelessness crisis on drug addiction.

"Researchers estimate that over 50 percent of people with opioid addictions in Seattle are homeless, and Seattle's Navigation Team, which is composed of outreach workers and police officers specially trained to interface with the homeless population, estimates that 80 percent of the homeless individuals they encounter in challenging encampments have substance abuse disorders," the lawsuit alleged.[465]

Funny how the housing affordability line goes out the window when they're not allowed to flat-out lie in a court filing without repercussions.

Sifting Through the Buzzwords

When the Radical Left calls for permanent supportive housing, it's just that: permanent. It comes with wraparound services to treat the homeless, when that person is ready. It's the "housing first" model with a low barrier to entry. That is, an addict may still use their drug of choice without any fear of eviction. There's little consideration given to recovering addicts in the same housing facilities who may be triggered—or offered drugs—by their neighbor smoking fentanyl. It's about getting as many people indoors as possible.

Throughout the pandemic, and well after it, Democrat lawmakers spent tax dollars to purchase or rent hotels and motels shuttered by the very COVID-19 pandemic policies they put in place. The goal was to fill them with the homeless, taking them off the street and addressing the oft-complained-about visible homeless making areas unsafe and unsanitary. They were half-baked plans and money pits.

Chicago mayor Lori Lightfoot spent $7 million to temporarily house homeless in 1,900 rooms for 13 months starting in March 2021,[466] after which they were all booted with little to no notice to shelters or other locations.[467] The city of Austin purchased a Candlewood Suites hotel for $9 million to house elderly homeless, but officials dragged their feet on renovations. Ironically, squatters destroyed the building, significantly pushing back renovations and plans.[468] King County executive Dow Constantine went on a hotel purchasing binge, with one La Quinta Inn & Suites property not far from schools.[469] Parents protested, but their concerns over safety were ignored, prompting a lawsuit against the county. Newly elected Los Angeles mayor Karen Bass committed $100 million to leasing motel rooms for the homeless,[470] but property owners were livid when the city would not make guarantees to cover damages by homeless occupants.[471]

The idea to utilize vacant rooms might sound promising on paper. It's much cheaper to retrofit a pre-existing property than to start from scratch as they are doing in Los Angeles with HHH. But in practice, the strategy is unimpressive. There is almost never a meaningful plan to actually help the homeless after they take a room. The hotels turn into sordid pigsties that were as contaminated as the encampments they escaped.

The *San Francisco Chronicle* investigated the homeless hotels in San Francisco under Mayor London Breed.[472] It's easy to see why her strategy failed. The rat infestation in one homeless hotel in the Tenderloin neighborhood was so bad that a resident pitched a tent in her own room to keep the rodents away. The hotel's homeless residents routinely fought, sometimes with knives and other weapons. Between 2020 and 2022, there were at least nine fatal overdoses at the hotel. The conditions were deplorable. And this property wasn't the exception.

The city's Department of Homelessness and Supportive Housing contracted with local nonprofits to run the 70 homeless hotels across the city. But they didn't do a very good job. From 2020 to 2022, 161 homeless suffered fatal overdoses while participating in the program. Police were frequently called because residents threatened staff, stabbed other residents, or set fire to the rooms. While providing wraparound services is the only way any of this can work, nonprofits were only getting $7 per day, per hotel room, to fund treatment. Much of the funds for the program went to maintenance and general upkeep. But it wasn't happening with any regularity or, if it did, it was quickly undone. Plumbing rarely worked, elevators broke down, and mold and mildew spread, with city building inspectors citing the properties over 1,600 times for violations.

The program was both a money pit for taxpayers and a death sentence for many homeless. The city tracked the progress of 515 men and women during and after the program. The goal of the temporary housing was to give them enough time to get their lives in order, seek wraparound services, land jobs, and save money so they can rent their own apartments or homes. That didn't happen. A quarter of the homeless died while in the program, 21 percent were back living on the streets, and 27 percent left the program but couldn't be tracked. Roughly 25 percent landed in other subsidized housing or living with friends and family. They were all let down by a system without rules, structure, meaningful supervision, or adequate funding. Meanwhile, homelessness citywide increased 56 percent.

Rules Matter

An Amazon employee was walking home early one evening in the Belltown neighborhood of Seattle when 41-year-old Wantez Tulloss spotted her. At the time, Tulloss had a lengthy criminal history, including first-degree robbery, theft, assault, and three violations of domestic violence no-contact orders. He was about to add another charge to the list. Video surveillance showed Tulloss approaching the woman from behind, dropping a bag dangling from his arm, and then striking her head with a bat he was carrying in his right hand. Police say he made full contact, causing a skull fracture that sent her to the ground in pain before she finally lost consciousness. It appears that Tulloss had intended to cause maximum harm. He didn't show any remorse. Tulloss returned to retrieve his shopping bag, walked away, and then grabbed a slice of pizza at a nearby restaurant.[473]

Tulloss is a bad guy. He was also a homeless man living in permanent supportive housing managed by one of Seattle's many service providers, Plymouth Housing. This provider offers a harm-reduction approach, which allows addicts to continue their addiction, judgment free. Indeed, their website notes that its staff creates a "nonjudgmental space" for its residents "to make changes if, and when, they are ready." Police and prosecutors were not so nonjudgmental, arresting and charging Tulloss with first-degree assault.

The homeless need rules and structure, more so the longer they've lived outside. If they're addicts or mentally ill, they desperately need treatment. Without rules and treatment, housing programs rarely work; all we've done is guarantee them a studio apartment where they can continue their destructive behavior without any consequences beyond death. If they don't have to pay rent, what's their incentive to find work? If they don't need to seek treatment, why would they quit smoking fentanyl or shooting up heroin? And if they're not getting mental health treatment, they continue to be a threat to themselves and others. That these programs offer few to no barriers to entry means they can also attract some of the worst in the homeless community.

Obviously, not everyone who enters these programs is dangerous like Tulloss. But if the program had standards for entry and actually worked to keep people accountable, a woman wouldn't likely have had her skull fractured. Maybe Tulloss would have sought treatment, if it was required. Instead, he was allowed to live carefree and ultimately allegedly commit a dastardly crime.

When Los Angeles mayor Bass announced her homeless hotel program, she had plenty reason to believe, based on Project Roomkey, that it wouldn't work. She moved forward anyway. This time, however, the failure of the initiative cannot be attributed to the idea itself, but to the actions of the homeless and their advocates.

Project Roomkey placed over 4,000 homeless in various hotels around the city. But there were actual rules, including curfews, a prohibition against drug use (or any criminal activity) anywhere on or off site, and a promise to keep the space tidy.[474] This is the start of a program that can work. But it earned rebuke from advocates and even homeless people who couldn't find the passion and time to find a job and save up for their own apartment, but formed the United Tenants Against Carceral Housing union. They complained of "prison-like" conditions, according to one homeless advocate, who complained that "when unhoused people are accepting the services that are offered, they are made to feel infantilized, they are made to feel like criminals." He argued these rules push the homeless away.[475] Ananya Roy, founding director of the Luskin Institute on Inequality and Democracy at University of California at Los Angeles, told local media she was once a fan of Project Roomkey, but after learning about the rules, she was discouraged, calling it "the most dehumanizing, prison-like housing."[476]

The homeless were told not to shoot up heroin in the lobby or in their rooms. They were asked to be respectful of the property they're not paying for. What indignities they suffered!

Obviously, the homeless union members were taken advantage of by Radical Left activists. What are the odds that any of the homeless knew what the term "carceral" meant, let alone be able to spell it. Comparing free hotel rooms to jail is delusional. Nevertheless, the complaints provided valuable insights into the role played by Radical Left activists and their supportive lawmakers in hindering efforts to find a solution to homelessness.

Democrats Hate Sweeps, Until They Don't

Rather than live in filth, surrounded by human waste, trash, and used needles, suffering actual indignities of living outside in the elements without access to plumbing or electricity, in clothes that haven't been cleaned since it last rained, the homeless are best suited in shelters where they can be safe and secure. Furthermore, they can receive assistance from case managers who specialize in guiding them toward the appropriate path. But the Radical Left's zealotry that the homeless are entitled to free housing as a human right has blocked efforts to alleviate homelessness and provide effective housing for those in need.

The Radical Left abhors homeless encampment sweeps. They claim they're evil, destructive, and hurt more than they help. The only time these critics seem to support sweeps is if it's to put the homeless into studio apartments. ACLU New York executive director Donna Lieberman calls sweeps "cruel," arguing it leaves the homeless "more vulnerable."[477] Mid-Minnesota Legal Aid and the ACLU of Minnesota went as far as to sue the city of Minneapolis for its sweeps, unsuccessfully arguing it was unconstitutional to destroy the personal property of the homeless.[478] Hugo Soto-Martinez successfully campaigned for Los Angeles City Council in 2022 on a message to end sweeps, calling them "ineffective, inhumane," while demanding permanent housing.[479] Portland Commissioner Jo Ann Hardesty made headlines in 2019 for a protest against a sweep, claiming to be "outraged that we are using public money to displace people that we cannot provide housing for."[480] Congresswoman Alexandria Ocasio-Cortez said she believes housing should be "legislated as a human right."[481]

A basic function for a city or county is to keep its sidewalks, parks, and other public areas clean and safe. As the COVID-19 pandemic began, many municipalities stopped sweeps, allowing encampments to take over. To say they swallowed some neighborhoods whole is an understatement. Los Angeles, San Francisco, New York, DC, Austin, Portland, and Seattle were simply overrun. And diseases quickly spread.

Encampments in Los Angeles were so bad that some spread medieval diseases like typhus and tuberculosis.[482] The 54 square blocks known as Skid Row were deemed a "typhus zone" thanks to a massive rat infestation and piles of uncollected trash.[483] Rather than sweep the area of its chronically homeless, men and women who are so far gone they will never get help unless you force it, then-mayor Garcetti authorized $300,000 for trash pickup, and sidewalk and street cleaning.[484] They received turn-down maid service.

San Francisco's homeless crisis became a national joke. The homeless were defecating everywhere and anywhere, which doesn't just impact the quality of life of residents, but spreads fecal-borne disease. Sam Miller created an app to map the city's poop problem. SnapCrap allowed San Franciscans to photograph evidence of the crappy situation residents found themselves in, then report it to the city for cleanup. The attention spurred the Department of Public Works to invest in a "Poop Patrol" of staffers who work to steam clean city sidewalks.[485]

Eventually, encampments grew so large that Democrat mayors were forced to act. Facing an escalating crisis already out of control, with diseases spreading, encampment crime rampant, and even liberal-to-a-fault residents fed up, mayors started to sweep more regularly. Of course, they faced opposition from the city's Radical Left activists.

Los Angeles banned encampments within 500 feet of schools and daycare centers. During a debate before the vote, one activist broke through a security barricade and charged at council members at their dais. Two officers were injured.[486]

Portland lawmakers went one step forward, banning encampments on sidewalks and restricting them to six sanctioned locations. The move was prompted by a 50 percent increase in homeless between 2019 and 2022, with over 700 individual encampments spread across the city. Various activists, including those with Stop the Sweeps PDX, responded with protestations and smears of any person or organization that supported sweeps.[487] At the state level, Oregon Democrats even introduced the "Right to Rest Act," which would decriminalize public encampments, awarding the homeless $1,000 if they were "harassed" into moving.[488]

In Washington, DC, Mayor Muriel Bowser initiated a pilot program to permanently clear homeless camps popping up around businesses, government offices, and tourist attractions. Some city council members tried to stop the sweeps, but failed on a 5 to 7 vote.[489]

But one city stood firmly against meaningful sweeps throughout most of the pandemic and into 2022. My hometown, Seattle, has a terrifyingly permissive attitude toward tent cities, but what it allowed to happen during COVID-19 was shocking. Although the city's residents had previously shown anti-sweep sentiment, it worsened thanks to activism by city council member Kshama Sawant and Seattle Public School board members.

Early in her political career, Sawant demanded Seattle must "build city-owned housing, and stop these inhumane sweeps."[490] She never backed off her position, maintaining a hostile attitude toward sweeps throughout her council career. She fought to maintain one controversial encampment, even after a felon living there was found with 30 rounds of assault rifle ammunition, brass knuckles, and several large knives. Protesters blocked garbage trucks from entering the area, catching the city off guard. How'd these hooligans know about the sweep when the schedule wasn't published anywhere? Sawant and her staff emailed the sweep schedules to area activists, who would then use Twitter to recruit others to fight back. At the time, Sawant disputed tipping off protesters. She maintained she was merely keeping the public informed about the goings on of a city department.[491]

Seattle's permissive attitude toward encampments rendered

nearly every Seattle park unusable. Downtown Seattle was unwalkable, with homeless addicts shooting up or smoking fentanyl in full view. You couldn't find parking around the city's stadiums, spots occupied by broken down RVs with homeless living in them. And the city wouldn't interfere. Between April and September 2019, the city of Seattle removed 451 encampments. During the same time period in 2020, that number was just seven.[492] As a resident, it's been alarming; as a journalist navigating the encampments for stories, it's dangerous and tragic.

Used needles littered children's playgrounds. One so-called "tent mansion" kept growing across the street from the Space Needle, featuring a keg to keep the occupants inebriated.[493] Hepatitis A spread at one camp, prompting a rare sweep that earned a protest. Seattle's recalcitrant, militant activists didn't care where the homeless set up camp; they believe it was a right to live where and how they wanted. Even if the encampments were a danger to the homeless or the pubic, they had defenders stopping sweeps and harassing me when I visited to cover stories. It created an ineluctable anxiety that something bad was going to happen. And, of course, it did.

City Hall Park, next to the county courthouse in downtown Seattle, resembled a third-world country. It's hard to adequately explain the bleak, dangerous conditions I saw (and smelled) at the park after dozens of homeless were allowed to set up a community of drug use and violence. It was tragically ironic that the encampment was located next to a courthouse where, in any sane world, its residents would be standing in front of a judge facing charges for their conduct.

A homeless, 35-year-old named Clint James Jory was just done serving a 21-month sentence for a series of random assaults against women. Police told me they believed he was living at the camp at City Hall Park. Six days after his July 2021 release, he was accused of committing a most despicable crime. Police say he snuck into the courthouse's women's restroom, where he waited nearly naked in a stall for a random victim. In this case, it happened to be a pregnant lawyer. Prosecutors say he "savagely attacked" her. Police say that with his pants hanging around his ankles, Jory covered her mouth and attempted to rape her. The victim cried for help, and a nearby sheriff's deputy who was walking by heard and intervened.[494] After being charged, Jory's parents confirmed their son is a meth addict who suffers from schizophrenia with auditory hallucinations.[495] Rather than get the help he needed, he was allowed to live carefree in an encampment that should never have been allowed to stand.

Courthouse staff were shocked, but not surprised. They had been complaining for months that the encampment was a danger, and for years that the neighborhood was imploding. The former King County sheriff John Urquhart and his chief of staff, Chris Barringer, were walking back to their offices in the courthouse when a homeless man, unprovoked, charged at them with a pair of scissors, ready to strike. Barringer turned around just in time, quickly pulling his sidearm, convincing the homeless man to stop. "Had we not turned around and squared off with him, I think he would have stabbed one or both of us in the back with the scissors," Barringer said to a local television station.[496]

The incident occurred in 2017, well before City Hall Park was taken over by the homeless. Staff were getting harassed and jurors attacked.[497] Eventually, the courthouse offered security escorts to staff who left the office at night. Rather than address the problems, the Seattle City Council insisted police not be involved. They were sensitive to claims that they were criminalizing homeless, a silly term meant to shame lawmakers into giving a pass to homeless criminals. Instead, then-council member Sally Bagshaw proposed putting ping-pong tables at the park and encouraging food trucks to set up. This would "activate" the park by encouraging everyday Seattleites to stop by, thereby pushing the homeless out.[498] Needless to say, fighting homeless crime with ping-pong tables didn't work. (Consider the déjà vu I experienced in April 2023 when Mayor Bruce Harrell, hoping to revitalize the same area, pitched pickleball tournaments and food trucks as a way to solve the homelessness crisis, as if hipsters sipping IPAs in between pickleball games will make any difference in the world.[499])

Seattle Democrats refused to protect adults from dangerous homeless people. Surely, you'd think they'd step up to help vulnerable children, right? Of course not. In April 2021, students were set to return to in-person classes after months of ineffective and emotionally damaging remote learning. But Broadview-Thompson K-8 students were greeted with a sprawling encampment at the park that borders its campus and playground. Over the pandemic, the Seattle Public School Board, which owns the park property, allowed the homeless to set up a community. Knowing that they wouldn't be removed, more homeless came to the area and set up camp. I visited the park many times, and it was never pleasant. The smell of urine through the lakeside park could make you gag; you could taste it. Trash was everywhere. The homeless would openly get high. As the school semester neared, parents wondered when the school board would sweep the encampment. In a statement, the district said "simply removing them from district property won't result in a permanent solution," given that the campers often "move between city- and district-owned properties." All that separated the school and its playground from the encampment was a flimsy fence, and parents were worried.

In an unusually bold move, the city was ready to sweep. Even city leaders understood the encampment posed an unacceptable risk to the students. But school board members kept the city off their property. I obtained emails that showed the school board president Chandra Hampson and then-director Zachary DeWolf instructing the city to stay away from not just the Broadview-Thompson encampment, but also the homeless that took over a park attached to a middle school in another neighborhood. They still had the audacity to ask for funding to help maintain the encampment and support its residents.

"I want to state very clearly this is not an ask for a sweep! I do not believe in sweeps," DeWolf emailed city staff.[500] "People experiencing homelessness need housing and resources, not traumatic sweeps of their livelihoods and belongings. I understand that the Council has allocated and assigned a lot of funding to support our neighbors experiencing homelessness. BUT we do need some support—we are bringing students back to classrooms and school buildings/campuses in a matter of a few weeks. Do you have any ideas for how to help?"

City staff and board members discussed options, but a sweep was eventually proposed by the city. It prompted Hampson and DeWolf to post a joint statement on Facebook saying sweeps are "decidedly inhumane and irresponsibly set people struggling with homelessness further into the margins." They demanded that "sweeps NEVER be performed on school grounds, adjacent or elsewhere in this City." A deputy mayor responded to warn them that even after extensive outreach, it's common that "some individuals do not accept offers of shelter until the posted day of removal, if at all." He warned that "many encampments are dangerous not only for children and the surrounding community but for the individuals living in the encampment."[501]

The board maintained their position, and opened the school with the encampment intact. Students and parents reported weapons, including a sword, and what was described as a human skull hanging from a tree—a sick decoration to make the property more their "own." I obtained video of prostitutes in revealing clothing walking in and out of the encampment. The school was forced into two lockdowns requiring emergency police response after a man believed to be from the encampment wandered into the school[502] and after the principal said their security guard "saw a person with what appeared to be a firearm on the other side of the fence, toward Bitter Lake."[503] There were at least two drug overdoses at the site, one fatal.[504] A sex offender lived there at one point. Eventually the school placed a green tarp over the fence, protecting the kids from seeing the camp and preventing the sex offender from being tempted to prey on innocent victims.

After weeks of pressure from the parents and even school staff, plus unwanted media coverage courtesy of my reports on *Tucker Carlson Tonight*, *America's Newsroom*, and *The Faulkner Focus*, the school board finally acted. They contracted with a small non-profit, Anything Helps, run by a former homeless addict named Mike Mathias, to help relocate the 70 homeless people who lived in the encampment. About one week after taking the reins, Mathias admitted to me that he asked a homeless addict to help "slam" him with meth (a term for intravenous drug use).[505]

"In July, I did agree to an offer made by a female camper to accept a shot of methamphetamine," Mathias told me. "She did attempt to administer this to me, and the event was short-lived and thankfully unsuccessful, but I regrettably admit that this occured [sic] nonetheless."

It was unsuccessful, but not for lack of trying. He said the homeless woman couldn't find a suitable vein. The county, which had agreed to work with Mathias to connect the homeless with housing, then halted the unofficial partnership. In a series of emails I obtained, it became clear the county hadn't even vetted Anything Helps, with one county staffer admitting to Mathias, "we do not have information about your organization's structure."

Slowly, the encampment was eventually cleared, with some residents accepting shelter at a homeless motel, and others refusing and simply moving to a different part of the city. That the drama unfolded the way it did was hardly a surprise to parents at the school, one of which decided to pull his kids out and move to another city. Protecting the homeless, even over innocent children, was commonplace. And it comes from a position that sweeps don't work. But they do.

The Carrot-and-Stick Approach to Homelessness

Cities that take a carrot-and-stick approach to the homeless have seen consistent results. More often than not, the homeless reject shelter, arguing they're disinterested in following rules or being separated from a spouse for the night. While it's certainly a position you and I might take, we're not living on the streets in desperate need of intervention. Perhaps living in Seattle has hardened me after seeing an anti-sweep policy at work, but there must be consequences to living on the streets, particularly for the ones who show no interest in changing. If they're unwilling to take us up on our offers, then we should stop offering sympathy. Endless tolerance does them no good.

A 10-minute drive over Lake Washington takes you to Bellevue, a city where parks aren't held hostage by the homeless. Why is it that, even during the pandemic, homelessness never rose to a crisis in Bellevue? It's simple: They didn't allow it. The city's police department does not tolerate encampments. But they approach the issue with compassion, working with local nonprofits to find shelter space for those living outside. The homeless either accept the help, get hassled every night, or leave the city completely. Whichever path they chose, it's one that doesn't end in a children's playground taken over by the homeless.[506] This, of course, doesn't solve homelessness, but it does get them connected with services and puts them on the right path.

When Democrats allow the homeless to roam the streets at night, living where they want, with no consequences, they're putting their residents and other homeless people at risk. One Portland-area homeless drug addict rocked the area and shocked the country.

Koryn Kraemer, a 25-year-old from Georgia, moved to Oregon in 2022. A former college goalkeeper for Oberlin College's soccer team, he was described as sweet and pleasant, but then things changed. Kraemer was renting a room in a home when the homeowner said he started mumbling to himself. Then he trashed the place and was summarily evicted.[507] He apparently spent several months living on the street, consumed by drugs. Early one morning, around 2:15 a.m., Kraemer reportedly attacked a 78-year-old homeless man on a light rail station platform in the suburb of Gresham.

A 911 dispatcher informed first responders: "A caller says the suspect is still on top of the victim and there's people standing around, not reacting to this... think he might be biting him, now." It turned out to be far worse than biting. Kraemer allegedly chewed off the victim's face and ear. "Police say that one patient's face is half chewed off, it appears," one dispatcher says. Another notes, "Our victim is most likely going to be a trauma injury, severe head trauma, possible fractured skull, missing one ear, at least."[508] First responders said the face-mastication was so damaging that they could see the victim's skull.

When police arrived, Kraemer actually thanked them for coming to *his* rescue. Police say he told them that the victim was a robot trying to kill him. Prosecutors say Kraemer confessed to spitting out the "flesh of the victim that he had consumed." Unsurprisingly, prosecutors report drugs and alcohol were involved, alleging Kraemer consumed alcohol, cannabis, and fentanyl pills prior to the attack.[509] It also took a while for police to identify Kraemer. He told them his name was "El Baker." In a sheer bit of irony that so painfully highlights the homeless crisis, the victim was identified as Gary Wayne Krussow. He was also a homeless man, battling drug addiction, and recently evicted from a house he was living in. Krussow previously served time for sex crimes involving a child.[510] These are the people taking over cities because the Radical Left allows them.

The Radical Left touts their laissez-faire approach as a way to offer the homeless dignity, rather than infantilizing them or burdening them with rules when they already live hardened lives. But sleeping outside in filth, without running water or electricity, near rat-infested trash heaps, is not dignified. There is a better way. In Albuquerque, New Mexico, they developed a plan that helped: Give the homeless jobs. Then-mayor Richard Berry, a Republican, had a novel concept. He actually listened to the homeless.

"There was a gentleman with a sign that says, 'will work,' so I came back to the office and told my staff, we're going to take these folks up on their offer," Mayor Berry said in 2015.[511] "Instead of being punitive and giving someone a ticket for standing on the corner panhandling, why don't we give them a better opportunity?"

That's exactly what he did, launching the "There's a Better Way" program. Along with a nonprofit, program officials drove around the city in a van, offering capable homeless people a job to pick up litter for $9 an hour. Men and women who felt lost, without any purpose or structure in their lives, found themselves experiencing what most do when cashing our first paycheck. We felt proud of ourselves. We accomplished something. We had purpose. You can never beat the feeling when you get that first paycheck. It's a great motivator, for most. And for the scores of homeless who didn't have that feeling in years, it inspired them to get their lives back in order. "I got to put some money in my pocket and I helped to clean up the community, it's a good feeling," a homeless worker told a local television station.[512]

When Mayor Berry left office, replaced by Democrat Tim Keller, the program lost its main cheerleader, and it earned the scrutiny of the city's inspector general.[513] An audit found it was not living up to its potential, inconsistently picking up workers and not doing enough to find new homeless people to participate. In 2017, it ended. But the concept works and should be one part of the approach to end homelessness. But not every homeless person can handle a job. The ones debilitated by addiction or mental illness need something more substantial.

Studies have shown that permanent supportive housing does not lead to better health outcomes for the homeless.[514] One reason is that the wraparound services, when offered, are not required. And in some cases, drug use is enabled or encouraged. And if someone is mentally ill, in many states, you can't merely commit them to treatment either due to laws, a lack of known family members, or a lack of viable treatment options.

Taking Control of the Streets

New York City mayor Eric Adams realized that if the city is capable of providing treatment, it might have to get aggressive in order to fill the beds. He announced in early December 2022 that he was empowering first responders to take a more liberal view of the involuntary commitment law.[515] City staff were previously working under the belief that you could only take such measures when an individual poses an imminent threat to themselves or others due to their mental illness. But Adams clarified that if they cannot meet their own "basic human rights," they are subject to commitment.

The idea received the blowback you'd expect from the Radical Left. "Mayor Adams continues to get it wrong when it comes to his reliance on ineffective surveillance, policing, and involuntary transport and treatment of people with mental illness," Coalition for the Homeless policy director Jacquelyn Simone said in a statement.[516] "Homeless people are more likely to be the victims of crimes than the perpetrators, but Mayor Adams has continually scapegoated homeless people and others with mental illness as violent." Some activists called this traumatic, while others said it violates a homeless person's civil rights.

California governor Gavin Newsom championed a similar approach in 2022, though it was focused on homeless suffering from psychotic disorders such as schizophrenia. Under the Community Assistance, Recovery, and Empowerment Act, judges can order individuals into intensive treatment if they're deemed unable to survive on their own while homeless and demonstrated that it would be the least restrictive path to recovery. They would be given legal counsel and case managers and helped to navigate a year-long treatment plan. Though it was "vehemently" opposed by the American Civil Liberties Union, which consistently fights to keep the homeless on the streets, Newsom pushed it through anyway.[517]

Much like the movement to normalize drug addiction that

claims it's stigmatizing to judge an addict's behavior, there's an equally dangerous push to suggest the mentally ill are not dangers to society and rarely commit violent crime. This assertion is a lie. Researchers have concluded that schizophrenics, for example, are "4 to 7 times more likely to commit violent crimes, such as assault and homicide, and 4 to 6 times more likely to exhibit general aggressive behavior, such as verbal and physical threats, compared with the general population."[518]

Like they do with addicts, the Radical Left tells this lie in an effort to keep the mentally ill from feeling stigmatized. But I'm not sure the mentally ill homeless, so far into their illness that they can't function and living in the bowels of a city, care about or recognize stigma. Nevertheless, they have the Radical Left serving as publicists trying to sell us on the idea that they pose no threat, so we won't force them into treatment. The Radical Left won't settle for anything short of permanently subsidized housing for the homeless.

Whatcha Gonna Do When the Word Police Come for You?

The Radical Left loathes the cops, yet paradoxically they love to word-police. They have been most successful in persuading media members to use different terms to characterize the homeless in an effort to slant coverage toward housing. They tell us to call the homeless "unhoused" or "individuals experiencing homelessness" (a wordy way to say "homeless"). There are more words and phrases for the homeless than effective programs to keep them off the streets.

The wokescolds on the Radical Left insist it's dehumanizing to use the term "homeless." It's not living around human waste and used needles that is damaging, but the term "homeless" that we ought to focus on. The Radical Left doesn't actually offer a coherent reason that saying "homeless" is "dehumanizing," though they try. Some argue the term "homeless" cannot be separated from a "toxic narrative" that blamed the homeless for crime and garbage littering our streets. They *are*, however, directly responsible for much of it.

Eve Garrow is a homelessness policy analyst at the ACLU of Southern California. "We've seen this before, words like transient or hobo are retired and no longer acceptable to use," Garrow told *Architectural Digest.*[519] "Homeless has become intertwined with narratives that are toxic. It deserves to be retired."

The rhetoric around the name change doesn't match reality. Unhoused.org, a "social impact startup," claims that the term "has derogatory connotations. It implies that one is 'less than,' and it undermines self-esteem and progressive change." The homeless are, in fact, "less than" the housed when they're living in filth and suffering. It's why we have a moral obligation to help; so they're treated like their lives matter as much as anyone else's.

The word "policing" is meant to push society toward a left-wing view of the issue. If we talk like the Left, we'll be more apt to do as they ask. Plus, changing words is so much easier than changing the reality of homelessness. It was an effective strategy, particularly since journalists are disproportionately liberal. And when you control the language, you can control the argument and narrative.

The Associated Press updated its stylebook in 2020 with the changes, making it clear that they take language cues from the Radical Left. "Homeless is generally acceptable as an adjective to describe people without a fixed residence. Avoid the dehumanizing collective noun the homeless, instead using constructions like homeless people, people without housing or people without homes," the AP declared.[520]

It was part of their effort to move toward what they call *person-first language*, with which they avoid centering a label around one's identity, because it doesn't say anything specific about who the person really is. It's an ironic reason, given the AP and most media outlets are hyperfocused on gender, religious, and racial identity. But calling someone "homeless" is one step too far? If the Radical

Left spent this much time actually tackling homelessness, perhaps they'd see more success.

Incentives, Accountability, Community, Results

It's obvious that Democrat policies are not helping the homeless; quite the opposite. According to HUD, four of the five states with the largest increases in sheltered homeless (those counted in shelters, transitional housing, and other temporary settings) from 2019 to 2021 were run by Democrats.[521] That implies those who are in temporary housing are not only staying in it, but the population is growing. This is the result of strategies that do not enforce rules or laws.

As children, we got dessert if we ate our vegetables. If we put in the hours to hit a stretch goal, we get a bonus at work. If you're attentive, caring, let your spouse pick the movie, throw in a foot rub every so often, you'll get a little extra treat after date night (and it doesn't even have to be your birthday!). Democrats seem to forget a basic truth of human nature: Incentives almost always work. And the programs that incentivize the homeless to be better see life-changing results, including self-sufficiency that a traditional housing-first model doesn't provide.

Community First! Village in Austin, Texas, is a residential community for the chronically homeless, run by Mobile Loaves and Fish, a faith-based organization. Its expansive campus stretches across 51 acres with micro-homes and RV homes, a culinary program and art house, gardens, and a community market. The roughly 460 residents are part of a community where every member strives to keep one another accountable. This is not a place to slack off or shoot up. There are rules, including no drug possession, no lawbreaking, a requirement to pay rent coming from federal or state benefits, along with a job you can hold on or off site. "You must pay rent, and do you know that we don't have a rent collection problem, and never have? Because everybody knows that they must pay rent," Community First! Village CEO Alan Graham said.[522] "When you pay rent, it turns out that you're invested. You have skin in the game. And every human needs to have skin in the game, and that's what is lacking out there on the streets."

In 2021, the residents earned a combined $1.2 million dollars through their jobs initiative.[523] In the culinary program, they can serve up homestyle meals at the Goodness Grill. If they're more creative, they can create products like ceramic mugs, jewelry, or paintings at the Community Art House that they can sell online or on site.

The volunteers at Community First! Village believe that "housing alone will never solve homelessness, but community will." They are right. Their community members have seen dramatic reductions in drug and alcohol use, with addicts getting the community support they need to stay sober.

The city of Marysville is a short drive north of Seattle, nestling the banks of the Snohomish River. Republican mayor Jon Nehring saw the city's homeless population not just growing in size, but growing in stubbornness, choosing to ignore requests to remove their encampments. Mayor Nehring then instituted a policy that proved to be effective. He instructed his police to offer the homeless two options: They either accept the help that's being offered, or they'll be arrested for whichever law they're breaking at the time (illegally camping or public drug use was the norm). The mayor and police officers preferred the homeless take the help, which they're happy to provide.

"Help means an initial assessment, and then a drug detox, or a substance abuse detox," Nehring told me when he first implemented the program in 2018.[524] "After that, a 30- to 60-day long term rehabilitation program. And then if they graduate from that, they move into transitional housing and job training, hopefully ultimately get a job, and be at least somewhat—if not fully—self-sufficient."

Nehring started to see results by December of that year, with 40 men and women not just entering but actually completing detox programs, 19 graduating from a long-term treatment program, and 37 securing housing. An added bonus was seeing a 20 percent decrease in crime that year. A few years later, despite the pandemic when other cities were allowing the homeless to take over their neighborhoods, Nehring kept his program in place and shared encouraging data with me. In 2021, 85 out of 87 homeless people completed their substance abuse treatment program, and all 30 were treated through a mental health assessment. The city was even able to secure housing for the 57 who requested it.[525]

It's Time to End the Homeless Industrial Complex

Covering the homeless crisis in Seattle and the greater metro area, I could not help but notice the same players and organizations are constantly awarded government grants to tackle an issue that's gotten worse under their watch. Yet, they keep getting larger budgets and government contracts. And they set themselves up to always excuse their failures.

In King County, Washington, a county-wide agency tasked with tackling homelessness had the temerity in January 2023 to demand nearly $12 billion dollars to solve homelessness. Its leadership said without those investments, which would be primarily spent on housing, homelessness would not improve.[526] Marc Dones, who headed the King County Regional Homelessness Authority, knew this request would never come to fruition. So why ask? It's a built-in excuse. When pressed why homelessness isn't improving, the simple retort is: "You didn't fulfil our budget request."

When programs are implemented by the homeless industrial complex, the homeless are promised a room or studio, but not a life to live free from an all-consuming health issue and a reliance on handouts. How do they get a job when they're high or mentally ill? Housing first, without rules or treatment, means the homeless never address what pushed them onto the streets in the first place. But it does mean the people in charge of the programs have job security. They're incentivized *not* to fix the problem.

Solutions are complex, time-consuming, and expensive. But a housing-first model that does not require those who need treatment to receive it will fail if the goal is to get people treatment and to a place of self-sufficiency. A study out of Ottawa, Canada, *Housing First for Adults with Problematic Substance Use*, compared homeless "with problematic substance use" in a two-year housing-first program versus those who had access to standard care sans a housing program. The addicts put in housing stayed there. But the ones without the housing-first program had both a greater decrease in drug use and improvements in mental health by 24 months. And not only did they report a greater increase in general quality of life, but they had better relationships with family members, a key role in getting off the streets and finding a true support structure. The decrease in drug use undoubtedly contributed to this. Most shockingly, at 24 months, those in the housing-first program reported *less* satisfaction with living conditions than their comparison group.[527]

Advocates argue that if you force services on the homeless, they will not stay in shelter or housing programs and return to the street. They're right, in some cases. But that's why cities must enforce laws, ensuring that camping in public or public drug use is not permitted. And permissive drug laws must be reversed for this to work. Concurrently, it's integral to stem the flow of illegal drugs crossing our borders and flooding our streets. If there's the choice between going into a structured program, with rules that include treatment for those who need it, and being harassed daily for living on the streets, the homeless will either accept a city or county's offer of help, succumbing to the relentless pressure to do so, or they will leave the city altogether. If neighboring cities take the same approach, the homeless will have few options. In the end, though, a constant push into services will eventually work, even for the most stubborn. Will it take time? Absolutely. But these are human beings and lost souls. It's worth it.

CHAPTER 7

THE SALT LAKE CITY MYTH

But Look at What *They* Did!

The Radical Left views Salt Lake City, Utah, as an inspiration, commonly citing the city as a success story for the housing-first model. Implemented under Democrat mayors since 2005, city leaders said they were able to cut the chronically homeless by roughly 90 percent between 2005 and 2015.[528] Though they were only dealing with about 2,000 people at the time, the city's approach was portrayed as proof that the housing-first model could work. All city leaders had to do was provide free housing to addicts and the mentally ill! If only it were that easy.

In the early 2000s, officials and residents in Salt Lake City noticed an increase in homelessness. It exploded into a crisis after the city hosted the XIX Olympics Winter Games. Desperate people from around the state and country came to Salt Lake in search of a job, attracted by the promise of brand-new facilities being built and others being upgraded. Park City, located just to the east of

Salt Lake, was undergoing development to be turned into a plaza featuring food stalls, concerts, and more.

With $1.9 billion poured into planning and hosting the games, local, state, and federal officials were under immense pressure to make the Olympics an achievement.

The host city bidding process had been marred by allegations of bribery and malfeasance, and with the whole world watching, officials were determined to make the games a success. A job explosion by 35,000 statewide was promised, and people came to fill the vacancies.[529]

The Olympics created more jobs, though nowhere near what was expected—only somewhere between 4,000 and 7,000, primarily in the leisure industry. Cesar Jimenez left Denver, Colorado, to get work in Salt Lake. The best he could find was shoveling snow, even with a background as a machinist. But at some point, the snow stopped falling, and his job proved ephemeral.[530] One year after the games, there was virtually no overall effect on employment in the city.[531] And those who were already broke and jobless before the Olympics found themselves without an income, back in the same position they were before they traveled to Utah. Jimenez ended up on the streets, living on a Skid Row near the railroad tracks downtown. There were plenty of similar stories, and the city needed to act.

The city turned an abandoned mattress factory into a makeshift emergency shelter that could handle 450 people. But it was not a pleasant place to stay. It was crowded, and it smelled. Drunken homeless would get into fights, the toilets overflowed, there was no hot water, and theft was common. "It's my first time homeless or in a shelter, and it's so messed up," Jimenez told the *New York Times*. Making matters worse for the homeless was the city was not especially hospitable, earning the dubious distinction of being named one of the 10 meanest cities to be homeless, since panhandling was illegal. The crisis worsened after the Olympic athletes and media left, and the city was forced into more substantial action over the next several years. And with the support of the Church of Jesus

Christ of Latter-day Saints (LDS), the city committed to a 10-year plan to end homelessness in 2005.

The city started with a pilot program in 2004,[532] with the 17 most problematic chronically homeless people they could find. These were men and women who were living outside for a year or more, were frequently using pricey emergency services, were suffering from addictions or mental illness, and were consistently spending time in jail. These people were given housing and case managers and were taught how to live again. After a year, city officials were pleased with the results. Of the 17 program participants, 14 were still in their homes. Three were dead. But it was a big enough success that the city deemed it time to scale up.

City leaders, nonprofit groups, and LDS volunteers worked to house as many homeless as they could, with the focus first on the chronically homeless. Officials identified available housing options and matched individual homeless people with the best housing situation for their specific needs. They also began to build units, a commitment that would continue over the next 10 years. But its residents weren't required to be clean or sober, nor have any mental health issue treated prior to the free housing. This required patience—and funding. When Bill Alkire lost his wife in 2000, he told the *San Francisco Chronicle* that he "crawled into a bottle, and didn't look back..." until he landed an apartment in one of the many housing units reserved for people like him. But recovery wasn't easy. He spent years in the housing continuing to drink but said persistent counseling offered by the city was finally successful. The cost to run the city's housing-first model? At the time, the cost was about $40 million, with half of the funding coming from donations from the LDS Church and other nonprofits.[533]

City leaders were ready to declare the housing-first model a triumph by 2015. Gordon Walker, then the director of the state Housing and Community Development Division, announced the state was "approaching a functional zero" on the chronically homeless. The news received national attention.

The *Washington Post* touted housing first as a "surprisingly simple way" to solve chronic homelessness.[534] A *San Francisco Chronicle* reporter said his hometown could learn a lot from Salt Lake. The initiative even earned the attention of *The Daily Show with Jon Stewart*, which could explain why so many younger activists heard about what a midsize city in a deeply conservative state was up to in the first place.

The Daily Show package featured the man who led the housing-first efforts, Lloyd Pendleton.[535] The program's biggest cheerleader, he proudly touted the city's success. "We did it by giving homes to homeless people. We gave homes to the homeless. Yes, it's simple. You give them housing, and you end homelessness," he said. As was typical of *The Daily Show*, it picked Fox News and FOX Business anchors and personalities to be the villains, splicing in clips of them observing the costs to simply house the homeless forever as both prohibitively high, but unreasonable, arguing it would disincentivize the homeless from working. But Pendleton pointed out it was much cheaper to give the homeless housing than it was to keep them on the streets—roughly $12,000 versus $20,000.

The housing-first model proved to be a big win for the city and the state, earning fawning press and inspiring city leaders and activists from across the country to fully embrace the housing-first model. It was a pivotal moment for the housing strategy, providing hope that it could finally solve the homelessness crisis. But the victory was declared way too soon. In fact, it was more like a failure.

After Victory, Homelessness Got Worse. Way Worse.

Inspired by the positive press, cities and activists nationwide adopted and celebrated the approach. No one appeared to follow up on how things were going in Salt Lake. To those who were paying close attention at the time, there were some red flags in declaring homelessness nearly solved. City leaders were focused on the *chronically homeless*, but media claimed that all *homelessness* was solved. That was hardly the case. And the way locals declared the program a success was dubious, at best. They saw keeping people in subsidized housing, not treating the underlying cause of the homelessness to begin with, as a win.

One year after declaring victory, homelessness was getting worse, not better. The state's largest homeless shelter, Road Home in Salt Lake, was always at capacity, with over 1,000 men, women, and children packed into tight quarters, triple bunks, or even on yoga mats lined up on the floor. The *Guardian* reported that some of the occupants spent more than 3,000 nights at the shelter. Was homelessness solved? Should they have declared victory? Should the media have offered such fanfare, reprinting press releases as stories? Glenn Bailey, executive director of a food pantry and thrift store called Crossroads, said, "Making a statement like that was in direct contrast to what you see on the street. It's an exaggeration. It wasn't helpful...since the recession, the largest single part of the homeless population that's grown is families with children, and youth."[536]

Homelessness has grown steadily across the state since 2016. In Salt Lake City, it's grown each year between 2018 and 2022, and those increases were seen across all housing categories (unsheltered, shelters, and transitional housing). The number of unsheltered in 2022 was twice that of 2018. And the category that Salt Lake lauded as its biggest success—chronic homeless—increased every year since 2015, representing 27 percent of the total homeless population in 2022, with those experiencing substance abuse or mental illness seeing only a slight one-year decline from its peak in 2021.[537] And the city's subsidized housing wasn't keeping up with demand, building only 600 new units by 2020.[538]

Not only did the crisis worsen, but the 2015 data showed that a 90 percent decline in chronically homeless was disingenuous, thanks to changes in reporting methodology. The *Salt Lake Tribune* noted that when state officials tallied the chronically homeless in 2005 for the Point in Time report, the city "used a multiplier to estimate the number of chronically homeless individuals across the entire year." The actual one-night count was 615, but the city estimated 1,932. In 2015, the city achieved their 90 percent drop in homelessness by comparing their estimate to a standalone one-night count. Had they compared apples to apples, the drop would have been 71 percent. That's still an achievement (if you define success by keeping people in subsidized housing without a guarantee that they've been treated), but a far cry from "approaching functional zero."[539]

In Come the Calvary of Activists

Desperate to get the crisis under control as homeless-driven crime ticked up and encampments started to proliferate in downtown, Salt Lake officials eventually turned to police operations and sweeps in 2017. The quality of life deteriorated thanks to violence and open drug use, particularly in and around the Rio Grande district in downtown, forcing then-governor Gary Herbert and the state legislature to convene a special legislative session.[540]

In one high-profile crime in the Rio Grande district, police said a homeless man attacked a minor league AAA baseball player in an attempted robbery near the city's largest homeless shelter. When the player didn't hand over his wallet, the homeless man reportedly hit the player over the head with a tire iron, slicing through his scalp. He suffered a concussion and required staples.[541] It was getting so bad, then-Utah house speaker Greg Hughes suggested, "you can have a discussion about the National Guard with a straight face."[542]

Operation Rio Grande, led by the Salt Lake City police in partnership with city agencies between 2017 and 2019, was a three-part enforcement initiative to address ongoing public safety issues that were driven, in large part, by or because of the homeless population. Democrat mayor Jackie Biskupski ordered Rio Grande Street temporarily closed to pedestrians and vehicles. It's where a large homeless population assembled because that's where services are provided. Then, the police went in.

There were over 1,000 arrests during the first month of the operation, many of them of drug dealers or users.[543] Most were misdemeanor arrests, with 676 released due to jail overcrowding or posting bail. "Everything we have learned after years of trying to deal with these problems tells us that we cannot arrest our way out of this problem," newly elected Salt Lake County mayor Ben McAdams said at the time. "The short-term gain of locking nonviolent people up brings long-term pain, as the fallout from arresting people and jailing individuals plays out in our community."

At the city jail, social workers and lawyers helped identify which arrestees would be eligible for a newly launched specialty drug court that allows addicts to go into treatment, instead of into jail with a permanent stain on their criminal record. With 618 of the arrestees accepting treatment, the city needed to ramp up its detox services. The plan was to open 256 new beds for treatment in various transitional housing locations around the city.

But not everyone was immediately put into treatment. And not everyone who was breaking the law was arrested. Soon, neighboring communities complained of spillover, with encampments popping up on their sidewalks. "We're seeing a lot more people just camping out now," said a 20-year homeowner about two miles away from Rio Grande Road. "A lot (of homeless tents) in the parks over here at Madsen Park and Jordan River Parkway." He told a local news station that he's never seen homelessness get so bad. "It's a little concerning because they're (the city and the state) moving them out of downtown, but they are just ending up over here. There are a lot of needles around, a lot of human waste bags. There are people camping on the overpass, and they're just throwing bags of waste down there. My dog got one the other day, and I'm like 'drop it drop it!"[544]

Some of the homeless from Salt Lake ventured all the way down to St. George, in southern Utah. "From a law enforcement stand point, what kind of individuals do we have coming to into the community? We have no idea what their criminal history is,"

Washington County sheriff Cory Pulsipher complained. Switchpoint, the city's only homeless shelter at the time, was frequently at capacity. Its director said they were not prepared for the influx of homeless from the north, and both locals and law enforcement were worried that with the homeless, crime would follow, particularly drug-related. "There's a whole culture that comes with it. Quite honestly, we want to do everything we can to help them get out of that culture, but we also have a duty to protect the residents that live here," Pulsipher said.[545]

Phase three of Operation Rio Grande was intended to connect those who finished treatment with jobs. It only connected 246 with work because phase two was failing. The vast majority of the operation budget was spent on the police, jails, and courts, with only 18 percent going toward substance abuse and mental health treatment, plus shelter and housing.[546] Why the imbalance? Because crime in the area was bad enough to require the funds be spent that way. City leaders also ran into the same problem other Democrat-run cities experienced when offering a more permissive approach to the homeless: Only 150 people agreed to the drug court program, despite making thousands of arrests by the end of the two-year operation.[547]

The operation faced fierce opposition from local activists screeching the same platitudes you'd hear in San Francisco, Seattle, New York, or Austin. They complained of criminalizing the homeless when the police were merely criminalizing criminals like drug dealers.

"Being homeless is not a crime, yet thousands of individuals living in or frequenting the Rio Grande neighborhood were detained, jailed and released with no additional help and the added burden of warrants, fines and a criminal record," the ACLU of Utah wrote in an eight-page report, a year into the effort, complaining that police "dominated" the operation. It complained that some arrested were for "active warrants," as if we're supposed to see that as a negative.[548] At the end of the two-year operation, the ACLU of Utah remained critical. They posited that the "aftershocks [of Operation Rio Grande] will continue to shape efforts to address the social issues involving homelessness in Salt Lake City. That's because the impact of arrests and fines do not easily vanish from people's list of troubles—especially those with limited resources—but reverberate, often derailing their efforts to rebuild their lives."[549]

Even when the city turned to sweeps without arrests, the activist class still complained. The homeless set up an unsanctioned encampment called Camp Hope, under an overpass on the west side of the city. It housed up to 200 people at one point, with rows of tents, trash strewn about, misery everywhere you looked. Before the sweeps, police or social workers offered the homeless resources, including shelter space, but people like Shawna Gardner declined.[550]

Gardner had been living on the streets for four years when the *Salt Lake Tribune* featured her in a story in 2020. She was the victim of domestic violence, one of the leading causes of homelessness among women. She found herself living at Camp Hope and was contacted by the city with offers of assistance. She said no to the shelter space because, according to the *Tribune*, "she doesn't like groups and has a hard time getting along with other women. Last time she was in a shelter, she thought some of the women were unsafe to be around."[551] It's stories like this that allow left-wing activists to form a narrative around the cruelty of sweeps, presenting women like Gardner as victims of an inhumane process that removes her from her home. But what is the city supposed to do when generous offers of help are routinely declined by irrational homeless who would rather sleep outside, vulnerable to both the elements and criminals, than go into shelter? If they leave her outside and she dies, which is an inevitability for every homeless left outside to suffer, the city is criticized for not doing enough. If they don't sweep, crime continues to soar, the quality of life for taxpayers continues to deteriorate, and the city is criticized too.

Activist Tyeise Bellamy with the Black Lives for Humanity

Movement emerged as a leader in the sweep resistance, in between demonizing cops as part of the greater Black Lives Matter movement. "I think their responsibility now is to realize that what they've done repeatedly has not worked," she told a local radio station.[552] "None of these abatements have been successful. And so their responsibility is to try something new." The city started working with her to help connect the homeless with services. But she was working against them, effectively helping shepherd the homeless to different encampments, warning them ahead of sweeps to collect their belongings and flee to a new location to set up camp. By doing that, she prevented the city's rapid intervention team from making another contact to bring folks indoors.[553] Bellamy hoped to create enough of a groundswell that residents would stand in the way of sweeps with her. She would post videos from sweeps claiming that the city was bulldozing people's homes (but it was mostly trash left over from the homeless).[554] At one point, she was sleeping at Camp Hope to help prevent future sweeps.[555]

Despite Bellamy's actions, Camp Hope was eventually cleared. But other encampments popped up, including Fort Pioneer, which became the city's largest unsanctioned encampment with between 150 and 200 occupants in 2022. A resident at the site for about four months, Stacey Johnson said it earned the moniker because "we're the pioneers of the unsheltered. We're the pioneers of change. And besides, I wanted to give Utah a little thrill."[556] These pioneers were chronically homeless, some drug addicts, and others with active arrest warrants.

Businesses Bear the Brunt

When COVID-19 hit, businesses were mostly shut down. The central business district saw most of its employees working remotely. By the end of 2022, when the pandemic was over, the area had 54 percent fewer office workers than it did pre-pandemic, with businesses continuing to adopt the work-from-home model. With a less activated area, the homeless easily took over. But they grew increasingly aggressive, forcing business owners who were in the area to organize and protect themselves, their staffs, and their customers.

Because their sidewalks and storefronts were occupied by the homeless, customers weren't coming in. The timing was especially difficult to cope with, given businesses were still trying to dig out of the COVID-19 economic hole foisted upon them thanks to pandemic shutdowns. Teresa Bowman had run Mid City Salon for 24 years by the end of the pandemic. She said the downtown area had "gotten really bad" with the homeless "constantly harassing us." She and her employees regularly cleaned up human waste, drug paraphernalia, and trash around the business. She didn't know how she was supposed to operate a business under those conditions, and she wasn't alone. "What I'm hearing from a lot of customers is they're getting aggressive. It's almost where people are scared to come now," Brett Delbridge, co-owner of Vape on Main, told a local news station. He said he's "seen numerous fights. I've seen people just getting assaulted. And it's just crazy—and it's just absolutely crazy how it's gotten to be out of control."[557]

Police say a homeless man robbed two banks, one in Salt Lake, threatening employees with "viral viruses" while demanding they give him money. Murphy James Hollie was reportedly wearing a medical mask when he entered the banks, handing tellers a note reading, "I have two small vials of viral problems," before demanding the money from the till. When he returned to one of the banks he allegedly targeted, police were called and able to make an arrest. In his backpack, they say they found a note that read in part, "I demand money" while claiming to have two "viral viruses" he pulled from a lab he claimed to have worked in.[558]

Southam Gallery Fine Art was located downtown for over 40 years, until the homeless crisis pushed them out. The mother-daughter co-owners were so bothered and concerned that they were willing to take on a space that cost them double the rent, with less foot traffic. But at least they wouldn't have to deal with homeless people camped out in the doorways and their customers would no longer be harassed by aggressive panhandlers. The owners would no longer have to pick up human feces or mop urine outside their door. They would no longer be trapped inside as a "crazy" homeless man terrorized them outside, nor would they face a middle-of-the-night alarm after a homeless man broke their shop window.[559] The art gallery wasn't the only business to ditch the area.

LatterDay Bride, which operated different locations in downtown since 2001, chose to leave the area altogether in summer 2022. The owner Nicole Thomas volunteered to help the homeless, and wanted to be a part of keeping the community safe and vibrant, but the amount of crime and homelessness was overwhelming. "I started noticing that I was developing some anxiety with it, and when we would get a yeller, that would walk by," Thomas told a local television station.[560] "We had something happen sometimes weekly. Sometimes we'd get three months, it wasn't a matter of if it would happen again. It was when will it happen again." She and her staff faced a number of challenges, including an employee suffering a concussion and bruised chest after being assaulted by a homeless family high on drugs. After one in the group promised to come back and burn the store down, Thomas was forced to hire armed security. Still, she lost employees who didn't feel safe. Then, in 2021, when a man who was wanted for sexual assault took refuge from police in her store, threatening employees and customers while disrobing, she made the agonizing decision to leave.

"I just decided at that moment that the definition of insanity is doing the same thing over and expecting a different result," said Nichole. "I woke up that next morning and I started looking at what my options would be to leave the downtown area."

The only thing that was helpful when dealing with the homeless was the weather. When it was cold, they generally stayed away. When it was warm, bookstore owner Ken Sanders says the problem was "out of control." He told UtahStories.com that, after 26 years, he contemplated closing his store and only selling online.[561]

Businesses near homeless shelters also saw a rise in crime and threatening behavior. Those who believe the Radical Left's claims that there's no correlation between homelessness and crime may seem surprised. In the Ballpark district, home to both the minor league baseball team and Gail R. Miller Homeless Resource Center, business owners had been under siege. Fights broke out frequently, with a machete-wielding mentally ill woman terrorizing the community. Robberies were common, and drug dealing and use was out in the open. One business owner installed eight security cameras to help catch anyone who broke in or caused problems around the shop.[562] The *Salt Lake Tribune* noted that violent crime soared in 2021, exceeding the neighborhood's three- and five-year averages.

Is This What Success Looks Like?

Salt Lake City found out the hard way that homelessness cannot be solved merely by housing people living outdoors. That's not how this works. On paper, sure, I suppose it makes sense. The problem is literally in the name, home*less*. But without addressing why they're homeless, their destructive behaviors continue. And, despite claims to the contrary, when you offer up free housing, it attracts more homeless. The same is true of permissive policies. If the homeless do not think they'll be hassled in a neighborhood, they will inhabit it.

Why did the city's initial drug diversion strategy fail in the Rio Grande Operation? Why do people say no to services? For the same reason they mostly fail everywhere else. The homeless are allowed to say no, while receiving little to no meaningful legal consequences when doing so.

A large portion of the homeless population are chronically homeless and have lost hope. Others choose not to change their lives. The programs offered only work for a small subsection of homeless who actually want to turn their lives around. The rest? They're seemingly content to waste their potential by living on the streets. It's not entirely their fault, of course. When you've lost hope, the idea of another government-run program or nonprofit initiative seems futile to entertain; they don't think they can be helped, which ironically keeps them from getting help. They've been failed before, they have little trust, and they just don't think it's worth their time to participate. You must be aggressive with these people.

The city's sweeps were ineffective because they were too slow to be implemented, and they allowed the homeless to move somewhere else for weeks or months at a time. And rather than distance itself from that approach, there's a city-wide push to create sanctioned encampments designated for the homeless to camp legally, park broken-down RVs or cars, and be connected with portable restrooms, cleaning stations, trash removal, and security. Council member Alejandro Puy, who took office in 2022, almost immediately endorsed the idea of "legalized camping grounds," suggesting the locations could be in church parking lots. Puy's newly elected colleague Victoria Petro-Eschler called the current situation chaotic, arguing, "We need to contain this and say this is where you're allowed to be." To her credit, Mayor Erin Mendenhall had offered an unequivocal no.[563]

That the idea is even seriously discussed shows you how far Salt Lake is from a solution. Rather than embrace ideas that work—housing contingent on treatment, rules, and small amounts of rent, with an end goal of releasing them from the grips of government handouts—we're seeing more of the same failed policies introduced and often implemented. And these failures are being ignored by other cities that are still pretending Salt Lake's housing-first model was a success to be replicated.

CHAPTER 8

FREE MONEY

Flirting with Universal Basic Income

Officials in Palm Springs, California, led by the city's first transgender mayor, were determined to offer a scheme giving transgender and nonbinary residents up to $900 a month for two years. They'd be able to spend the money however they want, a move meant to help low-income and homeless transgender locals get out of poverty. At the time, when I covered this program on *Tucker Carlson Tonight*, I declared it the nation's "wokest guaranteed income scheme."[564] But months later, leaders in San Francisco said, "Here, hold my beer!" and executed their own version.

If you identify as an aggressive, demiboy, woman of trans experience, San Francisco is eager to give you $1,200 a month, for up to 18 months, without any strings attached. The Guaranteed Income for Trans People (GIFT) program was announced in November 2022 by Mayor London Breed as part of its equity movement to help marginalized communities, no matter how small. Under the pilot program, 55 severely low-income (under $600 a month) transgender San Franciscans would be given funding to help "promote economic stability and recovery."[565] Given the income eligibility requirements, the program is mostly for the homeless transgender community. It even comes with access to "gender affirming medical and mental health care," along with case management and financial coaching.

"Even with our rich history of trans advocacy, we see that trans San Franciscans experience poverty at exponentially higher rates compared to the general population," said identity-obsessed Pau Crego, executive director of the San Francisco Office of Transgender Initiatives.[566] "This is especially the case for trans people of color, disabled trans people, trans elders, and other trans communities."

When the GIFT application was released, it went viral. It included 95 separate options under gender identity. It included the ones most people have heard of, such as "transgender woman/man" and "nonbinary." But it also included identities even members of the LGBT community had never heard of (I asked!): demiboy, sistergirl, feminine-of-center, multi-gender, xenogender, maverique, ninauposkitzipxpe, and gender outlaw. I couldn't even find some of the identities easily explained on Google when I was researching the story for a *Tucker Carlson Tonight* appearance. The list for sexual orientation was equally as absurd (if not offensive), including f—got, skoliosexual, BDSM/king, and other descriptors that are not really sexual orientations.[567]

The application read like a parody of how the Radical Left views gender and sexual orientation. But it wasn't a joke. And it was the epitome of how far the Radical Left has shifted the way our cities are run. They are obsessed with identity and enjoy playing intersectional politics. It's a perfect distinction between your average Democrat, who offers acknowledgment and respect for gender minorities, and the Radical Left, who demands you match their obsession with your own obsession. They try to find the most marginalized identity possible (many times wholly contrived for political purposes) to prove how "evolved" they are on the issues, whereas your average Democrat just wants to be thoughtful or polite. The reality is that there's literally no such thing as a skoliosexual nonbinary genderqueer. Is that supposed to be an attraction to people with crooked spines who pretend not to have a gender? It's an invention of the Radical Left. But it's the perfect identity for some gender radical with narcissist personality disorder to pretend to hold.

Much like the transgender people these programs seek to help, the program only *identifies* as a good idea. In reality, it's a more exclusive version of a socialist scheme to redistribute wealth called Guaranteed Income (or Universal Basic Income).

A Pretty Basic, Universal Scam

Radical Left mayors and wealthy Democrat donors created and funded Mayors for a Guaranteed Income as a way to tackle "income inequality," a somewhat nebulous term. Income inequality implies there's some kind of purposefully designed system that keeps people poor when personal habits and skill level play a significant role. But advocates believe guaranteed income is a "policy antidote to poverty and rising wealth and income inequality."[568]

The idea generally works like this: Select residents who meet specified criteria are given direct, monthly cash payments for between one and two years to spend how they see fit. The money is usually distributed on debit cards because not everyone who qualifies will have a bank account (some are extremely low income, and others are homeless). The idea is that allowing the recipients to spend money how they want will lift the stresses holding them back. They could use it on their rent, giving them extra money to spend on education to better themselves for a higher paying job. They could spend it on food so they don't have to choose between a car payment to get to work and feeding a family. They could even spend it on a much-needed medical procedure so they're not sidelined in the future by a health issue that keeps them from earning a paycheck.

As of January 1, 2023, there were 103 cities that have either shown interest in the concept or have actually started (or are about to start) a pilot program. They include large cities and small, from Atlanta, Newark, and Los Angeles to Tacoma, Washington; Evanston, Illinois; and Lansing, Michigan.

The first mayor-led guaranteed income program came out of Stockton, California, championed by then-mayor Michael Tubbs, a Democrat, in 2017. Called the Stockton Economic Empowerment Demonstration (SEED), the city randomly selected 125 qualifying residents to receive $500 per month for two years. This program's mere existence was reason enough for proponents to deem it a success. The whole point was to give people free money so their lives could be a little bit easier; thus, no matter what they spent it on, it would *always* be declared a success. In other words, these programs are designed to be lauded the second free money is distributed. That way, all the collective research can be used to justify expanding the program.

In Stockton, the city tracked how the money was spent and conducted interviews with participants. The program's own researchers, unsurprisingly, raved about the results. They said recipients were "less anxious and depressed, both over time and compared to the control group." But is this a meaningful result? They were giving people $500 a month with no strings attached. Who wouldn't feel less anxious and depressed about their financial situation with an extra $500? The research said the money was primarily spent on food at 36.92 percent, followed by sales/merchandise at 22.70 percent (this represented stores like Target, Walmart, and Costco; thus, researchers concluded this likely included money spent on food), utility bills at 11.34 percent, and vehicle maintenance at 8.77 percent. Though the program often uses the cost of healthcare and education as a reason to implement guaranteed income, the percentage that Stockton recipients used it on these was only 3.06 percent and 0.83 percent, respectively.[569]

Though there was hardly a causal relationship established, researchers claimed the $500 a month was leveraged to find full-time jobs by roughly 12 percent versus a 5 percent increase in full-time employment in the control group (though the control group started out by having more people employed at 32 percent than the guaranteed income group at 28 percent). Researchers argued the extra funds "enabled shifts in employment by giving recipients the emotional and financial capacity for risk taking." This was all enough for Tubbs to tell MSNBC, "Let's scream that from the mountaintops. The $500 allowed people to be entrepreneurial and bet on themselves."[570]

Left-wing media ate it up. Vox celebrated the stereotype-smashing research, noting that "Stockton's experiment shows what $500 per month in 'free money' can do for employment, mental health, and more."[571] A business columnist for the *Los Angeles Times* sang the program's praises, saying Stockton showed "the time has come for universal basic income."[572] Who knew a two-year program with only 125 recipients could be enough to inspire an entire country to take up the model? *RawStory* argued the program "blows up objections from conservative naysayers."[573]

Flawed Research by Design?

There's little doubt that $500 can help people, particularly if they're low income. But the research declaring victory was deeply flawed and woefully incomplete, in part because it was always meant as propaganda to be amplified by the left-wing press. But the data makes it hard to tell whether or not the program is worth the cost to adopt nationwide.

While the researchers and advocates celebrated how the money was spent, they were looking at extremely incomplete data. Researchers admit that roughly 40 percent of the money spent was not tracked because recipients either cashed it or transferred it to a bank account. They said this was due to "rational financial behavior" and their "prior experiences in the market and prior strategies for avoiding risk while managing household needs."[574] SEED could have created a rule to spend the money only via the debit card delivered to recipients, given the research is supposed to be of paramount importance, but they chose not to.

SEED saw an impressive 12 percent jump in employment, but there are severe limitations in interpreting the data.

First, the report doesn't say what kind of jobs they took, nor does it compare the length of time they spent searching for work prior to the study versus the control group. Did they all start looking at the same time? What industries were they looking in? How many of them had part time work (or gig economy jobs) as they were putting themselves through school? The control group had 5 percent more parents, 5 percent more black participants, and 6 percent fewer Asian participants, 15 percent more renters, and it was on average five years younger than the guaranteed income group. Couldn't at least some of this data play a role in who found jobs?

Second, the researchers concluded that the $500 a month allows for more risk-taking when looking for work. Not having to worry as much about finances allowed recipients, for example, to create more audacious employment goals or quit one job for an internship that could land them a higher income down the line. Fair enough. But do behaviors really change when participants know the free money will come to an end? We don't know the answer based on this study. Two years is far too short for meaningful data on behavioral changes.

The study's flaws did not matter to proponents. The point of the study was to promote heartwarming anecdotes about a single dad who used the money to buy a birthday cake for his kid, or a mom who was able to spend more time with her family instead of working extra hours for that $500 extra a month that could put food on the table. It was just enough to earn the guaranteed income movement some momentum. Though it wasn't enough to keep Tubbs in office. He was replaced by a Republican as the program was underway.

There Was Never Data to Back This Up

Guaranteed income has been described by Democrats as a promising tool to help tackle poverty. But to make that claim, you'd have to ignore mountains of data from a country that actually committed to honestly studying the program.

Finland was interested in the concept to both improve quality of life and the employment rate. The program was designed to encourage Finns to take on temporary or even low-paying jobs without the fear of losing benefits. Those jobs could ultimately lead to full-time, sustainable employment.

The country-backed program was open to a group of 2,000 unemployed Finns between the ages of 25 and 58. They received €560 (roughly $633 at the time) a month for two years starting in 2017, to be spent how they saw fit. They would continue to receive the payments even if they found full-time employment while enrolled.

The pilot program came with the same kinds of anecdotes we saw in Stockton. Juha Jarvinen called himself an "anarchist" father of six when he was featured on *Vice News*.[575] He was one of the 2,000 selected for the program. He says he put the money to good use, focused on starting up one of his many business ideas, like producing Shaman drums to sell online or to tourists. He complained that on government unemployment, the restrictions prevented him from focusing his time on his passions. He said the monthly, unconditional income "made it possible to create my own business. Before I needed to focus for what [the] employment office wants and now I can focus on what I want to do." He said, addressing concerns it could disincentivize people from looking for work, that €560 is not that much money, "so it doesn't make people just chill out or stay in their couches." As a frequent traveler to Europe, including Finland, I can attest that €560 doesn't go nearly as far as you might think. But neither does the guaranteed income scheme.

At the end of the pilot, the results were clear. There was no significant effect on the employment rate of the program participants and poverty was not reduced. The free money led to just six days of increased employment over a one-year period. Participants did say the money helped them make ends meet and made them happier, but that wasn't the point of the pilot, and we know that free money will generally make life easier and the beneficiaries happier.[576]

The experiment failed. And even if the goal was to make citizens happier, it would likely fail there too, with the added consequence of disincentivizing the very work you'd need to expand the tax base to fund such a program. In order to implement the program nationwide, in 2017 it would have required a significant tax raise, which would likely make people unhappy, especially since that tax raise would likely have led to fewer workers.

Ilkka Kaukoranta, chief economist at the Central Organization of Finnish Trade Unions, told *Vice* there's no easy way to fund the benefits without a massive tax hike against the workers. "If you pay everyone enough to live upon, that means that people don't have to work, which means that many would quite rationally, choose to work less." He said that if the pilot program's exact parameters were adopted nationwide, it would increase the budget deficit by 5 percent of the gross domestic product (GDP). He said a "more realistic scheme would involve a much higher rate of taxation to fund the benefits. And a higher rate of taxation means lower incentives to work."[577]

None of this mattered to Democrat-run cities that rushed to adopt the income scheme.

The city of Tacoma, Washington, a 40-minute drive south of Seattle, ended its one-year pilot in 2022, and before a report of the data was released, local media and the program's advocates declared it a success. Recipients were mostly single parents earning just enough to disqualify them from public assistance but not enough to comfortably get by. The $500 a month, the program's leaders said, was primarily spent on retail services, groceries, and utilities. The $6,000 over the year undoubtedly helped the families deal with Democrat-caused inflation that made the basics more difficult to pay for throughout the Biden administration. Advocates also framed the story around feel-good anecdotes about quality of life improving, with parents taking their kids to a Mariners game or a roller-skating rink. With that kind of image of success, who can say no to expanding the program?[578]

Guaranteed income transformed into a reparations programs in Oakland, California, when Democrat mayor Libby Schaaf announced her vision of a city "that has closed the racial wealth gap and where all families thrive. We believe that guaranteed income is the most transformative policy that can achieve this vision." In other words, the money was distributed on the basis of race. Whiteness renders Oakland residents unworthy of financial assistance because even acknowledging that whites can be poor would make it more difficult for the Radical Left to pound the "white privilege" drum. Indeed, the program's website claims that "wealth inequities [are] rooted in ongoing systemic racism" and says this idea dates back to the Black Panther Party.[579]

"There are huge gaps between people of color and our white residents. With the limited resources of this pilot, we would like to understand better how we can understand these disparities as well as address overall poverty," Schaaf told the *Washington Post*.[580]

These programs are primarily funded by private dollars donated by wealthy advocates for the program, like Twitter founder Jack Dorsey, who donated $18 million to Mayors for a Guaranteed Income.[581] He tweeted that he hoped the pilots "inform federal policy in the future." That's exactly the goal.

COVID-19 Unemployment Benefits Crippled the Economy

The federal government, along with state governments, effectively shut down most of the economy in early 2020 after the emergence of the COVID-19 virus. At the time, there was no vaccine, therapeutics, or much data on who it impacted and how bad an infection could be. The US economy lost a staggering 22 million jobs between February and April 2020.[582] Americans were hurting, and they were scared. But as weeks turned to months, the data became clearer: The virus had the greatest impact on the elderly and the severely immunocompromised, and for the rest of us, it was much like the flu. Kids were barely harmed by COVID. Yet, recalcitrant Democrat lawmakers were unwilling to move from their positions. The economy would stay shut down.

With bipartisan support, Congress passed the Coronavirus Aid, Relief, and Economic Security Act (CARES) on March 27, 2020. It was a $2.2 trillion stimulus bill meant to mitigate the economic effects of the pandemic and Democrat shutdown policies. It offered $1,200 direct payments to most adults and tax rebates for families, extended unemployment benefits, placed a 120-day moratorium on tenant evictions and mortgage foreclosures, funded the Paycheck Protection Program (PPP) to give businesses funds to keep their employees on the payroll, and deferred student loan payments. Eligible residents saw an enhanced benefit of $600 extra a month via Federal Pandemic Unemployment Compensation. Some people, like independent contractors and gig economy workers, received extra funds via Pandemic Unemployment Assistance.

Democrats weren't done spending. They passed the American Rescue Plan Act (ARPA) on March 10, 2021, which did not earn a single Republican vote in the House or Senate. It offered direct payments of $1,400 to most Americans, increased the federal minimum wage to $15 an hour, extended unemployment benefits for months, and offered rental and mortgage assistance to those falling behind.

While Democrats went on a spending spree, unwilling to foresee the inevitable inflation crisis it would create, local governments also introduced a number of policies or laws that they claimed were about helping residents get through the pandemic, but became more about offering handouts. The Radical Left, wherever they could, created programs driven by ideology, with a goal of making the public dependent on the government. Los Angeles County passed an eviction moratorium, allowing renters to be delinquent on their rent.[583] Boston opened up its unemployment insurance to gig workers, like Uber drivers.[584] The Seattle City Council handed out COVID relief dollars to illegal immigrants, no strings attached.[585]

CARES and ARPA were designed to keep people comfortable while out of the workforce. Local policies made it even easier, giving residents extra benefits while telling them they didn't have to pay rent. Most Americans took full advantage. Many of them didn't want to go back to work.

The National Bureau of Economic Research reviewed whether or not pandemic benefits reduced unemployment. They compared the 18 states that opted out of the Federal Pandemic Unemployment Compensation program in June 2021, three months earlier than the official September cutoff. It found that early-to-cut-off states saw 14.4 percent more 25- to 54-year-old unemployed workers finding jobs in July and August, compared to the unemployment benefit long haulers in other states. Moreover, the research found that "direct cash payments from various government programs, along with less opportunity to spend money due to social distancing measures, lead to substantially increased household savings."[586] It's obviously beneficial to save, but households were using the savings to stay out of the workforce longer. That explains why, throughout 2021, we saw high unemployment rates *and* high job openings.

Why was a New York dairy farmer, speaking with the *Daily Signal*, struggling to find workers, even though he offered $22 an hour? The unemployed told him that the unemployment benefits were worth more to them.[587] Why were restaurants and hotels struggling to find workers, especially since their industry was hit the hardest by COVID-19? The average worker in leisure and hospitality made $13.45 an hour, less than what they'd make being unemployed. Analysis by Noah Williams, director of the

Center for Research on the Wisconsin Economy at the University of Wisconsin–Madison, suggested roughly 40 percent of all American workers could earn more while on unemployment. Some saw more than *double* their pre-COVID-19 salaries. Workers in Maine and New Mexico would benefit the most. And that $600 boost provided for them the average American's full wage.[588]

Democrats (and some Republicans on the local level) paid Americans to stay unemployed during COVID. But we're supposed to believe that a guaranteed income scheme wouldn't have at least *some* negative impact on employment?

Some guaranteed income proponents argue that their idea will become reality out of necessity. The rise of machines and automation will put Americans out of work, and we'll need to do something to help sustain them. While their solution may be unserious, the concern is valid.

$15 Now! Unemployment Soon!

Seattle was home to the $15 Now movement, thanks to expert organizing by Socialist Alternative, a dues-paying members-only club committed to installing socialist policies in cities nationwide. Their leader is council member Kshama Sawant. Under her guidance, Seattle was one of the first large cities to adopt a mandatory $15 an hour minimum wage, up from the then $9.32 per hour requirement.

When Sawant was elected to office in 2013, representing the city's young, activist, and most Radical Left district, she was known as a firebrand. She'd characterize her targets with broad brushes, decrying all corporations as evil and greedy and all Democrats as bought and paid for. She said the working class was getting hosed by aforementioned corporations and Democrats. She was especially effective in courting young voters and activists who she convinced were victims of a capitalist system that doesn't value them.

Sawant's first major target was aircraft industry behemoth Boeing, a company that helped establish Washington State as an economic powerhouse. But in 2013, it would not commit to building 777X aircraft in Everett, where it operates the world's largest manufacturing plant. The company was looking for tax incentives to stay, but Democrat lawmakers were dragging their collective feet. There was growing concern that Boeing was not giving enough back to the state (as if half its workforce living in Washington, at the time, wasn't enough). With over 10,000 new jobs on the line, the state ultimately offered incentives to stay. But the union members had other plans, rejecting a contract that would have frozen their pensions. Boeing then started looking for a new home for the 777X.[589]

Hoping to court the company's machinists, with the ultimate goal of luring them to join Socialist Alternative to build the movement's war chest, Sawant declared war on Boeing. At a rally with workers and activists six days after the union rejected the contract extension, Sawant shouted, "The workers should take over the factories, and shut down Boeing's profit-making machine!" She said if Boeing took the 777X production to another state, it would be "nothing short of economic terrorism because it's going to devastate the state's economy."[590] Though she loathes corporations, she wanted Boeing to stay, though not under its then structure. She wanted workers to *literally* take "democratic ownership" of the factory.

"The only response we can have if Boeing executives do not agree to keep the plant here is for the machinists to say the machines are here, the workers are here, we will do the job, we don't need the executives. The executives don't do the work, the machinists do," she said.[591]

Sawant, a former Occupy activist and part-time community college economics instructor, doesn't know much about business or Boeing. That became clear when she told a local television station that under democratic ownership, "we can re-tool the machines to produce mass transit, like buses, instead of destructive, you know, war machines."[592] After city-wide media mockery, she turned to something much more in her wheelhouse, so-called workers' rights. And she was on a mission to pass a minimum wage hike in the city of Seattle.

To further establish credibility, Sawant vowed to only take a salary of $40,000 a year, the average workers' salary at the time. She said she would donate the remaining $117,000 to social justice causes. Local and national media loved the stunt along with the community. "This is not a question of charity," she told *New York Magazine*. "You simply cannot be so far removed from the values of the people you're representing."[593] Few journalists seemed interested to learn that she was reportedly funneling the "donations" to her own group, Socialist Alternative, which paid for her travel to push $15 Now nationwide.[594] They bought into the promise of $15 Now, she was a media star, and they served as her publicist.

Sawant led marches and strikes. She bullied opponents as corporate stooges. She partnered with like-minded, influential locals like Seattle venture capitalist Nick Hanauer (who was paying his workers around $9 an hour at the time he was demanding much smaller businesses pay $15).[595] She set her sights on chains like McDonald's, claiming they can easily afford a minimum wage hike, even though there were hardly any within city limits. The minimum wage was going to hit small businesses the hardest, but she rarely differentiated between them and corporations. McDonald's, Amazon, and Starbucks were demonized the same as a family-owned bakery, an independent book store, and a local coffee shop. Still, fast-food workers walked out of the job, demanding higher wages despite working "starter jobs" that require few skills, and it put pressure on government leaders to act.

Sensing the issue would lead to political clout, then-mayor Ed Murray swooped in and appointed a minimum wage advisory committee, tasking them to come up with a proposal to raise the minimum wage to $15. That's exactly what they did. And it went into effect April 1, 2015.

Large employers, defined as having over 501 employees worldwide, would pay $11 an hour, then $15 an hour by 2017. Small employers, with fewer than 500 employees, would slowly up the wage to $15 by 2019 (or 2021 if the employee receives tips). For 2022 through 2024, the wage would increase based on the consumer price index.

The plan had the support of the mayor and eight city council members. However, Sawant was not a fan. She argued it didn't go far enough and made too many concessions to business, such as not immediately implementing the hike. "We are not playing games here. Our work is far from done."[596]

This left-wing policy, propelled by the Radical Left, impacted businesses mostly the way critics warned, even as the city was experiencing an economic boom. It even made life harder for the very people it was supposed to help. Some businesses and nonprofits reported their employees asked for fewer hours soon after the minimum wage hike took effect. Full Life Care, which provides support for adults with chronic illnesses and physical or development disabilities, explained that five employees asked to reduce their hours in order to remain eligible for subsidized housing.[597] For other workers, they had no say in the matter; their employers cut their hours.

According to a study in the *American Economic Journal*, University of Washington (UW) researchers found "significant reductions in hours, particularly for less experienced workers." In fact, the average low-wage worker *lost* about $125 per month per job. While this helped employers avoid layoffs, it forced some employees to quit. Concurrently, new low-wage jobs were added at a slower pace. Indeed, the study found that "higher wages appear to deliver bigger paychecks to incumbent workers who earn low wages with limited upward mobility, but they also appear to curtail opportunities for new labor market entrants." This makes sense, of course. A number of business owners told me that if they're being forced to pay entry-level jobs a higher wage, they'll cease hiring at entry level, add more responsibilities, pay a bit more, and attract a higher caliber of applicants.[598] This hurt the low-skilled workers struggling to live in pricey Seattle the most.

Employment for low-wage earners became hard to come by, devastating young and immigrant workers with few skills and seniors who weren't able to leave the workforce due to cost-of-living concerns. Somewhat ironically, businesses paying higher wages signaled to landlords that they could get away with raising rents without impacting demand. What the Democrat council failed to consider was Amazon and other large corporations headquartered in Seattle were feeling the economic boom at the time, allowing them to pay their already high-salaried employees a bit more. And they were eating up the local rental supply, pushing the low-skilled workers, who couldn't find a job due to the minimum wage hike, farther out of the city.

At the time, Mayor Murray was unhappy with the findings from the UW researchers, which he had access to before its publication. The mayor contacted Michael Reich, an economics professor at the University of California at Berkley, asking him to provide a critique of the research and to publish his own observations. A week prior to the release of UW study, Reich reported his own results, which were, of course, glowing. Reich is an economist who epitomizes the Radical Left. He helped create the Union for Radical Political Economics, an anti-capitalist organization that embraces socialism. Unsurprisingly, he and his team were known to collaborate with labor unions to push a minimum wage.[599]

Emails revealed that the mayor's office imposed a deadline for Reich to finalize and publish his study before the UW researchers were scheduled to release their results.[600] The mayor's team even asked Reich to remove any reference to the UW study, emailing him, "Don't want your positive news to serve as a teaser for the UW study."[601] It was all a well-coordinated scam that led to positive coverage in the *New York Times* and the Associated Press. The mayor commissioned a study to downplay the effects of the minimum wage hike because he needed a political victory, even if it hurt the workers he said he wanted to help.[602] The city could have used the data to inform better policy moving forward, but instead, they ignored it.

Other cities followed suit and raised their minimum wage under a similar phased-in approach. New York City upped wages to $15 an hour for fast-food workers in 2015 and everyone else by December 2018. In 2022 and 2023, Los Angelinos saw a hike to $16.04, Portlanders to $15.45, and Minneapolitans to $15.19. Democrat-led cities are leading the way in paying workers more than they're worth, and the union interests pushing the legislation through were elated. This is where the unions underserve their members. These artificial hikes can only lead to fewer low-wage jobs, hurting lower-skilled Americans the most. Businesses are already reacting to the forced overpayment to employees by adopting automation.

Radical Left Hastened an Automated Future

Radical Lefties pushed businesses into automation much faster than the labor market would have otherwise engaged. By forcing businesses to pay employees much more than they're worth (respectfully, while I love my baristas, they're not worth $19 an hour when their jobs can be done by a Keurig), they incentivized decision makers to invest in technology to replace them. It's already putting people out of jobs.

Walk into a grocery market in Seattle, a movie theater in Los Angeles, or some sushi bar in New York, and you'll see self-checkout stands instead of clerks, automated kiosks instead of box office staff, and conveyor belts instead of waiters. Even before the minimum wage push, the American labor market was experiencing technology replacing jobs. So why wouldn't workers believe they'd be hastening their own demise by asking for so much more than they're worth?

Tipsy Robot on the Strip in Las Vegas replaced its bartenders with two robots that prepare up to 120 perfectly mixed and proportioned drinks per hour, with each cocktail taking somewhere between 60 and 90 seconds to make. Patrons enter their orders on an app, summoning two robotic arms to work. No more having to wave down a bartender who ends up hitting on your date. The only downside is the customer doesn't benefit from a heavy pour, but that's an upside to a business that gets to avoid throwing away potential profits.

McDonald's technology at a location in Fort Worth, Texas, is already threatening the jobs of fast-food workers—the very ones who organized job walkouts to demand more pay. It's a test concept that is almost entirely automated. Customers order on a kiosk inside the store or through an app and pick up their food at the drive thru. It was built to remove the human interaction from the experience.

Amazon has innovated automation technology in ways that will revolutionize grocery and retail, replacing workers along the way. Step into an Amazon Go, and it looks like the love child of a bodega and a Whole Foods. The signage is sleek and clean, the snacks upscale, with tasty food to go, while covering the basic grocery needs, such as meats and vegetables. Unlike your local Kroger, Publix, or Trader Joe's, there are no humans to interact with except, on occasion, the staffer who restocks shelves. It's completely cashier-less and cashless. You use your Amazon app or scan your palm for entry.

Through a sophisticated array of cameras and sensors, the Just Walk Out technology knows exactly what you take from the shelves and will charge you for it when you leave, using whatever credit card you have on file with Amazon. Change your mind and put your fried rice bowl or beef jerky back on the shelves, and you won't be charged. The first time I visited an Amazon Go, it felt like I was shoplifting, putting items directly in my bag like some of the homeless do at my local Target. I tried to trick the technology into charging me for items I'd put back on the shelves, but I failed each time. The technology is simply amazing. And it's being pitched to investors and business owners as a profitable way to run a business and deliver superior in-store experiences. Amazon directly sells the technology as able to "drive operational efficiencies" with improved "labor efficiency." And the technology is already expanding to third-party vendors, such as Lumen Field concessions in Seattle, Hudson shops in Dallas, TD Garden in Boston, and soon your local neighborhood grocery store.

The beauty of the technology is that businesses only pay for it once, don't need to worry about constant demands for more pay and fewer responsibilities, won't hear complaints about closing and opening a shop the next day, and will never have to worry about vacation or sick time (save the occasional technical upkeep). Democrats and their union allies continue to fail workers by ignoring the only thing they need to advance in the workforce: experience.

McDonald's workers make minimum wage *and will still be replaced* because the job they do requires very few skills. It used to be that these "starter jobs" were celebrated because they offered experience to those without any. They teach basic skills about running a cash register and interacting with customers. They help instill a work ethic, adopt a habit of showing up on time, and develop an ability to communicate on-the-job issues. They come with a modest paycheck not meant to sustain a family or an adult, but to teach you what you need to start a career. But a younger generation of workers, egged on by their so-called Democrat allies, developed a sense of entitlement where they should get what they want, where the boss works for them, and where the terms of employment are dictated by workers instead of management.

With the looming technological threats posing an existential threat to the labor industry, Democrats opted to pass legislation mandating how certain businesses should operate. Legislation even went as far as to tell businesses how to schedule employees.

San Francisco was the first city to pass a "predictive schedule" law, dubbed the Retail Workers Bill of Rights by the city's board of supervisors.[603] The Seattle City Council wasn't far behind, passing its own version called "secure scheduling" for large retailers and food-service workers.[604] Both laws are nearly identical.

Employers are required to give honest estimates of the hours an employee can expect to work, post work schedules a full two weeks in advance, offer at least 10 hours of time off between opening and closing shifts (known as "clopening"), and give available hours to existing part-time staff before making new hires. When employers make changes to schedules, they're expected to offer "predictability pay" of one hour of additional wages for every shift added after a schedule is posted. How in the world are you supposed to operate a restaurant, for example, under these conditions? A family-owned restaurant must tell staff two weeks in advance if they're needed, having no clue how busy they'll be. Seattle business owners told me that they simply under-staffed, cutting hours for employees who might have been needed, because they can't afford to pay employees on slow nights. And for the businesses that were able to successfully adapt, the COVID-19 pandemic changed everything. Restaurants or small grocery stores barely scraping by cut staff hours dramatically, or let staff go, unable to shoulder the burden of paying employees not to work because they predicted a shift incorrectly.

Inevitably, the Radical Left's coddling of American workers and interference with private businesses will push employers even closer to automating what they can. But no one is thinking this through, beyond a handful of futurists who support a pie-in-the-sky guaranteed income scheme. Though there's also a movement to give people free money that isn't part of a universal basic-income model.

The Tax Man Is Coming—But Only If You're White

Don Hines owns Yazoo BBQ in downtown Denver. With the encouragement of his father, Hines opened the restaurant with no previous industry experience. He just had passion and it paid off, earning rave reviews for the succulent, slow-cooked ribs and brisket. It was a hit, though Hines' father would never see it. He passed away two months before opening. Hines promised his father, on his death bed, that he wouldn't fail and he never looked back.[605]

Hines did his father proud, but soon the COVID-19 pandemic hit and the business barely survived. But, Yazoo kept delivering delicious meals and they were able to make it out of the pandemic—only to be hit by Denver's growing crime and homelessness crisis, while seeing his taxes balloon from $16,000 to $36,000 a year for a restaurant under 4,000 square feet. Hines was struggling.

On May 1, 2023, Hines stood in front of the Denver City Council and broke down in tears as he asked for help. "My customers are being harassed for food and money inside and outside my building every single day," he told the Council.[606] "Public urination and bowel movements of a disgusting degree during business hours and after hours. Strung out individuals totally out of control in and outside of the building. Destruction of property...graffiti of business vehicles and buildings. Vehicles broken into."

As he finished listing the issues facing his business and community, emotions took over. He didn't bother to hold back tears, or the whimper in his voice. He couldn't if he wanted to. Hines couldn't help but think of his father, on his death bed, and the vow he made to keep this restaurant a success.

"And I'm going to close with this. Dad: I'm doing my best but I'm going to fail because people aren't doing anything to help the little guy. And dad, I'm sorry," he said, looking down, before turning back to the Council to ask them to, "Please do y'alls job. Help the little guy. Thank you and have a good day because I definitely am not. It's a struggle."

A local news channel picked up the story the next day, featuring Hines' dilemma. The reporter reached out to Hines' councilmember, Candi CdeBaca. Judging by her statement, the councilmember didn't just understand his plight, but was ready to help.

"Mr. Hines's story is important and shows how much we need multi-pronged efforts to get him property tax relief, housing for the people living outside of his business, and infrastructure changes to improve the safety, lighting, and pedestrian access to his business," she said.

Finally, help could be on the way! If only Hines wasn't white.

CdeBaca made waves when elected in 2019 as a Democrat Socialist. During her re-election campaign in May, she outed herself as a racist who wasn't interested in helping Hines because of the color of his skin.

Days after Hines shared his story, CdeBaca attended a Greater Metro Denver Ministerial Alliance forum where she decried capitalism as being "built on stolen land, stolen labors, and stolen resources." She argued that she would use business improvement districts (BID), which are privately taxed but publicly sanctioned districts that provide supplemental services to help businesses, to install race-based taxes on white-owned businesses.

"I think there's a model that could be redistributive," she told the audience.[607] "Instead of a BID collecting extra taxation from the black and brown businesses that are struggling, you could be collecting those extra taxes from white-led businesses all over the city and redistributing them to black and brown owned businesses, who are not part of it, or are simply just black or brown owned. And that's one way to give back in the business fashion."

Though she argued the BID "steals from the community through taxation," she had no problem siccing it on white people. It didn't matter that Hines was struggling, thanks in large part to far-left policies CdeBaca supports. He was undeserving of help beause of his skin color. We used to call that kind of attitude racist. But in 2023, the Radical Left defined it as woke.

Reparations for Stephen Curry and LeBron James

"Despite now being nearly 160 years away from the Emancipation Proclamation, the vestiges of chattel slavery in the United States deeply and directly continue to have a harmful effect on the current era's social, economic, health, academic, legal, and cultural experiences and outcomes of Black and African American people in San Francisco," read a draft San Francisco Reparations Plan compiled by the San Francisco African American Reparations Advisory Committee.

California was never a slave state. Yet a group comprised of the Radical Left declared, "California and its localities meaningfully enforced and upheld slavery by perpetuating the racial caste system of subjugating Black Americans from the freedoms assured to them by the Declaration of Independence." The black San Francisco population was irreparably harmed by historical white supremacy, and they wanted their pound of flesh in the form of $5 million dollars in reparations for every eligible black resident over 18 years old, and a guarantee of $97,000 income for every low-income black resident over the next 250 years.

"A lump sum payment would compensate the affected population... and will redress the economic and opportunity losses that Black San Franciscans have endured, collectively, as the result of both intentional decisions and unintended harms perpetuated by City policy," the report said. But it also proposed wiping out all educational, personal, and credit card debt for black households. The proposal would cost roughly $100 billion, in a city with a $14 billion dollar budget and a $728 million deficit. Anyone who suffered through their 60-page draft has a more convincing argument that they're owed $5 million than black Americans.[608]

The only thing more humorous than the report, filled with historical hyperbole, are the Democrat lawmakers who were forced to take it seriously for fear of being labeled a sell-out to the progressive cause. And some in local media seemed eager to egg them on, with the *San Francisco Chronicle's* Justin Phillips writing, "What happens next will show whether San Francisco politicians are serious about confronting the city's checkered past, or are simply pretending to be."[609] The board of supervisors president Aaron Peskin told Phillips that he hopes the recommendations are approved. "There are so many efforts that result in incredible reports that just end up gathering dust on a shelf," Peskin said, presumably with a straight face. "We cannot let this be one of them."

It's not just San Francisco considering reparations. State-appointed members of a California reparations taskforce released a 500-page report (that lawmakers pretended to read) on the state's racist history, initially arguing black residents who lived in the state between 1933 and 1977 are owed hundreds of thousands of dollars due to historically racist policies.[610] Less than a year later, the amount owed ballooned to up to $1.2 million. "Reparations are not only morally justifiable, but they have the potential to address long-standing racial disparities and inequalities," Rep. Barbara Lee (D-California) claimed.[611] St. Louis mayor Tishaura Jones established a reparations committee to review how best to restore injustices from "slavery, segregation, and racism."[612] Until they conjure up their recommendations, the mayor signed a bill allowing progressives suffering from white guilt to voluntarily donate to a reparations fund to help "reverse generational wrongs."[613] Shelby County, Tennessee, which includes Memphis, lifted $5 million of federal COVID-19 relief dollars to allocate toward a feasibility study to offer reparations to descendants of slaves.[614]

One stain the Black Lives Matter (BLM) movement left on this country was instilling a belief for some black Americans that they're somehow owed payment for the historical sins of a country they never knew or experienced. But BLM adherents believe the country is founded on white supremacy; thus, black Americans can't escape the oppression responsible for any and all individual failures. Does no one see the absurdity in forcing Americans who were never slave owners to turn over tax dollars to Americans who were never slaves? And does no one see the racial resentment this can cause?

According to a Pew Research poll, a full 77 percent of black Americans support reparations for descendants of enslaved people. Only 18 percent of whites hold that same position. The results are equally stark when you break it down by ideology, with 48 percent of Democrats supporting some repayment versus 91 percent of Republicans saying absolutely not. But that's expected; it's an idea from the Radical Left, so Democrats will, of course, be more supportive. It's the age breakdown that is most curious. An astonishing 45 percent of adults under 30 support reparations, whereas only 18 percent of those 65 and older support it.[615] In other words, the generation *farthest away from slavery*, who grew up during a time of tiptoeing around racial issues to avoid the Twitter mob from canceling their careers, feel they're owed more than an older generation of Americans who likely did experience virulent racism.

Demanding reparations makes one a victim, and victimhood is quite powerful. It explains why the movement appears to be growing among younger Americans. But why does that generation feel entitled? It's what they were taught.

CHAPTER 9

INDOCTRINATION NATION

Teaching Your Kids to Hate (in the Name of Tolerance)

When parents sent their teens to 10th grade English class at Somers High School in Somers, New York, there was likely a basic expectation that they'd get a better understanding of how to craft a tight essay thesis, build supporting arguments with effective rhetorical devices, and deliver a conclusion that packs an unforgettable punch. Instead, they were taught that all whites are racist.[616]

Allison Ferrier passed out an assignment based on the book *Me and White Supremacy*, which promises to teach whites how to "dismantle the privilege within themselves so that they can stop (often unconsciously) inflicting damage on people of color, and in turn, help other white people do better too." Students were offered journaling prompts including, "How does your white fragility show up in conversations about race?" and "Have you ever weaponized your fragility against people of color?" That these statements essentially calling every kid a racist were posed as questions can almost be forgiven as parody. This can't be serious, can it? Oh, but it was.

Students and parents were rightly angered, complaining to the district's superintendent who immediately stepped in to cancel the lesson. Ferrier, who is white, was removed from the classroom for several days due to the controversy. She did, however, have her supporters with an overwhelmingly white group of mothers who love the idea of being woke on the issue of race. They have no shame in telling you of their so-called privilege. They won't actually give up any privilege because all they hope to do is earn social currency among other white mothers who proudly watch the *Reid Out* on MSNBC in some masochistic exercise in self-loathing.

After the Black Lives Matter (BLM) movement grew to prominence, an older generation of white progressives jumped at the chance to play White Savior, while simultaneously embracing the notion that they're inherently racist. The good news was they were taught they can fix historical and contemporaneous wrongs by acknowledging their so-called bigotry and offering handouts to black Americans who, apparently, are all victims of a white supremacist culture that's responsible for any and all ills. While these white adults were growing in number, BLM adherents knew there are only so many adults to convert to their cause. It's hard to mold the psyches of Americans with a lifetime of experiences and common sense that reminds them this country isn't as evil as they're being told. But there is a group with malleable minds waiting to be convinced of America's ills: children.

Left-wing educators transformed our nation's classrooms into cauldrons of hate. In the name of left-wing tolerance, they scolded white students for privilege they don't have, shamed their white fragility if and when students or parents complained, and presented progressive analysis of historical events as objective fact. Schools and districts became obsessed with identities, which they used to generalize a swath of students, treating them differently solely on the basis of their skin color. And we were all supposed to pretend *this* wasn't virulently racist.

Remote learning, a by-product of nonsensical COVID-19

mitigation policies with a loose connection to science, hurt America's children. Student grades plummeted as fast as their mental health. After years of advice to avoid planting your kid in front of a computer screen so you can send them outside to socialize with their peers, districts planted kids in front of a computer screen for hours a day as teachers lazily instructed them from home. The only positive element to come from remote learning was for the first time, parents (who were also forced to work from home) were able to hear what was being taught to their kids. And it shocked many, sparking a nationwide movement against critical race theory (CRT).

CRT is an academic framework for analyzing the intersection of race and racism in our society and institutions. It asserts that race is a social construct created by whites to oppress blacks, and that racism (and white supremacy, a phrase that lost its meaning when progressives weaponized it to attack anyone who disagreed with them) is embedded in our very way of life, from legal systems to public policies. Along with new commitments to fostering an "anti-racist" culture, Radical Left educators labeled all whites as oppressors and all blacks as oppressed, while telling white children that they benefit from unseen privilege giving them a leg up on their black classmates and friends.

At first, the Radical Left pretended schools were not teaching through a CRT lens, claiming it's a post-graduate or law-school level course that is wholly unattached to K–12. NBC News declared CRT an "amorphous, catch-all term used by the conservative movement as fodder for political debate," and that we were simply castigating curriculum that included Maya Angelou's poetry.[617] CNN claimed Fox News "engineered the panic over CRT" as "the perfect tool for scaring White conservative voters with made-up problems—for mobilizing them against the racial awakening of the past year."[618] MSNBC's Nicole Wallace simply declared that CRT "isn't real."[619]

Next, the claim was that conservatives were objecting to

teaching basic facts about America's founding, which included curriculum on segregation, slavery, red lining, and Jim Crow. It was a disingenuous claim that I found myself debating on Fox News early on during the controversy. On June 6, 2021, I was on a panel with liberal analyst Richard Fowler, who argued that CRT isn't something students see until they get to graduate school and that CRT proponents are simply demanding that we be "educated about the truth in American history. Basically, we had slaves in this country, we treated them pretty terribly. There was a thing called Jim Crow, during Jim Crow, African Americans were lynched, they weren't allowed to vote, they weren't given their rights. We had a failed war on drugs that impacted black people badly. I don't understand what's wrong with teaching the truths about American history and what's so wrong about that when it's actually what happened in this country."[620]

I responded with a little snark, explaining we're already teaching everything he just mentioned. Was he claiming that students leave schools without ever hearing about slavery? I told him there's not a single history textbook that doesn't talk about slavery. But to claim that it's historical fact to label one side oppressors and the other oppressed, while saying all white people hold white supremacist views, is evil and wrong. Fowler responded by asking me to name a classroom teaching CRT. It just so happened I was putting the finishing touches on a story about a classroom doing just that.

When you send your kid to biology class, you probably don't expect a lesson on white privilege. But at Canyon Park Middle School in Bothell, Washington, just outside of Seattle, students were asked to select their identities and privileges so that they can "figure out ways to dismantle systems of oppression." A mother filmed the lesson plan and shared it with me.[621]

Students were shown *What Is Privilege?*, a video produced by BuzzFeed. Adults of various identities were given a series of prompts, like if they can "show affection for your romantic partner in public without fear of ridicule or violence," "If you have ever tried to change your speech or mannerisms to gain credibility," or "If you would never think twice about calling the police when trouble occurs." If they agreed with the statement, they'd step forward. If they disagreed, they'd step back. The farthest forward in the group, in this case a white man, the more privilege they had. The farthest back, in this case a black gay woman and a black gay man, had the least privilege. "Just looking back and seeing like a bunch of people behind you is not a good feeling," one white male participant said, hoping to guilt other white people into believing they have some unearned privilege.

The teacher then gave students a worksheet called "Wheel of Power/Privilege," of which students were told, "this really is a good visual of intersectionality." Students were asked to circle their identities, which included "white skin" and "dark skin." Some of the identities, the teacher explained, were "marginalized by systems of oppression" that her students should be "working to dismantle." What does this have to do with science? Nothing. It was a left-wing educator foisting CRT-inspired lessons on her captive audience.

One district in Washington State went so far as to tell its teachers to defend CRT, but deny it was being taught in the classroom. I obtained a series of Puyallup School District memos from a concerned teacher. The memo contained talking points where staff was told to "reframe the discussion by sharing the goals and efforts within your district to ensure every student has access to an equitable education and what they need to be successful." They were given advice on how to defend CRT, pretending it's "not centered on blaming individuals or making anyone feel guilty. It focuses on understanding how race plays a role in how institutions like education serve people." And it included an article by left-wing partisan Dr. Shayla Griffin of Justice Leaders Collaborative. In an article distributed to the staff, she complains that the "far right co-opted" CRT as a means of "tapping into the fears of white Americans that they will lose something if people of color are treated more fairly."[622]

With dozens of examples being exposed nationwide every week, it was getting more difficult for the Radical Left to pretend CRT wasn't infecting the classroom. Parents were quite literally hearing the CRT coursework being taught from the laptop speakers of their elementary, middle, and high school students in remote learning sessions from the kitchen counter or dining room table. And despite the most passionate claims that the controversy was contrived, conservatives were winning. And schools either got defensive, or dug in their heels.

Hating America 101

Student athletes at Eastlake High School in Sammamish, Washington, an upscale neighborhood east of Seattle, were scheduled to play a football game the day before September 11, 2021, the 20th anniversary of the terrorist attacks that forever changed this nation. Students hoped to use the game to promote national unity, opting to celebrate a Patriot's Day theme for the game for which students were asked to wear red, white, and blue. It was a sweet and meaningful gesture from students not old enough to have experienced 9/11 themselves, but wise enough to understand the day's importance. But the gesture was deemed problematic by school administrators.[623]

The principal of Eastlake worried that American flag colors might offend the opposing team because the school is majority-minority. He explained his reasoning in an email to a parent who complained that the theme was cancelled. "Our leadership teachers made this decision and explained it to students," then-principal Chris Bede wrote. "I know tomorrow is 9/11 and understand the sacrifice and values our flag represents, but I think they just did not want to unintentionally cause offense to some who see it differently." Who at the opposing school could possibly find this offensive? And if it's deemed offensive, isn't that their problem? The school district would not explain directly when I inquired. But the district spokesperson explained, "Since it was not a home game, there was no opportunity to have an announcement about Patriot's Day and to share why students were dressed in red, white, and blue." It seems the district is unaware of how phones or email work. Students reached out to me to express their anger about the decision. But when you consider the Radical Left's takeover of education, this story is less shocking.

Students are being taught to hate this country. It's an intentional strategy to ensure that young students grow up to become Radical Left activists who will continue the ideological push on drug legalization, housing as a human right, police reforms, and reparations. When you hate your home, it's much easier to dismantle what's been built. The notion that American patriotism could trigger another school is an indication that the anti-American indoctrination is working.

Rather than teach this country's founding was on the basis of freedom and liberty in 1776, Radical Left activist Nikole Hannah-Jones posits the country was founded on slavery in 1619. Her thoroughly debunked history curriculum, the 1619 Project, is expressly centered on the country being borne to protect and maintain slavery. It is a contrived history, driven by a political agenda and presented through a CRT lens. And it was introduced to over 4,500 schools nationwide.[624]

Chicago Public Schools is one district that adopted the 1619 Project as part of its official curriculum. Students are taught to question whether or not America really is the Land of the Free. They learn that slavery created and perpetuated structural racial inequality that exists to this day. Capitalism is villainized as being "built on the work of enslaved people," and introduced to students initially through the story of fraudster and so-called "pharma bro" Martin Shkreli, who bragged that he took a $13.50 lifesaving antiparasitic drug and charged $750 a pill.[625] The America the Radical Left depicts is not one most people would want to live in without significant changes.

Left-wing educators in five schools in the Bellevue, Washington, School District teach an elective course titled, "Race in the United States," as told through a CRT lens. Literally. Students are taught "themes of social construction of race, movements as a catalyst for change, culture inclusion, institutionalized racism, and equity and social justice policy," according to a course syllabus. In one district school, high schoolers read the book *Critical Race Theory (Third Edition): An Introduction.*[626] The course's teacher, Lukas Michener, did not hide his intent. Writing for the National Education Association (NEA), the social studies teacher admitted, "The idea that we are neutral actors is false. We are not. We have lots of power. We meet with young people every day, and we want to ensure there is a just and equitable educational experience for all of them." It sounds inspiring to claim one's striving for equity, until you realize what that means to them. Michener, for example, bragged that he helped bring Black Lives Matter in Schools Week of Action into the classroom.[627]

Black Lives Matter in Schools Week of Action was adopted nationwide, using the controversial group's curriculum across multiple classrooms during the first week in February in public and private schools. It was inspired by a Seattle-area school that adopted BLM principles during a week of activism. The NEA says the purpose of the week is "to spark an ongoing movement of critical reflection and honest conversation and impactful actions in school communities for people of all ages to engage with issues of racial justice."[628] This is code for indoctrinating children into radical views on race and racism. Each day of the week was divided into BLM principles that would be imparted to students.

Monday focused on "restorative justice, empathy and loving engagement." In Washington, DC, schools, that means teaching empathy on the basis that society "offers vastly greater or lesser amounts of privileges based on accidents of birth, and rewards exploitation with wealth and power."[629] In the DeKalb County School District in Georgia, left-wing educators chose Dr. Nicole

Prad-Jennings to speak to students on mental wellness in the black community. She was a questionable choice as an inspirational speaker at the time, seeing that months earlier, in October 2021, she was charged with a misdemeanor for "family violence."[630]

For Tuesday, the curriculum is centered around "diversity and globalism." Students in Seattle Public Schools saw how they are "privileged" within the "Black global family that exists across the world in different regions."[631] The Oakland, California, Aurora School asked children to go home and "audit your family bookshelf to see how well it represents the diversity of our world."[632] Students also learned to become anti-Semites. The BLM at School curriculum team recommends a lesson plan on "Black + Palestinian Solidarity" in which students are asked to sign a petition to "end US military aid to Israel" and told that "Black people must stand firm with Palestine."[633]

Though it's completely disconnected from what you traditionally hear about BLM, the Wednesday curriculum highlighted the principles "trans affirming, queer affirming, and collective value." Young students in Philadelphia read the book *My Princess Boy* about a transgender four-year-old.[634] Denver Public Schools told parents they were "not necessarily teaching kids what transgender means," but they'd be reading to them books like *Julian Is a Mermaid* to expose them to the concept, and then "talk about what they notice and wonder" about the transgender character.[635] Teaching for Change, an education nonprofit that offers teachers curriculum for the Week of Action, recommended educators introduce transgender and nonbinary characters to elementary students, teach them how to use preferred pronouns, and that biology doesn't always determine if someone is a boy or girl.[636]

On Thursday, the focus is on "intergenerational, black families, and black villages" and disrupting Western concepts of the nuclear family. For teachers using the BLM curriculum starter kit, they're told that "Black Villages is the disruption of Western nuclear family dynamics and a return to the 'collective village' that takes care of each other. Globalism is our ability to see how we are impacted or privileged within the Black global family that exists across the world in different regions."[637]

In Evanston, Illinois, a 20-year veteran teacher sued Evanston/Skokie School District 65 over lesson plans around this week of action. Stacy Deemar argued the curriculum asked her to teach that " 'black' families and villages are 'the best/proper way' to have a family, and it's important to return to a family structure that 'takes care of each other' in contrast to the 'Western nuclear family.' " The lawsuit described one lesson plan for third graders: "During our lesson on whiteness, we discussed how white culture shows up in the way that we think about family structures. There is a belief that a 'normal' family consists of a mom, dad, son, daughter, and pet. We've learned that this isn't true." Fourth graders, the lawsuit alleges, were taught that the idea of the nuclear family is an example of white supremacy. The goal, Deemar believes, was to destroy the concept of family. She was instructed to display African proverbs around the class in a not-so-subtle way to push the concept of a collectivist family. One saying included, "it takes a village to raise a child."[638] (This is a concept that left-wing educators use to justify instilling in students a set of morals and values that conflict with what the parents wish their children to learn.)

Finally, Friday is all about black women and being "unapologetically black," which is the ideal, versus the racist "unapologetically white." Students in New York City public schools are told that society devalues black women.[639] Seattle educators focus on intersectionality, a framework that claims different identities (like being black and female) elicit different types discrimination.[640]

The curriculum is a daily, organized, and intentional attempt to push kids toward the radical BLM movement, while tainting the way they see the country. It's easy to see how Democrat cities will continue to deteriorate. When someone hates their country—its founding, its institutions, its system of governance—they're less likely to care about a city's destruction. They've convinced themselves they're making changes that will one day lead to a progressive utopia.

Hating the Police

Something Happened in Our Town is a children's book-turned-play about a community reeling after a white officer kills a black man. Schools around the country use it in their curriculum. The story offers some explicitly anti-police narratives meant to shape the way young people view cops. A character in the book declares the police shot the black man purely because of his skin color. Another character says that the cop "won't go to jail" because "cops stick up for each other. And they don't like Black men."

Parents might not expect this curriculum to land in their conservative cities or counties, but parents in Papillion, Nebraska, found out their elementary-age children were exposed to the story. The district admitted that it never vetted the book before students from kindergarten through sixth grade were shown a video based on the book. The book "got put on a resource list without being vetted and then it got shared with teachers. There was no way for teachers to know that that book was not vetted properly," Papillion–La Vista Community Schools communications director Annette Eyman told local media. Parents were upset, prompting the school to apologize, though local media mostly focused coverage on left-wing parents who think it's appropriate to discuss complex issues around "racial injustice" with young kids.[641]

The Radical Left hopes to dismantle policing. We've seen the impacts left-wing activism has had on the criminal justice system, siding with criminals over victims, making cities less safe as a result. But the activism is guaranteed to get more extreme as progressive educators are creating an army of police-hating youth who will graduate and continue the fight to abolish police.

Part of the BLM curriculum, along with supplemental materials and lessons educators presented in response to the death of George

Floyd, intends to demonize and villainize the police. Children are taught to hate and fear cops, which is the worst possible mindset to have when interacting with them. You're likely to act out, or unnecessarily increase the tension, which an officer will feel and wonder if you wish them harm. But it's hard to blame young Americans for distrusting police when they're fed a diet of anti-police indoctrination. It explains why so few students complain when school resource officers are booted from campus.

Some 1,700 students in Colorado were offered more explicitly anti-police messaging from staff at Denver South High School when administrators showed them a video, *Don't Be a Bystander: 6 Tips for Responding to Racist Attacks,* during a school assembly. The video explicitly warned against reporting hate crimes to the police because, "Armed police presence often escalates, rather than reduces, the risk of violence in a situation. Because police have been trained to see people of color, gender nonconforming folks and Muslims as criminals, they often treat victims as perpetrators of violence." The narrator tells students, "So, if the victim hasn't asked you to call the police, do not—I repeat—do not call the police." The Denver Police Foundation called the video "reprehensible."[642] They were underselling how truly disgusting the advice was.

Nationwide, teachers were allowed to adorn their classrooms with messages critical of police, echoing the demands of BLM radicals. A teacher at Fishers High School in Indiana displayed a student poster that read, "Defund the police?" A student in the classroom lost his brother, an Elwood police officer, six years earlier.[643] Elm City Montessori School in Connecticut flew the Black Lives Matter flag (in place of an American flag), while displaying "defund police" posters in its windows.[644] Catharine Blaine K–8 in Seattle proudly displayed "Black Lives Matter" on the school marquee.[645]

Some schools pushed kids into supporting BLM. A private school in DC, the Lowell School, recorded its kindergarten students marching in the hallway, chanting "Black Lives Matter" while holding signs supporting the cause. They posted the video on their Instagram account.[646] Farmington Public Schools in Michigan held a 21-day "equity challenge" in which students were encouraged to join a BLM protest.[647] And in order to join Eastlake High School's Link Crew, students had to pledge their support to Black Lives Matter.[648] The Radical Left isn't especially subtle here. And with such viciously anti-police messaging common in schools nationwide, it was no surprise that districts distanced the police from its campuses.

Schools Turn on Cops

When the Radical Left defunded and demonized cops post-Floyd, they did not spare school resource officers (SROs) protecting some of our most vulnerable citizens: children. The SRO programs were not just about protecting children from harm on campus, but also creating positive relationships between students and law enforcement. Students would get to know their SRO and build a trusting relationship that they could take into world post-graduation. When you break the narrative that cops mean them harm and prove to them the opposite, future interactions between the public and police would be less tense. But suddenly, these dedicated officers found themselves kicked off campus.

It started in Minneapolis, where the school board unanimously decided to cut ties with the local police department for on-campus protection.[649] What followed was a wave of similar actions at school districts across the country, decisions hastily taken to prove a commitment to the BLM movement. School boards banned SROs, claiming that black and Latino students felt uncomfortable in their presence. Democrat lawmakers argued SROs represented a racist example of over-policing our students, arguing that they make the schools *less* safe. In what seemed like one fell swoop, SRO programs shut down. Some school districts found out sooner than others that this was a mistake.

In October 2021, the Pomona Unified School District in California voted unanimously to boot the police from its school campuses, as officials embraced "reimaging school safety."[650] Prompted by community activists who pretended police on campus was traumatizing to 23,000 district students, the board fed into the Radical Left narrative that being around police is inherently dangerous. Student activists like Caroline Lucas celebrated the move as a "milestone" after complaining that black and Latino students were disproportionately arrested on campus. (Again, this lazy argument implies, without evidence, that white students are committing the same brazen acts that land black and Latino kids in hot water, without consequence.) Jesus Sanchez, cofounder of youth activist group *Gente Organizada*, made the bizarre claim that because Pomona has a large immigrant population, students would be suspicious of police because their only known contact with law enforcement is when they see a loved one deported.

"It's a feeling of fear. I don't feel safe," a 16-year-old Pomona student claimed to feel when she sees a cop on campus.[651] "I want to run away from them even though I haven't done anything."

For all the contrived talk about discomfort with police on campus, everything changed when there was a shooting a few blocks away. Four months after the decision to ditch cops, there was a shooting that left a 12-year-old with injuries from broken glass shattered by bullets.[652] Reminded of the safety risks of not having an officer nearby, not to mention the disincentive an officer on campus may serve to someone thinking about bringing a weapon to school, the school board voted to reinstate the SRO program.

"An incident such as this drives us, as leaders, to examine our practices and our protocols in caring for students and staff in regards to mental health, conflict mediation, emergency procedures, communication facilities, and safety," Superintendent Richard Martinez acknowledged during an October 20 school board meeting after the shooting.

In June 2020, the Denver School Board in Colorado unanimously voted to sever ties with the Denver Police Department, following the death of George Floyd. After a February 2023 shooting left a 16-year-old student dead at East High School, Superintendent Alex Marrero announced he was recommitted "to having an armed officer at each comprehensive high school." The decision came after students demanded the SROs return to campus.[653]

"I think the withdrawal a few years ago was a huge mistake. I knew it would lead to something like this and sure enough, it did," a high school senior told the *Denver Gazette*.

Didn't school leaders know about these inherent threats prior to the shooting? Of course they did. But they were swept up in the national anti-police campaign by BLM and their Democrat enablers. To be part of the left-wing "it crowd," the district opted to risk the safety and well-being of its students. But where Pomona and Denver school districts corrected a bad decision, others have not—even in the face of school violence.

SROs were replaced with restorative justice coordinators in the Madison, Wisconsin, School District.[654] But a commitment to de-escalation didn't stop high schoolers from brawling. In the year preceding the move, cops still found themselves stopping by the high schools to break up fights that the restorative justice coordinators couldn't. By November 21, officers responded to calls at the local schools averaging almost one every day.[655] One fight escalated to an all-campus affair at Madison East High School, sending five kids to the hospital. It took a police response of 15 officers to quell the chaos.[656] The next day, over a third of the student body stayed home after social media rumors spread of more violence to come, prompting the school to promise a change to security protocols.[657] Though they didn't commit to bringing back SROs, by early 2023 the conversation had begun, with the *Wisconsin State Journal* editorial board pleading with the district to make the right decision. They wrote in an editorial that it wasn't a question about whether or not police should be on campus because "they still go there almost every day." They said the real question is what kind of officer would you prefer respond to on-campus violence.

"Do we want officers who don't know and haven't developed relationships with students — officers who have to rush to emergencies at the high schools from other parts of the city after conflicts have spun out of control? That's what we have now, and it isn't working well," they offered.

That very question caused a penitent Montgomery County, Maryland, School District to undo its SRO reforms. Home to Bethesda, the county's population is majority-minority, with activists picking up the BLM mantle to push SROs off campus, arguing too many black and Latino kids were being contacted by police. In November 2020, Montgomery County council members Hans Riemer and Will Jawando began the push to dismantle the program.

Over the past three years, 460 students were arrested in the county, mostly for bringing drugs or weapons to school, along with fighting. Of those students, 382 (83 percent) were black or Latino. Did those kids bring drugs or weapons to school or get into fights? Yup. But too many of them were black or Latino, so punishing them was seen as racist. It was enough data to justify ending the program.[658] It didn't matter that roughly three quarters of the arrests were from school officials calling police, not from SROs on campus.[659] Democrat lawmakers wanted to end the so-called "school to prison pipeline," a Democrat metaphor pretending students are needlessly going to jail due to institutionalized racism.

"A big part of the harm is disproportionality in arrests, and having police officers in the building leads to arrests when you don't have to. When you look at what happens down the line, you hear the term 'school-to-prison pipeline,' a student gets arrested, particularly a student of color. We know half the students arrested are black students, despite their population," Jawando said. "We also know that students, for example, just like the general public, black students aren't more likely to use marijuana than white students, but they're getting arrested more for it. So that's part of the problem."[660]

The funding, he and other Democrats on the council argued, would be better suited toward restorative justice programs. In 2021, the program was cut after County Executive Marc Elrich pulled funding. In 2022, they took baby steps to bring it back—with some big restrictions.

With police out of the picture, students were committing more violent acts, including a school shooting that seriously injured a 15-year-old. County officials were forced to rethink their position. In early 2022, a plan had been hatched to call SROs "Community Engagement Officers" (CEOs) instead.[661] These CEOs will have designated work stations on campus, but won't be stationed there. They will serve as a liaison between the school and the local police and have direct contact with school staff. It's not a perfect solution; in fact, it's needlessly cumbersome, but it's better than nothing. And it's closer to fixing an error than what's happening in the Pacific Northwest's largest school districts.

Portland mayor Ted Wheeler promised in 2020 "to act immediately and aggressively to interrupt systems of institutional racism and injustice," which, apparently, included pulling SROs from Portland Public Schools and redirecting $1 million a year from the police to a program to support and nurture black children. By December 2022, the city was in talks with the Portland Police Bureau to potentially bring SROs back to campus. As for the $1 million to support black children, when a reporter with KOIN-TV asked if that promise was fulfilled, the mayor's office did not respond.[662] Perhaps they realized race-based support for children is immoral?

At Ingraham High School in North Seattle, a 15-year-old boy brought a gun to school and shot and killed a 17-year-old classmate following a verbal altercation over the gun. With no SRO on campus, the program pulled in June 2020, the teen was able to easily flee (in addition to think it permissible to bring a gun to campus in the first place). While the shooting reignited calls for gun control (even though there are already laws prohibiting a 15-year-old from possessing a gun), the mere idea of bringing SROs back to campus earned immediate rejection from student activists—the future of the Radical Right, trained by adults who share similar IQs. "Why are we having more armed people at our schools when we can train them on de-escalation tactics instead of bringing more guns into the schools?" one student asked.[663] Those de-escalation tactics didn't stop a classmate from being killed, did they?

It's not just that SROs were kicked off campus; it's that cops were demonized by the staff in lesson plans to the students, making the program's return much less likely and future interactions between students and police much more tense. For months, students were indoctrinated with messaging that cops are racist and oppressive and that it was the duty of the student body to take up the BLM mantle.

Each year, Seattle educators offer lesson plans for Black Lives Matter at School Week to students as early as kindergarten.[664] Educators are told that no matter their student's age, "they're not too young to talk about race" because "silence about race reinforces racism." During the 2021 school year, elementary students were taught that any incarceration of black people "is an act of state violence" and that we live "in a world where Black lives are systematically and intentionally targeted for demise." Any guesses which profession is to blame for this cruelly racist world? Seattle's anti-police sentiment even extends to officers called to in-progress emergencies.

Liban Harasam allegedly assaulted a young girl before stealing a student's backpack at Sand Point Elementary in Seattle in June 2022. Cops responded to the call, after the incident prompted a school lockdown, but an uncooperative principal forced police to let Harasam go free.[665]

When an officer arrived on campus, Harasam was seen on body camera footage wandering the campus, dropping items from the backpack he allegedly stole, before dropping it and leaving the campus. Principal Ric Baileykaze told the responding officer what had happened, but the officer needed to establish probable cause to detain Harasam (another result of Democrat's police reforms).

"Can we check with the student, see if there's anything missing? Because if I have to put hands on this guy, it's going to go south," the officer told Baileykaze.

Baileykaze then stonewalled the officer.

"I don't mean to tell you what to do at all, but we're good. We're good. I'll replace this stuff on my own. Thank you. Thank you," Baileykaze says as he begins walking away.

The officer told dispatch that the principal is "declining to talk to me."

Harasam was allowed to go free, but that's when police said he assaulted a delivery driver while attempting to steal his cell phone, and then injured an officer as he resisted arrest. Police told me at the time that the treatment Baileykaze gave the officer is nothing new; they encounter it frequently. After the arrest, the officer returned to the school to scold the principal.

"I couldn't have you walk away because I had nothing based off of what you said. Based on the law, we go enforce the laws. If we don't have a crime, I have no legal recourse to contact him other than a social contact, that he walked off, which he did. It wasn't until he tried robbing the DHL driver, that I had a crime and a felony at that. That could have been avoided if I knew that he had stolen a backpack at the time," the officer told him.

Clearly, Seattle educators and school board directors are stubbornly opposed to bringing police back on campus. Perhaps it's something in the water. But other school leaders and lawmakers around the country, once seemingly myopic thanks to their cult-like support of BLM, are starting to come around. And it's followed a foreseeable pattern: Make a decision to pull a safety measure, see an uptick in the behaviors the safety measures previously mitigated, and then reinstate the safety measure. Sometimes, however, it's too late, and the damage is done.

Everything Is Racist

Thanks to the mainstreaming of BLM activism, Radical Left educators (who are mostly white) were empowered to use explicitly partisan curriculum in the classroom. Much of it centered around analyzing subject matter through a race-obsessed lens that treats *everything* as racist. But to get young students to buy into the activism and commit to pursuing long-lasting societal change, educators had to first break them down with guilt. Students were told they're racist because American systems and institutions were made to uphold a power structure that delivered to them privilege they did not earn. And no matter how young, educators rushed to indoctrinate their students with left-wing orthodoxy.

Oak Middle School students in Orange County, California, were told to read and analyze a *Huffington Post* op-ed titled, "Why I'm a Racist," by contributor Jeff Cook, a "white American male... married to a beautiful blond-haired green-eyed woman... [with] two amazing blond-haired blue-eyed boys."[666] He says he was "raised to treat everyone equally, regardless of race" but he admits, "I'm probably still a racist." How can he be a racist if he, by his own measure, doesn't dehumanize or devalue people on the basis of skin color? He defines racism as being "uncomfortable with, ignorant of and distant from racial inequalities that exist in my country." And he acknowledges it's not "evil" to admit one is racist.[667]

To a white middle school student (and white guilt-ridden adult, for that matter), the message is clear: Structural racial inequities exist, and you don't feel guilty enough for them. The prompt to students is that if they want to avoid being viewed as a racist, they must accept the claims of racial inequities, no matter how far-fetched some examples may be. And they're encouraged to admit they're racist without feeling bad; the article aims to destigmatize the label, so long as you adopt a left-wing worldview.

To a black middle school student, it's a wake-up call: Their classmates are racist. This can't possibly create healthy relationships in the classroom. It could only lead to further division and racial segregation. What black kid would want to be friends with a white kid they're taught is racist simply for being white?

This indoctrination is intended to be subtle. It's the kind of assignment that an educator can defend as merely a thought exercise during which students can explore ideas without being explicitly told they *have* to agree. But they're being manipulated into agreement. It's rather twisted.

In the Olympia School District in Washington state, facing dwindling enrollment and subsequent funding, the school board was faced with difficult budget decisions. The board decided to cut music classes for fourth graders. But it wasn't a decision based solely on budget considerations. Director Scott Clifthorn justified the cuts by claiming the class is an example of white supremacy culture.

"We're a school district that lives in...is entrenched in...is surrounded by white supremacy culture. And that's a real thing," Clifthorne said. Then he launched into a faux-thoughtful monologue signaling his own virtues.

"There's nothing about strings or wind instrumental music that is intrinsically white supremacist. However, the ways in which it is and the ways in which all of our institutions, not just schools — local government, state government, churches, or neighborhoods — inculcate and allow white supremacy culture to continue to be propagated and cause significant institutional violence are things that we have to think about carefully as a community. And I think that we have to do that interrogation. And we have to address the ways in which it creates challenges for administering the educational day for our elementary learners while we retain the program," he said.[668]

Does any of that make any sense? Of course not. But, it doesn't have to. The goal is to speak of *everything* through a CRT lens.

In the nearby Tahoma School District in Washington, a volunteer Equity Team leader caused quite the stir with her TikTok account. Alicia Busch frequently posted racist and vulgar videos mocking white people as "amoral colonizers" who are dangerous because, "there is no safe place for BIPOC to exist when whiteness is present." She claimed that the "American dream is white supremacy."

"You too can achieve the American dream if only you work hard enough to conform to society's norms. And by 'society,' I mean white supremacy," she said in one video.[669] "And if you assimilate enough and if you reject — reject — all of your non-American culture, history, background, generational trauma and just get over it, so that you again can achieve the American dream, which is white supremacy. Isn't it lovely over here when you dehumanize yourself to the point where you are no longer recognizable? Not only are you not recognizable, but you have no culture of your own because it's lost to the American dream."

After I inquired about the videos with the district, thanks to parents who flagged the TikTok account to me, a spokesperson said Busch "offered to step away from the Equity Committee."

The Radical Left Tried to Make Segregation Trendy

New York's Lower Manhattan Community School, which is majority-minority, announced it would racially segregate junior high students for discussion about racial identity and social justice, with an eye toward undoing "the legacy of racism and oppression in this country that impacts our school community."[670] One might call separating students by race as racist and oppressive, but post-George Floyd, it was hip and evolved.

Schools began to embrace so-called "affinity groups" where students, teachers, and even parents are told to congregate exclusively with members of their own race to review curriculum, recieve training, or discuss school issues. Advocates say the goal is to create environments for racial minorities to feel more comfortable expressing themselves, free from the hostile, judgmental eye of whites. Groups for whites, however, are spaces to berate them for benefitting from the privilege society offers for being white. The practice was adopted nationwide.

Centennial Elementary in Denver planned a "families of color playground night" because school officials claimed it was a way to make black families "feel more included in our school community." The district said it was "committed to fostering, cultivating, and preserving a culture of inclusion and belonging, where our students, families and team members are safe and welcomed."[671] Nothing says inclusion and belonging like telling students they're unwelcome because of their skin color.

Seattle Public Schools and the Seattle Council of Parent Teacher Student Association hosted a series of race-based meetings as part of a "Listening Tour" to discuss, ironically, how to foster a more welcoming environment across the district. Sessions were held exclusively for black families, multigenerational African American black families, and Native American families. A district spokesperson told me that they "often use affinity groups" to "offer safe and welcoming spaces so that unique perspectives, input, and concerns can be shared with the superintendent." But there were no meetings specifically for Latino families. Why not? Are they less sensitive than black and Native American families, as the district implies?[672]

Race-based exclusions prompted a lawsuit against Wellesley Public Schools in Massachusetts after racial minority students were invited to an on-campus space "where members of historically marginalized groups can come together in a spirit of mutual support and understanding of shared experiences." The invitation from the district's superintendent, according to a lawsuit by the group Parents Defending Education, explicitly notes that it is a "safe space for our Asian/Asian-American and Students of Color, *not* for students who identify only as White." The email added, "If you identify as White, and need help to process recent events, please know I'm here for you as well as your guidance counselors. If you need to know more about why this is not for White students, please ask me!"[673] The district settled the lawsuit in February 2022, promising to end their racist practices.[674]

You're not supposed to question the necessity of affinity groups without getting an earful, as San Marcos High School student Jace Jonas found out. Alissa Piro was teaching virtually when Jonas said she announced a new Asian student union. In the chat box, Jonas wrote, "singling out a type of person for a club is racist. We should have an individual club for all races." Jonas told Fox News that it prompted Piro to yell, "G-dd—it!" before berating him. "She started berating me about how as a White male I get everything and it's my duty to look out for minorities and all these racist remarks against Whites and males. She later called me a moron," he explained. When he inquired about a "white student union," Piro was recorded as yelling, "You don't need a White student union, Jace. You get everything." The teacher was pulled from class for an investigation, and later apologized to Jonas. But the student's father says, despite previously earning straight As, "after that incident, he had a B in that class."[675]

While leftists tell us affinity groups are about comfort, it seems condescending and patently racist to implicitly label racial minorities as hypersensitive and incapable of communicating around those who don't look like them. Did anyone bother to truly ask blacks, Latinos, Asians, or any other group if they even wanted this? Kids aren't born racist. A young black boy and a young white boy will organically become friends unless they're taught to hate or distrust one another. If some children do, for whatever reason, feel uncomfortable around white people (or anyone who didn't look like them), wouldn't it be wiser and more unifying to address *why* they felt that way? Perhaps their feelings are borne out of years of nonstop race-baiters who financially benefit from tainting relationships. You know what could change minds and bring everyone together in more harmonious ways? Going to the same meetings, seeing white parents interact with educators and passionately defend their kids' interest just like black, Latino, Asian, and Native American families.

But we're no longer allowed to accept that holding negative views of people based solely on race is, in fact, racist. The Radical Left endorses affinity groups because it implies that white people, by their very whiteness, make others uncomfortable. Jackson, Michigan, school board member and equity consultant Kesha Hamilton made that exact case.

Hamilton, who is black, tweeted on December 18, 2022, that "Whiteness is so evil. it manipulates then says, I won't apologize for my dishonesty and trauma inducing practices and thinks you should applaud it for being honest about its ability to manipulate and be dishonest."[676] When she was asked to defend her racist tweet, generalizing all white people as evil and manipulative, she said she was actually addressing systemic racism, not white individuals.

"Whiteness is the system, the ideology, the belief, the thought that because your skin is white, you are superior to Black people," Jones said. "Because your skin is white you deserve better. Because your skin is white, you have better opportunities."

In other words, she really was talking about white individuals. Her comments caused a local firestorm, with parents declaring her language as "hurting society, not helping it." But she also had her supporters who said she was merely expressing her experiences because as "a woman in this American nation and a Black woman specifically is that sometimes others would rather I not exercise any of my rights as outlined in the Constitution. I do not apologize for exercising any of my rights."[677]

Of course, if a white parent or educator said "blackness is so evil," they'd be rightly ridiculed, scorned, and dismissed as a racist. Yet, targeting white people for derision solely on the basis of skin color is permitted because they're oppressors. To the Radical Left, this is a noble kind of racism with a goal of promoting equity.

Too Many Asians

In the wake of the so-called "racial awaking" post-Floyd, Thomas Jefferson High School for Science and Technology principal Ann Bonitatibus asked the school's mostly Asian students and immigrant parents to "think about your own journey and discovery of race and economic advantage in America." The email was bizarre, to say the least.

Bonitatibus said she was "awakened to see that our country's normal continues to be laced with racism that has plagued our nation since its founding" and asked that the school community "please think of privileges you hold that others may not." She then complained that the school does not reflect the racial composition of the district.

It was condescending White Knighting, with a liberal white lady lecturing a school that's 72 percent Asian that they should "consider colonialism's role in our country's history where certain classes exerted power over others as a means to economically exploit, oppress and enslave them."[678]

What in the world was the point of this email? It turns out, Bonitatibus was setting the stage to change the admissions process. The school had too many Asians and that needed to change. First, the admissions office nixed a tough admittance test where Asian students excelled. Then, she presented administrators with a new "holistic review" admission process where they take into account socioeconomic status of the students and if the student's household isn't English-speaking. The school maintained the new process did not consider race, but the so-called "Student Portrait Sheet" that students filled out would give significant hints as to their background.

This new approach dramatically cut the Asian population down by some 15 to 20 percent.[679] The Hispanic student population, meanwhile, went from between 1 percent and 5 percent to

11 percent. Black student enrollment shot up to 7 percent, from 1 percent to 2 percent. If race wasn't a factor, how did the school achieve these stats?

The Radical Left does not treat Asians as a minority group because they don't fit the preferred narrative. Academically, Asian students excel, often more so than white students, which conflicts with the Radical Left's insistence that this country is steeped in white supremacy to the detriment of racial minorities. If American systems were created to favor white people, why do Asians outperform whites? The Radical Left can't reconcile the positions, so they treat Asians as white.

In the North Thurston Public Schools in Washington State, Asian students were excelling. So much so that they were literally deemed "white" by the district so that it could better argue that systemic racism was keeping "students of color" from exceeding.

The district monitors student growth by various characteristics, including race. In one report on student achievement, the district examined the purported "opportunity gaps for historically underserved students of color." But the data wasn't as disproportionate as the district hoped when the data was measured against white students. The students of color were seeing marked improvements, getting closer to where white students were performing because Asian students were doing so well. Indeed, they were improving the fastest when it came to math and English, far better than white students at the time. To better argue that students of color were falling behind, the district broke out the data by "students of color" and "White/Asian" in its report.

A district website claimed that this was all done in error and that their "intent was never to ignore Asian students as 'students of color' or ignore any systemic disadvantages they too have faced." The statement claimed that they merely wanted to highlight that "our system is not meeting the instructional needs of our Black, Indigenous, Multi-racial, Pacific Islander and Latinx students." As

I reported at the time, the data was improving, showing the district was meeting the needs of students. But that reality didn't fit the talking point of systemic or institutionalized racism keeping students of color down.[680]

Math Is Racist: A Misleading Argument About Equity

Equity used to refer to equal access, but the Radical Left believes it means equal outcomes. If black and Hispanic students, in particular, do not perform as well as white students, progressives cite racism. It's the lazy disproportionality argument at work. Instead of focusing extra attention on the students who are falling behind—regardless of race—the Radical Left seeks to dismantle the very principles of the subject matter and rewrite it through a CRT lens. It's led to a movement declaring mathematics as racist.

Bankrolled by the Bill and Melinda Gates Foundation in 2021, a cabal of Radical Left nonprofits and educators introduced A Pathway to Equitable Math Instruction, a toolkit introducing "an integrated approach to mathematics that centers Black, Latinx, and Multilingual students in grades 6 to 8." The equity cabal claims math classes are rife with "white supremacy culture," actually arguing that when teachers "treat mistakes as problems by equating them with wrongness," it's racist because it "reinforces the ideas of perfectionism (that students shouldn't make mistakes) and paternalism (teachers or other experts can and should correct mistakes)." The Radical Left believes perfectionism and paternalism are characteristics of white supremacy culture.

The toolkit embraces the idea that black students do not view math the same way as white students, and that teaching them the "right" way to navigate algebra or calculus will reinforce white supremacy. "It allows the defensiveness of Western mathematics to prevail, without addressing underlying causes of why certain groups of students are 'underperforming,' a characterization that should also be interrogated," the toolkit argues. "It also presupposes that 'good' math teaching is about a Eurocentric type of mathematics, devoid of cultural ways of being."[681]

The belief that math is racist gained a following in Oregon, where the state's department of education offered a training session for teachers on the topic. It inspired math teachers like Muhammad Rahman, who told local media that he uses the toolkit to inform his approach with students. "There's something I might be doing that could be problematic, so just looking inside and trying to make sure I'm the best version of myself and make sure I'm teaching the best way I can to my students," Rahman explained.[682]

The coursework wasn't just meant to address the contrived issue of white supremacy in math courses. The more sinister angle was to teach students that capitalism is evil. The toolkit is meant to inspire students to challenge "the ways that math is used to uphold capitalist, imperialist, and racist views." How is this serving students? It's not. But it helps prime young minds to pursue an anti-capitalist agenda once they graduate. It's like they're being groomed to serve on the Portland City Commission.

Approaches espoused in the toolkit might be easier to justify to parents because they're promoted under the guise of equity. But when the Radical Left uses the term, it should be seen as a progressive code word used by those who want to dismantle the education system. It's gotten so absurd that they're even labeling harmless holidays racist.

Cancel Culture Comes for Halloween and Thanksgiving

Halloween used to be a fun holiday for kids, especially at school, when students were encouraged to dress up for the day and sit through spooky lesson plans filled with goofy puns that made classes fly by. Unhappy, lonely Radical Left educators now deem Halloween as promoting inequities and insensitivities among students.

Benjamin Franklin Day Elementary in Seattle hosted Halloween festivities until the school's Racial Equity Team, ghoulish volunteers who look for reasons to label everything "racist," stepped in.[683] The "Pumpkin Parade" featuring students in costumes was canceled so that the school could focus on its "foundational beliefs around equity for our students and families."

The crushing announcement was made in the school newsletter, claiming that "Halloween events create a situation where some students must be excluded for their beliefs, financial status, or life experience. Costume parties often become an uncomfortable event for many children, and they distract students and staff from learning. Large events create changes in schedules with loud noise levels and crowds. Some students experience over stimulation, while others must deal with complex feelings of exclusion. It's uncomfortable and upsetting for kids."[684]

The plan was to make all students equally miserable for the day. Rather than enjoy festivities, students would suffer through inclusive events like "thematic units of study about the fall," which includes a review of "autumnal artwork" while "sharing all the cozy feelings of the season." The school treated students like they were all 62-year-old widows on a weekend retreat to "find" themselves again.

Halloween isn't the only holiday the Radical Left has targeted. All celebrations must now be viewed through a racial justice lens.

Citing "conversations and concerns about the accuracy of the first Thanksgiving story," Stone Bank Elementary School in Oconomowoc, Wisconsin, cancelled a first-grade play because children dressing up as a Pilgrim or Native American was problematic to "the sensitivity of this time in our history," according to a school email to parents.[685] A fifth-grade performance of *A Christmas Carol* was cancelled after Radical Left parents complained that it mentioned God.[686] Similarly, Oneonta Elementary School in Imperial Beach, California, abruptly ditched its Christmas festivities to be more inclusive of students or staff who do not celebrate.[687] Inclusivity concerns marred the Easter egg hunt at Heritage Elementary in Madison, Alabama. The district opted to remove "Easter" from the event's name so as to not offend parents who don't celebrate the holiday.[688]

Parents Say Enough Is Enough

Parents in Loudoun County, Virginia, raised concerns about the direction of their school district. Their activism inspired an army of passionate mothers and fathers waking up to what was happening in their kids' schools. They started a movement that put the Radical Left on its heels and inspired millions of parents to stand up to educators who were lying about what was being taught in the classroom.

School board officials and educators told Virginia parents that CRT was neither taught in the classrooms nor a part of its equity plans. The district claimed it was simply having conversations, albeit tough ones, around race and racism. They argued the concept of CRT wasn't guiding their curriculum. "Loudoun County Public Schools does not teach Critical Race Theory (CRT) as part of its curriculum," insisted Loudoun County Public Schools (LCPS) spokesperson Wayne Byard. "CRT is not, and has never been, part of the social studies curriculum in Virginia."[689] They were lying.

A grassroots effort comprised of concerned parents, who were opposed to teaching kids to judge one another based on skin color or that white kids were being labeled oppressors, sprung to action. They quickly organized and brought receipts and anecdotes to school board meetings. It wasn't hard to find examples, and even teachers were willing to speak out as loudly as parents.

AP Government teacher Monica Gill explained that teachers were instructed to "disrupt and dismantle this systemic racism. And I can tell you, one thing that's for sure, it has been disruptive because there are parents who disagree with this ideology, there are teachers who disagree with it, there are students who disagree with it—and it is harmful."[690] Jeremy Wright, who leads the Instruction Learning Center at The North Star School, said the CRT influence would destroy "our culture at the schools."[691]

LCPS contracted with The Equity Collaborative for "Critical Race Theory Development" for its administrators.[692] And an email obtained by Fox News shows the district's former superintendent Eric Williams admitting staff training "align with the ideology of CRT."[693] Some staff training urged educators to stop being "color-blind" to race and, instead, be "color conscious."[694]

Lesson plans were also screenshot in a lawsuit against the district by Alliance Defending Freedom. It noted that eighth graders were taught racism against people of color is "based on a socially constructed racial hierarchy that privileges *white* people." Students were pushed to become "anti-racists" because when they don't make "anti-racist choices" in life, they "(un)consciously uphold aspects of white supremacy, white-dominant culture, and unequal institutions and society."[695]

While Loudoun County was getting media attention, in large part due to school board meetings that grew chaotic and contentious at times, parents in districts across the state were becoming more active in their communities. It helped propel longshot Republican candidate Glenn Youngkin into the governor's mansion. He took up the fight against CRT while his better-known Democrat opponent Terry McAuliffe scoffed at the issue, calling it a racist "dog whistle." But when he was previously governor, a leaked memo showed the Virginia Department of Education encouraged public schools to "embrace critical race theory" and "engage in race-conscious teaching and learning."[696] Conservatives weren't the only ones inspired to activism over CRT concerns.

When you lose San Francisco liberals, you know you've gone too far. That's exactly what the San Francisco School Board did, delivering a wake-up call to board members punished for focusing too much on CRT and not enough on academics.

Remote learning implemented due to the COVID-19 pandemic negatively affected students' academic progress. Test scores and grade point averages plummeted. Kids in San Francisco were no different, with the district's 49,000 students seeing its overall math proficiency rate drop from 51 percent before the pandemic to 46 percent after. English suffered less, but still dropped from 57 percent to 55 percent. Though educators boasted about their support for black lives throughout the pandemic, the proficiency gap between black and white students was staggering. Just 9 percent of black students in district schools were proficient in math, compared to 65 percent of whites.[697]

With such dramatic declines, parents expected the school board to help bring students to at least where they were pre-COVID. But school board members had other plans. They were to chase white supremacy from its districts by renaming 44 schools! In a 6 to 1 vote in January 2021, the district vowed to change the names of schools tied to racism, oppression, and slavery. Using Wikipedia (I'm not kidding), the school board found reason to remove the names of Herbert Hoover, Francis Scott Key, Thomas Jefferson, George Washington, Paul Revere, Theodore Roosevelt, Abraham Lincoln, and the senior senator from California, Diane Feinstein. Senator Feinstein's inclusion was a surprise, since she's unmistakably progressive. But when she was mayor of San Francisco in 1984, she replaced a Confederate flag from a city hall display after it was defaced. "It's a message to our families, our students and our community," school board member Mark Sanchez said. "It's not just symbolic. It's a moral message."

Parents and even Mayor London Breed criticized the exercise in wokeness, saying they're ignoring student struggles. But the *San Francisco Chronicle* claimed that board members "insisted that the renaming is timely and important, given the country's reckoning with a racist past. They have argued the district is capable of pursuing multiple priorities at the same time, responding to critics who say more pressing issues deserve attention."[698] Multiple priorities? On the night of this vote, the school board's agenda did not include a single issue related to academics or reopening schools.

By April, the backlash was too much for the school board to contend with. They voted unanimously to reverse course; Lincoln, Washington, Jefferson, and the others would remain. The same could not be said for the school board members. Three of the members were ousted by a parent-led recall campaign focused on anger that the schools were left closed for far too long. The school board president Gabriela López and members Alison Collins and Faauuga Moliga were unceremoniously booted from office with between 68 percent and 76 percent of voters sending them packing.[699] All that saved the other school board members was that they were not eligible for recall because they were recently elected.

It wasn't just renaming schools that did them in. They opted to mess with Asian American parents and their kids. That was a brutal mistake.

Lowell High is an elite school in San Francisco, one of the highest performers in California. But it wasn't diverse enough for the Radical Left, which saw a student population dominated by Asian and white students as inequitable. The school board forced the school's admissions practice to switch from merit-based to a lottery, which was supposed to help ensure enrollment was more diverse.

The change was successful in bringing in more black and Latino students, but average student grades tanked, with nearly a quarter of Lowell ninth graders earning a D or F in the Fall of 2021. The principal argued "half of our student body [being] new to in-person instruction at the high school level and absences among students/staff for COVID all explain this dip in performance."[700] But the older students in grades 10 through 12, who were admitted under the merit-based system, had only slight academic dips during COVID-19 lockdowns. It seemed clear that the new, lottery-selected students dragged the school's performance down. A biology teacher noted that "I have some students who have done no work the whole first grading period. I don't think some of these students would be doing well at any high school, which makes me wonder why they wanted to come to Lowell."[701]

The Asian American community was livid. Their children worked hard to earn a spot in the area's most elite high school, which came with it a sense of pride and a better chance at earning a spot in a top college or university. Parents viewed the move as anti-Asian.

Making matters worse were controversial tweets that school board president Collins posted in 2016 that gained attention during the recall. She complained that "many Asians...I know won't engage in critical race convos unless they see how they are impacted by white supremacy." She said, having grown up in mostly Asian American schools, that "Many Asian Am. Believe they benefit from the 'model minority' BS." She accused Asian Americans of using "white supremacist thinking to assimilate and 'get ahead.'" Collins even mentioned Lowell parents, which she said disparage "Black/Brown 'culture.'"[702] She could not, and did not, recover.

Left-wing school boards were suddenly in the spotlight, and parents were making moves. In Waukesha, Wisconsin, three Republican-backed candidates won school board seats in 2022 by campaigning against CRT.[703] Texas Republicans were able to flip a district State Board of Education seat, delivering more control to the conservative bloc of candidates who ran opposing CRT in the classroom.[704] The 11 Colorado candidates that centered campaigns around CRT won their respective races.[705] And all six school board members endorsed by Florida governor Ron DeSantis earned wins in 2022.[706] Overall, conservative candidates fighting CRT won big in 2022, earning 44 of the 58 seats they were running for, according to the 1776 Project PAC, which supported candidates fighting against the racist theory.[707]

These victories were huge. But they're not enough. Radical Left educators continue to indoctrinate students, convincing them that this country isn't worth fighting for and our institutions not worth maintaining. It will make it that much easier to continue the progressive fight once these students graduate and enter the real world. But in the meantime, the Radical Left will lay the groundwork for their students to continue years down the road.

CHAPTER 10

UNLIVABLE CITIES

Well, Someone Needs to Pay to Destroy These Cities

When the latest Census Bureau data was released in 2022, New York officials knew they would see a population dip, but not as dramatic as it turned out to be. Fleeing from crime and homelessness, over 524,000 New Yorkers fled between 2020 and 2022, giving the state the largest population loss of any state in the country.[708] In 2020, the exodus was so severe that the state lost a congressional seat. It was easy to see why so many left.

The crime crisis was out of control, with daily headlines of tragic drive-by murders, brutal subway assaults, and repeat offenders being released from jail just a few hours after arrest. You couldn't avoid homelessness in the state's largest cities, with trash strewn around a region that's used to having some grit but not be as filthy as a dump. Local leaders no longer seemed to have pride in their cities and state. And yet, the cost of living was still through the roof, even after a short COVID-related respite. Rent in Manhattan hit an average $5,249 in November 2022, up nearly 20 percent over a year with most landlords requiring an annual income of 40 times the monthly rent.[709] And despite record high subway crime, facing a $3 billion deficit in 2025, the Metropolitan Transportation Authority planned to raise tolls and subway fares by 5.5 percent.

Wealthy New Yorkers ditched the state during the pandemic and didn't return. Earners making between $150,000 and $750,000 fell by nearly 6 percent between 2019 and 2020. The numbers were worse for those earning more than $750,000, with a 10 percent increase in exiles during the same time period.[710] They could afford the rent, and it's not like the state (or New York City specifically) hasn't gone through crime spikes before. So, what was different this time? Staggering tax hikes pursued by an insatiable Radical Left.

According to the Heritage Foundation, New Yorkers shoulder the highest share of personal income in taxes and the highest individual income tax rate. They have the second-highest state and local corporate income tax collections per capita and pay the sixth highest capital-stock tax rate. Their property taxes and local sales tax rate are the fourth highest in the nation. How can anyone justify paying that much for the quality of life that is nowhere near what it once was? Under then-mayor Bill de Blasio, with few improvements under Eric Adams, life in New York was flatly unpleasant, especially to those who experienced life under local Republican leadership when crime and cost of living were down.

"We might be getting near that tipping point where we do make it economically unsustainable for enough of those folks to stay here," New York comptroller Thomas DiNapoli told Bloomberg News.[711] "There's no doubt there's been a net migration of taxpayers at the upper end. It should be a concern for everybody."

The state economy took a more than $19.5 billion blow as a result of the exodus.[712] But New York was not alone. Democrat-run California saw nearly 510,000 locals flee to escape the same issues as New York, namely a crime and homelessness crisis, plus crippling cost of living. States with less crime and lower cost of living, like Florida, Texas, Idaho, and Tennessee, were seeing population surges. Texas and Florida alone gained 900,000 and 700,000 new residents respectively. You'd think that Democrat leaders would take the hint and perhaps replicate some policies, or at least attitudes, taken by Republican-led states, right? Wrong. They dug in their heels.

Punishing the Wealthy

President Barack Obama was on the campaign trail in 2012, delivering a speech in Roanoke, Virginia, on a warm summer evening, explaining that the only way to return to a time where the "American dream" was attainable would be to tax the wealthy. It was a mostly typical stump speech full of strawman arguments and disingenuous characterizations of Republican economic views, blaming them for the slowest job growth in decades (which actually occurred under Democrat leadership). But there was a moment during the speech that revealed the Radical Left's philosophy and disdain for the wealthy (which they falsely assume describes all business owners).

"There are a lot of wealthy, successful Americans who agree with me because they want to give something back," Obama bellowed with the trademark mix of swagger and smarm. "They know they didn't. Look, if you've been successful, you didn't get there on your own. You didn't get there on your own. I'm always struck by people who think, well, it must be because I was just so smart. There are a lot of smart people out there. It must be because I worked harder than everybody else. Let me tell you something, there are a whole bunch of hardworking people out there. If you were successful, somebody along the line gave you some help. There was a great teacher somewhere in your life. Somebody helped to create this unbelievable American system that we have that allowed you to thrive. Somebody invested in roads and bridges. If you've got a business, you didn't build that! Somebody else made that happen.

The Internet didn't get invented on its own. Government research created the Internet so that all the companies could make money off the Internet."[713]

"You didn't build that!" Isn't that statement the perfect encapsulation of Democrat beliefs? That the government is responsible for your successes, not you. But the opposite is true. You paid the teacher's salary, you paid for the roads to be built, and you paid for the employees who helped create a successful business. On the surface, Obama's statement seems more delusional than radical, but it's that attitude that justifies the long arm of the government taking increasing control of your life.

Democrat-run states that lost high tax earners needed to make up the money to pour into some of the very same programs, strategies, and schemes that scared away the population to begin with. So, they again leaned into high tax earners to shoulder the burden, usually under the hackneyed argument that the wealthy have to "pay their fair share." Additionally, states inhospitable to businesses, offering an increasingly difficult-to-justify tax structure, pushed major corporations away.

Under pressure from the Radical Left, then-governor Andrew Cuomo raised the state tax rate on New Yorkers' wealthiest in 2021. Those making between $5 million and $25 million were taxed at 10.3 percent and those making over $25 million were taxed at 10.9 percent. The top 1 percent of earners in the state already pay 40 percent of the taxes, while responsible for job creation and funding local economies through high-end purchases. How are they not already paying their fair share? And while the taxes are supposed to be phased out at 2027, good luck finding a Democrat tax plan that ever goes away. Additionally, state Democrat lawmakers are angling to tax long-term capital gains. Every bit of income will be taxed and distributed in ways that do not make their lives better. Surely, this will push even more of the wealthy out of New York, especially if the quality of life suffers at the same time.

Ken Griffin runs Citadel, a multimillion-dollar hedge fund and was Illinois' richest resident. But Democrats couldn't keep him in the state, attempting to bleed him of his financial success, because he was fed up with area crime. Griffin announced in June 2022 that he was moving to Miami because Florida offered a better corporate environment and wasn't plagued by violent crime. He told the *Wall Street Journal*, "If people aren't safe here, they're not going to live here. I've had multiple colleagues mugged at gunpoint. I've had a colleague stabbed on the way to work. Countless issues of burglary. I mean, that's a really difficult backdrop with which to draw talent to your city."[714] Reporter and author Adam Lashinsky called this move "pathetic," arguing the state "nurtured him and built his empire and he just says, 'okay, buh-bye.'"[715]

With the wealthy pulling out of Democrat states, Radical Left lawmakers banded together to make them pay the price. "Let's make sure if they move, they have nowhere else to go because we're all taxing them together," Washington State senator Noel Frame (D-Seattle) said in January 2023.[716] Frame introduced a 1 percent "wealth tax" against Washingtonians (worth over $250 million) on their financial assets, such as stocks and bonds. The year prior, the Democrat-controlled state legislature imposed a 7 percent capital gains tax, even though income taxes are unconstitutional.[717] But the far-Left state Supreme Court redefined capital gains to be an excise tax so that it would be constitutional. The Court's majority argued their new definition was necessary because Washington's "upside-down tax system perpetuates systemic racism by placing a disproportionate tax burden on BIPOC residents."[718]

California targeted the wealthy with a "worldwide net worth" over $1 billion with an additional 1.5 percent tax on top of everything else they pay. They would even impose it on the wealthy after they leave the state. It's a way to further push the fiction that these success stories were *only* made possible because of the state government, when they were actually earned in spite of California taxes and policies.

Democrats choose not to address their spending. They just look for other sources of revenue when their running low on cash, and they do it even as residents reject the idea. For example, Washington State voters overwhelmingly rejected the capital gains tax via a nonbinding advisory vote. They were ignored. California Proposition 30, which taxed personal income above $2 million, was also rejected by a wide margin. Yet Democrats keep pushing forward, to the benefit of Republican states.

The War on Cars

Democrat lawmakers claim to support the Average Joe, arguing Republicans are on the side of corporate America, which they claim destroys the middle class. Yet it's Democrat-run cities, propelled by the Radical Left, crushing the average American earner, making it increasingly difficult to live there by embracing a war on cars.

The Radical Left endorses an urbanist-at-all-cost mentality. They want you out of your cars and living near your workplace so you can either bike, bus, or walk to the office, which helps save the environment from the ill effects of carbon dioxide and other in-air pollutants. But it's also driven by perhaps a more subconscious desire to control your life and reimagine the American dream. Unlike buses or trains, which work on a fixed schedule, cars gave us more than a convenient means of travel; they have offered us the freedom to go where we please, when we please. And it's not just home ownership, but car ownership, that embodies the American dream. But with an increasing number of Radical Left activists believing the country is founded on white supremacy, they won't be especially hospitable to us reaching that dream.

No matter the motivation, the war on cars meant tearing up roads, paid for by drivers, to hand over to carless residents to bike or bus around town, often without having to pay for the anti-car infrastructure projects. It's a pretty great deal for those without a car, but it makes life more expensive for scores of locals.

Democrat-run cities, particularly on the West Coast, do not hide their goal, which is to make driving so difficult and guilt-inducing that you give up and opt for a cleaner mode of transportation. Los Angeles will make its notoriously anxiety-inducing commutes even worse when the city adds up to 100 miles of bus-only lanes by 2027. Transit in Los Angeles is as slow as everyone else's commute because buses are stuck in traffic like everyone else. But under an "equity" transit strategy, bus lanes will be erected in areas of already high traffic. The justification is that because low-income Los Angelinos are heavy bus users and racial minorities, they are more worthy of commute assistance. It doesn't matter that only 6 percent of residents use the bus; their intersectional identities are all that matters.[719]

Denver's anti-car mayor Michael Hancock doesn't like the idea of single-occupant drivers, decrying the "shocking" stat that 73 percent of city commuters drive alone to and from work. He'd rather they take a bus, so he's promised to "dedicate more travel lanes as transit only and make bus service more accessible to everyone." But it continues to be a futile exercise in government spending. As Hancock invested billions on transit improvements, transit commuting only rose by 1.1 percent between 2000 and 2016, whereas solo driving rose to 76 percent in 2016.[720] Yet, the anti-car mayor and Radial Left activist class continued their push, permanently removing parking spots across the city and gutting its downtown core of traffic lanes, using the COVID-19 pandemic for cover.[721] It's somewhat ironic because during and after COVID-19, transit hit record lows as commuters eschewed buses for the comfort of their personal vehicles. Indeed, the *New York Times* called the pandemic "an existential crisis for transit."[722] Yet, Democrat-run cities and states in areas dominated by car travel tripled down on their spending for transit, hoping to sway the small percentage of commuters back.

Portland, Oregon, is replacing scarce parking with trees and grass.[723] San Francisco has been lowering speed limits to a 20-mile-per-hour crawl.[724] Seattle has been tearing up already congested streets to add bike lanes, as part of a commitment to 100 miles of protected lanes by 2024.[725] Washington State even plans to eventually ban right-hand turns in almost all circumstances, a supposed nod to pedestrian and bike commuter safety, but a not-so-thin attempt to inconvenience drivers enough for them to ditch their cars.[726]

The effort to change America's car culture on the West Coast hasn't yet come to fruition. While East Coast cities like New York, Boston, and DC rely heavily on transit and pedestrian travel, West Coast cities can never fully commit to a car-free future. While New York built upward, Los Angeles built outward, making transit commuting unlikely for most people who travel far distances to get to and from work. And cities like San Francisco and Seattle, which had high transit use pre-COVID-19, created unintended consequences.

The Radical Left has effectively priced people out of their cities with their war on cars. Those who live close to work are more likely to commute via transit, bicycle, or foot. That means housing costs will reflect the median pay of the businesses in the immediate area. Amazon is headquartered in neighborhoods in and around downtown Seattle and house about 75,000 six-figure salaried tech workers and corporate managers who have been incentivized to live near the office because the city has killed parking and replaced car lanes with bike- and bus-only lanes. It's considerably more convenient to work nearby than face a daunting commute from the suburbs.

To accommodate the Amazon employees, property owners either upgraded their housing supply or built new complexes from scratch, knowing they'd be able to charge upward of $3,000 a month for a tiny studio or one-bedroom apartment because the local Amazon workforce would be able to afford it. At the same time, to help impede car ownership, the city stopped requiring parking spots be commensurate with the number of apartment dwellers. With limited housing supply (thanks to poor local planning where city leaders refused to compromise views of the picturesque Puget Sound, Elliot Bay, Lake Union, and Lake Washington by severely capping the number of city high-rise buildings), rents went through the roof, pushing out low- and middle-income workers to the fringes of the city (or outside of Seattle entirely) where it's more affordable but also harder to commute from.

If a middle-income worker managed to find an affordable apartment complex, they cannot rely on a car. The intentional lack of parking spaces resulted in criminally high monthly parking fees in most Seattle apartments of upward of $280 a month. And forget about home ownership. By enticing high-paid tech workers to live close to the office, city leaders ceded the housing market to the richest locals to purchase, further pushing prices up and making home ownership nearly impossible for low- and middle-income locals.

Seattle, like other left-wing cities, tried to help those they priced out of the city by raising the minimum wage, which did little to address the housing market, but did force small businesses like retail, restaurants, coffee shops, grocery stores, and local entertainment venues to raise their prices to make up for the increase in cost of doing business in the city. That means that the minimum wage increase didn't go nearly as far as progressives had hoped.

The Radical Left knows it can't *fully* end American's reliance on cars, so they step in to force you into the vehicles they support. The State of California will ban the sale of new gas-powered vehicles in 2035 after the California Air Resources Board issued the rule in 2022. It's meant to force car manufacturers to produce cleaner vehicles and reduce the state's dependence on oil, cutting some 50 percent in car pollution by 2040 along the way. The move triggered over a dozen, mostly Democrat-run states into the same policy, including Oregon, Washington, Colorado, and New Jersey.[727]

It's another example of an ideologically inspired policy decision that will make life worse for its residents. Electric vehicles (EVs) are still prohibitively expensive for many Americans, and the investments to create infrastructure to handle such a vehicle transition will cost trillions.

Where, exactly, will apartment dwellers plug in their EVs? With only about 41,000 charging stations nationwide, what about everyday drivers? A family that's making the drive from Bakersfield to San Diego or Los Angeles to the Bay Area for a weekend getaway will likely need a charge on the way. Where should they plug in if they run low on juice during the drive? Even if in the unlikely event that states install new EV charging infrastructure to accommodate the new vehicles, the costs would be astronomical, forcing tax hikes.

Seattle City Light started to install charging stations around the city in 2022. Each location, which can only handle one or two vehicles, cost anywhere between $11,000 and $25,000 *each*.[728] To install so-called quick-charge stations, it'll cost a city, county, or state between $20,000 and $50,000 per station, on top of the labor and maintenance costs.[729]

To install a home charging system allowing for 120 volts, which gets you roughly 60 miles per charging hour, it'll set a family back at least $600, on top of the monthly electricity fees. How much more money will Americans be forced to pay in electricity, with costs already on the rise? Those costs surged nearly 15 percent nationwide in 2022.[730] And can the energy infrastructure withstand the demand progressives are forcing on it? California was hit with a miserable heat wave in August 2022, with residents turning on their air conditioners en masse. Governor Gavin Newsom warned Californians to conserve energy, including by unplugging their EVs. "As California's grid [nearly] suffered from blackouts under the strain of the heat waves in 2022, the question remains as to whether the Californian grid will be ready for a tidal wave of demand brought on by EVs," Rami Reshef, CEO of the hydrogen fuel cell company GenCell, told *Newsweek*.[731]

Washington and California state Democrats have been eager to push drivers into EVs, but they foresee an obvious problem. Like many other states, a statewide gas tax funds transportation infrastructure projects. As drivers move toward EVs, there's considerably smaller budgets for costly projects to fix bridges and highways. The Democrat response is one that benefits urbanists while potentially crippling rural residents. The Washington State Transportation Commission, backed by Democrat lawmakers, is recommending a road usage charge to ultimately replace the gas tax. Drivers would pay 2.5 cents for every mile they drive, a system Democrats hope to implement by 2028.[732] In California, lawmakers are considering a fee of 1.8 cents per mile, which would average out to about $115 a month for the typical commuter.[733]

The states are still working through legitimate privacy concerns. Should the government be able to track where and when we drive via a GPS device they would install (or force car manufacturers to install)? But more troublesome is that rural residents get shafted. Some have to drive miles just to get to the nearest grocery store, or even longer to visit the nearest hospital. They'll be paying more in road usage fees than the Seattleite or Los Angelino who will walk to their nearby Whole Foods but will benefit from the rural driver's mileage fees for the times they end up using the roads (whether in a car, in transit, on a bicycle, or on foot). In fairness to Democrats, their vision never intended to include rural areas or even the suburbs. They're remnants of America's racist history.

Reverse Gentrification

"Language matters," declared Seattle city councilwoman Teresa Mosqueda.[734] " 'Single family' zoning may seem to some as merely a planning term, but we know historically it has been used to further exclusionary practices and discriminatory policies of the past. If Seattle is going to be an equitable and just city, then we must also apply that same lens to our zoning code. After years of discussion, we are acting on what we know is right to undo the legacy of exclusion that exists within our planning documents—starting with how we talk about our neighborhoods."

In the summer of 2021, the Seattle City Council took on the monumental and controversial task of rezoning through a social equity lens. Like others in the Radical Left, the council members view suburbs as racist and home ownership as an underserved privilege enjoyed primarily by white people. Both concepts must be dismantled and rebuilt. It was a position that existed for years, though wasn't taken especially seriously. But the Black Lives Matter (BLM) movement inspired Radical Left politicians to view housing through a racial justice and equity lens.

Insufferably self-righteous faux think pieces started to appear, damning America's "racist" zoning laws. Progressive editorialist Jerusalem Damas declared in Vox, "it's time to sue the suburbs" arguing that the federal government "must open up the floodgates for civil rights organizations, developers, and its own Justice Department to begin suing the worst offenders of exclusionary zoning." She says the legal argument doesn't have to prove the intent of the zoning laws was racism. Rather, under the "disparate impact standard," plaintiffs would only have to show that it led to discrimination against a protected class.[735]

One reason for local pushback to rezoning is that it would change the character of the community. It neither makes sense nor is aesthetically pleasing to shove a massive apartment complex in between row after row of Spanish colonial-style homes. There were also communities that were zoned precisely to stay small so that homeowners and renters could escape the feeling of living in a large city. But to Elizabeth Winkler in the *Washington Post*, that position is "sinister," because its true intent is to keep the poor and working-class black locals from moving in. "Across the country, American communities employ 'snob zoning' policies that forbid builders from constructing apartment buildings or impose minimum residential lot requirements. They are often presented as driven by concerns that building smaller units could change the character of a community. Some ordinances even exclude modest single-family homes in the name of preserving a neighborhood's 'aesthetic uniformity,'" she complained.[736]

Lawmakers were convinced that now was the best time to dismantle single-family zoning. And that's exactly what they did, passing zoning changes to effectively implement a reverse gentrification. They didn't like that suburbs or neighborhoods were affluent and white, so they granted developers the right to erect apartment complexes and duplex or triplex dwellings.

California lawmakers passed legislation intended to squeeze multiple units into single-family zones and to build more housing around public transit, which its low-income residents must take since the state makes driving unaffordable. They claimed single-family zoning is rooted in white supremacy because a real estate developer in the 1900s used it to discriminate against black homeowners or renters because he thought they'd bring property values down.[737] The Berkeley City Council passed a resolution in 2021 to denounce the racist history of single-family housing, vowing to pursue a two-year plan to add multi-unit dwellings to neighborhoods around the city. Then-council member Lori Droste, a privileged white lady allured by the BLM movement, said the effort was "to address systemic racism. We can't address racial and economic segregation unless we address zoning reform, that's definitely true." She, and others, did manage to express that residents in single-family housing aren't racist; they're just living in what the council hopes to turn into the vestiges of a white supremacist past.[738]

BLM-inspired housing changes were already tried in Minneapolis, when the city council passed a 2018 plan called "Minneapolis 2040," which ended single-family zoning on the 70 percent of land that, up until this change, prohibited multi-family dwellings. It also ended parking requirements for developments. Advocates claimed this was a YIMBY (which stands for, "yes in my backyard") success story, pointing to declining rents in the years following the single-family zoning ban. Yet by August 2022, it failed to generate substantial new housing with just 97 new units built. Analysis by *Bloomberg News* suggested the city was on pace to add just 1 percent of new units by 2040.[739]

This isn't to suggest there wasn't an increase in housing supply that helped drive down rents (nor does this mean development won't ramp up). There *was* an increase in duplexes and triplexes being built, but they weren't developed on land previously zoned exclusively for single-family dwellings. Instead, as an analysis in *Reason* pointed out, the buildings popped up along commercial corridors. And ending the parking requirements seemed to have incentivized more developments (though that will come with the unintended consequences of making car ownership more onerous in a city where driving is nearly required).[740] It's also worth noting that prices for single-family homes increased.[741]

More housing can obviously drive down rents, but when policy is inspired by a ridiculous claim of racism, you might not see left-wing leaders focused on thoughtful and strategic growth. How often does the Radical Left make an ideological change only to then abandon further leadership all together, content with the initial virtue signal. Is a triplex going to make a difference in a suburb with single-family housing, or would you get better results by allowing (or even requiring) developers to build more stories where high-rises and large complexes already exist? And what impact do these changes have on families? Parents chose to live in single-family homes because they generally come with much more room and outdoor space so they can grow and be comfortable. The newer multi-unit dwellings aren't especially spacious (there are $3,800 a month two-bedroom apartments in Seattle with just 892 square feet of indoor space and no grassy backyards to play with the kids and pets), making it difficult to raise or grow a family.

If those in charge get mired in the equity argument surrounding policy, they won't nurture any meaningful change or address the unintended consequences of their actions. Cities that capped development heights was a result of poor planning, and that wasn't the result of white supremacy. Those city planners and leaders didn't think the areas would attract as many people as they did.

Would the Food Network Approve?

The Radical Left wants to force you onto buses paid for with higher taxes and push you into multi-unit households without a lot of space or a yard. But they're not done with their demands. They also don't want you cooking on gas stoves, so the Radical Left hopes to ban the appliances in new construction.

Commissioner Richard Trumka Jr. of the US Consumer Product Safety Commission (USCPSC) said his agency planned to take action against the dangers posed by cooking on gas stoves. They emit air pollutants including carbon monoxide, which is easily addressed by cracking a window or turning on the overhead stove fan. But suddenly the USCPSC was alarmed about the health impacts, telling *Bloomberg News* that these stoves are "a hidden hazard. Any option is on the table. Products that can't be made safe can be banned."[742] The comments came about a month after Senator Cory Booker (D-New Jersey) and Congressman Don Beter (D-Virginia) sent a letter to the agency asking them to address the "cumulative burden" that gas stove emissions have on black and Latino families. They were looking at cooking through a racial justice lens, which explains why most people who learned of the possible ban dismissed it as Radical Left nuttiness. But for some, there were consumer and business concerns. Some 40 percent of American households have a gas stove, and the food industry relies on them.

If you listened to left-wing media, this entire controversy was made up by Fox News. *Politico* dismissed the issue, claiming it was just conservatives finding "a new punching bag."[743] A panel on

MSNBC's *Morning Joe* declared it one of many "conspiracy theories" borne out of "a small kernel of something."[744] NPR featured a reporter to explain how conspiracy theories work, claiming the Right pushed the lie to fit "nicely into ready-made stories about government control or tyranny. The feds are going to come to your house and take something. And so another worldview gas stoves fit very well is the supposed absurdity of the Left."[745] But it *is* an example of the absurdity on the Left. Gas stove bans are already happening, and the Biden White House plan to support a ban was unintentionally and prematurely exposed.

California has the highest percentage of households that cook using natural gas (70 percent) and has been ground zero for the gas stove ban movement. In 2019, Berkeley became the first city in the nation to ban gas hookups in new construction, both residential and commercial. The United States Court of Appeals for the Ninth Circuit unanimously struck the ban down in 2023, but not before the legislation inspired 50 other California cities to implement similar rules. Los Angeles and Santa Barbara require new residential and commercial buildings to be built all-electric, offering an exemption only for commercial cooking. San Francisco, Glendale, and Oakland have implemented the ban for newly constructed buildings.[746]

New York governor Kathy Hochul quietly added a proposal to ban gas-powered stoves in new home and commercial construction. She did not want to bring much attention to the proposal, making only an ambiguous reference to banning "the sale of any new fossil fuel-powered heating equipment by 2030."[747] In New York City, a ban was already in place.

There's been considerable pushback from the food industry, with chefs noting they can't provide high-quality meals on electric stovetops. Restaurateur James Mallios told the *New York Post*, "I've cooked with electric in outdoor markets—like Urbanspace—and it sucked. It takes forever, and people don't like the results. You can't char—it doesn't work the same way." Restaurateur Stratis Morfogen warned that a ban "will tank it and bring growth to a half and destroy our industry." He declared the move a "total farce to appease the woke movement."[748]

Trumka, who's cooking bona fides likely extend to eating meals paid for by eco-lobbyists, dismissed the concerns from chefs. "There is this misconception that if you want to do fine-dining kind of cooking, it has to be done on gas. It's a carefully manicured myth," he said.[749]

The commissioner laid the groundwork for a future debate. And while left-wing media outlets downplayed the issue, the Biden administration was seriously considering the ban months before Trumka's interview. He wrote an October 25, 2022, memo declaring there was enough evidence on the dangers of gas stoves to forward a proposed gas stove ban, especially since "lower-cost, safer alternatives are available."[750] He advocated for a notice of proposed rulemaking (NPR) in 2023 "proposing to ban gas stoves in homes. The additional work needed to complete an NPR is primarily economic; the available health and scientific evidence on illnesses caused by the relevant gasses at the concentrations present in homes with gas stoves already exists."

He continued, "The need for gas stove regulation has reached a boiling point. CPSC has the responsibility to ban consumer products that emit hazardous substances, particularly, when those emissions harm children, under the Federal Hazardous Substances Act."

The idea of a gas stove ban isn't as surprising as one might think. Seattle banned gas heating in new construction or for replacement heating systems in older buildings, ensuring that all buildings will eventually have gas-free heating. Beginning in 2030, California homeowners will only be able to replace their gas-powered hot-water heaters with zero-emission equipment. Burlington, Vermont, even banned gas-powered leaf blowers.

The bans are part of a greater effort to control the American people, forcing them to adapt habits that, in their view, will fight climate change and so-called environmental racism where black and Latino households face harsher consequences due to environmental hazards. And they're baby steps to the ultimate plan of banning gas-powered vehicles nationwide. But ultimately the message is clear: If you want to live in cities run by the Radical Left, you must live as they tell you.

CLOSING THOUGHTS

GET ACTIVATED

WHEN I INFILTRATED ANTIFA IN SEATTLE, toured homeless encampments in Portland, dug into the policing data in Chicago, and pressed any lawmaker who would agree to come on my radio show to defend their positions, I did it with one goal in mind: to shine a spotlight on the issues few in the media will discuss openly and honestly. Someone had to do it because you deserve to know what's happening and why.

Local media from Chicago to Chattanooga, Los Angeles to Laredo, or New York to Norfolk do not tell you the full story about what's happening in your community. And when they cover important news, it's all transactional: *This happened there because of this and that.* They give you basic facts, throw in some lousy man-on-the-street reaction, and then move on to a hastily produced puff piece about a three-legged pug in need of a forever home or advice from your community's oldest living resident to live as long as she. (Spoiler: It's *always* to drink one Dr. Pepper a day and to smile more.) The most important stories sometimes garner the least amount of coverage, and it rarely connects the dots on *why* something is happening. Crime is up in San Antonio because of the open border. School scores are in the toilet in San Francisco because educators spend more time indoctrinating your kids than teaching them basic knowledge. Portland homicides, Seattle overdoses, and New York theft are soaring because of light-on-crime policies. Does your local news media tell you that directly?

After finishing the first draft of this book, I took the light-rail train to SeaTac Airport to give a speech in Las Vegas. Luggage in hand, I couldn't take an elevator to the station platform because they were occupied by druggies smoking fentanyl. None of the elevators worked because the agency in charge of transit is too busy focusing on equity initiatives for its staff. When I hopped on the train, there were three homeless people occupying much of the space, one sprawled out across multiple seats, another hunched over, passed out. The third was getting high. How did it get this bad? How did instances like this turn from occasional to the norm? I bet you have similar experiences in your own communities.

I wrote this book to help you better understand the motivation and strategies from the Radical Left. As importantly, I hoped to connect the dots between Radical Left legislation, policy, strategies, and initiatives and how the worst policies are spreading nationwide. For many of you who moved to the suburbs or to a red county to escape the madness, you quickly realized the futility of running away. Others should be warned: You can't escape the Radical Left. Their influence will infect your community next.

Ask yourself if you're happy with where you live and how you're living. Do you feel safe and secure? Do you think your kids are being cared for at school? Do you have the freedoms to live your life as you see fit? Probably not, or you likely wouldn't have made it to the end of this book.

So, now what? You've learned about the Radical Left—their motivations, strategies, and policies. What do you do with this information? The answer depends on how much you care about your communities and country, and what you want to leave your kids and grandkids. If you're like me, you see a country on life support that you so desperately want to save. Great. Then save it!

What do you want to change in your community? Start by picking one issue. Are you passionate about keeping drug consumption sites from your neighborhood? Do you want to help the homeless the way Community First! Village in Austin was able to? Are you concerned with what's being taught in your kid's schools, or do you want to fight against unfair taxes?

Picking an issue to get behind is the first step to returning your community to a place of sanity. Don't try to take on too much at once. Be realistic, then get *activated*.

I often tell my radio and podcast audience that if they truly want to enact change, they have to get activated. This means different things to different people. To me, it means getting involved in a way that's reasonable and can have a measurable effect. While I've donated time (and money) to homelessness outreach, I'm blessed to have a large platform to expose what's happening. But you can be as influential as anyone behind a microphone, in front of a camera, or behind a keyboard. You can be that one constituent who spends that one minute to send that one email to that one lawmaker on that one issue you're passionate about, convincing him or her that they're on the wrong side. For others, you can donate money or time to a campaign you believe in. For the exceptionally committed, you'll organize like-minded friends, family, and neighbors for a specific cause.

Community groups formed nationwide to put pressure on local lawmakers to do something about used needles left in parks. Concerned citizens organized a successful recall against an out-of-control DA. Parents decided to fight for their kids and oust school board members who weren't taking care of their kids. Chefs are fighting to keep a crucial tool in their restaurants, knowing the gas stove is key to their survival. Every movement starts with *one* motivated person who sacrifices time and energy for the good of the community.

The Radical Left is relatively small in number, yet they have so much power and influence over our lives. But they only hijacked our country because we let them. They amassed power by manipulating or gaming the system, while the rest of us weren't noticing. Billionaire activist George Soros knew the fastest way to enact the changes he wanted was to pour money into DA races because those positions have enormous amount of power and discretion. It was a successful strategy. Antifa radicals used threats of violence to silence opposition. It worked. President Joe Biden just stopped enforcing border security and, before any of us knew it, we had an influx of illegal immigrants coming into the country. Before we realized what was happening, our way of life and our cities changed. But now you *know* their strategies, making it that much easier to fight back and win.

America is at a crossroads. We'll either stay on a path charted by the Radical Left, or we'll map out a new course, one that wrestles back control. We can continue to follow the Radical Left's destructive policies, or we can return to common sense strategies that help those most in need, while ensuring we preserve what we love most about our communities. There are way more of us, the silent majority, than there are of them, the loud minority. We ought to act like it.

I won't lie. It can be depressing and maddening to think about how the Radical Left is destroying American cities. What they've done to places I love makes me angry. Maybe you're worried or angry about what's happening to the communities you love too. But I've come to realize we don't have to feel depressed, worried, or angry. Instead, we should feel inspired to change. And I hope you'll work hard to do what you can to defeat the Radical Left and undo their damage. Isn't this country worth saving? Because if we don't act fast, we'll go from exploring what's *killing* America to what *killed* America.

ACKNOWLEDGEMENTS

WHO WOULD HAVE THOUGHT I'd write a book, or host a successful radio show, or appear on Fox News so often? Not me. That's not to say that I didn't want to do all those things, but it's hard to imagine achieving them on my own. Of course, I didn't do any of this on my own.

First, thank you for buying this book or listening to the audio book. There are a lot of options on the market, and you chose me. Sure, I might have harassed some of you via my radio show or on Twitter, but you didn't *have* to listen. So, thank you. Want me to write another one? Buy a few more copies and give them out as gifts.

I want to thank everyone in my life (current and past) who put up with my workaholism, which got in the way of friendships at times. Thanks to my agents Paul Anderson, John McConnell, and AJ Rice for their guidance and (mostly) suppressing annoyance at my manic texts (seriously, there were a lot of manic texts). Thanks to my friend Dan Fine for dealing with my strong personality without expressing exhaustion or annoyance, Ben Shapiro for his friendship and supporting my work, Brandi Kruse for her loyalty and encouragement, Shannon Bream for her kindness and guidance, Harris Faulkner for taking time out of writing her own book to advise me, Pete Hegseth for his enthusiasm, and, of course, Tucker Carlson for giving me the opportunity to be a small part of what was the best news show on television. It always felt surreal when I appeared on his show. It never lost its excitement. Tucker inspires my work and informs how I investigate and tackle stories; I've grown and developed as a journalist because of him.

Most of you would not know who I was if not for the TV producers and bookers who took a chance on me and kept inviting me back. Thank you to Alex (who is responsible for my first-ever Tucker and Fox News appearance; I am forever indebted), Lexi, Samantha, Eldad, Johnny, Justin, Brigid, Sean, Ari, Preston, Brynn, Kourtney, Sara, Chelsea, and Jack. And if not for the trust of Stuart Varney, Trace Gallagher, Kennedy, Lawrence Jones, Rachel Campos Duffy, Will Cain, Kayleigh McEnany, Brian Kilmeade, Dana Perino, Bill Hemmer, Dan Bongino, Guy Benson, Hegseth, Bream, and Faulkner, I'd not have the privilege of appearing in front of millions of people a week. Thanks to Greg, who has been behind the camera for 99% of my appearances and always anticipates anything I need, and Anne, who does my makeup while I sarcastically respond to everything she says.

I'd like to thank my editor Alex Pappas and his team for working tirelessly to make this book better than I ever could on my own. Alex decided I was worth the risk of giving me blank pages to fill with my thoughts, and I worked hard to ensure he didn't regret it.

And thank you to Paul Morsink. He was my high school English teacher and the one who helped me develop a passion for writing. When we're in high school, we tend not to thank the people who meant the most to us in that moment in time. I regret not telling him at the time that he sparked in me an interest in writing. And given the controversial topics covered in this book, I hope he doesn't regret inspiring me.

NOTES

1 Jason Rantz, "Rantz: Tacoma Cop Who Drove out of Crowd Was Swarmed, Threatened by Mob," *MyNorthwest*, January 23, 2021, https://mynorthwest.com/2499586/rantz-mob-surrounded-threatened-safety-of-tacoma-cop-who-drove-out-of-crowd/

2 Alta Spells, "Tacoma Police Officer Drives through Crowd, Leaving at Least One Person Injured, Officials Say," CNN, January 24, 2021, https://www.cnn.com/2021/01/24/us/tacoma-officer-drives-through-crowd/index.html

3 Elwyn Lopez (@ABCNews), "Police SUV Seen Plowing through Crowd in Tacoma, Washington," YouTube, January 24, 2021, https://www.youtube.com/watch?v=Td4EIRhmKyM

4 Craig Sailor and Allison Needles, "Tacoma Police Car Plows through Crowd of Pedestrians Gathered at Downtown Street Race," *Tacoma News Tribune*, January 24, 2021, https://www.thenewstribune.com/article248726860.html

5 Jason Rantz, "Jason Rantz: I Was Inside Antifa Riots in Tacoma—This Is What I Saw," Fox News, January 26, 2021, https://www.foxnews.com/opinion/antifa-riots-tacoma-jason-rantz

6 Seattle Fire Department (@SeattleFire), "In response to protests," Twitter, May 30, 2020, 12:34 a.m., https://twitter.com/SeattleFire/status/1266588744359874560

7 Jonathan Choe (@choeshow), "Breaking: Violence in Downtown Seattle," Twitter, May 30, 2020, 5:46 p.m., https://twitter.com/choeshow/status/1266848427746324480

8 Brandi Kruse (@BrandiKruse), "Rioter took A-15," Twitter, May 30, 2020, 7:16 p.m., https://twitter.com/BrandiKruse/status/1266871105186193408

9 Jason Rantz, "WATCH: Security Guard Bravely Disarms Rioters of AR-15 in Seattle Protest," *MyNorthwest*, May 30, 2020, https://mynorthwest.com/1902233/watch-security-guard-bravely-disarms-rioters-of-ar-15-in-seattle-protest/

10 Jason Rantz (@jasonrantz), "Mayor Durkan: Demonstrators threw Molotov cocktails," Twitter, May 30, 2020, 9:21 p.m., https://twitter.com/jasonrantz/status/1266902588034650117

11 Jason Rantz (@jasonrantz), "Frozen water bottles thrown," Twitter, May 30, 2020, 9:37 p.m., https://twitter.com/jasonrantz/status/1266906662507393025

12 Jason Rantz (@jasonrantz), "Total chaos in Downtown Seattle as looting is out of control," Twitter, May 30, 2020, 7:29 p.m., https://twitter.com/jasonrantz/status/1266919709032583168

13 Kshama Sawant (@cmkshama), "The outrage on Seattle's streets today," Twitter, May 30, 2020, 10:52 p.m., https://twitter.com/cmkshama/status/1266925408231976961

14 Jason Rantz (@jasonrantz), "Seattle activists—the agitators, not the peaceful," Twitter, June 1, 2020, 1:33 a.m., https://twitter.com/jasonrantz/status/1267328352056049664

15 Seattle City Council, "Council Briefing 6/1/20," Explore Videos, Seattle Channel, https://www.seattlechannel.org/videos?videoid=x114383

16 Seattle City Council, "Council Briefing 6/1/20."

17 Seattle City Council, "Council Briefing 6/1/20."

18 Jason Rantz (@jasonrantz), "This is devolving into chaos," Twitter, June 20, 2020, 12:21 a.m., https://twitter.com/jasonrantz/status/1267672549011283968

19 Seattle Times Staff, "Seattle-Area Protests: March during Sixth Day of Action after George Floyd's Killing Draws Massive Crowd Around City Hall," *Seattle Times*, June 3, 2020, https://www.seattletimes.com/seattle-news/seattle-area-protests-mayor-jenny-durkan-to-meet-with-protest-leaders-today-as-demonstrators-prepare-for-sixth-day-of-action-after-george-floyds-death/?utm_source=link&utm_medium=social#update-12824660

20 Seattle Times Staff, "Seattle-Area Protests."

21 Seattle Times Staff, "Seattle Police Use Blast Balls, Pepper Spray to Try to Disperse Saturday Protesters," *Seattle Times*, June 6, 2020, https://www.seattletimes.com/seattle-news/seattle-area-protests-demonstrators-prepare-for-ninth-day-of-action-after-george-floyds-killing/?utm_source=link&utm_medium=social#update-12832729

22 Seattle Police Department (@SeattlePD), "At about 7:30 p.m. demonstrators outside," Twitter, June 6, 2020, 11:42 p.m., https://twitter.com/SeattlePD/status/1269474731717087233
23 Jason Rantz (@jasonrantz), "SPD Chief Carmen Best confirms arson," Twitter, June 7, 2020, 1:14 a.m., https://twitter.com/jasonrantz/status/1269497873336397826
24 Jason Rantz (@jasonrantz), "One thing Seattle cops are still dealing with," Twitter, June 7, 2020, 1:23 a.m., https://twitter.com/jasonrantz/status/1269500144342298624
25 Seattle Times Staff, "Seattle Police Use Blast Balls, Pepper Spray to Try to Disperse Saturday Protesters," *Seattle Times*, June 6, 2020, https://www.seattletimes.com/seattle-news/seattle-area-protests-demonstrators-prepare-for-ninth-day-of-action-after-george-floyds-killing/?utm_source=link&utm_medium=social#update-12833614
26 Teresa Mosqueda (@TeresaCMosqueda), "STOP. @MayorJenny @carmenbest @SeattlePD JUST STOP," Twitter, June 6, 2020, 11:33 p.m., https://twitter.com/TeresaCMosqueda/status/1269472527400591360
27 Jason Rantz (@jasonrantz), "Just now: @CMDanStrauss claims or implies," Twitter, June 7, 2020, 3:19 a.m., https://twitter.com/jasonrantz/status/1269529483758858243
28 Seattle Times Staff, "Seattle Police Use Blast Balls, Pepper Spray to Try to Disperse Saturday Protesters," *Seattle Times*, June 6, 2020, https://www.seattletimes.com/seattle-news/seattle-area-protests-demonstrators-prepare-for-ninth-day-of-action-after-george-floyds-killing/
29 Seattle Times Staff, "Seattle Police Use Blast Balls, Pepper Spray to Try to Disperse Saturday Protesters."
30 Joe Nguyen (@meetjoenguyen), "Protesters are peaceful but this doesn't look like peace," Twitter, June 7, 2020, 2:03 a.m., https://twitter.com/meetjoenguyen/status/1269510228468396032?ref_src=twsrc%5Etfw
31 Jason Rantz, "Rantz: Seattle Councilmember Defends 'Kill Yourselves' Threat to Cops at Protest," *MyNorthwest*, June 7, 2020, https://mynorthwest.com/1927020/rantz-man-threatens-murder-cops-seattle-protest-councilwoman/
32 Jason Rantz (@jasonrantz), "Protesters claim SPD instigates violence," Twitter, June 7, 2020, 4:10 p.m., https://twitter.com/jasonrantz/status/1269723405751705600?s=20&t=6LNAr7g_p0wp5Vf4dLrRPQ
33 Jason Rantz (@jasonrantz), "Chief @carmenbest calls out people falsely claiming 'brutality,'" Twitter, June 7, 2020, 10:38 p.m., https://twitter.com/jasonrantz/status/1269820948581986305?s=20&t=6LNAr7g_p0wp5Vf4dLrRPQ

34 KING-5 Staff, "Protesters Remove Barricade at Seattle's East Precinct on Capitol Hill," KING-TV, June 8, 2020, https://www.king5.com/article/news/local/washington-protests-seattle-demonstrations-real-time-updates-live-blog-monday-june-8/281-fe44844b-f212-457b-be77-2fc280bb678d

35 Isolde Raftery, "We Know Who Made the Call to Leave Seattle Police's East Precinct Last Summer, Finally," KUOW Radio, July 9, 2021, https://www.kuow.org/stories/we-know-who-made-the-call-to-seattle-police-s-east-precinct-last-summer-finally

36 Seattle Police Department (@spdblotter), "Chief Best Address to Officers," YouTube, June 11, 2020, https://youtu.be/iH0BwJdw28I

37 Daniel Beekman and Lewis Kamb, "As Police Were Abandoning East Precinct, Seattle Officials Drafted Plan to Give Station to a Black Lives Matter Group," *Seattle Times*, January 30, 2022, https://www.seattletimes.com/seattle-news/politics/as-police-were-abandoning-spd-east-precinct-seattle-officials-drafted-plan-to-give-station-near-chop-to-a-black-lives-matter-group/

38 Esmy Jimenez and Isolde Raftery, "'They've Given Us the Precinct.' Seattle Police Backs Away, and Protesters Take Back Pine," KUOW, June 8, 2020, https://www.kuow.org/stories/they-gave-us-east-precinct-seattle-police-backs-away-from-the-barricade

39 Jimenez and Raftery, "'They've Given Us the Precinct.' Seattle Police Backs Away, and Protesters Take Back Pine."

40 Nick Givas, "Seattle News Crew Attacked as Police Leave Precinct, Newly Released Video Shows," Fox News, June 17, 2020, https://www.foxnews.com/us/seattle-news-crew-attacked-as-police-leave-precinct-newly-released-video

41 Seattle Times Staff, "Seattle-Area Protests: Demonstrators Back on Capitol Hill after Occupying City Hall," *Seattle Times*, June 9, 2020, https://www.seattletimes.com/seattle-news/seattle-area-protests-live-updates-for-tuesday-june-9/?utm_source=link&utm_medium=social#update-12840167

42 Seattle Times Staff, "Seattle-Area Protests: Demonstrators Back on Capitol Hill after Occupying City Hall."

43 Seattle Times Staff, "Seattle-Area Protests: Demonstrators Back on Capitol Hill after Occupying City Hall."

44 Jonathan Choe, "Council Member Sawant Let Protesters into City Hall to Show It Belongs to the People," KOMO-TV, June 10, 2020, https://komonews.com/news/local/council-member-sawant-let-protesters-into-city-hall-to-show-it-belongs-to-the-people

45 Seattle Times Staff, "Seattle-Area Protests: Demonstrators Back on Capitol Hill after Occupying City Hall."

46 Seattle Times Staff, "Seattle-Area Protests: Demonstrators Back on Capitol Hill after Occupying City Hall."

47 Jason Rantz, "I'm Reporting from Seattle's CHOP. Here's What It's Really Been Like," *The Daily Signal*, June 29, 2020, https://www.dailysignal.com/2020/06/29/im-reporting-from-seattles-chop-heres-what-its-really-been-like/

48 Rantz, "I'm Reporting from Seattle's CHOP. Here's What It's Really Been Like."

49 Dan Simon, "Protesters Have Occupied Part of Seattle's Capitol Hill for a Week. Here's What It's Like Inside," CNN, June 15, 2020, https://www.cnn.com/2020/06/15/us/seattle-capitol-hill-autonomous-zone-monday/index.html

50 Reuters Staff, "Trump Suggests Governors Call in National Guard to 'Dominate the Streets,'" Reuters, June 5, 2020, https://www.reuters.com/article/us-minneapolis-police-protests-trump/trump-suggests-governors-call-in-national-guard-to-dominate-the-streets-idUSKBN23C258

51 Bill Chappell, "'Go Back to Your Bunker,' Seattle Mayor Tells Trump in Spat over Protests," National Public Radio, June 11, 2020, https://www.npr.org/sections/live-updates-protests-for-racial-justice/2020/06/11/874690470/go-back-to-your-bunker-seattle-mayor-tells-trump-in-spat-over-protests

52 Jay Inslee (@JayInslee), "A man who is totally incapable of governing," Twitter, June 11, 2020, 12:51 a.m., https://twitter.com/JayInslee/status/1270941712320352258

53 Rebecca Perry (@Rebecca_Perry), "Gov. Inslee on so-called 'autonomous Zone," Twitter, June 10, 2020, 7:16 p.m., https://twitter.com/Rebecca_Perry/status/1270857416955981825

54 Mike Baker, "Free Food, Free Speech and Free of Police: Inside Seattle's 'Autonomous Zone,'" *New York Times*, June 11, 2020, https://www.nytimes.com/2020/06/11/us/seattle-autonomous-zone.html

55 Simon, "Protesters Have Occupied Part of Seattle's Capitol Hill for a Week. Here's What It's Like Inside."

56 Ian Schwartz, "Seattle Mayor Durkan: CHAZ Has a 'Block Party Atmosphere,' Could Turn into "Summer of Love,'" *Real Clear Politics*, CNN, June 12, 2020, https://www.realclearpolitics.com/video/2020/06/12/seattle_mayor_durkan_chaz_has_a_block_party_atmosphere_could_turn_into_summer_of_love.html

57 Kelly Weill, "Local Businesses Love the 'Domestic Terror' Zone in Seattle, Actually," *Daily Beast*, June 12, 2020, https://www.thedailybeast.com/local-businesses-love-the-domestic-terror-autonomous-zone-in-seattle-actually

58 Schwartz, "Seattle Mayor Durkan: CHAZ Has a 'Block Party Atmosphere,' Could Turn into 'Summer of Love.' "
59 Puget Sound John Brown Gun Club. Accessed January 2023, https://psjbgc.org/
60 Casey Martin (@caseyworks), "Just spoke with 2 people at #CHAZ entrances with AR-15s," Twitter, June 11, 2020, 4:06 a.m., https://twitter.com/caseyworks/status/1270990666542141440
61 Simon, "Protesters Have Occupied Part of Seattle's Capitol Hill for a Week. Here's What It's Like Inside."
62 Raz Simone (@RazSimone), "Yes I WAS a 'pimp' not like that tho," Twitter, June 24, 2020, 6:38 p.m., https://twitter.com/razsimone/status/1275921224963551235
63 Alex Kasprak, "Does This Video Show Raz Simone Handing Out Guns in Seattle's CHOP," Snopes, June 23, 2020, https://www.snopes.com/fact-check/raz-simone-guns/
64 Jason Rantz (@jasonrantz), "This man kept bumping into me," Twitter, June 13, 2020, 5:36 p.m., https://twitter.com/jasonrantz/status/1271919349423411200/photo/1
65 Kyle (@kesags), "Pretty sure Jason Rantz has entered the Autonomous Zone," Twitter, June 13, 2020, 4:55 p.m., https://twitter.com/kseags/status/1271909054504263680?
66 Jason Rantz, "Rantz: Alleged Seattle Arsonist Near CHOP Arrested, AK-47 Found Nearby," *MyNorthwest*, June 17, 2020, https://mynorthwest.com/1959063/rantz-seattle-chop-arsonist-arrested-weapons-found/
67 Jason Rantz, "Rantz: Alleged Seattle Arsonist Near CHOP Arrested, AK-47 Found Nearby."
68 Jason Rantz, "Rantz: Alleged Seattle Arsonist Near CHOP Arrested, AK-47 Found Nearby."
69 Jason Rantz, "Rantz: Alleged Seattle Arsonist Near CHOP Arrested, AK-47 Found Nearby."
70 Jason Rantz, "Rantz: Confusion as Seattle Activists Change CHAZ to CHOP," *MyNorthwest*, June 13, 2020, https://mynorthwest.com/1945236/rantz-chaz-chop-name-change/
71 Daisy Zavala Magana, "CHOP Protester Sentenced to 2 Years in Prison for Lighting Fire Outside Seattle Police East Precinct," *MyNorthwest*, October 5, 2021, https://www.seattletimes.com/seattle-news/law-justice/chop-protester-sentenced-2-years-in-prison-for-lighting-fire-outside-seattle-police-east-precinct/
72 Rich Smith, "CHOP Medic Intervened in a Sexual Assault in Cal Anderson," *The Stranger* (slog), June 19, 2020, https://www.thestranger.com/slog/2020/06/19/43938596/chop-medic-intervened-in-a-sexual-assault-in-cal-anderson

73 Brandi Kruse (@BrandiKruse), "The addition of concrete barriers," Twitter, June 16, 2020, 1:05 p.m., https://twitter.com/BrandiKruse/status/1272938368423231489
74 Anthony Derrick, "City of Seattle Engages with Capitol Hill Organized Protest to Make Safety Changes," Office of the Mayor, City of Seattle, June 16, 2020, https://durkan.seattle.gov/2020/06/city-of-seattle-responds-to-the-capitol-hill-organized-protest/
75 Jason Rantz, "Rantz: CHOP Seattle Activists Already Blocking Lanes City Opened," *MyNorthwest*, June 16, 2020, https://mynorthwest.com/1953935/rantz-chop-seattle-blocking-lanes-city-opened/
76 Stephanie Klein, "Police Release Body Cam Footage after CHOP Shooting," *MyNorthwest*, June 20, 2020, https://mynorthwest.com/1968889/seattle-police-investigate-shooting-chop/
77 Stephanie Klein, "Kshama Sawant Releases Statement on Shooting at the CHOP," *MyNorthwest*, June 20, 2020, https://mynorthwest.com/1969263/kshama-sawant-statement-shooting-chop/
78 Stephanie Klein, "Kshama Sawant Releases Statement on Shooting at the CHOP."
79 Cole Miller (@ColeMillerTV), "Here's the full statement from @CHOP," Twitter, June 21, 2020, 1:41 a.m., https://twitter.com/ColeMillerTV/status/1274578220545798145
80 Tim Stelloh, "Officials Tell Protesters to Leave Seattle's 'Autonomous Zone,'" NBC News, June 22, 2020, https://www.nbcnews.com/news/us-news/officials-tell-protesters-leave-seattle-s-autonomous-zone-n1231821
81 Associated Press Staff, "Seattle Protesters: We Are Here to Dismantle Systemic Racism," KING-TV, June 25, 2020, https://www.king5.com/article/news/local/seattle-protesters-we-are-here-to-dismantle-systemic-racism/281-5029ffa8-5cad-46c1-ac7b-b75b597b043e
82 Associated Press Staff, "Seattle Protesters: We Are Here to Dismantle Systemic Racism."
83 *Free Capitol Hill* (blog), "The Demands of the Collective Black Voices at Free Capitol Hill to the Government of Seattle, Washington," Medium.com, June 9, 2020, https://medium.com/@seattleblmanon3/the-demands-of-the-collective-black-voices-at-free-capitol-hill-to-the-government-of-seattle-ddaee51d3e47
84 Halie Golden, "Seattle Will Move to Dismantle 'Chaz' Occupied Protest Zone, Mayor Says," *The Guardian*, June 23, 2020, https://www.theguardian.com/us-news/2020/jun/22/seattle-dismantle-chaz-protest-zone
85 Theron Zahn (@TheronZahnKOMO), "BREAKING: SDOT crews have backed down," Twitter, June 26, 2020, 11:16 a.m., https://twitter.com/TheronZahnKOMO/status/1276534750174314497

86 Preston Phillips (@PrestonTVNews), "JUST IN: Seattle Mayor Jenny Durkan's office says Seattle PD won't return," Twitter, June 26, 2020, 3:53 p.m., https://twitter.com/PrestonTVNews/status/1276604485511479297

87 Jason Rantz (@jasonrantz), "After a guy with a bloody eyebrow took shelter," Twitter, June 26, 2020, 3:14 p.m., https://twitter.com/jasonrantz/status/1276594672194838528

88 Rebecca Moss and Ashley Hiruko, "Family of Teen Killed in CHOP Zone Alleges Seattle's Failings Enabled 'State-Created Danger,'" *Seattle Times*, July 19, 2022, https://www.seattletimes.com/seattle-news/times-watchdog/family-of-16-year-old-killed-in-chop-zone-alleges-seattles-failings-enabled-a-state-created-danger/; David Gutman and Sydney Brownstone, "'Everybody Down!' What Happened at the Shooting That Killed a Teenager and Led to CHOP's Shutdown," *Seattle Times*, July 8, 2020, https://www.seattletimes.com/seattle-news/everybody-down-what-happened-at-the-chop-shooting-that-killed-a-teenager-and-led-to-the-areas-shutdown/

89 Seattle Police Department (@SeattlePD), "As of 7:45 a.m., officers have made 23 arrests," Twitter, July 1, 2020, 10:57 a.m., https://twitter.com/SeattlePD/status/1278342077311406081

90 Seattle Police Department (@SeattlePD), "Officers are investigating several vehicles," Twitter, July 1, 2020, 9:35 a.m., https://twitter.com/SeattlePD/status/1278321414655770632

91 Jason Rantz (@jasonrantz), "Small group of protesters around CHOP are now chanting," Twitter, July 1, 2020, 11:28 a.m., https://twitter.com/jasonrantz/status/1278349714535014405

92 Jason Rantz, "Rantz: Seattle Experienced a Violent Riot Against Police, Not a Protest," *MyNorthwest*, July 26, 2020, https://mynorthwest.com/2048957/rantz-seattle-riot-not-protest-anti-police/

93 Jason Rantz (@jasonrantz), "The peaceful protesters destroyed a Starbucks," Twitter, July 25, 2020, 8:51 p.m., https://twitter.com/jasonrantz/status/1287188641903607810

94 Rantz, "Rantz: Seattle Experienced a Violent Riot Against Police, Not a Protest."

95 Jason Rantz, "Rantz: Rioters Tried to Burn Seattle Police Alive, Sealed Door during Fire at East Precinct," *MyNorthwest*, August 25, 2020, https://mynorthwest.com/2114190/rantz-rioters-burn-seattle-police-alive-sealed-door/

96 US Attorney's Office, Western District of Washington, "Alaska Man Sentenced to 20 Months in Prison for Arson Conspiracy for August 2020 Fire at Seattle Police East Precinct," news release, May 24, 2020, https://www.justice.gov/usao-wdwa/pr/alaska-man-sentenced-20-months-prison-arson-conspiracy-august-2020-fire-seattle-police

97 Jason Rantz, "Rantz: Video Shows Activists Launching Molotov Cocktails at Seattle Police Union Building," *MyNorthwest*, August 26, 2020, https://mynorthwest.com/2117542/rantz-video-shows-activists-launching-molotov-cocktails-at-seattle-police-union-building/

98 Jason Rantz, "Rantz: Former Dem State Rep's Son Suspected of Hitting Officer in Head with Bat," *MyNorthwest*, September 28, 2020, https://mynorthwest.com/2194005/rantz-former-dem-state-reps-son-arrested-officer-bat-head/

99 Daisy Zavala Magana, "Kirkland Man Who Hit Officer with Bat during Seattle Demonstration Sentenced," *Seattle Times*, March 16, 2022, https://www.seattletimes.com/seattle-news/law-justice/kirkland-man-who-hit-officer-with-bat-during-seattle-demonstration-sentenced/

100 Jason Rantz, "Rantz: Ex-lawmaker's Son Charged in Planning Sophisticated Attacks against Seattle Police," *MyNorthwest*, October 16, 2020, https://mynorthwest.com/2238652/rantz-ex-lawmakers-son-sophisticated-attack-seattle-police-charged/

101 Danielle Wallace, "Seattle Realtor, Stepson of Ex-Dem Lawmaker Became 'Protest Buddies,' Charged with Arson Attack on Precinct," Fox News, October 21, 2020, https://www.foxnews.com/us/seattle-protest-buddies-arson-police-assault

102 KIRO-TV Staff, "Man Sentenced for Attack on Seattle Officer during 2020 Demonstration," KIRO-TV, March 11, 2022, https://www.kiro7.com/news/local/man-sentenced-attack-seattle-officer-during-2020-demonstration/MS6TJKZ7LBAQ5NZACH77ZAQJ7M/

103 Yaron Steinbuch, "Rep. Jerry Nadler Calls Violence from Antifa in Portland a 'Myth,'" *New York Post*, July 27, 2020, https://nypost.com/2020/07/27/jerry-nadler-calls-violence-from-antifa-in-portland-a-myth/

104 *State of Washington v. Shannon B. Blake,* No. 35601-9-III, January 22, 2019, https://www.courts.wa.gov/opinions/pdf/356019_unp.pdf

105 *State v. Blake,* Supreme Court, February 25, 2021, WA Reports Public Access Cuil PAW Document Page (lexis.com)

106 SB 5476, https://app.leg.wa.gov/billsummary?BillNumber=5476&Year=2021&Initiative=false

107 Jim Brunner, "King County Prosecutor Dan Satterberg Says He's Now a Democrat," *Seattle Times*, May 29, 2018, https://www.seattletimes.com/seattle-news/politics/king-county-prosecutor-dan-satterberg-says-hes-now-a-democrat/

108 Dan Satterberg, "Crackdown on Immigrants Undermines Public Safety," *Seattle Times*, March 24, 2017, https://www.seattletimes.com/opinion/crackdown-on-immigrants-undermines-public-safety/

109 Nicholas Kristof, "Seattle Has Figured Out How to End the War on Drugs," *New York Times*, August 23, 2019, https://www.nytimes.com/2019/08/23/opinion/sunday/opioid-crisis-drug-seattle.html

110 Kristof, "Seattle Has Figured Out How to End the War on Drugs."

111 Jason Rantz, "Rantz: Homeless Bazaar Selling 'Stolen' Clothes, Booze Takes over Prime Seattle Location," *MyNorthwest*, July 25, 2021, https://mynorthwest.com/3032314/rantz-homeless-bazaar-stolen-seattle/

112 Evan Bush and Andy Manix, "City Attorney Pete Holmes Apologizes for Taking Pot to Work," *Seattle Times*, July 11, 2014, https://www.seattletimes.com/seattle-news/marijuana/city-attorney-pete-holmes-apologizes-for-taking-pot-to-work/

113 King County Public Health Database, "Overdose Deaths," https://kingcounty.gov/depts/health/examiner/services/reports-data/overdose.aspx

114 Jason Rantz, "Rantz: Seattle Running Out of Dead Body Storage Due to Fentanyl ODs," *MyNorthwest*, January 22, 2023, https://mynorthwest.com/3788318/rantz-seattle-running-out-of-dead-body-storage-due-to-fentanyl-ods/

115 Daniel Beekman, "Seattle Court Agrees to Vacate Misdemeanor Marijuana Convictions Prosecuted Before Legalization," *Seattle Times*, September 24, 2022, https://www.seattletimes.com/seattle-news/politics/seattle-court-agrees-to-vacate-misdemeanor-marijuana-convictions-prosecuted-before-legalization/

116 *City of Seattle v. Defendant*, Preliminary Findings of Fact, Conclusions of Law and Order re: City's Motion to Dismiss Possession of Marijuana Charges, September 11, 2018, https://news.seattle.gov/wp-content/uploads/2018/09/MarijuanaOrder.pdf

117 Amelia Templeton, "Oregon Becomes 1st State in the US to Decriminalize Drug Possession," Oregon Public Broadcasting, November 3, 2018, https://www.opb.org/article/2020/11/04/oregon-measure-110-decriminalize-drugs/

118 Simon Gutierrez, "Proposed Initiative Aims to Reduce Meth Distribution in Oregon," KPTV-TV, March 8, 2020, https://www.kptv.com/2020/03/09/proposed-initiative-aims-reduce-meth-distribution-oregon/

119 Simon Gutierrez, "Proposed Ballot Measure Would Change How Oregon Handles Drug Addiction," KPTV-TV, February 11, 2020, https://www.kptv.com/2020/02/12/proposed-ballot-measure-would-change-how-oregon-handles-drug-addiction/

120 Gutierrez, "Proposed Initiative Aims to Reduce Meth Distribution in Oregon."

121 Gutierrez, "Proposed Ballot Measure Would Change How Oregon Handles Drug Addiction."

122 Dirk VanderHart,"Oregon's Pioneering Drug Law Raises More Questions than Answers in Early Months," Oregon Public Broadcasting, October 27, 2021, https://www.opb.org/article/2021/10/27/oregon-pioneering-drug-law-raises-more-questions-than-answers-early-months/

123 Dirk VanderHart, "Addiction Experts Tell Oregon Lawmakers the State Has Been Too Lax on Drug Use," Oregon Public Broadcasting, September 21, 2022, https://www.opb.org/article/2022/09/21/oregon-decriminalize-drugs-measure-110-addiction-treatment/

124 Mental Health and Addiction Certification Board of Oregon, "Oregon Data Extracted from the National Survey on Drug Use and Health," December 2021, https://mhacbo.org/media/2021_epidemiology.pdf

125 Oregon Criminal Justice Commission, "Analysis of Oregon's Publicly Funded Substance Abuse Treatment System: Report and Findings for Senate Bill 1041," September 2019, https://www.oregon.gov/cjc/CJC%20Document%20Library/SB1041Report.pdf

126 Oregon Health Authority, "Opioids and the Ongoing Drug Overdose Crisis in Oregon," September 2022, https://sharedsystems.dhsoha.state.or.us/DHSForms/Served/le2479_22.pdf

127 Oregon Health Authority, "Opioid Overdose Public Health Surveillance Update," December 21, 2022, https://www.oregon.gov/oha/PH/PREVENTIONWELLNESS/SUBSTANCEUSE/OPIOIDS/Documents/monthly_opioid_overdose_related_data_report.pdf

128 Keith Humphreys testimony, Senate Interim Committee on Judiciary and Ballot Measure 110 Implementation, September 21, 2022, https://olis.oregonlegislature.gov/liz/2021I1/Committees/SJD110/2022-09-21-08-30/MeetingMaterials

129 Keith Humphreys testimony, Senate Interim Committee on Judiciary and Ballot Measure 110 Implementation, September 21, 2022, https://olis.oregonlegislature.gov/liz/2021I1/Committees/SJD110/2022-09-21-08-30/MeetingMaterials

130 Blair Best, " 'We're Done with Portland': Some Residents Move Away over What They Say Is the City's Lack of Response to Homeless Camps," KGW-TV, August 29, 2022, https://www.kgw.com/article/news/local/homeless/portland-residents-move-washington-over-lack-response-homeless-camps/283-6eea7e53-4a56-4296-97cc-f8fe106818c7

131 Simon Gutierrez, "City of Portland Struggling with Rampant Property Crime," KPTV-TV, November 15, 2022, https://www.kptv.com/2022/11/15/city-portland-struggling-with-rampant-property-crime/

132 Bobby Allyn, "Justice Department Promises Crackdown on Supervised Injection Facilities," National Public Radio, August 30, 2018, https://www.npr.org/sections/health-shots/2018/08/30/642735759/justice-department-promises-crackdown-on-supervised-injection-sites

133 Michael Nedelman, "Philadelphia Takes Bold Step toward Opening Drug Injection Sites," CNN, January 24, 2018, https://www.cnn.com/2018/01/24/health/philadelphia-supervised-injection-sites/index.html

134 Hoag Levins, "LDI Pilot Grant Funds Evaluation Study of Philadelphia's Safe Injection Facility Concept," University of Pennsylvania, January 28, 2018, https://ldi.upenn.edu/our-work/research-updates/ldi-pilot-grant-funds-evaluation-study-of-philadelphias-safe-injection-facility-concept/

135 Elana Gordon, "Mapping Project to Assess Best, Worst Locations for Philly Safe Injection Site," WHYY Radio, February 22, 2018, https://whyy.org/articles/mapping-project-assess-best-worst-locations-philly-safe-injection-site/

136 Mark Stevenson and MaryClaire Dale, "Mexico Depicts Philadelphia Street Scenes in Anti-drug Ads," Associated Press, November 11, 2022, https://abcnews.go.com/Health/wireStory/mexico-depicts-philadelphia-street-scenes-anti-drug-ads-93126359

137 Jason Rantz, "Rantz: I Visited Vancouver's Devastating, Dangerous Safe-Injection Neighborhood," *MyNorthwest*, October 31, 2017, https://mynorthwest.com/799135/visiting-insite-safe-injection/

138 Mike Howell, "Philadelphia Mayor Visits Vancouver's Drug Injection Sites," VancouverIsAwesome.com., August 8, 2019, https://www.vancouverisawesome.com/local-news/philadelphia-mayor-kenney-injection-sites-vancouver-bc-1945052

139 Bobby Allyn, "Justice Department Promises Crackdown on Supervised Injection Facilities" National Public Radio, August 30, 2018, https://www.npr.org/sections/health-shots/2018/08/30/642735759/justice-department-promises-crackdown-on-supervised-injection-sites

140 Bobby Allyn, "Desperate Cities Consider 'Safe Injection' Sites for Opioid Users," National Public Radio, January 10, 2018, https://www.npr.org/sections/health-shots/2018/01/10/576757086/desperate-cities-consider-safe-injection-sites-for-opioid-users

141 Timothy Nerozzi, "NYC Health Department's Heroin-Fentanyl Poster Sparks Anger from Top City Council Republican," Fox News, May 27, 2022, https://www.foxnews.com/us/nyc-health-department-heroin-fentanyl-poster-anger-city-council-republican

142 Melissa Klein, "City to Junkies: Don't Be Ashamed to Get High," *New York Post*, May 28, 2022, https://nypost.com/2022/05/28/city-tells-junkies-not-to-be-ashamed-to-get-high/

143 "Respect to Connect: Undoing Stigma," The National Harm Reduction Coalition, February 2, 2021, https://harmreduction.org/issues/harm-reduction-basics/undoing-stigma-facts/

144 Jason Rantz, "Rantz: Seattle Public Health Will Give Needles to Minors, Community Pushes Back," *MyNorthwest*, April 4, 2022, https://mynorthwest.com/2748522/rantz-seattle-public-health-needles-minors/

145 Jason Rantz, "Rantz: Seattle Public Health Will Give Needles to Minors, Community Pushes Back," *MyNorthwest*, April 4, 2022, https://mynorthwest.com/2748522/rantz-seattle-public-health-needles-minors/

146 EdHat Staff, "Four-Year-Old Pricked by Used Needle at Local Park," EdHat.com., October 23, 2018, https://www.edhat.com/news/four-year-old-pricked-by-used-needle-at-local-park

147 Alys Martinez, "Parents Demand Answers after 4-Year-Old Son Was Pricked by Discarded Needle at Park," KEYT-TV, October 23, 2018, https://keyt.com/news/2018/10/23/parents-demand-answers-after-4-year-old-son-was-pricked-by-discarded-needle-at-park/

148 Griffin Kelly, "'Woke' NYC Starbucks Now a Haven for Junkies, Drunks, and Homeless," *New York Post*, August 13, 2022, https://nypost.com/2022/08/13/squatters-take-over-noho-starbucks/

149 Amy Clancy, "Starbucks Baristas Poked by Discarded Needles," KIRO-TV, April 23, 2019, https://www.kiro7.com/news/local/starbucks-baristas-poked-by-discarded-needles-1/845466157/

150 Ana Sofia Nauf, "Starbucks Baristas Are at Risk of Being Poked by Dirty Needles," *The Stranger*, April 20, 2016, https://www.thestranger.com/news/2016/04/20/23980766/starbucks-baristas-are-at-risk-of-being-poked-by-dirty-needles

151 Jason Rantz, "Rantz: Seattle Homeless Shelter Buys Heroin Pipes with City Funds, Teaches Rectal Injection Method," *MyNorthwest*, February 21, 2021, https://mynorthwest.com/2593799/rantz-seattle-shelter-city-fund-heroin-pipes-injection/

152 Jason Rantz, "Rantz: Seattle Homeless Shelter Buys Heroin Pipes with City Funds, Teaches Rectal Injection Method," *MyNorthwest*, February 21, 2021, https://mynorthwest.com/2593799/rantz-seattle-shelter-city-fund-heroin-pipes-injection/

153 Jason Rantz, "Rantz: Seattle Homeless Shelter Buys Heroin Pipes with City Funds, Teaches Rectal Injection Method," *MyNorthwest*, February 21, 2021, https://mynorthwest.com/2593799/rantz-seattle-shelter-city-fund-heroin-pipes-injection/

154 Elizabeth Heckman, "Business Owners 'Shaking Their Heads' as Boston Gives Free Crack Pipes to Addicts: 'All of Us Are Suffering,'" Fox News, December 9, 2022, https://www.foxnews.com/media/business-owners-shaking-heads-boston-gives-free-crack-pipes-addicts-us-suffering

155 California Department of Health Care Services, "Recovery Incentives Program: California's Contingency Management Benefit," January 2023, https://www.dhcs.ca.gov/Pages/DMC-ODS-Contingency-Management.aspx

156 Seattle Office of City Auditor, "Action Is Needed to Explore Ways to Offer an Evidence-Based Treatment for People Who Use Methamphetamine,"

October 24, 2022, https://www.seattle.gov/documents/Departments/CityAuditor/auditreports/Methamphetamine_Audit_Published_10-24-22.pdf

157 Jim Kenney and Larry Krasner, "Criminalizing Crack Addiction Was a Mistake. Philly's Approach to Opioids Must Be Different," *Philadelphia Inquirer*, February 15, 2018, https://www.inquirer.com/philly/opinion/commentary/opioid-safe-injection-sites-cues-comprehensive-user-engagement-philadelphia-jim-kenney-larry-krasner-20180215.html

158 US Department of Justice, "2020 Drug Enforcement Administration National Drug Threat Assessment," March 2021, https://www.dea.gov/sites/default/files/2021-02/DIR-008-21%202020%20National%20Drug%20Threat%20Assessment_WEB.pdf

159 Charles Couger, "Convicted Murderer Vows to Get LA DA Gascon's Name Tattooed on His Face in Audio Obtained by Fox News," Fox News, April 18, 2022, https://www.foxnews.com/media/convicted-murderer-gascons-name-tattoo-audio

160 Maloy Moore, Ryan Menezes, and James Queally, "Here Are the Mega-Donors and Police Unions Pouring Millions into the L.A. County District Attorney Race," *Los Angeles Times*, November 3, 2020, https://www.latimes.com/projects/la-district-attorney-race-top-donors/

161 James Queally, "George Gascón Takes Office, Facing Test on Campaign Vows," *Los Angeles Times*, December 7, 2020, https://www.latimes.com/california/story/2020-12-07/george-gascon-campaign-promises-la-county-district-attorney

162 Charles Couger, "Convicted Murderer Vows to Get LA DA Gascon's Name Tattooed on His Face in Audio Obtained by Fox News," Fox News, April 18, 2022, https://www.foxnews.com/media/convicted-murderer-gascons-name-tattoo-audio

163 Brianna Herlihy, "Study Debunks 'Red State Murder' Claim from Hillary Clinton, Democrats," Fox NewsFox News, November 4, 2022, https://www.foxnews.com/politics/new-study-debunks-red-state-high-crime-claim-by-hillary-clinton-democrats

164 Larry Krasner, "Krasner: Racism Hides Best in Our Beliefs About Crime," *Philadelphia Tribune*, November 23, 2020, https://www.phillytrib.com/special_sections/raceinamerica/justice/krasner-racism-hides-best-in-our-beliefs-about-crime/article_b2654cdc-79b5-5784-ac1a-10e4968218c2.html

165 Kim Foxx, "To Tackle Violence, It Is Vital That We Reckon with Race," *Chicago Sun Times*, December 7, 2020, https://chicago.suntimes.com/2020/12/7/22160123/kim-foxx-institutional-racism-system-racism-chicago-violence-states-attorneys-office

166 Danielle Wallace and Marta Dhanis, "NYC Judge Drops Murder Charge against Bodega Worker after Manhattan DA Backtracks," Fox News,

July 19, 2022, https://www.foxnews.com/us/manhattan-da-moves-drop-murder-charge-nyc-bodega-worker-deadly-stabbing

167 FOX 5 News York (@fox5ny), "Outrage after Manhattan Bodega Worker Charged with Murder," YouTube, July 8, 2022, https://www.youtube.com/watch?v=E2Wygod9Zzk&ab_channel=FOX5NewYork

168 Caitlyn Shelton, "Outrage Mounts over Prosecution of NYC Bodega Clerk," NewsNation, July 12, 2022, https://www.newsnationnow.com/on-balance-with-leland-vittert/outrage-mounts-over-prosecution-of-nyc-bodega-clerk/

169 Jason Rantz, "Rantz: WA Democrats' Bill Says It's 'Racial Equity' to Go Easy on Drive-by Murderers," *MyNorthwest*, December 28, 2021, https://mynorthwest.com/3293353/rantz-wa-democrats-bill-says-its-racial-equity-to-go-easy-on-drive-by-murderers/

170 George Gascón (@GeorgeGascon), "For decades we attached felony consequences too low-level offenses," Twitter, December 7, 2020, 3:52 p.m., https://twitter.com/georgegascon/status/1336050949165465602

171 Office of Juvenile Justice and Delinquency Prevention, "Arts-Based Programs and Arts Therapies for At-Risk, Justice-Involved, and Traumatized Youths," May 2016, https://ojjdp.ojp.gov/mpg/literature-review/arts-based-programs-for-youth.pdf

172 Michael Ruiz, "Los Angeles DA Gascon's Office Lands 5-Month Probation Camp Sentence for Teen Who Mowed Down Mom and Infant," Fox News, June 3, 2022, https://www.foxnews.com/us/los-angeles-da-gascon-sentence-teen-mom-infant-video

173 Michael Ruiz and Bill Melugin, "Venice Hit-and-Run Driver Who Plowed into Mom, Baby in Stolen Car Is Murdered after Light Sentence," FOX Los Angeles, January 20, 2023, https://www.foxla.com/news/venice-hit-and-run-mom-baby-stolen-murdered-after-light-sentence-gascon

174 Tammy Mutasa, "Teen Robbery Suspects on House Arrest on the Run after Cutting Off Electronic Monitors," KOMO-TV, March 22, 2022, https://komonews.com/news/operation-crime-justice/teen-robbery-suspects-on-house-arrest-on-the-run-after-cutting-off-electronic-monitors

175 Alfred Charles, "2 Teen Fugitive Suspects in Pawn Shop Robbery Now Prime Suspects in Tacoma Pot Shop Murder," KOMO-TV, March 24, 2022, https://komonews.com/news/local/2-teen-fugitive-suspects-in-pawn-shop-robbery-now-prime-suspects-in-tacoma-pot-shop-murder

176 KING 5 Staff, "Teen Pleads Not Guilty in Robbery That Led to Deadly Shooting of Tacoma Pot Shop Employee," KING-TV, April 20, 2022, https://www.king5.com/article/news/crime/teen-pleads-not-guilty-robbery-deadly-shooting-tacoma-pot-shop/281-2a13f0b4-d0d9-4e41-82fe-514790eabfb6

177 FOX 32 News Staff, " 'Shocks the Conscience': Chicago Police Arrested 11-Year-Old for Carjacking, Brown Says," WFLD-TV, November 29, 2021, https://www.fox32chicago.com/news/shocks-the-conscience-chicago-police-arrested-11-year-old-for-carjacking-brown-says

178 WWLTV (@wwltv), "Mayor Upsets Victims by Showing Up at Sentencing in Support of Attacker's Family," YouTube, August 19, 2022, https://www.youtube.com/watch?v=oevZciXo2_c&ab_channel=WWLTV and MissyWilkinson and Mike Perlstein, "Teen Carjacker Was Graduate of Cantrell Internship Program for Juvenile Offenders," NOLA.com, August 22, 2022, https://www.nola.com/news/crime_police/article_800aa538-2263-11ed-896a-d33357e666d1.html

179 WWLTV, "Mayor Upsets Victims by Showing Up at Sentencing in Support of Attacker's Family."

180 Mark Menard, "Cantrell 'Personally Worked' to Guide Teen Accused of Costco Carjacking Away from Crime," WWL Radio, February 7, 2022, https://www.audacy.com/wwl/news/local/cantrell-personally-worked-with-alleged-costco-carjacker

181 Menard, "Cantrell 'Personally Worked' to Guide Teen Accused of Costco Carjacking Away from Crime."

182 *Washington v. Bassett,* October 18, 2018, https://law.justia.com/cases/washington/supreme-court/2018/94556-0.html

183 Sara Jean Green, "Ruling Offers Hope for Man Sentenced to Life for Killing His Family as Teen," *Seattle Times*, April 29, 2017, https://www.seattletimes.com/seattle-news/law-justice/ruling-offers-hope-for-man-sentenced-to-life-for-killing-his-family-as-teen/

184 19 News Investigation Team, "Murder Suspect Anthony Kennedy Strangled Girlfriend in 2019, Court Records Show," WOHZ-TV, November 20, 2022, https://www.cleveland19.com/2022/12/01/murder-suspect-anthony-kennedy-strangled-girlfriend-2019-court-records-show/

185 Cleveland Municipal Court, "Domestic Intervention Education and Training (D.I.E.T.)," https://clevelandmunicipalcourt.org/judicial-services/court-programs-services/diet

186 Sia Nyorkor, "Cleveland Man on the Run after Allegedly Murdering Live-in Girlfriend, Burying Body in Pennsylvania," WOHZ-TV, November 29, 2022, https://www.cleveland19.com/2022/11/29/wanted-anthony-kennedy-suspected-murdering-adrianna-taylor/

187 George Gascón, "Sentence enhancements," Twitter, March 4, 2021, https://twitter.com/georgegascon/status/1367567441564340226

188 George Gascón, "Gang enhancements," Twitter, March 4, 2021, https://twitter.com/GeorgeGascon/status/1367567447469920258

189 Evan Sernoffsky, "SF DA-Elect Chesa Boudin Sets New Course in Gang Cases, Citing Charges 'Infused with Racism,'" *San Francisco Chronicle*,

December 14, 2019, https://www.sfchronicle.com/crime/article/SF-DA-elect-Chesa-Boudin-sets-new-course-in-gang-14906018.php

190 "Attorney General's Annual Report on CalGang for 2021," California Department of Justice, https://oag.ca.gov/system/files/media/ag-annual-report-calgang-2021.pdf

191 Joey Nuñez Estrada, Tamika Gilreath, Ron Avi Astor, and Rami Benbenishty, "A Statewide Study of Gang Membership in California Secondary Schools," *Youth & Society* 48, no. 5 (September 2016): 720-736, https://www.researchgate.net/publication/274537197_A_Statewide_Study_of_Gang_Membership_in_California_Secondary_Schools

192 Pramila Jayapal (@RepJayapal), "Today we marked up H.R. 2152 in the Judiciary Committee," Twitter, March 7, 2018, 3:28 p.m., https://twitter.com/RepJayapal/status/971482701835456514

193 Gabrielle Fonrouge, "Dems Demand Answers from NYC Prosecutors on Use of 'Excessive' Cash Bail," *New York Post*, November 22, 2021, https://nypost.com/2021/11/22/dems-demand-answers-from-nyc-prosecutors-on-use-of-cash-bail/

194 Tucker Carlson, "Tucker Carlson: Normal People Don't Want Criminal Justice Reform, They Want Criminal Justice Enforcement," Fox News, January 3, 2020, https://www.foxnews.com/opinion/tucker-carlson-criminal-justice-reform-enforcement and https://560theanswer.com/columnists/mike-gallagher/video/tucker-explains-how-bail-reform-has-been-a-national-disaster

195 Lee Hunter, "What You Need to Know about Ending Cash Bail," Center for American Progress, March 16, 2020, https://www.americanprogress.org/article/ending-cash-bail/

196 John Clark, "Mother Blames New York's No-Cash Bail Law for Daughter's Murder," MyStateline.com, November 2, 2022, https://www.mystateline.com/news/mother-blames-new-yorks-no-cash-bail-law-for-daughters-murder/

197 Aliza Chasan, Jay Dow, and Anthony DiLorenzo, "Feces Attack Suspect Released without Bail, Arrested Again in Connection with Brooklyn Hate Crime," PIX-TV, Masrch 2, 2022, https://pix11.com/news/local-news/feces-attack-suspect-released-without-bail-arrested-again-in-connection-with-brooklyn-hate-crime/

198 Bobby Allyn, "New DA Telling Philly Prosecutors Not to Seek Bail for Defendants in Low-Level Crimes," WHYY Radio, February 21, 2018, https://whyy.org/segments/new-da-telling-philly-prosecutors-not-seek-bail-defendants-low-level-crimes/

199 Philadelphia Police Department, "Crime Mapper," Crime Maps & Stats, https://www.phillypolice.com/crime-maps-stats/

200 Philadelphia Police Department, "Crime Stats Reports: 2021," https://drive.google.com/drive/folders/1gV8ivfKbcQqPoskcQiozESm71Eug_il1

201 Chuck Goudie, Barb Markoff, Christine Tressel, and Ross Weidner, "Cook County Electronic Monitoring Program, Used Widely, Slammed in New Report," WLS-TV, September 24, 2021, https://abc7chicago.com/cook-county-electronic-monitoring-sheriff-tom-dart-chicago-appleseed-center-for-fair-courts/11045139/

202 Jennifer Smith, "Nearly 100 People Charged with Murder Are Free to Walk Streets of Chicago Thanks to Woke Bail Reform: Judge Refuses to Jail Suspects Accused of Violent Crimes Despite Pleas from Cops and the Mayor," DailyMail.com, January 11, 2022, https://www.dailymail.co.uk/news/article-10391037/Nearly-100-people-charged-murder-free-walk-streets-Chicago-thanks-woke-bail-reform.html

203 Andy Grimm, "Chief Judge Shoots Down Lightfoot's Request for Moratorium on Electronic Monitoring for Most Violent Offenders," *Chicago Sun Times*, January 4, 2022, https://chicago.suntimes.com/2022/1/4/22867152/tim-evans-shoots-down-lightfoots-request-moratorium-electronic-monitoring-most-violent-offenders

204 State of Illinois, Circuit Court of Cook County, "Chief Judge Timothy C. Evans Responds to Mayor Lori Lightfoot's Request on Electronic Monitoring," news release, January 18, 2022, https://www.cookcountycourt.org/MEDIA/View-Press-Release/ArticleId/2914/Chief-Judge-Timothy-C-Evans-responds-to-Mayor-Lori-Lightfoot-s-request-on-Electronic-Monitoring

205 Chicago CBS Staff, "No Bail for Devontay Anderson, Third and Final Suspect Charged in Slaying of 7-Year-Old Jaslyn Adams," CBS News, July 21, 2021, https://www.cbsnews.com/chicago/news/devontay-anderson-charged-murder-7-year-old-jaslyn-adams/

206 Sam Charles, "Before He Was Charged in Jaslyn Adams' Death, Demond Goudy's Life Was Marked by Violence," AWGN-TV, April 30, 2021, https://wgntv.com/news/wgn-investigates/before-he-was-charged-in-jaslyn-adams-death-demond-goudys-life-was-marked-by-violence/

207 "READI Chicago Is an Innovative Response to Gun Violence in Chicago," READI Chicago, https://www.heartlandalliance.org/readi/

208 Jason Rantz, "Rantz: Judge Marcus Naylor Released Homeless Suspect in Dog Murder, Who Just Skipped Hearing, Is At-Large," *MyNorthwest*, June 3, 2021, https://mynorthwest.com/2946225/rantz-judge-marcus-naylor-released-homeless-suspect-in-dog-murder-who-just-skipped-hearing-is-at-large/

209 Olivia LaVoice, "'She's All I Had:' Man Speaks Out after Stranger Kills His Dog in Random Downtown Seattle Attack," KCPQ-TV, June 1, 2021, https://www.q13fox.com/news/unacceptable-victim-whose-dog-was-kicked-and-killed-in-seattle-speaks-out-after-suspect-released-from-jail

210 Chelsia Rose Marcius and Sean Piccoli, "Suspect Arrested in Brooklyn Subway Killing Was on Supervised Release," *New York Times*, October 6,

2022, https://www.nytimes.com/2022/10/06/nyregion/brooklyn-subway-slashing-arrest.html

211 Steven Vago and Allie Griffin, "Dad of Subway Slasher Victim Slams Courts after Suspect's Latest Attack," *New York Post*, October 7, 2022, https://nypost.com/2022/10/07/dad-slams-courts-after-nyc-subway-slasher-alvin-charles-kills-stabs-another-victim/

212 Jonah E. Bromwich, "Manhattan D.A. Acts on Vow to Seek Incarceration Only for Worst Crimes," *New York Times*, January 6, 2022, https://www.nytimes.com/2022/01/06/nyregion/alvin-bragg-manhattan-da.html

213 Joe Marino, Tina Moore, Ben Feuerherd, and Bruce Golding, "Knife-Wielding Suspect Has Felony Charge Reduced under Manhattan DA Alvin Bragg's Policies," *New York Post*, January 11, 2022, https://nypost.com/2022/01/11/manhattan-da-alvin-bragg-reduces-armed-robbers-felony-charge/

214 Joe Marino and Bruce Golding, "Ex-con Would Have Faced 'Long Time in Jail' If Not for New Manhattan DA: Judge," *New York Post*, January 12, 2022, https://nypost.com/2022/01/12/ex-con-would-have-faced-lengthy-sentence-if-not-for-alvin-bragg-judge/

215 Melissa Klein, "NYC Convictions Plummet, Downgraded Charges Surge under Manhattan DA Bragg," *New York Post*, November 26, 2022, https://nypost.com/2022/11/26/convictions-plummet-downgraded-charges-surge-under-manhattan-da-bragg/

216 Reuven Fenton, David Meyer, Steven Vago, and Jorge Fitz-Gibbon, "Eric Adams Insists Subways Still Safe and There Is Only 'Perception of Fear,'" *New York Post*, January 16, 2022, https://nypost.com/2022/01/16/nyc-mayor-eric-adams-says-subway-riders-only-have-perception-of-fear/

217 David Meyer, Craig McCarthy, and Gabrielle Fonrouge, "Killings in NYC Subway System Skyrocket to Highest Level in 25 Years—Even as Ridership Plummeted," *New York Post*, October 11, 2022, https://nypost.com/2022/10/11/nyc-subway-murders-jump-to-highest-levels-in-25-years-data/ and Brenton Blanchet, "Fatally Stabbed Man Marks 11th New York City Subway System Killing of 2022," *People*, December 10, 2022, https://people.com/crime/new-york-subway-man-fatally-stabbed-marks-11th-killing-2022/

218 Craig McCarthy, "NYC Mayor Eric Adams Blames Media for 'Perception' of Surging Subway Crime," *New York Post*, October 20, 2022, https://nypost.com/2022/10/20/eric-adams-blames-media-for-perception-of-crime-surging-in-nyc-subways/

219 Caroline Downey, "Hochul Accuses Zeldin of 'Hyperventilating' about Crime, Says He's 'Trying to Scare People,'" *National Review*, November 7, 2022, https://www.nationalreview.com/news/hochul-accuses-zeldin-of-hyperventilating-about-crime-says-hes-trying-to-scare-people/

220 Brie Stimson, "Gavin Newsom Joins Truth Social to Call Out 'Republican lies,' Perceived 'Red State Murder Problem,'" Fox News, June 17, 2022, https://www.foxnews.com/politics/gavin-newsom-truth-social-republican-lies-red-state-murder-problem

221 Rafael A. Mangual, "Dems' Shameless Ploy to Blame Crime Rise on 'Red States,'" *New York Post*, October 11, 2022, https://nypost.com/2022/10/11/dems-shameless-ploy-to-blame-crime-rise-on-red-states/

222 Ben Adler, "Republican-Controlled States Have Higher Murder Rates Than Democratic Ones: Study," Yahoo! News, April 4, 2022, https://news.yahoo.com/republican-controlled-states-have-higher-murder-rates-than-democratic-ones-study-212137750.html

223 Jeremy Kohler and Tom Scheck, "St. Louis' Murder Total Has Fallen, but Some Killings Went Uncounted," ProPublica, March 31, 2022, https://www.propublica.org/article/st-louis-murder-total-has-fallen-but-some-killings-went-uncounted

224 Rafael Mangual, "Dems' Shameless Ploy to Blame Crime Rise on 'Red States,'" *New York Post*, October 11, 2022, https://nypost.com/2022/10/11/dems-shameless-ploy-to-blame-crime-rise-on-red-states/

225 Nick Smith, "New Orleans Police Hire Civilians to Combat Officer Shortage," *The Hill*, September 26, 2022, https://thehill.com/homenews/state-watch/3661803-new-orleans-police-hire-civilians-to-combat-officer-shortage/

226 Emma Colton, "New Orleans Closes 2022 with Sky-High Homicide Rate Not Seen in Decades: 'Horrific,'" Fox News, January 9, 2023, https://www.foxnews.com/us/new-orleans-closes-2022-sky-high-homicide-rate-decades-horrific

227 FOX 8 Staff, "New Orleans Mayor Doesn't 'Embrace' City's Title as 'Murder Capital' of U.S.," WVUE-TV, September 27, 2022, https://www.fox8live.com/2022/09/27/new-orleans-mayor-doesnt-embrace-citys-title-murder-capital-us/

228 NBC Chicago Staff, "Chicago Weekend Shootings: More Than 50 Shot, 9 Fatally, in Memorial Day Weekend Violence," NBC Chicago, May 31, 2022, https://www.nbcchicago.com/news/local/chicago-weekend-shootings-at-least-48-shot-8-fatally-in-memorial-day-weekend-gun-violence/2845854/

229 Rising (@thehill), "Batya Ungar-Sargon: CNN's Brian Stelter Downplays US Crime Wave, Devalues True Victims of Violence," YouTube, January 26, 2022, https://www.youtube.com/watch?v=NIZw_95PjHM&ab_channel=TheHill

230 Zachary Faria, "CNN Determines the Real Problem with the Surge in Homicides Is Fox News's Coverage," *Washington Examiner*, January 24, 2022, https://www.washingtonexaminer.com/opinion/cnn-determines-the-real-issue-with-the-surge-in-homicides-is-fox-newss-coverage

231 John Gramlich, "What We Know about the Increase in U.S. Murders in 2020," Pew Research Center, October 27, 2021, https://www.pewresearch.org/fact-tank/2021/10/27/what-we-know-about-the-increase-in-u-s-murders-in-2020

232 John Gramlich, "What the Data Says (and Doesn't Say) about Crime in the United States," Pew Research Center, November 20, 2020, https://www.pewresearch.org/fact-tank/2020/11/20/facts-about-crime-in-the-u-s/

233 Mike D'Onofrio, "Philadelphia Homicides Hit Historic Level in 2021," Axios Philadelphia, January 10, 2022, https://www.axios.com/local/philadelphia/2022/01/10/philadelphia-record-homicides-2021-police

234 Jacob Schermerhorn, "Rochester's Homicide Surge," *Rochester Beacon*, February 3, 2022, https://rochesterbeacon.com/2022/02/03/rochesters-homicide-surge/

235 Sara Cline, "2021 Was a Record Year for Homicides in Portland," Oregon Public Broadcasting, January 15, 2022, https://www.opb.org/article/2022/01/15/2021-was-a-record-year-for-homicides-in-portland/

236 Public Policy Institute of California, "Proposition 47 Linked to Increase in Some Property Crimes, but Not Violent Crime," news release, June 13, 2018, https://www.ppic.org/press-release/proposition-47-linked-to-increase-in-some-property-crimes-but-not-violent-crime/

237 Erik Ortiz and Jacob Ward, "After San Francisco Shoplifting Video Goes Viral, Officials Argue Thefts Aren't Rampant," NBC News, July 14, 2021, https://www.nbcnews.com/news/us-news/after-san-francisco-shoplifting-video-goes-viral-officials-argue-thefts-n1273848

238 NBC Bay Area Staff, "San Francisco Targets Closing Early Due to Rise in Thefts," NBC Bay Area, July 2, 2021, https://www.nbcbayarea.com/news/local/san-francisco-targets-closing-early-due-to-rise-in-thefts/2585683/

239 Roland Li, "Exclusive: Man Died from Overdose at S.F. Whole Foods Months before Closure," *San Francisco Chronicle,* April 12, 2023, https://www.sfchronicle.com/bayarea/article/sf-whole-foods-closure-overdose-17893301.php

240 J.D. Morris and Roland Li, "After Nordstrom Store Closures, What Can San Francisco Do to Stop the Retail Exodus?" *San Francisco Chronicle*, May 3, 2023, https://www.sfchronicle.com/sf/article/after-nordstrom-closures-s-f-stop-retail-exodus-18074794.php

241 Roland Li and Sam Whiting, "Westfield Mall Blamed 'Rampant Criminal Activity' for Nordstrom Closing in S.F. Here's What the Data Says," *San Francisco Chronicle*, May 3, 2023, https://www.sfchronicle.com/sf/article/westfield-mall-blamed-nordstrom-closure-criminal-18076486.php

242 Katherine Cook, "'People Feel Unsafe': Portland Coffee Shop Closes Downtown Location," KGW, April 11, 2023, https://www.kgw.com/article

/money/business/coava-coffee-closes-downtown-portland-location/283-d688b500-43ad-46c7-8568-af7e806f0b49

243 Kyle Iboshi, "After 19 Shoplifting Incidents in a Year, a Store at Washington Square Mall Is Calling It Quits," *KGW*, March 3, 2023, https://www.kgw.com/article/news/investigations/store-washington-square-mall-closes-shoplifting/283-312cb798-1a0a-49fd-9c3f-fe53d4669ca1

244 Robert Higgs, "Large City Losing Another Retailer, REI, due to Thefts, Break-Ins, Security Issues," *Cleveland*, April 18, 2023, https://www.cleveland.com/business/2023/04/large-city-losing-another-retailer-rei-due-to-thefts-break-ins-security-issues.html

245 Jason Rantz, "Rantz: Seattle Judge Releases Homeless, Prolific Shoplifter Caught Stealing 70-inch TV," *MyNorthwest*, January 26, 2022, https://mynorthwest.com/3326387/rantz-seattle-judge-releases-prolific-shoplifter/

246 Joe Marino, "NYPD Brass Rip Bail Reform While Shouting Out Recently-Freed Repeat Offender on Live TV," *New York Post*, November 28, 2022, https://nypost.com/2022/11/28/nypd-brass-rip-bail-reform-cite-yet-another-outrageous-case-of-recidivist/

247 Spectrum News NY1 (@NY1), "Police Commissioner Keechant Sewell and Chief of Department Kenneth Corey," interview, Twitter, November 28, 2022, 7:36 a.m., https://twitter.com/NY1/status/1597207835204407296

248 Chelsea Prince, "Man Shot in Phipps Plaza Movie Theater over Seat Dispute, Police Say," *Atlanta Journal Constitution*, December 21, 2021, https://www.ajc.com/news/crime/man-shot-in-buckhead-movie-theater-over-seat-dispute-police-say/HUYKBO22AREGNEPXC7YXLKSB54/

249 Jon Shirek, "Police Report: Man Put Gun to Woman's Head, Knocked Her into Pavement in Lenox Square Parking Deck Robbery," WATL-TV, April 15, 2021, https://www.11alive.com/article/news/local/buckhead/lenox-square-mall-parking-lot-robbery-buckhead-atlanta/85-1ddc1c7d-466a-495e-8184-73e3c2bd5279

250 Alexis Stevens, "Lenox Square Shooting: Security Guard Recovering, Two Teens in Custody," *Atlanta Journal Constitution*, June 14, 2021, https://www.ajc.com/news/crime/breaking-possible-shooting-at-lenox-square-prompts-large-police-presence/BYAVTILIORGRRDJ56GYTKGCLB4/

251 Bill White, "Buckhead City. It's Time," Insider Advantage, August 21, 2021, https://insideradvantage.com/2021/08/02/buckhead-city-its-time/

252 Wilborn Nobles, "Atlanta Mayor Slams Buckhead Cityhood Leader for His Ties to Donald Trump," *Atlanta Journal Constitution*, December 21, 2021, https://www.ajc.com/news/atlanta-news/atlanta-mayor-slams-buckhead-cityhood-leader-for-his-ties-to-donald-trump/O7KIXEPFK5GYPEB65JLQQYTBRA/

253 Tucker Carlson, "Tucker Carlson: CNN Hates the Idea of Buckhead Trying to Leave the City of Atlanta," Fox News, June 15, 2021, https://www.foxnews.com/opinion/tucker-carlson-cnn-hates-buckhead-trying-leave-atlanta
254 Wilborn Nobles, "Atlanta Mayor Slams Buckhead Cityhood Leader for His Ties to Donald Trump," *Atlanta Journal Constitution*, December 21, 2021, https://www.ajc.com/news/atlanta-news/atlanta-mayor-slams-buckhead-cityhood-leader-for-his-ties-to-donald-trump/O7KIXEPFK5GYPEB65JLQQYTBRA/
255 Marisa Lagos, "The Troy McAlister Case Is a Flash Point in the Drive to Recall SF DA Chesa Boudin. Should It Be?," KQED, May 18, 2022, https://www.kqed.org/news/11914457/how-the-troy-mcalister-case-became-a-flashpoint-in-the-drive-to-recall-sf-da-chesa-boudin
256 Lagos, "The Troy McAlister Case."
257 Action News 5 Staff, "'Don't Come Near Me:' Blytheville Police Release Details of Officer-Involved Shooting Investigation," WMC-TV, May 2, 2019, https://www.actionnews5.com/2019/05/02/blytheville-police-releasing-details-officer-involved-shooting-investigation/
258 Joseph Wulfsohn, "NBC Allegedly Tells Reporters Not to Use Word 'Riots' in George Floyd Coverage," Fox News, May 28, 2020, Fox Newshttps://www.foxnews.com/media/nbc-news-george-floyd-coverage
259 Joseph Wulfsohn, "MSNBC's Ali Velshi Says Situation Not 'Generally Speaking Unruly' While Standing Outside Burning Building," Fox News, May 29, 2020, https://www.foxnews.com/media/msnbc-anchor-says-minneapolis-carnage-is-mostly-a-protest-as-building-burns-behind-him
260 Joy Reid (@JoyAnnReid), "Let me repeat this for those inventing the idea of 'Black Lives Matter riots,'" Twitter, August 29, 2020, 2:28 p.m., https://twitter.com/JoyAnnReid/status/1299775888385605632
261 Jon Levine, "CNN's Don Lemon Defends Antifa Despite Violence: 'No Organization Is Perfect,'" The Wrap, August 31, 2018, https://www.thewrap.com/cnns-don-lemon-defends-antifa-despite-violence-no-organization-is-perfect/
262 The Daily Caller, "Here is Chris Cuomo comparing Antifa members to the brave soldiers," screengrab, Facebook, June 6, 2019, https://www.facebook.com/DailyCaller/photos/here-is-chris-cuomo-comparing-antifa-members-to-the-brave-soldiers-who-stormed-t/10156281000426770/
263 CBS News Staff, "LA City Council Approves LAPD Budget Cuts; Department Temporarily Stops Overtime Pay," KCAL-TV, June 16, 2020, https://www.cbsnews.com/losangeles/news/los-angeles-city-council-approves-lapd-budget-cuts-department-temporarily-stops-overtime-pay/
264 Dakota Smith and David Zahniser, "L.A. Reallocates LAPD Funds a Year after George Floyd Death," *Los Angeles Times*, May 26, 2021,

https://www.latimes.com/california/story/2021-05-26/lapd-funds-reallocation-george-floyd

265 Stephanie Pagones, "Seattle City Council Approves 18% Police Budget Decrease, Reportedly One of Biggest Cuts Nationwide," Fox News, November 24, 2020, https://www.foxnews.com/us/seattle-city-council-police-department-budget

266 Everton Bailey Jr., "Portland Mayor Pledges to Divert Millions from Police Bureau, Ban Chokeholds in City Reforms," *The Oregonian*, June 9, 2020, https://www.oregonlive.com/portland/2020/06/defund-portland-police-units-to-reinvest-in-communities-of-color-among-citys-reform-plans-mayor-says.html

267 Jonathan Dienst and Courtney Copenhagen, "Most Riot, Looting Cases from Last Year Dropped by NYC DAs," NBC New York, June 18, 2021, https://www.nbcnewyork.com/news/local/crime-and-courts/most-riot-looting-cases-from-last-year-dropped-by-nyc-das/3114714/

268 Dienst and Copenhagen, "Most Riot, Looting Cases from Last Year Dropped by NYC DAs."

269 Brittany Bernstein, "De Blasio: Black Lives Matter Protests Exempt from Large-Event Ban," *National Review*, July 10, 2020, https://www.yahoo.com/lifestyle/blasio-black-lives-matter-protests-115502505.html

270 Dana Rubinstein and Jeffery C. Mays, "Nearly $1 Billion Is Shifted from Police in Budget That Pleases No One," *New York Times*, June 30, 2020, https://www.nytimes.com/2020/06/30/nyregion/nypd-budget.html

271 Sarah Al-Arshani, "Hundreds of Officers Quit the Minneapolis Police Department after George Floyd Was Killed. The Department Is Reportedly Still Struggling to Recruit," *Insider*, October 23, 2022, https://www.yahoo.com/news/hundreds-officers-quit-minneapolis-police-135604068.html

272 CBS News Staff, "Former Minneapolis Police Officer Talks About His Decision to Leave: 'I Did It Out of Principle,'" WCCO-TV, May 16, 2021, https://www.cbsnews.com/minnesota/news/former-minneapolis-police-officer-talks-about-his-decision-to-leave/

273 Tony Plohetski, "How Calls to 'Defund the Police' Took Austin to a Crossroads of Police Reform," *Austin American-Statesman*, August 31, 2021, https://www.statesman.com/in-depth/news/politics/2021/09/01/austin-police-department-budget-cuts-stirs-debate-over-police-reform/5536198001/

274 Bethany Blankley, "Interim Chief: Austin Police Department in 'Dire Crisis' after Defunding," *The Center Square*, July 19, 2021, https://www.thecentersquare.com/texas/interim-chief-austin-police-department-in-dire-crisis-after-defunding/article_f1cf3332-e8b2-11eb-a76c-afc3b5f2ca55.html

275 Leo Stallworth, "LASD Stats Show 94% Jump in Homicides in LA County over 2-Year Span, Sheriff Villanueva Says," ABC Los Angeles, January 19, 2022, https://abc7.com/los-angeles-county-crime-statistics-homicide-murder/11489644/

276 Josh Cain, "'They're Worn Out': LAPD Contends with Hundreds of Officer Resignations, Retirements after Protests, Pandemic Break Out." *Los Angeles Daily News*, August 6, 2021, https://www.dailynews.com/2021/08/06/theyre-worn-out-lapd-contends-with-hundreds-of-officer-resignations-retirements-after-protests-pandemic-break-out/

277 Kristin Thorne, "NYPD Officers Quitting in Record Numbers amid Growing Issue over New York City Crime," ABC New York, October 29, 2022, https://abc7ny.com/nypd-police-officers-patrick-lynch-quitting/12372321/

278 Jason Rantz, "Rantz: Seattle Councilmember Lisa Herbold Suggests SPD Fire White Cops," *MyNorthwest*, July 19, 2020, https://mynorthwest.com/2032503/rantz-herbold-seattle-fire-white-police-defund/

279 Hanna Scott, "Hatred of Police, Lack of Support and Politics among Reasons for SPD Exodus in Exit Interviews," *MyNorthwest*, October 19, 2020, https://mynorthwest.com/2246464/hatred-police-lack-support-politics-spd-exit-interviews/

280 Hana Kim, "Report Finds It Takes Seattle Police Longer to Respond to High-Priority Calls Compared to Previous Years," FOX Seattle, June 14, 2022, https://www.q13fox.com/news/police-response-times-are-dramatically-up-for-people-in-need-the-most-in-seattle

281 Natalie Swaby, "2020 Had the Highest Number of Seattle Homicides in 26 Years," KING-TV, January 12, 2021, https://www.king5.com/article/news/crime/in-2020-seattle-saw-the-highest-number-of-homicides-in-26-years/281-9409d828-afcf-45f0-8caf-a90b19d56877

282 Nigel Jaquiss, "Mayor Ted Wheeler Agrees to Disband the Portland Police Bureau's Gun Violence Reduction Team," *Willamette Week*, June 9, 2020, https://www.wweek.com/news/2020/06/09/mayor-ted-wheeler-agrees-to-disband-the-portland-police-bureaus-gun-violence-reduction-team/

283 City of Portland Police Bureau, "Shooting Incident Statistics: Jan 2020–Mar 2023," https://www.portlandoregon.gov/police/81203

284 Maxine Bernstein, "55 Homicides in Portland in 2020—the Most in 26 Years—Involved Victims from 8 Months Old to 71," *The Oregonian*, January 5, 2021, https://www.oregonlive.com/crime/2021/01/55-homicides-in-portland-in-2020-the-most-in-26-years-involved-victims-from-8-months-old-to-71.html

285 Sara Cline, "2021 Was a Record Year for Homicides in Portland," Oregon Public Broadcasting, January 15, 2022, https://www.opb.org/article/2022/01/15/2021-was-a-record-year-for-homicides-in-portland/

286 Maxine Bernstein, "Portland's 101 Homicides in 2022 Set New Record: 'At Some Point, We Have to Be Tired of Burying Our Children,'" *The Oregonian*, January 9, 2023, https://www.oregonlive.com/crime/2023/01/portlands-101-homicides-in-2022-set-new-record-at-some-point-we-have-to-be-tired-of-burying-our-children.html

287 Peter Hermann, "Homicides in D.C. Hit 16-Year High; Shootings Also Have Spiked," *Washington Post*, December 31, 2020, https://www.washingtonpost.com/local/public-safety/homicides-rise-washington/2020/12/31/59dd659e-3953-11eb-bc68-96af0daae728_story.html

288 Martin Austermuhle, "D.C. Surpasses 2020 Homicide Tally with 199 Killings So Far This Year," DCist.com, November 16, 2021, https://dcist.com/story/21/11/16/dc-surpasses-2020-homicide-tally/

289 Emma Colton, "San Francisco Defunded the Police Before Reversing Course the Next Year amid Calls for 'Accountability,'" Fox News, August 16, 2022, https://www.foxnews.com/us/san-francisco-defunded-police-reversing-course-next-year-calls-accountability

290 Emma Colton, "Burlington, Vermont, Reeling from Highest Number of Homicides in Decades after Defunding Police," Fox News, December 12, 2022, https://www.foxnews.com/us/vermonts-largest-city-pays-bloody-price-cutting-police-force

291 CBS News Staff, "LAPD to Move More Officers to Patrol, Downsize Air Support, Robbery/Homicide Divisions," KCAL-TV," November 7, 2020, https://www.cbsnews.com/losangeles/news/lapd-to-move-more-officers-to-patrol-downsize-air-support-robbery-homicide-divisions/

292 Paul LeBlanc, "Clyburn Says 'We've Got to Have Police Officers' after Tlaib Calls for 'No More Policing,'" CNN, April 13, 2021, https://www.cnn.com/2021/04/13/politics/jim-clyburn-rashida-tlaib-policing-cnntv/index.html

293 Kimberly Kindy, "Half of the Nation's Largest Police Departments Have Banned or Limited Neck Restraints since June," *Washington Post*, September 6, 2020, https://www.washingtonpost.com/graphics/2020/national/police-use-of-force-chokehold-carotid-ban/

294 Atrium Health Wake Forest Baptist, "Study Finds Vascular Neck Restraint Used by Law Enforcement Officers Is Safe and Effective," news release, November 1, 2022, https://newsroom.wakehealth.edu/news-releases/2022/11/study-finds-vascular-neck-restraint-used-by-law-enforcement-officers-is-safe-and-effective

295 Daniel Beekman, "Seattle City Council Bans Police Use of Tear Gas and Chokeholds as Protests for Black Lives Continue," *Seattle Times*, June 15, 2020, https://www.seattletimes.com/seattle-news/politics/seattle-city-council-bans-police-use-of-tear-gas-and-chokeholds-as-protests-for-black-lives-continue/

296 Associated Press Staff, "Elected Officials Must OK Tear Gas Use by

Cops in Washington under Compromise Plan," KING-TV, April 22, 2021, https://www.king5.com/article/news/politics/state-politics/police-tear-gas-use-washington-lawmakers-compromise-plan/281-9fc3eddd-5e56-4720-b18f-0a2958dffd90

297 Jason Rantz, "Rantz: Dem Law Led to K-9 Line of Duty Death but Seattle Activists Blame Police," *MyNorthwest*, January 9, 2022, https://mynorthwest.com/3305941/rantz-dem-law-k-9-death-seattle-activists-police/

298 Rantz, "Rantz: Dem Law Led to K-9 Line of Duty Death."

299 Sarah Rumpf-Whitter, "California Bill Would Ban Police Dogs from Arrests, Crowd Control; Cites Racial Bias, Trauma," Fox News, March 21, 2023, https://www.foxnews.com/politics/california-bill-would-ban-police-dogs-arrests-crowd-control-citing-racial-bias-trauma

300 Phil Murphy (@GovMurphy), "We MUST address the systemic and implicit biases," Twitter, August 27, 2020, 5:35 p.m., https://twitter.com/GovMurphy/status/1299098209751629825

301 Craig Mauger, "Michigan Senate Unanimously Approves Requiring Implicit Bias Training for Police," *The Detroit News*, June 4, 2020, https://www.detroitnews.com/story/news/local/michigan/2020/06/04/mich-senate-panel-votes-require-implicit-bias-training-police/3142904001/

302 Jason Rantz, "Rantz: Seattle City Training Docs Teach White People Are Racist 'Oppressors,' Black People Are Victims," *MyNorthwest*, October 4, 2021, https://mynorthwest.com/3174847/rantz-seattle-city-training-whites-racist-blacks-victims/

303 Martin Kaste, "NYPD Study: Implicit Bias Training Changes Minds, Not Necessarily Behavior," National Public Radio, September 10, 2020, https://www.npr.org/2020/09/10/909380525/nypd-study-implicit-bias-training-changes-minds-not-necessarily-behavior

304 Kaste, "NYPD Study: Implicit Bias Training Changes Minds."

305 Jordan Levy, "Philly Becomes the First Big U.S. City with a Law Banning Minor Traffic Stops," *Billy Penn*, March 3, 2022, https://billypenn.com/2022/03/03/philly-becomes-the-first-big-u-s-city-with-a-law-banning-minor-traffic-stops/

306 David Kirkpatrick, Steve Eder, Kim Barker, and Julie Tate, "Why Many Police Traffic Stops Turn Deadly," *New York Times*, October 31, 2021, https://www.nytimes.com/2021/10/31/us/police-traffic-stops-killings.html

307 KGET-TV Staff, "KCSO Releases Summary of Deadly Officer-Involved Shooting Near Fort Tejon," KGET-TV, August 12, 2019, https://www.kget.com/news/crime-watch/kcso-releases-summary-of-officer-involved-shooting-near-fort-tejon/

308 Felicia Jordan, "Cincinnati Police Department Revises Rules for Vehicle Pursuits," WCPO-TV, March 1, 2022, https://www.wcpo.com/news

/local-news/hamilton-county/cincinnati/cincinnati-police-revise-rules-for-vehicle-pursuits

309 Chicago Police Department, "Emergency Vehicle Operations–Eluding and Pursuing," Department Directives System General Order G03-03-01, August 15, 2020, https://directives.chicagopolice.org/#directive/public/6607

310 Jason Rantz, "Rantz: WA Dems Responsible as 41,330 Cars Stolen, Now Try to Ban Police Traffic Stops," *MyNorthwest*, December 14, 2022, https://mynorthwest.com/3750213/rantz-wa-democrat-responsible-41330-cars-stolen-ban-police-traffic-stops/

311 AJ Janavel, "Washington State Patrol Stepping Away from Puget Sound Auto Theft Task Force," FOX 13, December 16, 2022, https://www.q13fox.com/news/washington-state-patrol-stepping-away-from-puget-sound-auto-theft-task-force

312 Jason Rantz, "Rantz: Astonishing 10,000% Increase in Catalytic Converter Theft due to WA Democrat's Law," *MyNorthwest*, June 20, 2022, https://mynorthwest.com/3525709/rantz-astonishing-10000-increase-catalytic-converter-theft-wa-democrats-law/

313 Bart Schaneman, "Rash of Robberies Has Washington State's Cash-Only Cannabis Industry on Edge," *Marijuana Business Daily*, February 15, 2022, https://mjbizdaily.com/rash-of-robberies-has-washington-states-cash-only-cannabis-industry-on-edge/

314 Jason Rantz, "Rantz: Alleged Hostage Taker Cites Dem Law to Warn Seattle Cops Not to Chase Him," *MyNorthwest*, June 13, 2022, https://mynorthwest.com/3511940/rantz-alleged-hostage-taker-cites-dem-law-to-warn-seattle-cops-not-to-chase-him/

315 Jason Rantz, "Rantz: Seattle Police Policy Would Let DUI Suspects Flee Even if in Stolen Car," *MyNorthwest*, October 9, 2022, https://mynorthwest.com/3665807/rantz-seattle-police-policy-let-dui-suspect-flee-stolen-car/

316 Matt, Johnson, "Atlanta Police Begins No-Chase Policy Effective Immediately," WSB-TV, January 3, 2020, https://www.wsbtv.com/news/local/atlanta/atlanta-police-sets-no-chase-policy-effective-immediately/NMXS6JZ6LRBBPP2FE5KMY25RAY/

317 Asian Simone Burns, "Atlanta Police Alter 'No-Chase' Policy," *Atlanta Journal Constitution*, January 4, 2021, https://www.ajc.com/news/breaking-atlanta-police-alter-no-chase-policy/ZMGZG5DKCVDSZMTFYUMOGEHAT4/

318 Neil Vigdor, "What to Know about the Police Shooting of Adam Toledo," *New York Times*, April 16, 2021, https://www.nytimes.com/2021/04/16/us/adam-toledo-chicago-police-shooting.html

319 NBC Chicago Staff, "No Charges for Officers in Fatal Shootings of Adam Toledo, Anthony Alvarez," NBC Chicago, March 15, 2022, https://www

.nbcchicago.com/news/local/chicago-politics/no-charges-for-officers-in-fatal-shootings-of-adam-toledo-anthony-alvarez/2783566/

320 Tim Fitzsimons, "'Why Are You Shooting Me?' Video Shows Chicago Fatally Shooting Anthony Alvarez," NBC News, April 28, 2021, https://www.nbcnews.com/news/us-news/why-are-you-shooting-me-video-shows-chicago-police-fatally-n1265682

321 Fitzsimons, "'Why Are You Shooting Me?'"

322 Julie Bosman and Ellen Almer Durston, "Hundreds March in Chicago, Protesting Police Shooting of Adam Toledo, 13," *New York Times*, April 16, 2021, https://www.nytimes.com/2021/04/16/us/chicago-police-shooting-protests.html

323 Matt Masterson, "Chicago Police Unveil Finalized Foot Pursuit Policy," WTTW-TV, June 21, 2022, https://news.wttw.com/2022/06/21/chicago-police-unveil-finalized-foot-pursuit-policy

324 Madeline Kenney, "Slain Chicago Police Officer 'Wanted to Do Good for the World,' Brother Says," *Chicago Sun Times*, August 8, 2018, https://chicago.suntimes.com/news/2021/8/8/22615487/chicago-police-officer-killed-ella-french-wounded-suspects-arrested-west-englewood-david-brown

325 Stefano Esposito, "Brothers Charged in Fatal Shooting of Chicago Police Officer Denied Bail," *Chicago Sun Times*, August 10, 2021, https://chicago.suntimes.com/crime/2021/8/10/22618563/brothers-emonte-eric-morgan-fatally-shooting-chicago-police-officer-ella-french-denied-bail

326 Madeline Buckley, "Officer Carlos Yanez Jr., Wounded in Shooting that Killed Ella French, Attends Court Hearing for the First Time: 'This Was Not Easy for Him to Be Here,'" *Chicago Tribune*, December 2, 2021, https://www.chicagotribune.com/news/breaking/ct-ella-french-carlos-yanez-court-20211202-i336uc6535abbnh3w5ezl3n7ea-story.html

327 Matt Rosenberg, "It's Open Season on Chicago Police: Shootings at Cops Up Fourfold in 2020, 2021," *Madison St. Clair Record*, June 8, 2022, https://madisonrecord.com/stories/626998281-it-s-open-season-on-chicago-police-shootings-at-cops-up-fourfold-in-2020-2021

328 WGN News (@wgntv), "WATCH: Charges Announced in Fatal Shooting of Chicago Police Officer Ella French," press conference, YouTube, August 9, 2021, https://www.youtube.com/watch?v=FhhRq6cejWQ&ab_channel=WGNNews

329 CBS News Staff, "'We've Got to Be Bold': Chicago Mayor Lori Lightfoot on Reforming the Police in the Wake of George Floyd's Death," CBS News, June 11, 2020, https://www.cbsnews.com/news/lori-lightfoot-chicago-mayor-reform-police-death-george-floyd/

330 Adam Andrzejewski, "Democratic Mayors Defunded Their Police, While Spending Millions on Their Own Police Protection," *Forbes*, June

1, 2020, https://www.forbes.com/sites/adamandrzejewski/2021/07/20/democratic-mayors-defunded-their-police-while-spending-millions-on-their-own-police-protection/?sh=391f5c39d86b

331 Yaron Steinbuch, "Chicago Cops Turn Backs on Mayor Lori Lightfoot after Fatal Police Shooting," *New York Post*, August 10, 2021, https://nypost.com/2021/08/10/chicago-cops-turn-back-on-lori-lightfoot-after-police-shooting/

332 Jim Ryan, "Multnomah Co. DA's Office Won't Prosecute Many Arrested in Portland Protests," *The Oregonian*, August 11, 2020, https://www.oregonlive.com/portland/2020/08/multnomah-county-da-to-announce-protest-policy-watch-live.html

333 Minyvonne Burke, "Portland Police Officers Resign En Masse from Crowd Control Unit after Officer Is Indicted," NBC News, June 18, 2021, https://www.nbcnews.com/news/us-news/entire-portland-police-crowd-control-unit-resigns-after-officer-indicted-n1271309

334 Jonathan Levinson and Conrad Wilson, "Civil Trial against Portland Starts in 2020 Use of Force Case, Dozens to Follow," Oregon Public Broadcasting, September 27, 2022, https://www.opb.org/article/2022/09/27/portland-racial-justice-protester-civil-trial-police-use-of-force/

335 Levinson and Wilson, "Civil Trial against Portland Starts."

336 Brent Weisberg, "DA Mike Schmidt Announces Portland Police Officer Indicted over August 2020 Use of Force Incident," news release, Multnomah County District Attorney (website), June 15, 2021, https://www.mcda.us/index.php/news/da-mike-schmidt-announces-portland-police-officer-indicted-over-august-2020-use-of-force-incident

337 Jason Rantz, "Rantz: Seattle City Dept. Defends Vicious All-Staff Email Labeling Cops White Supremacists," *MyNorthwest*, June 7, 2021, https://mynorthwest.com/2952103/rantz-seattle-city-dept-defends-vicious-all-staff-email-labeling-cops-white-supremacists/

338 Rantz, "Rantz: Seattle City Dept. Defends Vicious All-Staff Email Labeling Cops White Supremacists."

339 Dan Rodricks, "Q&A: Brandon Scott on 'Defunding Police,' the BLM Protests and His Victory in Baltimore's Mayoral Primary," *The Baltimore Sun*, June 19, 2020, https://www.baltimoresun.com/opinion/columnists/dan-rodricks/bs-md-rodricks-0621-20200619-32gdaghypndwlobbj2bsfu7auq-story.html

340 Ron Cassie, "Why Baltimore's Protests Are So Peaceful," Bloomberg News, June 4, 2020, https://www.bloomberg.com/news/articles/2020-06-04/why-baltimore-s-george-floyd-protest-is-different

341 Julian Baron, "Baltimore City Spent $3.6M Last Year on Protection for Top City Officials," FOX 5 News, May 12, 2021, https://foxbaltimore.com/news/local/baltimore-city-spent-36m-last-year-on-security-protection-for-top-city-officials

342 Matthew Green, "SF Mayor Breed Unveils Plan for Reinvesting $120 Million from Police into Black Communities," KQED, February 25, 2021, https://www.kqed.org/news/11862094/sf-mayor-breed-unveils-plan-for-reinvesting-120-million-from-police-into-black-communities

343 Adam Andrzejewski, "Democratic Mayors Defunded Their Police, While Spending Millions on Their Own Police Protection," *Forbes*, June 1, 2020, https://www.forbes.com/sites/adamandrzejewski/2021/07/20/democratic-mayors-defunded-their-police-while-spending-millions-on-their-own-police-protection/

344 Cori Bush (@CoriBush), "We're going to defund the police and refund our social services," Twitter, October 18, 2020, 8:02 p.m., https://twitter.com/coribush/status/1317979379042078720

345 Joe Schoffstall, "Cori Bush's Campaign Paid Her Husband for Security Services—but He Doesn't Have a Private Security License," Fox News, February 28, 2023, https://www.foxnews.com/politics/cori-bushs-campaign-paid-husband-security-services-doesnt-have-private-security-license

346 Emily Crane, "Cori Bush Will Pay $200K for Private Security—but Still Wants to Defund Police," *New York Post*, August 5, 2021, https://nypost.com/2021/08/05/cori-bush-will-pay-200k-for-private-security-but-still-wants-to-defund-police/

347 Becky Willeke, "St. Louis Has Highest Murder Rate in U.S. in 2020; Other Crimes Decreasing," FOX 2 St. Louis, September 30, 2021, https://fox2now.com/news/missouri/st-louis-has-highest-murder-rate-in-u-s-in-2020-other-crimes-decreasing/

348 Jamaal Bowman (@JamaalBowmanNY), "We're fighting in your memory, Tamir," Twitter, December 29, 2020, 5:45 p.m., https://twitter.com/JamaalBowmanNY/status/1344051941140275202

349 Jon Levine, "Jamaal Bowman Requested Special Police Protection for His Yonkers Home," *New York Post*, June 26, 2021, https://nypost.com/2021/06/26/jamaal-bowman-requested-police-protection-for-yonkers-home/

350 Jason Rantz, "Rantz: Sawant Claims Seattle Cops Told to 'Orchestrate Violence' Before Riots," *MyNorthwest*, June 3, 2020, https://www.mynorthwest.com/1907464/rantz-kshama-sawant-seattle-cops-orchestrate-riots/

351 Jason Rantz, "Rantz: Police-Defunding Seattle CM Demands Protection as Residence Targeted by Feces," *MyNorthwest*, October 15, 2022, https://mynorthwest.com/3675116/rantz-police-defunding-seattle-demands-protection-residence-targeted-feces-sawant/

352 Gregory Pratt, "After Mayor Lori Lightfoot Says She's 'Quite Shocked' President Trump Hadn't Weighed in on Chicago Looting, He Repeats Offer to Send Federal Help," *Chicago Tribune*, August 11, 2020, https://

www.chicagotribune.com/politics/ct-chicago-looting-trump-offers-federal-help-20200811-3su4njj4b5g5fe5ceggvqesxzm-story.html

353 NBC Chicago Staff, "'No Question:' Lightfoot Says Chicago Police Budget Will Increase in New Fiscal Year," NBC Chicago, August 11, 2021, https://www.nbcchicago.com/news/local/no-question-lightfoot-says-chicago-police-budget-will-increase-in-new-fiscal-year/2588315/

354 WSJ Editorial Board, "Refunding the San Francisco Police," *Wall Street Journal*, December 16, 2021, https://www.wsj.com/articles/refunding-the-san-francisco-police-london-breed-crime-11639696468

355 Emma Colton, "San Francisco Defunded the Police Before Reversing Course the Next Year amid Calls for 'Accountability,'" Fox News, August 16, 2022Fox News, https://www.foxnews.com/us/san-francisco-defunded-police-reversing-course-next-year-calls-accountability

356 Adam Manno, "Portland REFUNDS the Police: Department Gets an Extra $5.2M as City Faces Greatest Cop Shortage in Decades and Record Number of Homicides after Slashing $15M from the Budget over Defund the Police Movement," *Daily Mail*, November 17, 2021, https://www.dailymail.co.uk/news/article-10214459/Portland-US-cities-looking-refund-police.html

357 City News Service Staff, Los Angeles, "LA City Council Approves Revised $11.8B Budget for 2022-23," Spectrum News 1, May 18, 2022, https://spectrumnews1.com/ca/la-west/politics/2022/05/18/los-angeles-city-council-to-review-2022-23-budget

358 Nicco Pelicano, "Austin Police Department Sees Largest Budget Increase in History a Year after It Was 'Defunded,'" Hilltop Views, September 21, 2021, https://www.hilltopviewsonline.com/24083/news/austin-police-department-sees-largest-budget-increase-in-history-a-year-after-it-was-defunded/

359 Peter Nickeas and Omar Jimenez, "Voters Will Decide on the Future of Policing in Minneapolis. The Question Goes Beyond 'Defunding the Police,'" CNN, November 3, 2021, https://www.cnn.com/2021/10/29/us/minneapolis-police-future-vote/index.html

360 Doug Seaton and James Dickey, "Minneapolis Needs a Fully-Funded Police Department," *Minneapolis Post*, December 7, 2022, https://www.minnpost.com/community-voices/2022/12/minneapolis-needs-a-fully-funded-police-department/

361 Theo Keith, "Minneapolis, St. Paul End Tumultuous 2021 by Increasing Police Spending," FOX 9, December 10, 2021, https://www.fox9.com/news/minneapolis-st-paul-end-tumultuous-2021-by-increasing-police-spending

362 Snejana Farberov, "Chicago's Mayor-Elect Warns against 'Demonizing' Rampaging Teens after Unrest," *New York Post*, April 17, 2023,

https://nypost.com/2023/04/17/chicagos-mayor-elect-warns-against-demonizing-rowdy-teens/

363 Illinois Policy, "Brandon Johnson Refuses to Condemn Looting During 2020 Riots (Repeatedly)," WGN News, March 12, 2023, https://www.youtube.com/watch?v=O3JUqZGN1hE&ab_channel=IllinoisPolicy

364 Savannah Eadens, "'Deadliest' Block in Portland Now Quiet after Community Safety Division Addresses Drug Dealing, Prostitution," *The Oregonian*, January 1, 2023, https://www.police1.com/crime-prevention/articles/deadliest-block-in-portland-now-quiet-after-community-safety-division-addresses-drug-dealing-prostitution-z4cipSsUtvm7jria/

365 Bobby Cuza, "NYPD, MTA Say They're Turning the Tide on Subway Crime," Spectrum News, February 7, 2023, https://www.ny1.com/nyc/all-boroughs/transit/2022/12/13/nypd—mta-say-they-re-turning-the-tide-on-subway-crime

366 NBC News (@NBCNews), "Florida Couple Stabbed to Death While Bicycling Near Daytona Beach Home," YouTube, March 8, 2022, https://www.youtube.com/watch?v=HWQjFB-bLpk&ab_channel=NBCNews

367 Brenda Altman, "Omg Robin is so awesome," Facebook, March 5, 2022, https://www.facebook.com/photo?fbid=126655303245878&set=ecnf.100077042260462

368 Clair Metz (@clairmetzwesh), "@ChiefJakari @DaytonaBchPD on murder of couple," WESH-TV interview, Twitter, March 6, 2022, 5:28 p.m., https://twitter.com/clairemetzwesh/status/1500599213218017281

369 Frank Fernandez, "Daytona Beach Police Identify 2 People Killed in Stabbing Sunday on North Wild Olive Ave," *The Daytona Beach News-Journal*, March 7, 2022, https://www.news-journalonline.com/story/news/local/volusia/2022/03/07/daytona-beach-stabbing-north-wild-olive-ave-neighbors-speak-out/9409648002/

370 Vicki Karr, "State Attorney: Jean Macean Indicted in Murders of Brenda, Terry Aultman at Daytona Beach Bike Week," FOX 35 Orlando, March 29, 2022, https://www.fox35orlando.com/news/state-attorney-jean-macean-indicted-in-murders-of-brenda-terry-aultman-at-daytona-beach-bike-week

371 Denver City Council meeting, August 28, 2017, https://denver.granicus.com/player/clip/10550?view_id=180&meta_id=242616&redirect=true&h=64e184d33381234690a269c0ec048ecf

372 Joe Rubino and Nick Coltrain, "Nearly 150 Migrants Unexpectedly Dropped in Downtown Denver, Prompting City to Open Emergency Shelter," *Denver Post*, December 7, 2022, https://www.denverpost.com/2022/12/07/denver-migrants-emergency-shelter/

373 Jared Polis, "Colorado Takes Action to Assist Migrants in Completing Their Journeys," Colorado Governor Jared Polis (newsletter), January

3, 2023, https://www.colorado.gov/governor/news/9356-colorado-takes-action-assist-migrants-completing-their-journeys

374 Jon Anuta, "NYC Mayor Doubles Down on Criticism of Colorado, Federal Government over Migrants," January 4, 2023, *Politico*, https://www.politico.com/news/2023/01/04/eric-adams-criticism-colorado-asylum-seekers-00076423

375 Andy Newman and Raul Vilchis, "A Migrant Wave Tests New York City's Identity as the World's Sanctuary," *New York Times*, August 20, 2022, https://www.nytimes.com/2022/08/20/nyregion/nyc-migrants-texas.html

376 Newman and Vilchis,"A Migrant Wave Tests New York City's Identity."

377 NYC: Official Website of New York City, "Mayor Bill de Blasio Signs into Law Bills to Dramatically Reduce New York City's Cooperation with U.S. Immigration and Customs Enforcement Deportations," news release, November 14, 2014, https://www.nyc.gov/office-of-the-mayor/news/520-14/mayor-bill-de-blasio-signs-law-bills-dramatically-reduce-new-york-city-s-cooperation-with#/0

378 Rozina Sabur, "New York Opens Controversial Migrant 'Tent City' with Sofas and TVs," *The Telegraph*, October 19, 2022, https://www.telegraph.co.uk/world-news/2022/10/19/new-york-opens-controversial-migrant-tent-city-sofas-tvs/

379 NYC: Official Website of New York City, "Mayor de Blasio and Officials Applaud the Department of Justice for Ending Grant Limitations on 'Sanctuary Cities,'" news release, April 29, 2021, https://www.nyc.gov/office-of-the-mayor/news/325-21/mayor-de-blasio-officials-applaud-department-justice-ending-grant-limitations-on

380 Annie Correal, "Man Accused of Murdering Woman, 92, Should Have Been Deported, ICE Says," *New York Times*, January 14, 2020, *New York Times*, https://www.nytimes.com/2020/01/14/nyregion/92-year-old-woman-queens-murder.html

381 Snejana Farberov, "Convicted Rapist Attacks His Wheelchair-Bound Victim after Release from Jail," *Daily Mail*, June 21, 2019, https://www.dailymail.co.uk/news/article-7167421/Convicted-rapist-attacks-wheelchair-bound-victim-release-jail.html

382 Jason Rantz, "Gael Tarleton," interview, Jason Rantz Show on KTTH Radio Seattle, June 28, 2019, https://omny.fm/shows/the-jason-rantz-show/gael-tarleton

383 Sara Jean Green, "White Center Man Convicted of Rape Accused of Attacking Victim Days after His Release from Jail," *Seattle Times*, June 18, 2019, https://www.seattletimes.com/seattle-news/law-justice/white-center-man-convicted-of-rape-accused-of-attacking-victim-days-after-his-release-from-jail/

384 King County Sheriff's Office PIO (@kingcosoPIO), "#Update on the

search for Francisco Carranza-Ramirez," Twitter, June 20, 2019, 1:20 p.m., https://twitter.com/kingcosoPIO/status/1141757705125683200

385 Brandi Kruse, "Rapist Accused of Attacking Victim after Release Believed to Have Fled to Mexico," FOX 13 News, June 20, 2019, https://www.q13fox.com/news/rapist-accused-of-attacking-victim-after-release-believed-to-have-fled-to-mexico

386 Essex Porter, "Ice Criticizes Sanctuary Laws in Murder of Federal Way Teen," KIRO-TV, October 11, 2019, https://www.kiro7.com/news/local/ice-criticizes-sanctuary-laws-in-murder-of-federal-way-teen/996519679/

387 Rantz, "Gael Tarleton."

388 Maxine Bernstein, "ICE Put Hold Months Ago on Undocumented Immigrant Now Accused of Killing Wife," *The Oregonian*, November 1, 2018, https://www.oregonlive.com/clackamascounty/2018/11/ice_immigration_detainer_place.html

389 Jayati Ramakrishnan, "Portland Man Gets Life in Prison for Killing Partner, Dumping Her Body Near Summer Camp," *The Oregonian*, September 9, 2019, https://www.oregonlive.com/crime/2019/09/portland-man-pleads-guilty-to-killing-wife-dumping-her-body-near-a-summer-camp.html

390 Fox News Staff, "Deputies in Portland Investigated by Own Department for Cooperating with ICE Agents," Fox News, October 23, 2017, https://www.foxnews.com/politics/deputies-in-portland-investigated-by-own-department-for-cooperating-with-ice-agents

391 Chelsea Wicks, "Sheriff Reese Investigates Deputies Helping ICE," KOIN-TV, February 23, 2017, https://www.koin.com/news/sheriff-reese-investigates-deputies-helping-ice/

392 Michael T. Light, Jingying He, and Jason P. Robey, "Comparing Crime Rates between Undocumented Immigrants, Legal Immigrants, and Native-Born US Citizens in Texas," *Proceedings of the National Academy of Sciences of the United States of America*, December 7, 2020, https://www.pnas.org/doi/10.1073/pnas.2014704117#sec-6

393 Michaelangelo Landgrave and Alex Nowrasteh, "Illegal Immigrant Incarceration Rates, 2010–2018: Demographics and Policy Implications," CATO Institute, April 21, 2020, https://www.cato.org/publications/policy-analysis/illegal-immigrant-incarceration-rates-2010-2018-demographics-policy

394 Christian Gunadi, "Does Immigrant Legalization Affect Crime? Evidence from Deferred Action for Childhood Arrivals in the United States," University of California at San Diego, October 17, 2019, https://economics.ucr.edu/wp-content/uploads/2019/11/JMP-Christian-Gunadi.pdf

395 Louis Casiano and Bill Melugin, "Los Angeles County DA Gascon Issues Directives to Avoid 'Adverse Immigration Consequences," Fox News, December 6, 2022, https://www.foxnews.com/politics/los-angeles-county-da-gascon-issues-directives-avoid-adverse-immigration-consequences

396 Fares Sabawi, "2021Was San Antonio's Deadliest Year since 1994, Data Shows," KSAT-TV, January 7, 2022, https://www.ksat.com/news/local/2022/01/07/2021-was-san-antonios-deadliest-year-since-1994-data-shows/

397 Jonathan Cotto, "Crimes in San Antonio Increased in 2022, New Data Shows," KSAT-TV, January 17, 2023, https://www.ksat.com/news/local/2022/12/01/homicides-jump-as-crime-up-nearly-12-in-san-antonio/. Michael Karlis, "Mexico City, Other Large Latin American Cities Now Have Lower Homicide Rates than San Antonio," *San Antonio Current*, January 3, 2023, https://www.sacurrent.com/news

398 Mario Diaz, "Houston Homicide Numbers Continue to Skyrocket in 2022," NBC Houston, February 8, 2022, https://www.click2houston.com/news/investigates/2022/02/08/houston-homicide-numbers-continue-to-skyrocket-in-2022/

399 Brooke Taylor, "Homicide Rate in Houston Is Up, Despite a Program Designed to Drive Down Crime," ABC Houston, August 9, 2022, https://abc13.com/one-safe-houston-program-crime-crackdown-homicide-rates-up-in/12113466/

400 Rebecca Salinas, "Cartel Leader Indicted in San Antonio; Arrest Caused Retaliatory Shooting, Burnings on Border," KSAT-TV, March 17, 2022, https://www.ksat.com/news/texas/2022/03/17/cartel-leader-indicted-in-san-antonio-arrest-caused-retaliatory-shooting-burnings-on-border/

401 KSAT 12 (@KSATnews), "Cartels Found to Have Stolen Seven Vehicles in San Antonio Area, Sheriff Says," YouTube, November 17, 2022, https://www.youtube.com/watch?v=jQCceyue8KI&ab_channel=KSAT12

402 Yami Virgin, "Cartel War Has Ties in South Texas, but Not Just on the Streets," NBC San Antonio, July 27, 2020, https://news4sanantonio.com/news/local/cartel-war-has-ties-in-south-texas-but-not-just-on-the-streets

403 FOX 26, "Mexican Drug Cartels Infiltrating Houston Neighborhoods DEA Special Agent in the Hot Seat," interview, FOX 26 Houston, August 11, 2019, https://www.fox26houston.com/whats-your-point/mexican-drug-cartels-infiltrating-houston-neighborhoods-dea-special-agent-in-the-hot-seat

404 US Immigration and Customs Enforcement, "ICE Houston Arrests 9 Criminal Aliens Wanted for Illegally Reentering US," news release, January 6, 2021, https://www.ice.gov/news/releases/ice-houston-arrests-9-criminal-aliens-wanted-illegally-reentering-us

405 Dave Kovaleski, "ICE Arrests 45 Illegal Immigrants in Houston Area," *Homeland Preparedness News*, August 15, 2018, https://homelandprepnews.com/stories/29969-ice-arrests-45-illegal-immigrants-in-houston-area/

406 Alex Nowrasteh, "Illegal Immigrants Aren't Responsible for the Rise in Homicides in Houston, Texas," CATO Institute, May 4, 2022, https://www.cato.org/blog/illegal-immigrants-arent-responsible-rise-homicides-houston-texas

407 Nowrasteh, "Illegal Immigrants Aren't Responsible for the Rise in Homicides in Houston, Texas."

408 Jon Kamp, Jose de Cordoba, and Julie Wernau, "How Two Mexican Drug Cartels Came to Dominate America's Fentanyl Supply," *Wall Street Journal*, August 30, 2022, https://www.wsj.com/articles/mexico-drug-cartels-fentanyl-overdose-sinaloa-jalisco-11661866903

409 Brian Mann, "2022 Was a Deadly (but Hopeful) Year in America's Opioid Crisis," NPR, December 31, 2022, https://www.npr.org/2022/12/31/1145797684/2022-was-a-deadly-but-hopeful-year-in-americas-opioid-crisis

410 DEA Intelligence Program—Strategic Intelligence Section, "Fentanyl Flow to the United States," DEA-DCT-DIR-008-20, Drug Enforcement Administration, January 2020, https://www.dea.gov/sites/default/files/2020-03/DEA_GOV_DIR-008-20%20Fentanyl%20Flow%20in%20the%20United%20States_0.pdf

411 Jon Kamp, Jose de Cordoba, and Julie Wernau, "Inside the Mexican Cartels That Rule Fentanyl Smuggling," *Wall Street Journal*, September 20, 2022, https://www.wsj.com/story/inside-the-mexican-cartels-that-rule-fentanyl-smuggling-48b5c665

412 US Attorney's Office, Southern District of California, "Fentanyl Seizures at Border Continue to Spike, Making San Diego a National Epicenter for Fentanyl Trafficking; U.S. Attorney's Office Prioritizes Prosecutions and Prevention Programs," news release, Department of Justice, August 11, 2022, https://www.justice.gov/usao-sdca/pr/fentanyl-seizures-border-continue-spike-making-san-diego-national-epicenter-fentanyl

413 Phillip Bump, "Most Fentanyl Is Seized at Border Crossings—Often from U.S. Citizens," *Washington Post*, October 4, 2022, https://www.washingtonpost.com/politics/2022/10/04/border-fentanyl-seizures-americans/

414 Pramila Jayapal (@PramilaJayapal), "Over 90% of fentanyl is brought into the country by U.S. citizens," Twitter, February 9, 2023, 5:45 p.m., https://twitter.com/PramilaJayapal/status/1623815262418993154

415 Martin Weil, "D.C. Mayor's Statement Opposes President Trump's 'Threats' of Deportations," *Washington Post*, June 21, 2019, https://www.washingtonpost.com/local/public-safety/dc-mayors-statement-opposes-president-trumps-threats-of-deportations/2019/06/21/c355f1e8-948c-11e9-b58a-a6a9afaa0e3e_story.html

416 Anthony Derrick, "Mayor Durkan Condemns Trump Administration's Threat to Escalate ICE Raids This Weekend," news release, Office

of the Mayor, City of Seattle, July 11, 2019, https://durkan.seattle.gov/2019/07/mayor-durkan-condemns-trump-administrations-threat-to-escalate-ice-raids-this-weekend/

417 Lexi Sutter, "'Back Off:' Lori Lightfoot Issues Strong Rebuke of President Trump's Immigration Policies," NBC Chicago, June 22, 2019, https://www.nbcchicago.com/news/local/chicago-mayor-lori-lightfoot-strongly-worded-rebuke-donald-trump-policies/145814/

418 Nouran Salahieh, "'Inhumane, Disgraceful and Dangerous': Mayor Garcetti Responds to Trump's Threat to Deport Millions of Immigrants," KTLA-TV, June 18, 2019, https://ktla.com/news/inhumane-disgraceful-and-dangerous-mayor-garcetti-responds-to-trumps-threat-to-deport-millions-of-immigrants/

419 Eliott McLaughlin, "ICE Has Begun Raids to Round Up Undocumented Immigrants, Official Says," CNN, July 15, 2019, https://www.cnn.com/2019/07/14/politics/ice-raids-undocumented-immigrants/index.html

420 Jordan Fabian, "Only 35 Arrested in ICE Raids Touted by Trump," *The Hill*, July 23, 2019, https://thehill.com/homenews/administration/454314-only-35-arrested-in-ice-raids-touted-by-trump/

421 Joel Rose, "Many Americans Falsely Think Migrants Are Bringing Most of the Fentanyl Entering U.S.," National Public Radio, August 18, 2022, https://www.npr.org/2022/08/18/1118271910/many-americans-falsely-think-migrants-are-bringing-most-of-the-fentanyl-entering

422 Bob Ortega and Rob O'Dell, "River of Drugs Runs through Rio Grande Valley," *USA Today*, March 30, 2014, https://www.usatoday.com/story/news/nation/2014/03/30/rio-grande-is-hot-spot-for-pot-smugglers/7066181/

423 Associated Press Staff, "Drug Smuggling Tunnel with Rail System Uncovered on US-Mexico Border," *The Guardian*, May 16, 2022, https://www.theguardian.com/us-news/2022/may/16/california-drug-smuggling-tunnel-us-mexcio-border

424 Brian Flood, "Mainstream Morning News Ignores Massive Migrant Caravan Heading to US Border," Fox News, October 26, 2021, Fox Newshttps://www.foxnews.com/media/mainstream-morning-news-ignores-massive-migrant-caravan

425 Paul Krugman, "Notes on Immigration," *New York Times*, March 27, 2006, https://archive.nytimes.com/krugman.blogs.nytimes.com/2006/03/27/notes-on-immigration/

426 Mohammad Fazel Zarandi, Jonathan S. Feinstein, and Edward H. Kaplan, "Yale Study Finds Twice as Many Undocumented Immigrants as Previous Estimates," *Yale Insights*, September 21, 2018, https://insights.som.yale.edu/insights/yale-study-finds-twice-as-many-undocumented-immigrants-as-previous-estimates

427 Julia Ainsley, "Migrant Border Crossings in Fiscal Year 2022 Topped 2.76 Million, Breaking Previous Record," NBC News, October 22, 2022, https://www.nbcnews.com/politics/immigration/migrant-border-crossings-fiscal-year-2022-topped-276-million-breaking-rcna53517

428 Adam Shaw, Bill Melugin, and Griff Jenkins, "Over 73,000 'Got-aways' at Southern Border in November, Highest Ever Recorded," Fox News, December 1, 2022, Fox Newshttps://www.foxnews.com/politics/73000-gotaways-southern-border-november-highest-ever-recorded

429 Jeffery C. Mays and Annie Correal, "New York City Gives 800,000 Non-citizens Right to Vote in Local Elections," *New York Times*, December 9, 2021, https://www.nytimes.com/2021/12/09/nyregion/noncitizens-voting-rights-nyc.html

430 EdSource Staff, "Judge Throws Out S.F. Law Allowing Non-citizens to Vote in School Board Elections," Education Source, August 1, 2022, https://edsource.org/updates/judge-throws-out-s-f-law-allowing-non-citizens-to-vote-in-school-board-elections

431 2020 Democratic Platform, https://democrats.org/where-we-stand/party-platform/

432 Joe Schoffstall and Adam Shaw, "Liberal Group Lands $171M Gov't Contract That Could Reach $1B to Help Illegal Immigrants Avoid Deportation," Fox News, July 14, 2022, Fox Newshttps://www.foxnews.com/politics/liberal-group-171m-govt-contract-could-hit-1b-illegal-immigrants-avoid-derportation

433 Seattle Legal Defense Network, "Have You or Someone You Know Received a Notice from Immigration Court or Been Detained by ICE?," Office of Immigrant and Refugee Affairs, City of Seattle, 2023, https://www.seattle.gov/iandraffairs/programs-and-services/immigration-legal-defense

434 LAIst, "LA's Pilot Fund for Undocumented Immigrants to Get Free Legal Services Is Here to Stay," Boyle Heights Beat, May 12, 2022, https://boyleheightsbeat.com/las-pilot-fund-for-undocumented-immigrants-to-get-free-legal-services-is-here-to-stay/

435 Faiza Mahamud, "Rights Advocates Say Minneapolis Must Issue City IDs to Residents, Unveil List of 'Pro-Immigrant' Demands," *Star Tribune*, July 21, 2022, https://www.startribune.com/rights-advocates-minneapolis-must-issue-city-ids-to-residents-unveil-list-of-pro-immigrant-demands/600192070/

436 Paul Crookston, "Stacey Abrams: 'Blue Wave' Is 'Comprised of Those Who Are Documented and Undocumented,'" *Washington Free Beacon*, October 12, 2018, https://freebeacon.com/politics/dem-candidate-abrams-blue-wave-comprised-documented-undocumented/

437 Michelle Goldberg, "We Can Replace Them," *New York Times*, October 29, 2018, https://www.nytimes.com/2018/10/29/opinion/stacey-abrams-georgia-governor-election-brian-kemp.html

438 Cong. Rec. S4938 (daily ed. July 19, 2021) (statement of Sen. Durbin), https://www.congress.gov/117/crec/2021/07/19/167/126/CREC-2021-07-19-pt1-PgS4938-3.pdf

439 Blanca Barragan, "Ballot Measure HHH," Curbed Los Angeles, October 11, 2016, https://la.curbed.com/2016/10/11/13238618/explain-ballot-measure-hhh-los-angeles

440 "Los Angeles, California, Homelessness Reduction and Prevention Housing, and Facilities Bond Issue, Measure HHH (November 2016)," *BallotPedia*, https://ballotpedia.org/Los_Angeles,_California,_Homelessness_Reduction_and_Prevention_Housing,_and_Facilities_Bond_Issue,_Measure_HHH_(November_2016)

441 Brenda Gazzar, "ELECTION 2016: LA's Proposition HHH to House Homeless Gets Early Support," *Los Angeles Daily News*, November 9, 2016, https://www.dailynews.com/2016/11/09/election-2016-las-proposition-hhh-to-house-homeless-gets-early-support/

442 Barragan, "Ballot Measure HHH."

443 Kristen Bell, "Kristen Bell Urges 'Yes' Vote on LA Prop HHH for Homeless Funding: 'I Refuse to Look at People I Have to Step over on the Street as Animals,'" *The Hollywood Reporter*, November 3, 2016, https://www.hollywoodreporter.com/lifestyle/lifestyle-news/kristen-bell-urges-yes-vote-la-prop-hhh-homeless-funding-i-refuse-look-at-people-i-have-step-st-943261/

444 Courtney Friel, "Election Results: L.A. Voters Approve Measure to Spend $1.2 Billion to House the Homeless," Los Angeles Times in KTLA-TV, November 9, 2016, https://ktla.com/news/local-news/election-results-l-a-voters-approve-measure-to-spend-1-2-billion-to-house-the-homeless/

445 Associated Press Staff, "Los Angeles Is Spending Up to $837,000 to House a Single Homeless Person," Associated Press at KTLA-TV, February 24, 2022, https://ktla.com/news/los-angeles-is-spending-up-to-837000-to-house-a-single-homeless-person/

446 Ron Galperin, "The Problems and Progress of Prop. HHH," Los Angeles Controller report, February 23, 2022, https://controller.lacity.gov/audits/problems-and-progress-of-prop-hhh

447 Morning Briefing Staff, "US Homeless Deaths Spike Wasn't from Covid: It Was Overdoses," KFF Health News, May 31, 2022, https://khn.org/morning-breakout/us-homeless-deaths-spike-wasnt-from-covid-it-was-overdoses/

448 Doug Smith and Benjamin Oreskes, "Homeless Population's Mental Illness, Substance Abuse Under-Reported," *Los Angeles Times*, October 7, 2019, https://www.latimes.com/california/story/2019-10-07/homeless-population-mental-illness-disability

449 Sean Coffey, "Study Confirms Serious Health Problems, High Trauma Rates among Unsheltered People in U.S.," UCLA Newsroom, October

7, 2019, https://newsroom.ucla.edu/releases/serious-health-conditions-trauma-unsheltered-homeless

450 Stories Staff, "LA Mayor on the Affordable Housing Crisis," Habitat for Humanity, https://www.habitat.org/stories/la-mayor-affordable-housing-crisis

451 NW Reporter Staff, "Seattle Mayor Rolls Out Plans to 'Bend the Arc' So More People Can Live in the City," Northwest Multiple Listing Service, August 14, 2019, https://www.nwmls.com/seattle-mayor-rolls-out-plans-to-bend-the-arc-so-more-people-can-live-in-the-city/

452 Amanda Ruiz, "Mayor Steve Adler: Austin Could End Homelessness in 3 Years," FOX 7 Austin, August 26, 2022, https://www.fox7austin.com/news/mayor-adler-austin-homeless-crisis

453 "San Francisco Homeless Count and Survey: 2022 Comprehensive Report," Applied Survey Research, September 19, 2022, https://hsh.sfgov.org/wp-content/uploads/2022/08/2022-PIT-Count-Report-San-Francisco-Updated-8.19.22.pdf

454 "Full 2022 Point in Time Count Report Shows COVID-19 Added to Unsheltered Homelessness," November 9, 2022, Multnomah County, https://www.multco.us/multnomah-county/news/full-2022-point-time-count-report-shows-covid-19-added-unsheltered

455 "A Snapshot of Homelessness in the Colorado Balance of State Continuum of Care: 2022 Homeless Point-in-Time Study Sheltered Count," Colorado Coalition for the Homeless, 2022, https://www.coloradocoalition.org/sites/default/files/2022-08/2022%20Homelessness%20Point-in-Time%20Study%20-%20CO%20BoS%20CoC%20-%20Sheltered%20Count%20Only_0.pdf

456 Green Doors, "Austin & Travis County Homelessness Facts," https://www.greendoors.org/facts/austin-data.php

457 "Homelessness in Los Angeles County," Los Angeles Almanac, 2022, https://www.laalmanac.com/social/so14.php

458 "Point-in-Time Count." King County Regional Homelessness Authority. 2022, https://kcrha.org/data-overview/king-county-point-in-time-count/

459 Gillian Flaccus and Geoff Mulvihill, "Growing Homeless Camps Contrast with West Coast Tech Wealth," *Denver Post*, November 6, 2017, https://www.denverpost.com/2017/11/06/homeless-explosion-west-coast/

460 KUOW Staff, "5 Questions: City Council Candidates in Central Seattle," KUOW Radio, October 28, 2019, https://www.kuow.org/stories/5-questions-for-council-candidates-in-central-seattle

461 Dan Strauss, "Ballard Commons Grand Reopening!," Seattle City Council member home page, December 7, 2022, https://strauss.seattle.gov/ballard-commons-update/

462 Claire Withycombe, "Inslee Wants WA to Borrow $4B to Build Housing and Shelter. How Would That Work?" *Seattle Times*, January 30, 2023,

https://www.seattletimes.com/seattle-news/politics/inslee-wants-wa-to-borrow-4b-to-build-housing-and-shelter-how-would-that-work/

463 Christopher Rufo, "Seattle Under Siege," *City Journal*, Autumn 2018, https://www.city-journal.org/seattle-homelessness

464 All Home, "2020 Count Us In," July 29, 2020, https://kcrha.org/wp-content/uploads/2020/07/Count-Us-In-2020-Final_7.29.2020.pdf

465 *City of Seattle v. Purdue Pharma*, September 28, 2017, https://www.seattle.gov/documents/Departments/CityAttorney/OpioidLitigation/SeattleComplaint-Opioid.pdf

466 TRD Staff, "Hotel Julian Rented Out 1,900 Rooms over the Past Year," The Real Deal, March 15, 2022, https://therealdeal.com/chicago/2022/03/15/foia-shows-chicago-paid-downtown-hotel-7m-to-shelter-homeless/

467 FOX 32 (@FOX32Chicago), "Chicago Relocates Homeless from Hotel They've Stayed in for a Year during Pandemic," YouTube, February 23, 2022, https://www.youtube.com/watch?v=3hu6jtnXxb4&ab_channel=FOX32Chicago

468 Paul Best, "Austin Hotel Purchased for $9M to Become Homeless Shelter Is Vandalized: 'Nearly Every Door Is Bashed In,'" Fox News, May 12, 2022, Fox Newshttps://www.foxnews.com/us/austin-hotel-purchased-homeless-shelter-vandalized-nearly-every-door-bashed-damage

469 AP Staff, "Kirkland, King County Sued over Converting Hotel to Permanent Housing for the Homeless," Associated Press, April 6, 2022, https://www.kiro7.com/news/local/kirkland-king-county-sued-over-converting-hotel-permanent-housing-homeless/UTG2JZKT5ZAP5CJRONDG2IZKPU/

470 Josh Haskell, "Teams Begin Moving Homeless from Encampments into Hotels, Motels under Mayor Karen Bass' New Plan," KIRO-TV, December 21, 2022, https://abc7.com/mayor-karen-bass-los-angeles-moving-homeless-into-hotels-inside-safe-initiative/12596917/

471 Evan Symon, "LA Motel Owners Fight Back against Mayor Bass' Homeless Housing Plans," *California Globe*, December 20, 2022, https://californiaglobe.com/articles/la-hotel-motel-owners-fight-back-against-mayor-bass-homeless-housing-plans/

472 Joaquin Palomino and Trisha Thadani,"Broken Homes," *San Francisco Chronicle*, April 26, 2022, https://www.sfchronicle.com/projects/2022/san-francisco-sros/

473 Jason Rantz, "Rantz: Seattle Police Say Video Shows Homeless Man Hitting Woman in Head with Bat," *MyNorthwest*, February 8, 2022, https://mynorthwest.com/3340830/rantz-police-video-shows-homeless-man-hitting-woman-heat-with-bat/

474 "Project RoomKey – Program Rules," March 15, 2021, https://www.documentcloud.org/documents/21115146-project-roomkey-program-rules-final-031521

475 Clare Busch, "Members of LA's Unhoused Community Form Union, Demand Changes to Project Roomkey," KNX News, May 21, 2021, https://www.audacy.com/knxnews/news/local/la-homeless-form-union-demand-changes-to-project-roomkey

476 Busch, "Members of LA's Unhoused Community Form Union, Demand Changes to Project Roomkey."

477 NYCLU Staff, "NYCLU Statement on NYPD Sweep of Unhoused Encampment in the East Village," news release, ACLU of New York, April 6, 2022, https://www.nyclu.org/en/press-releases/nyclu-statement-nypd-sweep-unhoused-encampment-east-village

478 MinnPost Staff, "Judge Declines to Stop Sweeps of Minneapolis Homeless Encampments," *The Glean*, October 30, 2020, https://www.minnpost.com/glean/2020/10/judge-declines-to-stop-sweeps-of-minneapolis-homeless-encampments/

479 Hugo Soto-Martínez (@HugoForCD13), "Last week we rallied against ineffective, inhumane policy," Twitter, August 2, 2022, 1:09 p.m., https://twitter.com/HugoForCD13/status/1554514645787897857

480 Sophie Peel, "City Commissioner Jo Ann Hardesty Condemns Use of Boulders to Expel Portland Homeless Camps," *Willamette Week*, July 18, 2019, https://www.wweek.com/news/city/2019/07/18/city-commissioner-jo-ann-hardesty-condemns-use-of-boulders-to-expel-portland-homeless-camps/

481 Aris Folley, "Ocasio-Cortez: Housing Should Be Legislated as a Human Right," *The Hill*, May 31, 2019, https://thehill.com/homenews/house/446287-ocasio-cortez-housing-should-be-legislated-as-a-human-right/

482 Anna Gorman, "Medieval Diseases Are Infecting California's Homeless," *The Atlantic*, March 8, 2019, https://www.theatlantic.com/health/archive/2019/03/typhus-tuberculosis-medieval-diseases-spreading-homeless/584380/

483 Dennis Romero and Andrew Blankstein, " 'Typhus Zone': Rats and Trash Infest Los Angeles' Skid Row, Fueling Disease," NBC News, October 14, 2018, https://www.nbcnews.com/news/us-news/typhus-zone-rats-trash-infest-los-angeles-skid-row-fueling-n919856

484 Nathan Wilson, "Leaked City Documents Give Protesters Heads-Up on Homeless Camp Cleanups," KIRO-TV, August 16, 2018, https://www.kiro7.com/news/local/leaked-city-documents-give-protesters-heads-up-on-homeless-camp-cleanups/814642305/

485 Amy Graff, " 'SnapCrap' App Invites San Francisco Residents to Report Poop on City Streets," SFGate, October 4, 2018, https://www.sfgate.com/bayarea/article/SnapCrap-app-San-Francisco-poop-feces-dirty-street-13281837.php

486 Lawrence Richard, "Protesters Disrupt Los Angeles City Council Vote on Banning Homeless Encampments Near Schools," Fox News, August

10, 2022, https://www.foxnews.com/us/protesters-disrupt-los-angeles-city-council-vote-banning-homeless-encampments-near-schools

487 Stop The Sweeps PDX (@StopSweepsPDX), "Fighting against sweeps and those who profit, " Twitter, https://twitter.com/stopsweepspdx

488 Andrew Mark Miller, "Oregon Democrats Propose 'Right to Rest Act' Decriminalizing Public Camping as Homeless Crisis Surges," Fox News, April 28, 2023, https://www.foxnews.com/us/oregon-democrats-propose-right-rest-act-decriminalizing-public-camping-homeless-crisis-surges

489 Sara Cline, "In an About-Face, Liberal US Cities Target Homeless Camps," KGW-TV, March 10, 2022, https://www.kgw.com/article/news/local/liberal-cities-homeless-camps-seattle-portland-sacramento-crackdown/283-687c4ed6-97a1-481d-bb16-f5a700e0ba96

490 Kshama Sawant, "Stop Inhumane Sweeps of Homeless Encampments!," Kshama's Council home page, January 19, 2016, https://sawant.seattle.gov/stop-inhumane-sweeps/

491 Wilson, "Leaked City Documents Give Protesters Heads-Up on Homeless Camp Cleanups."

492 Jason Rantz, "Seattle Homelessness Explodes, with No End in Sight," FOX Business, November 13, 2020, https://www.foxbusiness.com/politics/seattle-homelessness-no-end

493 Jason Rantz, "Rantz: Seattle's Homeless 'Tent Mansion' Grows, Adds a Keg," *MyNorthwest*, June 5, 2018, https://mynorthwest.com/1008929/rantz-seattles-homeless-tent-mansion-grows-adds-a-keg/

494 Alfred Charles, "Man Held for Attempted Rape of King County Female Courthouse Worker, Seattle Police Say," KOMO-TV, July 29, 2021, https://komonews.com/news/local/man-held-in-sexual-assault-of-king-county-courthouse-worker-seattle-police-say

495 Charles, "Man Held for Attempted Rape of King County Female Courthouse Worker."

496 Joel Moreno, "Sheriff Nearly Stabbed Outside King County Courthouse," KOMO-TV, August 29, 2017, https://komonews.com/news/local/sheriff-nearly-stabbed-outside-king-county-courthouse#!

497 Christine Clarridge, "From 2017: Judges Complain It's Unsafe, Unsanitary Outside King County Courthouse in Seattle," *Seattle Times*, July 11, 2017, https://www.seattletimes.com/seattle-news/law-justice/judges-complain-its-unsafe-unsanitary-outside-county-courthouse-in-seattle/

498 Jason Rantz, "Seattle Council Member to Fight Crime with Ping-Pong Balls," *MyNorthwest*, June 22, 2018, https://mynorthwest.com/1026756/seattle-council-member-to-fight-crime-with-ping-pong-balls/

499 Jason Rantz, "Rantz: Mayor Thinks Pickleball Can Solve Seattle Crime, Fentanyl Crisis," *MyNorthwest*, April 25, 2023, https://mynorthwest.com/3876574/rantz-pickleball-solve-seattle-fentanyl-crime-crisis/

500 Jason Rantz, "Rantz: School Board Members Demanded Seattle Not Sweep Homeless Encampments from Schools," *MyNorthwest*, April 5, 2021, https://mynorthwest.com/2745058/rantz-school-board-members-demanded-seattle-not-sweep-homeless-encampments-from-schools/

501 Rantz, "Rantz: School Board Members Demanded Seattle Not Sweep Homeless Encampments from Schools."

502 KTTH Staff, "Outreach Worker: We Need 'Right Resources' for Homeless Camp Near Seattle School," *MyNorthwest*, May 23, 2021, https://mynorthwest.com/2916062/homeless-camp-by-seattle-school-unsanitary/

503 Jason Rantz, "Rantz: Seattle School with Encampment Went on Lockdown over Firearm Sighting," *MyNorthwest*, April 27, 2021, https://mynorthwest.com/2849037/rantz-seattle-school-with-encampment-went-on-lockdown-over-firearm-sighting/

504 Kara Kostanich, "Parents, Neighbors Concerned about Growing Homeless Encampment on Seattle School Property," KOMO-TV, May 18, 2021, https://komonews.com/news/project-seattle/parents-neighbors-concerned-about-growing-homeless-encampment-on-seattle-school-property

505 Jason Rantz, "Rantz: Seattle Nonprofit Contractor Shot Meth with Homeless Woman He Was Tasked to Help Near School," *MyNorthwest*, December 8, 2021, https://mynorthwest.com/3273913/rantz-seattle-contractor-meth-homeless-woman-school/

506 KIRO Newsradio Newsdesk, "Why Are There No Homeless Camps in Bellevue Public Parks?" *MyNorthwest*, April 14, 2021, https://mynorthwest.com/2801465/bellevue-public-homeless-camps-approach/

507 Mike Benner, "Gresham MAX Attack Suspect Claimed Victim Smelled Like a Robot, DA's Office Says," KGW-TV, January 4, 2023, https://www.kgw.com/article/news/crime/gresham-max-attack-suspect-court/283-8f5fce55-6e6a-4af7-ad62-d5e1f98a53cf

508 Tucker Carlson and Jason Rantz, "Homeless Man in Gruesome Attack," from *Tucker Carlson Tonight* (original broadcast January 5, 2023), YouTube, https://www.youtube.com/watch?v=NvmMiyDS2qA&ab_channel=JasonRantz

509 Office of the District Attorney, "DA Mike Schmidt Announces Arraignment of Koryn Kraemer, 25, for Assault," news release, Multnomah County District Attorney (website), April 2021, https://www.mcda.us/index.php/news/da-mike-schmidt-announces-arraignment-of-koryn-kraemer-25-for-assault

510 Mike Benner, "Victim of Vicious Attack at MAX Stop in Gresham Identified by Authorities," KGW-TV, January 5, 2023, https://www.kgw.com

/article/news/local/victim-of-vicious-attack-at-max-stop-in-gresham-identified/283-e720e0c4-f739-4d01-8c88-a8468f940e5c

511 Francesca Washington, "Albuquerque Homeless Work Program Coming to an End This Month," KRQE-TV, September 12, 2019, https://www.krqe.com/news/albuquerque-metro/albuquerque-homeless-work-program-coming-to-an-end-this-month/

512 Washington, "Albuquerque Homeless Work Program Coming to an End This Month."

513 Francesca Washington, "Inspector General: Albuquerque Homeless Work Program Not Reaching Full Potential," KRQE-TV, November 11, 2019, https://www.krqe.com/news/albuquerque-metro/inspector-general-better-way-program-not-reaching-full-potential/

514 National Academy of Sciences, Engineering, and Medicine; Health and Medicine Division; Board on Population Health and Public Health Practice; Policy and Global Affairs; Science and Technology for Sustainability Program; Committee on an Evaluation of Permanent Supportive Housing Programs for Homeless Individuals, "3, Evidence of Effect of Permanent Supportive Housing on Health," in *Permanent Supportive Housing: Evaluating the Evidence for Improving Health Outcomes among People Experiencing Chronic Homelessness* (Washington, DC: National Academies Press, July 11, 2018), https://www.ncbi.nlm.nih.gov/books/NBK519591/

515 Zachary B. Wolf, "A Hard Look at New York's Controversial New Approach to the Homeless," CNN, December 3, 2022, https://www.cnn.com/2022/12/03/politics/nyc-hospitalize-mentally-ill-what-matters/index.html

516 Jacquelyn Simone, "Coalition for the Homeless' Statement on Mayor Adams' Mental Health Address and Legislative Agenda," news release, November 29, 2022, https://www.coalitionforthehomeless.org/press/coalition-for-the-homeless-statement-on-mayor-adams-mental-health-address-and-legislative-agenda/

517 Steven Felschundneff, "New 'Care Court' Aims to Treat Severe Mental Illness," *The Claremont Courier*, January 19, 2023, https://claremont-courier.com/latest-news/new-care-court-aims-to-treat-severe-mental-illness-72152/

518 W Cho, WS Shin, I An, M Bang, DY Cho, and SH Lee, "Biological Aspects of Aggression and Violence in Schizophrenia," *Clinical Psychopharmacology and Neuroscience* 17, no 4 (November 20, 2019): 475–486, https://www.ncbi.nlm.nih.gov/pmc/articles/PMC6852683/

519 Nicholas Slayton, "Time to Retire the Word 'Homeless' and Opt for 'Houseless' or 'Unhoused' Instead?," *Architectural Digest*, May 21, 2021, https://www.architecturaldigest.com/story/homeless-unhoused

520 Patrick Maks, "Previewing a New AP Stylebook," Associated Press, May 1, 2020, https://blog.ap.org/products-and-services/previewing-a-new-ap-stylebook

521 Meghan Henry, Tanya de Sousa, Colette Tano, Nathaniel Dick, Rhaia Hull, Meghan Shea, Tori Morris, and Sean Morris, Abt Associates, "Point-in-Time Estimates of Sheltered Homeless: Part 1 of the 2021 Annual Homeless Assessment Report (AHAR) to Congress," Office of Community Planning and Development, US Department of Housing and Urban Development, February 2022, https://www.huduser.gov/portal/sites/default/files/pdf/2021-AHAR-Part-1.pdf

522 "Homelessness: The Reality and the Solution," short documentary video, Cicero Institute, https://ciceroinstitute.org/homelessness-the-reality-and-the-solution/

523 Mobile Homes and Fishes, home page, https://mlf.org/

524 KTTH Staff, "Marysville Comes Up with Creative Solution for Homeless Problem," *MyNorthwest*, December 7, 2018, https://mynorthwest.com/1211486/marysville-mayor-homeless-problem-social-workers/

525 Mayor Jon Nehring shared the two-year data sets with me.

526 Greg Kim, "Ending Homelessness in King County Will Cost Billions, Regional Authority Says," *Seattle Times*, January 26, 2023, https://www.seattletimes.com/seattle-news/homeless/ending-homelessness-in-king-county-will-cost-billions-regional-authority-says/

527 Rebecca A. Cherner, Tim Aubry, John Sylvestre, Rob Boyd, and Donna Pettey, "Housing First for Adults with Problematic Substance Use," *Journal of Dual Diagnosis* 13, no. 3 (July–September, 2017): 219–229, https://pubmed.ncbi.nlm.nih.gov/28414579/

528 Kelly McEvers, "Utah Reduced Chronic Homelessness by 91 Percent; Here's How," National Public Radio, December 10, 2015, https://www.npr.org/2015/12/10/459100751/utah-reduced-chronic-homelessness-by-91-percent-heres-how

529 Robert Baumann, Bryan Engelhardt, and Victor A. Matheson, "The Labor Market Effects of the Salt Lake City Winter Olympics," College of Holy Cross, Department of Economics Faculty Research Series, Paper No. 10-02, May 2010, https://web.holycross.edu/RePEc/hcx/HC1002-Matheson-Baumann-Engelhardt_SLCOlympics.pdf

530 Charlie Leduff, "OLYMPICS: THE STREETS; Loitering Behind the Clean Streets," *New York Times*, February 14, 2002, https://www.nytimes.com/2002/02/14/sports/olympics-the-streets-loitering-behind-the-clean-streets.html

531 Robert Baumann, Bryan Engelhardt, and Victor A. Matheson, "Employment Effects of the 2002 Winter Olympics in Salt Lake City, Utah," *Journal of Economics and Statistics* (Jahrbuecher fuer Nationaloekonomie

und Statistik), De Gruyter, 232 no. 3 (June 2012): 308–317, https://ideas.repec.org/a/jns/jbstat/v232y2012i3p308-317.html

532 Lloyd Pendelton, "The Housing First Approach to Homelessness," TEDMED, TED Talk, 2016, https://www.ted.com/talks/lloyd_pendleton_the_housing_first_approach_to_homelessness?language=en

533 Kevin Fagan, "What S.F. Can Learn from Salt Lake City," *San Francisco Chronicle*, https://www.sfchronicle.com/archive/item/What-S-F-can-learn-from-Salt-Lake-City-30428.php

534 Terrence McCoy, "The Surprisingly Simple Way Utah Solved Chronic Homelessness and Saved Millions," *Washington Post*, April 17, 2015, https://www.washingtonpost.com/news/inspired-life/wp/2015/04/17/the-surprisingly-simple-way-utah-solved-chronic-homelessness-and-saved-millions/

535 Comedy Central's *The Daily Show,* January 7, 2015, https://www.cc.com/video/lntv3q/the-daily-show-with-jon-stewart-the-homeless-homed

536 Maria L. La Ganga, "Utah Says It Won 'War on Homelessness,' but Shelters Tell a Different Story," *The Guardian*, April 27, 2016, https://www.theguardian.com/us-news/2016/apr/27/utah-homeless-shelters-housing-first

537 "Salt Lake County Point-in-Time Count," End Utah Homelessness, https://endutahhomelessness.org/salt-lake-valley/salt-lake-county-pit-count/

538 Bethany Rogers, "Utah Was Once Lauded for Solving Homelessness—The Reality Was Far More Complicated," *Salt Lake Tribune*, May 11, 2020, https://www.sltrib.com/news/politics/2020/05/11/utah-was-once-lauded/

539 Rogers, "Utah Was Once Lauded for Solving Homelessness."

540 Ben Winslow, "Governor to Call Special Session on 'Operation Rio Grande' Issues Next Week," FOX 13 Salt Lake City, September 13, 2017, https://www.fox13now.com/2017/09/13/governor-to-call-special-session-on-operation-rio-grande-issues-next-week

541 Christopher Smart, "Minor League Las Vegas Baseball Player Attacked by Homeless Salt Lake City Man, Police Say," *Salt Lake Tribune*, July 4, 2017, https://archive.sltrib.com/article.php?id=13641208&itype=storyID

542 Christopher Smart, "Escalating Violence around Homeless Shelter Has Utah House Speaker Asking: Is This a Job for the National Guard?," *Salt Lake Tribune*, July 6, 2017, https://archive.sltrib.com/article.php?id=5475873&itype=CMSID

543 Katie McKellar, "Over 1,000 Arrests Made in Operation Rio Grande as 37 New Treatment Beds Open," KLS TV, September 7, 2017, https://www.ksl.com/article/45717402/over-1000-arrests-made-in-operation-rio-grande-as-37-new-treatment-beds-open

544 Danica Lawrence, "Some Neighbors Are Frustrated with the Impact 'Operation Rio Grande' Is Having on Their Neighborhoods," FOX 13, August 21, 2017, https://www.fox13now.com/2017/08/21/some

-neighbors-are-frustrated-with-the-impact-operation-rio-grande-is-having-on-their-neighborhoods

545 D.J. Bolerjack, "Operation Rio Grande Forcing Hundreds of Homeless to Southern Utah Cities," KUTV, September 7, 2017, https://kutv.com/news/local/operation-rio-grande-forcing-hundreds-of-homeless-to-southern-utah-cities

546 Bethany Rodgers and Taylor Stevens, "Nearly 80% of the Money Budgeted for Operation Rio Grande Was Used for Policing, Jail Beds, and Court Costs," *Salt Lake City Tribune*, December 13, 2020, https://www.sltrib.com/news/politics/2020/12/13/nearly-money-budgeted/

547 Rodgers and Stevens, "Nearly 80% of the Money Budgeted for Operation Rio Grande."

548 American Civil Liberties Union of Utah and Smart Justice Utah, "Calculating the Real Cost of Operation Rio Grande," October 16, 2018, https://media.good4utah.com/nxsglobal/good4utah/document_dev/2018/10/16/ACLU_UT-CalcCostORG-Embargoed_1539727608016_59188554_ver1.0.pdf

549 Katie McKellar, "ACLU Says Operation Rio Grande Created 'Long-Term Damage,'" *Deseret News*, November 4, 2019, https://www.deseret.com/utah/2019/11/4/20947955/operation-rio-grande-aclu-salt-lake-utah

550 Sara Tabin, "Homeless Camps Have Been Cleared Out in Salt Lake City. Unhoused People Say They Don't Know Where They Will Stay Now," *Salt Lake Tribune*, December 13, 2020, https://www.sltrib.com/news/2020/12/12/homeless-camps-have-been/

551 Bethany Rodgers, "ACLU Says Operation Rio Grande Was 'Designed as a Hammer,' and Arrest Figures Show It," *Salt Lake Tribune*, October 16, 2018, https://www.sltrib.com/news/politics/2018/10/16/aclu-says-operation-rio/

552 Emily Means, "Camp Last Hope Closes as Activist and Salt Lake City Officials Come to the Table Together," KUER 90.1, February 3, 2021, https://www.kuer.org/politics-government/2021-02-03/camp-last-hope-closes-as-activist-and-salt-lake-city-officials-come-to-the-table-together

553 Paighten Harkens and Rick Egan, "Rio Grande Confrontations Show Tensions Rising among Salt Lake City's Homeless," *Salt Lake Tribune*, January 14, 2023, https://www.sltrib.com/news/2023/01/14/help-us-tensions-build-among/

554 Black Lives for Humanity Movement (@BlackLivesforHumanity-Movement), "This is the abatement that gave birth to 'Camp Last Hope,'" Facebook, November 7, 2021, https://www.facebook.com/BlackLivesforHumanityMovement/videos/617996129472257

555 Emily Means, "'Camp Last Hope' Provides Shelter for People Displaced by Salt Lake Encampment Cleanups," KUER 90.1, December 22, 2020, https://www.kuer.org/politics-government/2020-12-22/camp-last-hope-provides-shelter-for-people-displaced-by-salt-lake-encampment-cleanups

556 Emily Means, "'There Is Nowhere for Us to Go'—Unsheltered People React to Tear Down of Salt Lake City Encampment," KUER 90.1, February 17, 2022, https://www.kuer.org/race-religion-social-justice/2022-02-17/there-is-nowhere-for-us-to-go-unsheltered-people-react-to-tear-down-of-salt-lake-city-encampment

557 Amy Nay, "Downtown Salt Lake City Business Owners Say Some Homeless Individuals Are Creating Unsafe Environment," FOX 13, July 15, 2022, https://www.fox13now.com/news/local-news/downtown-slc-business-owners-say-some-homeless-individuals-scare-customers-away

558 Derick Fox, "Homeless Man Allegedly Threatens Banks with Viral Viruses and 'Demands Money,'" ABC4, December 23, 2022, https://www.abc4.com/news/wasatch-front/homeless-man-allegedly-threatens-banks-with-viral-viruses-and-demands-money/

559 Del Leonard Jones, "Homeless Population Forces Prominent Business to Leave Downtown Salt Lake City," Utah Stories, January 11, 2023, https://utahstories.com/2023/01/homeless-population-forces-prominent-business-to-leave-downtown-salt-lake-city/

560 Spencer Joseph, "Local Bridal Shop Leaves Downtown Salt Lake City after Complaints of Crime, Homeless Population," FOX 13, July 27, 2022, https://www.fox13now.com/news/local-news/local-bridal-shop-leaves-downtown-salt-lake-city-after-complaints-of-crime-homeless-population

561 Del Leonard Jones, "Homeless Population Forces Prominent Business to Leave Downtown Salt Lake City," Utah Stories, January 11, 2023

562 Paighten Harkins, "Ballpark Residents Inundated by Crime Feel Unsafe, Unheard by Salt Lake City Leaders, *Salt Lake Tribune*, May 10, 2022, https://www.sltrib.com/news/2022/05/10/ballpark-residents/

563 Matt Canham, "Should Utah Give Homeless People a Place to Camp? Here Are Arguments for and against," *Salt Lake Tribune*, November 25, 2021, https://www.sltrib.com/news/politics/2021/11/25/should-utah-give-homeless/

564 Yael Halon, "Palm Springs Moves to Pay Transgender, Non-binary Residents: Jason Rantz," Fox News, April 5, 2022, https://www.foxnews.com/media/palm-springs-transgender-residents-pay-jason-rantz

565 "San Francisco Launches New Guaranteed Income Program for Trans Community," Office of the Mayor, SF.GOV, November 16, 2022, https://sf.gov/news/san-francisco-launches-new-guaranteed-income-program-trans-community

566 "San Francisco Launches New Guaranteed Income Program for Trans Community."

567 "G.I.F.T. Guaranteed Income for Transgender People" (application for residents of San Francisco), https://www.giftincome.org/apply

568 "About Us," Mayors for Guaranteed Income, https://www.mayorsforagi.org/about
569 Stacia West, Amy Castro Baker, Sukhi Samra, and Erin Coltrera, "Preliminary Analysis: SEED's First Year," https://static1.squarespace.com/static/6039d612b17d055cac14070f/t/603ef1194c474b329f33c329/1614737690661/SEED_Preliminary+Analysis-SEEDs+First+Year_Final+Report_Individual+Pages+-2.pdf
570 MSNBC Interview with Katy Tur, March 3, 2021, https://www.msnbc.com/katy-tur/watch/one-california-city-ran-a-universal-basic-income-experiment-employment-rates-went-up-101934661618
571 Sigal Samuel, "When a California City Gave People a Guaranteed Income, They Worked More—Not Less," Vox, March 6, 2021, https://www.vox.com/future-perfect/22313272/stockton-basic-income-guaranteed-free-money
572 Michael Hiltzik, "Stockton Shows the Time Has Come for Universal Basic Income," *Los Angeles Times*, March 6, 2023, https://www.latimes.com/business/story/2021-03-06/stockton-study-universal-basic-income
573 Ray Hartmann, "Groundbreaking Progressive Program Blows Up Objections from Conservative Naysayers," RawStory, March 4, 2021, https://www.rawstory.com/universal-basic-income/
574 West, Baker, Samra, and Coltrera, "Preliminary Analysis: SEED's First Year."
575 "Finland Is Giving Citizens $660 a Month for Free as an Experiment," *Vice News Tonight* (HBO), October 31, 2017, https://www.youtube.com/watch?v=vwjNrxVd-1E&ab_channel=VICENews
576 Minna Ylikanno, Olli Kangas, Signe Jauhiainen, and Miska Simanainen, "Evaluation of the Experiment," in *Experimenting with Unconditional Basic Income* (Gloucestershire: Edward Elgar Publishing Ltd., 2021), 44–54, https://www.researchgate.net/publication/353833411_Evaluation_of_the_experiment
577 "Finland Is Giving Citizens $660 a Month for Free as an Experiment."
578 Alexandra Yoon-Hendrick, "How Tacoma's Yearlong Guaranteed Income Experiment Fared," *Seattle Times*, January 5, 2023, https://www.seattletimes.com/seattle-news/how-tacomas-yearlong-guaranteed-income-experiment-fared/
579 Oakland Resilient Families website, accessed January 15, 2023, https://oaklandresilientfamilies.org/about
580 Teo Armus, "Oakland Will Give Some Families of Color $500 a Month, One of the Biggest Tests Yet for Guaranteed Income," *Washington Post*, March 24, 2021, https://www.washingtonpost.com/nation/2021/03/24/oakland-guaranteed-income-race-wealth/
581 Allen Kim, "Twitter CEO Jack Dorsey Donated $15 Million to Help Fund Program for Guaranteed Income to Residents in Need," CNN,

December 9, 2020, https://www.cnn.com/2020/12/09/us/jack-dorsey-guaranteed-income-trnd/index.html

582 "Employment Recovery in the Wake of the COVID-19 Pandemic," Bureau of Labor Statistics, December 2020, https://www.bls.gov/opub/mlr/2020/article/employment-recovery.htm

583 Jaclyn Cosgrove, "L.A. County Extends COVID-19 Eviction Moratorium through September," *Los Angeles Times*, June 22, 2021, https://www.latimes.com/california/story/2021-06-22/la-county-extends-covid19-eviction-moratorium-through-september

584 Erin Tiernan, "Massachusetts Opens Unemployment Applications to Gig Workers, Self-Employed," *Boston Herald*, April 20, 2020, https://www.bostonherald.com/2020/04/20/massachusetts-opens-unemployment-applications-to-gig-workers-self-employed/

585 Kamaria Hightower, "City of Seattle Launches $16 Million Seattle Relief Fund to Help Low-Income Residents Impacted by the COVID-19 Pandemic," news release, Office of the Mayor, City of Seattle, October 25, 2021, https://durkan.seattle.gov/2021/10/175036/

586 Harry J. Holzer, R. Glenn Hubbard, and Michael R. Strain, "Did Pandemic Unemployment Benefits Reduce Employment? Evidence from Early State-Level Expirations in June 2021," National Bureau of Economic Research, December 2021, https://www.nber.org/system/files/working_papers/w29575/w29575.pdf

587 Rachel Greszler, "Fact Check: Was Biden Right about Federal Unemployment Benefits Having No Effect on Jobs Report?," *The Daily Signal*, May 12, 2021, https://www.dailysignal.com/2021/05/12/fact-check-was-biden-right-about-federal-unemployment-benefits-having-no-effect-on-job-report/

588 Greg Iacurci, "It Pays to Stay Unemployed. That Might Be a Good Thing," CNBC, May 9, 2020, https://www.cnbc.com/2020/05/09/it-pays-to-stay-unemployed-that-might-be-a-good-thing.html

589 Steven Greenhouse, "Union's Rejection Puts Future Home of Boeing 777X in Doubt," *New York Times*, November 14, 2013, https://www.nytimes.com/2013/11/15/business/unions-rejection-puts-future-home-of-boeing-777x-in-doubt.html

590 Gary Horcher, "Seattle City Councilmember-Elect Shares Radical Idea with Boeing Workers," KIRO TV, November 19, 2013, https://www.kiro7.com/news/seattle-city-councilmember-elect-shares-radical-id/246045525/

591 Horcher, "Seattle City Councilmember-Elect Shares Radical Idea with Boeing Workers."

592 Horcher, "Seattle City Councilmember-Elect Shares Radical Idea with Boeing Workers."

593 Kevin Roose, "Meet the Seattle Socialist Leading the Fight for a $15 Minimum Wage," *New York Magazine*, May 26, 2014, https://nymag.com/intelligencer/2014/05/kshama-sawant-seattle-socialist.html

594 Kevin Schofield, "Kshama Sawant: The Art of the Self-Deal," Seattle City Council Insight, April 20, 2018, https://sccinsight.com/2018/04/20/kshama-sawant-the-art-of-the-self-deal/

595 Dyer Oxley, "Seattle CEO Pushing for $28 Minimum Wage, Only Pays $9," *MyNorthwest*, May 13, 2016, https://mynorthwest.com/291249/the-capitalist-who-wants-to-pay-a-28-minimum-wage/

596 Seattle Times Staff, "Calls for Immigration, Wage Reform on Mostly Peaceful May Day," *Seattle Times*, May 2, 2014, https://www.seattletimes.com/seattle-news/calls-for-immigration-wage-reform-on-mostly-peaceful-may-day/

597 Natasha Chen, "Nonprofit Employer: Workers Requested Reduced Hours to Stay in Subsidized Housing," KIRO TV, June 8, 2015, https://www.kiro7.com/news/nonprofit-worker-reduced-hours-requested-stay-subs/43270246/

598 Ekaterina Jardim, Mark C. Long, Robert Plotnick, Emma van Inwegen, Jacob Vigdor, and Hilary Wething, "Minimum-Wage Increases and Low-Wage Employment: Evidence from Seattle," *American Economic Journal: Economic Policy* 14, no. 2 (2022): 263-314, https://www.aeaweb.org/articles?id=10.1257/pol.20180578

599 Jason Rantz, "Rantz: Seattle Minimum Wage Study Appears Insanely Biased," *MyNorthwest*, June 21, 2017, https://mynorthwest.com/669659/rantz-seattle-minimum-wage-study-appears-insanely-bias/

600 Dan Springer, "Seattle Sought Report Confirming Minimum Wage Benefits," Fox News, June 29, 2017, Fox Newshttps://www.youtube.com/watch?v=5Ck_NKkJ41g&t=121s&ab_channel=FoxNews

601 Michael Saltsman, "The 'Smoking Gun' Emails That Show Advocates, Academics Coordinated to Boost $15," *Forbes*, June 26, 2017, https://www.forbes.com/sites/michaelsaltsman/2017/07/26/the-smoking-gun-emails-that-show-advocates-academics-coordinated-to-boost-15/?sh=1f7a0d04706d

602 Daniel Person, "The City Knew the Bad Minimum Wage Report Was Coming Out, So It Called Up Berkeley," *Seattle Weekly*, June 26, 2017, https://www.seattleweekly.com/news/seattle-is-getting-an-object-lesson-in-weaponized-data/

603 Retail Workers Bill of Rights, http://retailworkerrights.com/get-the-facts/

604 Janet I. Tu, "Seattle City Council Approves Worker-Scheduling Law," *Seattle Times*, September 19, 2016, https://www.seattletimes.com/business/retail/seattle-council-approves-worker-scheduling-law/

605 Samantha Spitz, “Downtown Restaurant Owner Brought to Tears during Plea to Council,” KDVR, May 2, 2023, https://kdvr.com/news/local/downtown-restaurant-owner-brought-to-tears-during-plea-for-action/

606 Denver City Council General Public Comment Session, May 1, 2023, https://denver.legistar.com/DepartmentDetail.aspx?ID=43798&GUID=6AAA099D-DF37-4951-AFA0-7AB4EF939E61

607 Candi CdeBaca (@candiforcouncil), May 4, 2023, https://www.tiktok.com/@candiforcouncil/video/7229416516251421995

608 San Francisco African American Reparations Advisory Committee, “DRAFT San Francisco Reparations Plan,” December 2022, https://sf.gov/sites/default/files/2023-01/HRC%20Reparations%202022%20Report%20Final_0.pdf

609 Justin Phillips, “$5 Million for Each Longtime Black Resident? S.F. Has a Bold Reparations Plan to Consider,” *San Francisco Chronicle*, January 15, 2023, https://www.sfchronicle.com/bayarea/justinphillips/article/sf-reparations-black-17716918.php

610 Lil Kalish, “Reparations Task Force: State Could Owe Black Californians Hundreds of Thousands of Dollars,” Cal Matters, September 26, 2022, https://calmatters.org/california-divide/2022/09/reparations-task-force/

611 Anders Hagstrom, “California Reparations Panel Approves Payments of up to $1.2 Million to Every Black Resident,” Fox News, May 7, 2023, https://www.foxnews.com/politics/california-reparations-panel-approves-payments-1-2-million-every-black-resident

612 Travis Cummings, “City of St. Louis Addresses Systemic Injustice with New Reparations Commission,” KSDK-TV, December 8, 2022, https://www.ksdk.com/article/money/city-of-st-louis-addresses-systemic-injustice-with-new-reparations-commission/63-2c207a70-c5a1-44c7-9faf-727cf08c5f28

613 Associated Press, “St. Louis Mayor Signs Bill Allowing Voluntary Reparations,” *US News and World Report*, April 2, 2022, https://www.usnews.com/news/best-states/missouri/articles/2022-04-02/st-louis-mayor-signs-bill-allowing-voluntary-reparations

614 Katherine Burgess, “Shelby County to Study Reparations to Descendants of Slaves, Allocates $5 Million,” Memphis Commercial Appeal, February 22, 2023, https://www.commercialappeal.com/story/news/local/2023/02/22/shelby-county-allocates-5-million-creates-committee-to-study-reparations/69932671007/

615 Carrie Blazina and Kiana Cox, “Black and White Americans Are Far Apart in Their Views of Reparations for Slavery,” Pew Research Center, November 28, 2022, https://www.pewresearch.org/fact-tank/2022/11/28/black-and-white-americans-are-far-apart-in-their-views-of-reparations-for-slavery/

616 News 12 Staff, "Teacher to Return to Somers HS after 'White Fragility' Lesson Was Stopped Mid-Way," News 12, November 11, 2022, https://bronx.news12.com/teacher-to-return-to-somers-hs-after-white-fragility-lesson-was-stopped-mid-way

617 Phil McCausland, "The Teaching of Critical Race Theory Isn't Happening in Classrooms, Teachers Say," NBC News, July 1, 2021, https://www.nbcnews.com/news/us-news/teaching-critical-race-theory-isn-t-happening-classrooms-teachers-say-n1272945

618 Brandon Tensley, "The Engineered Conservative Panic over Critical Race Theory, Explained," CNN, July 8, 2021, https://www.cnn.com/2021/07/08/politics/critical-race-theory-panic-race-deconstructed-newsletter/index.html

619 Townhall.com (@townhallcom), "This is INSANE," Twitter, November 2, 2021, 8:29 p.m., https://twitter.com/townhallcom/status/1455693642866298887

620 Jason Rantz and Richard Fowler, "Parents Push Back against Critical Race Theory," Fox News Live, June 6, 2021, https://www.foxnews.com/video/6257662174001

621 Jason Rantz, "Rantz: Teacher Uses Science Class to Label White Middle Schoolers Privileged Oppressors," *MyNorthwest*, June 9, 2021, https://mynorthwest.com/2937573/rantz-teacher-uses-science-class-to-call-white-middle-schoolers-privileged-oppressors/

622 Jason Rantz, "Rantz: District Tells Staff to Defend Critical Race Theory, but Deny They Teach It," *MyNorthwest*, September 20, 2021, https://mynorthwest.com/3133091/rantz-district-defend-critical-race-theory-deny/

623 Jason Rantz, "Rantz: High School Cancels 9/11 Tribute, Says It Could Offend Some Students," *MyNorthwest*, September 12, 2022, https://mynorthwest.com/3141211/rantz-high-school-cancels-9-11-tribute-says-it-could-offend-some-students/

624 Hannah Farrow, "The 1619 Project Curriculum Taught in over 4,500 Schools—Frederick County Public Schools Has the Option," Medill News Service, July 21, 2020, https://dc.medill.northwestern.edu/blog/2020/07/21/the-1619-project-curriculum-taught-in-over-4500-schools-frederick-county-public-schools-has-the-option/#sthash.1JXiO3FD.dpbs

625 U.S. History Teachers in Chicago Public Schools Curriculum, https://1619education.org/builder/lesson/american-institutions

626 Jason Rantz, "Rantz: Bellevue High School Teaches Critical Race Theory with Intent to Create Activists," *MyNorthwest*, April 6, 2022, https://mynorthwest.com/3420690/rantz-bellevue-high-school-teaches-critical-race-theory-crt/

627 Lukas Michener, "Lukas Michener: Uniting for Social Justice with NEA," National Education Association, June 16, 2020, https://www

.nea.org/professional-excellence/leadership-development/member-spotlight/lukas-michener-uniting-social

628 NEA edjustice, "Black Lives Matter at School," National Education Association, https://neaedjustice.org/black-lives-matter-at-school/

629 D.C. Area Educators for Social Justice, "D.C. Area Black Lives Matter at School Week of Action," accessed January 28, 2023, https://www.dcareaeducators4socialjustice.org/black-lives-matter/resources/older-children#lessons

630 Houston Keene, "Georgia School District Hosts BLM Event Featuring Speaker Charged with 'Family Violence,'" Fox News, February 3, 2022, Fox Newshttps://www.foxnews.com/politics/georgia-school-district-hosts-blm-school-event-featured-speaker-charged-family-violence

631 Seattle Public Schools, "Black Lives Matter at School Week Educator Resource Guide," accessed January 28, 2023, https://mysps.seattleschools.org/wp-content/uploads/2021/01/2021-BLMAS-Week-ducator-esource-uide.pdf

632 Aurora School, "Black Lives Matter Week of Action: Jan 31–Feb 4," https://auroraschool.org/blog/black-lives-matter-week-of-action-jan-30-feb-5

633 BLM@School Curriculum Team, "TOPIC – Black + Palestinian Solidarity," https://www.are.na/blm-school-curriculum-team/topic-black-palestinian-solidarity

634 David Sheridan, "The Case for Teaching Black Lives Matter in Schools," National Education Association, February 8, 2017, https://neaedjustice.org/2017/02/08/black-lives-matter-schools/

635 Janet Oravetz, "After Entering Elementary School under 'False Pretenses,' Man Was Verbally Abusive, Principal Says," NBC Denver, January 25, 2022, https://www.9news.com/article/news/crime/centennial-elementary-security-incident/73-2bcb539a-ac7b-4736-9126-70d2c4324e4f

636 D.C. Area Educators for Social Justice, "Introduction of Transgender and Nonbinary Identities with I Am Jazz," Teaching for Change, https://www.dcareaeducators4socialjustice.org/black-lives-matter/resources/early-childhood-elementary

637 Houston Keene, "Schools Across America Implement BLM Week of Action That Calls for 'Disruption of Western Nuclear Family,'" Fox News, February 2, 2022, https://www.foxnews.com/politics/schools-across-america-blm-week-action-nuclear-family

638 *Deemar v. Board of Education of the City of Evanston/Skokie*, June 29, 2021, https://www.fairforall.org/content/pdfs/profiles/2021-06-29-deemar-v-district-65.pdf

639 Public BLM at NYC Schools, "Teaching the 13 Principles of BLM," Last accessed April 29, 2023, https://drive.google.com/drive/folders/1704IpimoxEeipQnDHrPh8DaTQzO1Z5S7

640 Andrea Chorney and Elisa M. Yzaguirre, "Lesson Title: Unapologetically Black Women Poets (Adapted from Teaching Tolerance)," Seattle Public Schools, https://drive.google.com/drive/folders/1nIxvtLYdM-rmTRhnLZ_vnLd7HNTPULqu

641 Jose Zozaya, " 'Crossed the Line': Papillion-La Vista Responds to Controversy over Kids' Book on Racial Injustice," KETV-TV, April 12, 2021, https://www.ketv.com/article/school-district-teachers-union-respond-to-controversy-over-childrens-book-on-racial-injustice/36100697

642 Luige Del Puerto, "Video Shown to Denver South Students: Do Not Call the Police in Case of Racist Attack," *The Denver Gazette*, August 23, 2022, https://denvergazette.com/news/education/video-shown-to-denver-south-students-do-not-call-the-police-in-case-of-racist/article_403d4c10-2337-11ed-aa14-cf230fb15ee7.html

643 WTHR-TV Staff, "Attorney for HSE Schools to Investigate 'Defund the Police' Poster in Classroom with Fallen Officer's Brother," WTHR-TV, August 19, 2022, https://www.wthr.com/article/news/local/fishers-high-school-classroom-defund-police-sign-noah-shahnavaz-brother/531-4fca3415-b22b-44ea-9c9b-1f807b81e2c3

644 Libs of TikTok (@libsoftiktok), "Elementary school in Connecticut featuring the BLM flag," Twitter, January 18, 2023, 9:42 a.m., https://twitter.com/libsoftiktok/status/1615721254576693248/photo/1

645 Jason Rantz, "Rantz: Seattle Public Schools Teaching Radical BLM, Anti-police Lessons to K-5 Students," *MyNorthwest*, January 31, 2021, https://mynorthwest.com/2525568/rantz-seattle-public-schools-radical-blm-anti-police-lessons/

646 Hank Berrien, "WATCH: Kindergartners March Chanting 'Black Lives Matter' at Posh Private D.C. School," *The Daily Wire*, February 7, 2022, https://www.dailywire.com/news/watch-kindergartners-march-chanting-black-lives-matter-at-posh-private-d-c-school

647 Mark Hicks, "Farmington District Launched 'Equity Challenge,' Protests Erupted," *The Detroit News*, January 12, 2022, https://www.detroitnews.com/story/news/local/oakland-county/2022/01/11/farmington-district-launched-equity-challenge-protests-erupted/9164886002/; and Libs of TikTok (@libsoftiktok), "A Michigan school held a 21 day equity challenge," Twitter, December 22, 2021, 2:46 p.m., https://twitter.com/libsoftiktok/status/1473741667391967236

648 Jason Rantz, "Rantz: HS Teachers Demanded Students Pledge Support of BLM and Abortion," *MyNorthwest*, June 7, 2022, https://mynorthwest.com/3506560/rantz-eastlake-high-school-pledge-support-blm-abortion/

649 Lauren Camera, "Momentum Stalls in Fight to Remove Police from Schools," *US News and World Report*, May 25, 2021, https://www.usnews.com/news/education-news/articles/2021-05-25/momentum-stalls-in-fight-to-remove-police-from-schools

650 Melissa Gomez, "Pomona Schools Defund Police, Re-imagine School Safety," *Los Angeles Times*, July 7, 2021, https://www.latimes.com/california/story/2021-07-02/pomona-unified-defund-school-police
651 Gomez, "Pomona Schools Defund Police, Re-imagine School Safety."
652 Hayley Smith, "Pomona Schools Defunded Police; a Shooting Brings Them Back," *Los Angeles Times*, November, 5, 2021, https://www.latimes.com/california/story/2021-11-05/pomona-schools-defunded-police-a-shooting-brings-them-back
653 Nicole C. Brambila and Julia Cardi, "Denver Public Schools to Bring Police Officers Back to Schools in Light of East High Shooting," *Denver Gazette*, March 22, 2023, https://denvergazette.com/news/education/denver-public-schools-to-bring-police-back/article_1240fde6-c90b-11ed-ad71-9f12da010498.html
654 Sarah Schwartz, "These Districts Defunded Their School Police. What Happened Next?," *Education Week*, June 4, 2021, https://www.edweek.org/leadership/these-districts-defunded-their-school-police-what-happened-next/2021/06
655 Wisconsin State Journal Editorial Board, "Bring Back SROs to Help Stem Violence in Madison Schools," *Wisconsin State Journal*, November 14, 2021, https://www.agupdate.com/opinion/editorial/bring-back-sros-to-help-stem-violence-in-madison-schools/article_afa34940-08d1-5109-88a8-ceaa7b6baa27.html
656 Elizabeth Beyer, "Melee Outside East High Draws Heavy Police Response, Pepper Spray, Ambulances," *Wisconsin State Journal*, November 9, 2021, https://madison.com/news/local/education/local_schools/watch-now-melee-outside-east-high-draws-heavy-police-response-pepper-spray-ambulances/article_8e1a2f1c-f76d-5ce1-8ae1-df1fd0d3f6cb.html
657 Elizabeth Beyer, "More than a Third of East High School Students Stay Home; District Promises Security Changes," *Wisconsin State Journal*, November 10, 2021, https://madison.com/wsj/news/local/education/local_schools/more-than-a-third-of-east-high-school-students-stay-home-district-promises-security-changes/article_57ae7b18-ce48-535e-a1cc-24b427d86388.html#_ga=2.12841136.60373578.1672555929-841611893.1672555929
658 Caitlynn Perez, "Council Members Want to End MCPS School Resource Officer Program," Moco360, November 17, 2020, https://bethesdamagazine.com/2020/11/17/council-members-want-to-end-mcps-school-resource-officer-program/
659 Kolbie Satterfield, "Montgomery County Council Discusses Ending SRO Program in Schools," WUSA-TV, February 4, 2021, https://www.wusa9.com/article/news/education/montgomery-co-could-end-sro-program/65-f4dd38a0-4ff2-4971-ae77-0e7faf30b214

660 Satterfield, "Montgomery County Council Discusses Ending SRO Program in Schools."

661 Laura Wainman, "Police Coming Back to Montgomery County Schools, Now Known as Community Engagement Officers," WUSA-TV, April 26, 2022, https://www.wusa9.com/article/news/education/community-engagement-officers-montgomery-county-public-schools/65-8475c60e-4c4f-4bed-9c46-6b6d07245532

662 KOIN-TV broadcast, "Bringing School Resource Officers Back, PPS in Early Talks to Return Officers to Schools," video, KOIN-TV, December 15, 2022, https://www.koin.com/video/bringing-school-resource-officers-back-pps-in-early-talks-to-return-officers-to-schools/8238282/

663 Jake Chapman, "New Push to Potentially Bring School Resource Officers Back to Seattle Public Schools," KIRO-TV, November 17, 2022, https://www.kiro7.com/news/local/new-push-potentially-bring-school-resource-officers-back-seattle-public-schools/ABQMFM7H6RHAJB5QIRGCHPIV3A/

664 Black Lives Matter in School: Background Information and Teacher Guide, https://www.seattlewea.org/file_viewer.php?id=10521

665 Jason Rantz, "Rantz: After Seattle Principal Stonewalled Police, Suspect Allegedly Assaulted Two Victims," *MyNorthwest*, November 16, 2022, https://mynorthwest.com/3706947/rantz-seattle-principal-stonewalled-police-suspect-allegedly-assaulted-two-victims/

666 Audrey Conklin, "California Middle Schoolers Get 'Uncomfortable' Assignment of Huffington Post Op-Ed, 'Why I'm a Racist,' " Fox News, June 3, 2021, https://www.foxnews.com/us/california-middle-schoolers-huffington-post-op-ed

667 Jeff Cook, "Why I'm A Racist," *The Huffington Post*, July 15, 2016, https://www.huffpost.com/entry/why-im-a-racist_b_57893b9ee4b0e7c873500382

668 Jason Rantz, "Rantz: School Board Cuts Music Class over 'White Supremacy,' 'Institutional Violence'," *MyNorthwest*, April 23, 2023, https://mynorthwest.com/3877315/rantz-school-music-class-white-supremacy/

669 Jason Rantz, "Rantz: School Equity Leader Out after Racist and Vulgar TikTok Videos Spread," *MyNorthwest*, October 11, 2021, https://mynorthwest.com/3182734/rantz-school-equity-leader-racist-tiktok/

670 Elizabeth Rosner and Selim Algar, "Manhattan School to Sort Kids by Race During Social Justice Discussions," *New York Post*, November 18, 2021, https://nypost.com/2021/11/18/manhattan-school-to-sort-kids-by-race-during-social-justice-discussions/

671 Sam Dorman, "Denver Elementary School under Fire for Planning 'Families of Color Playground Night,' " Fox News, December 15, 2021, Fox Newshttps://www.foxnews.com/us/denver-school-playground-families-color

672 Jason Rantz, "Rantz: Seattle Public Schools to Hold Racially Segregated 'Listening Tour' with Superintendent," *MyNorthwest*, April 11, 2022, https://mynorthwest.com/3430733/rantz-seattle-public-schools-racially-segregated-listening-tour-superintendent/

673 Sam Dorman, "MA School District's Racially Segregated 'Healing Space' Explicitly Excluded White Students: Complaint," Fox News, May 20, 2021, Fox Newshttps://www.foxnews.com/us/massachusetts-segregated-healing-space-white-students

674 Phililp Marcelo, "Wellesley School District Settles Suit by Conservative Group over Student Affinity Groups," Associated Press, February 8, 2022, https://www.wbur.org/news/2022/02/08/wellesley-parents-defending-education-lawsuit-settlement-boston

675 Yaron Steinbuch, "California Teacher Suspended for Berating Students during Zoom Class," *New York Post*, April 13, 2021, https://nypost.com/2021/04/13/california-teacher-suspended-for-berating-students/

676 Martin Slagter, "'Whiteness' Remarks by Jackson School Board Member Defended, Criticized during Tense Meeting," MLive, January 17, 2023, https://www.mlive.com/news/jackson/2023/01/whiteness-remarks-by-jackson-school-board-member-defended-criticized-during-tense-meeting.html

677 Slagter, "'Whiteness' Remarks by Jackson School Board Member Defended, Criticized during Tense Meeting."

678 Thomas Jefferson High School for Science and Technology, newsletter, June 7, 2020, https://content.govdelivery.com/accounts/VAEDUFCPS/bulletins/28f8d9f

679 Robert Barnes and Hannah Natanson, "Supreme Court Lets Thomas Jefferson High School Admissions Policy Stand," *The Washington Post*, April 25, 2022, https://www.washingtonpost.com/politics/2022/04/25/supreme-court-high-school-admissions-race/

680 Jason Rantz, "Rantz: District Reclassified Asians with Whites When They Did Too Well Academically," *MyNorthwest*, December 15, 2020, https://mynorthwest.com/2365883/rantz-district-reclassified-asians-with-whites-when-they-did-too-well-academically/

681 Jason Rantz, "Rantz: Bill and Melinda Gates Foundation Bankrolls 'Math Is Racist' Lunacy," *MyNorthwest*, February 17, 2021, https://mynorthwest.com/2604518/rantz-bill-and-melinda-gates-foundation-bankrolls-math-is-racist-lunacy/

682 Lincoln Graves, "Debate Emerges over Racism and White Supremacy in Oregon Math Instruction," KATU-TV, February 26, 2021, https://mynbc15.com/news/nation-world/debate-emerges-over-racism-and-white-supremacy-in-math-instruction

683 Jason Rantz, "Rantz: Seattle School Cancels Halloween over 'Equity,' Says Black Kids Don't Celebrate," *MyNorthwest*, October 12, 2021,

https://mynorthwest.com/3183712/rantz-seattle-elementary-school-cancels-halloween-equity-concerns/

684 Rantz, "Rantz: Seattle School Cancels Halloween over 'Equity,' Says Black Kids Don't Celebrate."

685 Dr. Susan Berry,"School Cancels First-Grade Thanksgiving Play: Concerns about 'Accuracy' and 'Sensitivity,'" Breitbart, November 27, 2019, https://www.breitbart.com/politics/2019/11/27/school-cancels-first-grade-thanksgiving-play-concerns-accuracy-sensitivity/

686 Christina Butler, "School Cancels Play Following Complaints about Famous Line, Education Concerns," WHTM-TV, December 15, 2016, https://www.abc27.com/news/school-cancels-play-following-complaints-about-famous-line-education-concerns/

687 Derek Staahl, "South Bay Elementary School Cancels Christmas Show, Upsetting Some Parents," ABC San Diego, December 20, 2019, https://www.10news.com/south-bay-elementary-school-cancels-christmas-show-upsetting-some-parents

688 Crystal Bonvillian, "Madison School's Easter Egg Controversy Has Officials Dealing with Fallout from National Media Exposure," AL.com, March 28, 2013, https://www.al.com/breaking/2013/03/madison_schools_easter_egg_con.html

689 Tyler O'Neil, "Virginia School Districts Deny Teaching Critical Race Theory Even in the Face of Evidence," Fox News, November 11, 2021, Fox Newshttps://www.foxnews.com/politics/virginia-school-districts-deny-teaching-critical-race-theory-evidence

690 Sam Dorman, "Virginia Teacher Says Critical Race Theory Has Damaged Community as Frustrated Parents Demand Changes," Fox News, April 16, 2022, Fox Newshttps://www.foxnews.com/us/loudoun-county-critical-race-theory-divided

691 Joe Karwacki, "Loudoun County Teacher Speaks out on Critical Race Theory: 'This Isn't What I Signed Up For,'" Fox News, June 14, 2021, Fox Newshttps://www.foxnews.com/media/loudoun-county-teacher-speaks-out-critical-race-theory-this-isnt-what-i-signed-up-for

692 Karwacki, "Loudoun County Teacher Speaks out on Critical Race Theory."

693 Sam Dorman, "Virginia County Officials Acknowledge Critical Race Theory Influences, Aligns with Their Work," Fox News, June 15, 2021, https://www.foxnews.com/us/virginia-loudoun-officials-acknowledge-critical-race-theory-influences-work

694 *C.I. v. Albemarle County School Board,* December 22, 2021, https://adfmedialegalfiles.blob.core.windows.net/files/CIcomplaint.pdf

695 *C.I. v. Albemarle County School Board.*

696 Ann Dailey Moreno, "Document Reveals McAuliffe Admin Pushed Va. Schools to 'Embrace' Critical Race Theory," *The National Desk*,

October 15, 2021, https://wset.com/news/nation-world/documents-reveal-mcauliffe-pushed-virginia-schools-to-teach-critical-race-theory

697 Jill Tucker, "California and S.F. Reading and Math Test Scores a Gut Punch for School Districts," *San Francisco Chronicle*, October 24, 2022, https://www.sfchronicle.com/bayarea/article/California-reading-and-math-scores-finally-show-17530574.php

698 Jill Tucker, "Washington and Lincoln Are Out. S.F. School Board Tosses 44 School Names in Controversial Move," *San Francisco Chronicle*, January 26, 2021, https://www.sfchronicle.com/education/article/Washington-and-Lincoln-are-out-S-F-school-board-15900963.php

699 Laura Meckler, "San Francisco Recalls School Board Members Seen as Too Focused on Racial Justice," *The Washington Post*, February 16, 2022, https://www.washingtonpost.com/education/2022/02/16/san-francisco-school-board-recall/

700 Richard Cano, "New Data Shows Shift at Lowell High School: More Students Given Failing Grades after Admissions Change," *San Francisco Chronicle*, May 25, 2022, https://www.sfchronicle.com/sf/article/lowell-high-admissions-17196603.php

701 Nathan Heller, "What Happens When an Élite Public School Becomes Open to All?," *The New Yorker*, March 7, 2022, https://www.newyorker.com/magazine/2022/03/14/what-happens-when-an-elite-public-school-becomes-open-to-all

702 Jill Tucker, "San Francisco School Board Member Criticized for Racist Tweets in 2016 Aimed at Asian Americans," *San Francisco Chronicle*, March 19, 2021, https://www.sfchronicle.com/local-politics/article/SFUSD-school-board-member-criticized-for-racist-16039069.php

703 Aubrie Spady, "Waukesha School Board Election: GOP-Backed Candidates Take 3 Seats after Critical Race Theory Controversy," Fox News, April 7, 2022, https://www.foxnews.com/politics/school-election-republican-critical-race-theory

704 Brian Lopez, "Texas Republicans against 'Critical Race Theory' Win Seats on the State Board of Education, Strengthening Its GOP Majority," *The Texas Tribune*, November 9, 2022, https://www.texastribune.org/2022/11/08/texas-state-board-education-election-results/

705 Jake Epstein, "11 Colorado School Board Candidates Backed by a New Conservative PAC That Rails against Critical Race Theory All Won Their Races," *Insider*, November 4, 2022, https://www.insider.com/colorado-school-board-candidates-anti-critical-race-theory-sweep-races-2021-11

706 Andrew Atterbury, "DeSantis, Conservatives Score More Florida School Board Wins," *Politico*, November 8, 2022, https://www.politico.com/news/2022/11/08/desantis-conservatives-school-board-00065794

707 Eric Ortiz, "School Board Candidates Who Opposed Critical Race Theory, Mask Mandates Win," NBC News, November 3, 2022, https://www.nbcnews.com/news/education/school-board-candidates-opposed-critical-race-theory-mask-mandates-win-rcna4420

708 Sophie Mann, "Woke Exodus! California and New York Have Each Lost More than Half MILLION Residents since April 2020—as People Flee Due to Surging Home Prices and Out-of-Control Crime," *Daily Mail*, December 26, 2022, https://www.dailymail.co.uk/news/article-11575181/Woke-exodus-California-New-York-lost-half-MILLION-residents-July-2020.html

709 Keith Griffith and Stephen M. Lepore, "Average Manhattan Rent Rocketed to $5,249 in November—Up 19% in a Year—as Property Experts Say That Only a Recession Will Help Lower Prices Again," *Daily Mail*, December 2022, https://www.dailymail.co.uk/news/article-11519585/Average-Manhattan-rent-rocketed-5-249-November-19-year.html

710 Megan Henney, "Wealthy New Yorkers Fled City en Masse as High-Tax State Exodus Persists," FOX Business, December 7, 2022, https://www.foxbusiness.com/money/wealthy-new-yorkers-fled-city-en-masse-high-tax-state-exodus-persists

711 Martin Z. Braun, "New York Risks Losing Wealthiest over High Taxes, Comptroller Says," Bloomberg News, December 14, 2022, https://www.bloomberg.com/news/articles/2022-12-14/new-york-risks-losing-wealthiest-residents-if-taxes-keep-rising?leadSource=uverify%20wall

712 Steve Bittenbender, "New York Loses $19.5 Billion in Population Exodus, IRS Confirms," *The Center Square*, May 28, 2022, https://www.thecentersquare.com/new_york/new-york-loses-19-5-billion-in-population-exodus-irs-confirms/article_c805dfd6-dde6-11ec-8d0e-4f667cd41881.html

713 Barack Obama, "Remarks by the President at a Campaign Event in Roanoke, Virginia," Obama White House Archives, July 13, 2012, https://obamawhitehouse.archives.gov/the-press-office/2012/07/13/remarks-president-campaign-event-roanoke-virginia

714 John Clark, "Illinois' Richest Man Ditches Chicago for Miami, Says Employees Don't Feel Safe," MyStateline.com, June 23, 2022, https://www.mystateline.com/news/national/illinois-richest-man-ditches-chicago-for-miami-says-employees-dont-feel-safe/

715 *Cavuto Live*, "California Considers Wealth Tax for Residents Who Leave Blue State," Fox News, January 28, 2023, https://www.foxnews.com/video/6319422693112

716 Laura Mahoney, Donna Borak, and Michael J. Bologna, "Tax-the-Rich Blue States Want to Leave Wealthy 'Nowhere to Hide,'" Bloomberg Tax Report, January 19, 2023, https://news.bloombergtax

.com/daily-tax-report-state/tax-the-rich-blue-states-want-to-leave-wealthy-nowhere-to-hide

717 Melissa Santos, "Wealth Tax Prospects Doubtful—But Tax Reform Isn't Dead," Axios, January 20, 2023, https://www.axios.com/local/seattle/2023/01/20/wealth-tax-washington-state-tax-reform

718 Jason Rantz, "Rantz: Dems Defend WA Supreme Court's Racist Capital Gains Tax Ruling," *MyNorthwest*, March 29, 2023, https://mynorthwest.com/3866485/rantz-dems-defend-wa-supreme-courts-racist-capital-gains-tax-ruling/

719 Danielle Muoio and Katie Balevic, "Here Are the 9 North American Cities with the Best Public Transit Systems," Yahoo! News, January 4, 2023, https://news.yahoo.com/9-north-american-cities-best-165214869.html

720 Randal O'Toole, "Denver Mayor's Anti-car Agenda Doubles Down on Failed Policies," Complete Colorado, January 9, 2018, https://pagetwo.completecolorado.com/2018/01/09/denver-mayors-anti-car-agenda-doubles-down-on-failed-policies/

721 Tim Jackson, "Anti-car Agenda Undermines Denver's Economic Recovery," *Denver Gazette*, December 22, 2020, https://gazette.com/denver-gazette/anti-car-agenda-undermines-denver-s-economic-recovery/article_3ec7588c-43b2-11eb-9531-3f572935920a.html

722 Nicole Gelinas, "Mass Transit, and Cities, Could Grind to a Halt without Federal Aid," *New York Times*, July 3, 2020, https://www.nytimes.com/2020/07/03/opinion/coronavirus-mass-transit.html

723 Taylor Griggs, "PBOT Pilot Program Aims to Replace Parking with Trees," Bike Portland, November 16, 2022, https://bikeportland.org/2022/11/16/pbot-pilot-project-will-replace-parking-with-trees-367205

724 "San Francisco Lowers Speed Limits in Targeted Business Districts under New State Law," news release, Office of the Mayor, City of San Francisco, January 13, 2022, https://sfmayor.org/article/san-francisco-lowers-speed-limits-targeted-business-districts-under-new-state-law

725 Seattle Department of Transportation, "Seattle Bicycle Master Plan," 2021–2024 Implementation Plan, May 2021, https://www.seattle.gov/documents/Departments/SDOT/BikeProgram/BMP_Imp_Plan_2021_FINAL.pdf

726 Chris Sullivan, "Will Banning Free Right Turns Make Our Roads Safer?," *MyNorthwest*, February 2, 2023, https://mynorthwest.com/3798439/will-banning-free-right-turns-make-our-roads-safer/

727 Emma Newburger, "California Bans the Sale of New Gas-Powered Cars by 2035," CNBC, August 25, 2022, https://www.cnbc.com/2022/08/25/california-bans-the-sale-of-new-gas-powered-cars-by-2035.html

728 Kurt Schlosser, "Seattle City Light to Install Electric Vehicle Chargers at Curbside Locations Across City," Geekwire, July 6, 2022, https://

www.geekwire.com/2022/seattle-city-light-to-install-electric-vehicle-chargers-at-curbside-locations-across-city/

729 Chris Courtney, "How Much Does It Cost to Install an EV Charger?," Carvana (blog), July 18, 2021, https://blog.carvana.com/2021/07/how-much-does-it-cost-to-install-an-ev-charger/

730 Utility Dive, "Electricity Prices Surged 14.3% in 2022, Double Overall Inflation: US Report," January 19, 2023, https://www.utilitydive.com/news/electricity-prices-inflation-consumer-price-index/640656/

731 Aleks Phillips, "The Problem with Gavin Newsom's Climate Change Agenda," *Newsweek*, January 18, 2023, https://www.newsweek.com/california-gavin-newsom-climate-change-extreme-weather-electric-vehicles-1774425

732 Drew Mikkelsen, "Washington Drivers Would Pay 2.5 Cents per Mile under Recommendation," KING-5, December 13, 2022, https://www.king5.com/article/news/local/drivers-would-pay-per-mile-under-recommendation/281-51c31deb-efaa-4f22-bd97-97e26e002ef0

733 Daryl Hopkins, "Paying by the Mile for California Roads, Infrastructure," *Capitol Weekly*, February 9, 2022, https://capitolweekly.net/paying-by-the-mile-for-california-roads-infrastructure/

734 Teresa Mosqueda, "Today I'm excited to announce long-awaited legislation recognizing the diversity of Seattle's neighborhoods with a name change to 'single family' zones," @CMTMosqueda, Twitter, June 28, 2021, 2:03pm, https://twitter.com/CMTMosqueda/status/1409618449882501134

735 Jerusalem Demsas, "America's Racist Housing Rules Really Can Be Fixed," Vox, February 17, 2021, https://www.vox.com/22252625/america-racist-housing-rules-how-to-fix

736 Elizabeth Winkler, " 'Snob Zoning' Is Racial Housing Segregation bsy Another Name," *The Washington Post*, September 25, 2017, https://www.washingtonpost.com/news/wonk/wp/2017/09/25/snob-zoning-is-racial-housing-segregation-by-another-name/

737 Erin Baldassari and Molly Solomon, "The Racist History of Single-Family Home Zoning," KQED, October 5, 2020, https://www.kqed.org/news/11840548/the-racist-history-of-single-family-home-zoning

738 Supriya Yelimeli, "Berkeley Denounces Racist History of Single-Family Zoning, Begins 2-Year Process to Change General Plan," Berkeleyside, February 24, 2021, https://www.berkeleyside.org/2021/02/24/berkeley-denounces-racist-history-of-single-family-zoning-begins-2-year-process-to-change-general-plan

739 Justin Fox, "What Happened When Minneapolis Ended Single-Family Zoning," Bloomberg News, August 20, 2022, https://www.bloomberg.com/opinion/articles/2022-08-20/what-happened-when-minneapolis-ended-single-family-zoning

740 Christian Britschgi, "Eliminating Single-Family Zoning Isn't the Reason Minneapolis Is a YIMBY Success Story," Reason, May 11, 2022, https://reason.com/2022/05/11/eliminating-single-family-zoning-isnt-the-reason-minneapolis-is-a-yimby-success-story/

741 Yonah Freemark and Lydia Lo, "Effective Zoning Reform Isn't as Simple as It Seems," Bloomberg News, May 24, 2022, https://www.bloomberg.com/news/articles/2022-05-24/the-limits-of-ending-single-family-zoning

742 Ari Natter, "US Safety Agency to Consider Ban on Gas Stoves amid Health Fears," Bloomberg News, January 9, 2023, https://www.bloomberg.com/news/articles/2023-01-09/us-safety-agency-to-consider-ban-on-gas-stoves-amid-health-fears h

743 David Iaconangelo, "4 Things to Know about the Gas Stove Frenzy," *Politico*, January 14, 2023, https://www.politico.com/news/2023/01/14/gas-stove-firestorm-00077760

744 Lindsay Kornick, "GOP Meltdown over Gas Stoves Proves They're Addicted to Conspiracies like 'Bad Bathtub Meth': MSNBC Analyst," Fox News, January 16, 2023, https://www.foxnews.com/media/gop-meltdown-gas-stoves-proves-addicted-conspiracies-bad-bathtub-meth-msnbc-analyst

745 A. Martinez, "The Facts and Strategy Behind the Outrage over Rumors of a Ban on Gas Stoves," National Public Radio, January 20, 2022, https://www.npr.org/2023/01/20/1150228734/the-facts-and-strategy-behind-the-outrage-over-rumors-of-a-ban-on-gas-stoves

746 Soumya Karlamangla, "How the Gas-Stove Debate Has Played Out in California," *New York Times*, January 18, 2023, https://www.nytimes.com/2023/01/18/us/gas-stove-debate-california.html

747 Jennifer Gould, "Gov. Hochul Quietly Sneaks in Proposal to Ban Sale of Gas Stoves, Fuels Outrage Across New York," *New York Post*, January 11, 2023, https://nypost.com/2023/01/11/hochuls-plan-to-ban-sale-of-gas-stoves-fuels-outrage/

748 Gould, "Gov. Hochul Quietly Sneaks in Proposal to Ban Sale of Gas Stoves."

749 Ari Natter, "US Safety Agency to Consider Ban on Gas Stoves amid Health Fears," Bloomberg News, January 9, 2023, https://www.bloomberg.com/news/articles/2023-01-09/us-safety-agency-to-consider-ban-on-gas-stoves-amid-health-fears

750 Thomas Catenacci, "Internal Biden Admin Memo Shows It Was Serious about Banning Gas Stoves before Public Uproar," Fox News, February 2, 2023, https://www.foxnews.com/politics/internal-biden

ABOUT THE AUTHOR

JASON RANTZ is the host of *The Jason Rantz Show*, a top-rated, influential afternoon-drive talk show on Western Washington's dominant conservative talk station, KTTH 770 AM / 94.5 FM in Seattle. The show reaches tens of thousands of live listeners and more through the show's podcast. He is a frequent guest on Fox News, where he regularly reports and analyzes the madness in progressive cities.